THE BIBLE
IN
AUSTRALIA

Meredith Lake is a historian of religion, society and culture in Australia, with a PhD from the University of Sydney. Her books include a student guide to *The Bible Down Under* (2016) and a study in social welfare from the Great Depression to the present, *Faith in Action: HammondCare* (2013).

THE BIBLE
IN
AUSTRALIA
A CULTURAL HISTORY

MEREDITH LAKE

NEWSOUTH

A NewSouth book

Published by
NewSouth Publishing
University of New South Wales Press Ltd
University of New South Wales
Sydney NSW 2052
AUSTRALIA
newsouthpublishing.com

© Meredith Lake 2018
First published 2018

10 9 8 7 6 5 4 3 2 1

ISBN: 9781742235714 (paperback)
        9781742244146 (ebook)
        9781742248585 (ePDF)

 A catalogue record for this book is available from the National Library of Australia

Design Josephine Pajor-Markus
Cover design Peter Long
Cover images Steve Hamblin/Alamy Stock Photo; Svetlan/ Shutterstock
Printer Griffin Press

CONTENTS

INTRODUCTION: UNDER THE SKIN

Koby Abberton emerges like a shark on to the sand at Maroubra Beach. Tattooed from shoulder to shoulder, his body bares letters like teeth: 'My brothers keeper'. The phrase proclaims Abberton's fierce loyalty to the Bra Boys, the infamous surfer tribe he leads. It defines the us-and-them mentality he and his Maroubra crew have forged in confrontation with 'outsiders' and in defiance of police.

'My brother's keeper' comes from the Bible. In the book of Genesis, chapter four, Cain attempts to dodge responsibility for his murdered sibling Abel by asking God: 'Am I my brother's keeper?' The question sums up Cain's disregard for his brother's life. The Bra Boys have grabbed the phrase and turned its old meaning upside down.

Abberton's tattoo is suggestive of the Bible's place in twenty-first-century Australia. It floats in fragments across the surface of popular consciousness. There are traces almost everywhere, even in the hypermasculine subculture of a suburban beach. At the same time its religious elements have sunk into the deep; its older meanings are readily subverted and reshaped. But even in a truncated form, adrift from theology and even faith, the Bible can still mark out identities and provide people with a creed. In the Bra Boys' case, it even retains secular missionaries. In 2012, Abberton launched a 'brothers keeper' surfwear label, with a concept store on Maroubra's Marine Parade. The shop wall was emblazoned with a mashup of Psalm 23 and Genesis 4: 'As I walk through the valley of the shadow of death I shall fear no evil except God for I am my brother's keeper'. The same sentence was printed on board shorts in a 'shadow of death' range, and there is a video on YouTube showing Abberton painting out the design.

The Bible's changing place in Australian culture, over the few hundred years since it was first hauled across the water and on to a Sydney beach, offers a rich and surprising history. There is even a wonderful true story about the crew of the *Gorgon*, sailing back to England from the penal settlement on Norfolk Island in 1792. Hauling in a shark they had caught and cutting it open, they were astonished to find inside 'a Prayer Book, Quite fresh, not a leaf of it defaced'. The book had been inscribed with the name of a convict presumably lost at sea during the original voyage out to New South Wales: 'Francis Carthy, cast for death in the Year 1786 and Repreaved the Same day at four oClock in the afternoon'.[1]

The cargo of the First Fleet included hundreds of Scriptures, in hard copy, unloaded at Sydney Cove and distributed at the discretion of the chaplain. Fragments of the Bible were also transmitted by European colonists through common and formal speech, in various kinds of writing, and even in the inscriptions on convicts' bodies. A significant minority of people transported to Australia had tattoos based on the Bible. Convict George Dakin, for example, was marked with Proverbs 14:9, 'Fools mock at sin'. Fourteen-year-old Joseph Dummet had an Adam and Eve tattoo along with the admission 'the serpent beguiled me & I did Eat'. John Oldershaw had a crucifixion scene above the ominous words of Amos 4:2, 'Prepare to meet thy God'. Joseph Lamb, a thief, bore a warmer encouragement from the Psalms, 'Love God for he is good to all'.[2] Many more were marked with crosses or other scriptural scenes and symbols. From the outset of its Australian career, the Bible has been more than a book. It has belonged not only to the upright or the educated: it is a word for all kinds of people.

The Bible still gets under Australian skin. Whatever opinions people may hold about the state of the churches, the integrity of Christian belief, or even the nature of secularism, it is clear that religion has not gone away. In the early twenty-first century, it is a major topic of public conversation – often a deeply polarising one. The story of the Bible in Australia offers a fresh perspective. It invites us to reconsider some competing myths. One is that Australia, since the convicts, has been a doggedly secular society and culture. Another is that Australia is (or was, or should be) a straightforwardly Christian nation. The often surprising history of the Bible here disrupts both assumptions. It enables a richer, more interesting and expansive story.

BUT WHAT IS THE BIBLE? I'VE BEEN USING THE TERM AS IF IT is obvious, and in a sense it is. According to the *Macquarie Dictionary*, it is the collection of sacred writings of the Christian religion, comprising the Old Testament and the New Testament; or a copy of the text of these writings. This definition matches well with common usage, but we need to dive deeper to do good history. After all, in what sense are these 'sacred writings'? What of the seven books labelled Apocrypha, rejected by Protestants but accepted as Scripture by Catholics? And the Old Testament is hardly old to Jewish believers.

Part of what is so interesting about 'the Bible' is that it does not really exist. Or rather, it does not exist in a static or self-evident way: the Bible is a fluid thing, ever-changing. In different times and places, and among different communities, it has comprised different books, in different orders, in different translations and editions. Over centuries, and at a truly astonishing rate in modernity, it has changed and been changed by the proliferating forms, languages, contexts and communities in which it appears. Now more than ever, there's an ocean of competing answers to the question of the Bible – not least its sacredness, authority, interpretation and meaning.

By the time the Bible was introduced to Australia, the major debates about which books were in and which were out were well and truly over. The question of translation was more or less settled for that era, too. In English, there was the King James or Authorised version of 1611, comprising sixty-six books in two Testaments, sometimes with the Apocrypha bound separately in between (without the status of holy writ). This was by far the most common version that circulated in Australia until well into the twentieth century. However, the King James Bible was rarely if ever the only one. Catholics certainly preferred others – initially the Douay-Rheims, later the Knox Bible and the Jerusalem Bible – approved by the Vatican and incorporating the Deutero-canonical books to make a total of seventy-three.

The multiplication of translations and the publication of all kinds of new editions is one of the remarkable stories of the nineteenth and twentieth centuries. But even in the relative calm of the late eighteenth century, and as far from the historic centre of Christianity as the British colonies of Australia, the Bible was already a many-splendoured thing: an object, a text, a source of stories and ideas; a word read, gossiped, preached, tattooed; and seen as everything from a resented imposition to the very Word of God.

FROM SUCH BEGINNINGS, THE BIBLE'S AUSTRALIAN CAREER could only be interesting. It has mattered as a core part of the colonial inheritance from Britain; because of its dynamic place in culture; and because of its transformative role in the life of faith. Or to put it another way, the Bible has mattered to Australia in three main guises – the globalising Bible, the cultural Bible and the theological Bible.

The globalising Bible

The Bible was initially transmitted to Australia from elsewhere, and relatively recently at that. This is important, though not because it is unusual, for the Bible is not really indigenous to any one place or people: as a library of composite texts, it has always been a multi-author, multi-lingual and multi-cultural thing – even in the original Bible lands. The bare fact of the Bible's introduction from overseas means its presence in Australia has been shaped by major global movements of people, cultures and ideas. The Bible matters because it is a key element of the Australian experience of globalisation. It is part of what connects Australians to other places and peoples.

This globalising quality is a longstanding part of the Bible's history. The books that comprise the New Testament were themselves written in the midst of Christian expansion. They provide a glimpse into the cultural and theological challenges of initial church growth beyond Palestine into parts of Europe and Asia Minor. The next few centuries of Christian history are marked by its geographical spread and adaptation, including among the peoples of Asia. By the tenth century, Christian traders, travellers and missionaries had carried their faith beyond India to China, and possibly even as far as the trading ports of western Malaya and northern Sumatra.[3] If subsequent history had been different, perhaps Asian Christians might have eventually conveyed the Bible to Australia.

As it was, European imperialism introduced the Bible to Australia, and gave it some very significant characteristics. The first relates to its specifically *European* source. Conveyed to Australia by British colonisers, and reinforced by decades of British immigration, the Bible did not arrive 'clean', so to speak, but thick with existing associations and applications, accrued through centuries of British and more broadly European history. It arrived not as a 'blank text' open to any possible interpretation, but embedded in a particular if porous community, culture and tradition.

One of the European Bible's most important features was its long (though not uncontested) standing as the revealed Word of God: it came to Australia backed by centuries of belief that it contained the knowledge of salvation and the ultimate truth about the world. Granted such import and authority, the European Bible had long been considered, debated and fought over. From the conversion of the Roman emperor Constantine and the emergence of Christendom to the sixteenth-century Reformations and the readjustments of the Enlightenment, there were myriad ramifications for European thought, state and society.

By the late eighteenth century, the Bible's history in Europe had informed and partly produced much of what Europeans took as basic to their own civilisations. For example:

- the very form of the book, the codex, and a form of modernity intimately associated with the written word;
- a sense of linear time – alpha and omega, beginning and end – and a vision of history utterly unlike that of Indigenous Australians;

- certain ideas about government, society, the environment and human nature;
- a vernacular language itself shaped by various translations of the Bible, and a literature resplendent with biblical phrases, narratives, characters and themes.

I am not suggesting that the Bible produced these in any simple way. It is a complex text which has always given rise to multiple interpretations and applications. In addition, European reflection on the Scriptures has always been informed by non-Christian impulses and traditions – classical, humanist and Enlightenment, for example. These too had substantial consequences for Europe and its colonial outposts, including Australia. Nevertheless the Bible was critical to many of the cultural products Europeans exported to the world during the age of empire. Transplanted to Australia by colonising Britons, these living artefacts of the Bible's European history were interwoven into the story of this place. The consequences proved transformative for Australia.

Second, the Bible was conveyed to Australia as part of a specifically *imperial* movement of people, institutions and ideas. The first and most dominant form of the globalising Bible in Australia was European and imperial. From the outset, the Bible was associated with the colonising projects of transporting convicts, appropriating Aboriginal land, and forming settler societies. To understand its long-term significance in Australian life, we need to consider not only the transmission of its European cultural products, but the messy realities of culture contact and the dynamics of colonial power.

The precise relationships between Christianity and colonialism are very complex. But part of the reason the Bible still matters in Australia today is because it was part of the long dark history of the frontier. It is not just that Prime Minister Paul Keating alluded to the Golden Rule – do to others what you would have them to do you (Matthew 7:12) – in his famous Redfern Speech of 1992, or that the language of Kevin Rudd's 2008 Apology to the Stolen Generations had a biblical provenance. In profound ways, the Bible helped shape the very dynamics of British colonialism. The colonists' understandings of Scripture infused everything from dispossession and personal violence to humanitarian denunciations of settler greed and cruelty.

Crucially for contemporary Australia, the Bible did not remain the cultural or even the theological property of the invading Europeans. Though colonists and especially missionaries often imposed the European Bible on Aboriginal communities, from very early on, Indigenous people found ways to reappropriate and reinterpret it for themselves. Since at least the mid-nineteenth century, and in especially visible ways since the 1960s, Indigenous Australians have drawn on the Bible to demand just treatment. The history of Indigenous rights movements, as well as the emergence of Indigenous churches, point to the extraordinary potency of the Bible in Australian history – as both a tool of imperial oppression and a text of liberation. The Bible remains deeply important for Australia today, because it is at once an embedded part of our European inheritance, and a source for subverting colonial power and reconciling the nation. It is a text that crosses and reshapes cultural boundaries.

The Bible and culture

'I am not a Christian', wrote the left-leaning intellectual Clive Hamilton in 2015, 'but I believe that the cultural legacy of Christianity runs deep and should not be discarded wholesale':

The King James Bible, for instance, has profoundly shaped our use of language, the language of the atheist as much as the parish priest. The Book of Job is perhaps the deepest meditation we have on the human condition. And the New Testament's stock of parables and stories imbues our moral thinking, generally in positive ways.

The Bible should be 'approached critically, and not treated as holy writ', Hamilton added. But 'in western societies like ours, a rounded education includes this legacy'. His point about 'the cultural riches of the Bible' was clearly made.[4]

In early twenty-first-century Australia, such statements are readily made by atheists and Christians, conservatives and progressives. Prior to becoming Prime Minister, for example, Liberal leader Tony Abbott nominated the Bible as the most important 'great text ... at the core of our civilisation'.[5] His Labor nemesis, Prime Minister Julia Gillard, also insisted that 'our culture is steeped in Christian traditions ... Understanding the Bible is one of the keys to Western culture and if you don't have the key it can be very, very difficult to unlock'.[6] Such formulations are not universally accepted, and the implications for school education are fiercely debated (which is partly why these statements were made in the first place). But the Bible's dynamic relationship to culture — now, and in the past — rewards investigation. In Australia, the Bible has played a significant role in culture both as a way of life, and as expressed in the arts. It has been a reference point for generations of ordinary Australians, and a stimulating influence on the creative imagination.

The very idea of the Bible as a great text of our civilisation, a treasure trove of cultural riches, is not a timeless or universal commonplace. It has a history of its own. Prior to the eighteenth century, Europeans understood the value and authority of the Bible in overwhelmingly theological terms: it was the Word of God. But in the context of the Enlightenment and in the face of new critiques, a host of scholars and literati developed a new model of authority that stood apart from religious belief: the Bible as cultural heritage.[7] Emerging particularly from Germany and England during the eighteenth and early nineteenth centuries, this idea of the 'cultural Bible' became widely influential. It did not immediately displace the theological Bible: for many nineteenth- and even twentieth-century Europeans, the cultural Bible existed alongside the Bible as the Word of God, barely distinguishable from it. In Britain and her Australian colonies, believers commonly upheld the King James as a splendid embodiment of both qualities. But if Hamilton and Gillard are any guide, Enlightenment scholars ultimately succeeded in laying a foundation for valuing the Bible in cultural terms, even after faith has gone.

This cultural or 'Enlightenment' Bible proved remarkably adaptable to the end of Western Christendom. Newly framed in terms of shared cultural assumptions, rather than faith, it informed new visions of citizenship, rooted not in the religion of the state but in particular national identities. It influenced the ways people imagined themselves and their community, the kind of society they were building. Its impact was marked: for example, in forming a respectable, post-penal society; during the debates about nation around the time of federation; and amid the collapse of old certainties during the 1960s and after.

Of course, the Bible is not inherently Western, let alone British. The migrating locus of the Christian church from Europe to the majority world – Africa, Asia – is a highly significant global trend. But the Bible's potency in Australia, and the longevity of its influence, has stemmed partly from its European – and more specifically its British – cultural associations and credentials. This helps to explain why the decline of Christianity in Australia does not entail the decline of the Bible, but rather its transformation.

The theological Bible and the life of faith

The Bulletin magazine served up a real treat to readers in January 1904. It had collected a whole list of opprobrious slang for a clergyman: sky-pilot, devil-dodger, gospel-puncher, amen-snorter and Bible-banger. That last term – 'Bible-banger' or 'Bible-basher' – is an original Australian contribution to the riches of the English language. *The Bulletin*'s is the first known usage in print.[8] For more than a century now, it has expressed an irreverent strain in Australian culture, especially intolerance for over-zealous or moralising types. (Consider Randolph Stow's literary depiction of 'Bible bashers and humourless clods', or Prime Minister Gough Whitlam's derision of Queensland Premier Joh Bjelke-Petersen as a 'Bible-bashing bastard'![9])

However, even in the generation that invented Bible-basher as a phrase, anticlerical individuals could retain a deep regard for Scripture itself. 'I am a strong Labour man and Socialist', wrote one worker from North Queensland in 1910. When it comes to the 'condemnation of cant and hypocrisy and of most parsons and bishops and churches and their ways I am with it all the way'.

> But why not leave us and our Bible (dear old Bible! grand old Bible!) alone … there are many like myself to whom the very name of Jesus, Saviour and Christ, is a sacred thing, not to be lightly spoken.[10]

There is more than a hint of protest here. But it goes to show that the relationships between people's religious beliefs, church perceptions and attitude to the Bible are not always straightforward. The Bible's reception by the wider population, and the strength of its influence in society, is related to but not synonymous with the reception and influence of the churches.

This book is alert to secular uses of the Bible – from appeals to the cultural Bible to Koby Abberton's tattoo. But it also keeps a close eye on specifically Christian institutions and movements – which, after all, have played such a key role in placing the Bible before the people, and lent authority to particular interpretations. In places it begins to burrow into the experience of those who, 'through the living and eternal word of God … have been born again' (1 Peter 1:23). In this, it takes seriously what many Australians – though not many of their historians – have taken seriously before: the Bible as the Word of God.

In theological terms, the Bible's sacred character may be the only real basis for its significance to Australia. According to Scripture itself, the Word of God is 'alive and active' (Hebrews 4:12) – or as the King James version has it, 'quick and powerful'. It has an agency and an impact of its own:

> So also will be the word that I speak (says the Lord)—
> it will not fail to do what I plan for it;
> it will do everything I send it to do
> (Isaiah 55:11 (Good News Translation)).

In every generation since the Bible first came to Australia, there have been people who have expected God's Word to work, and who have personally understood what the famous Australian preacher James Jefferis meant when he said 'there is a power in the Bible itself, in the spirit of its teaching, in the revelation it makes of God and His love'. For such people, the Bible is no dead letter, to be appreciated in merely cultural terms: it is a word to be believed, a means of knowing the living God. To quote Jefferis again:

> The Bible itself is nothing unless its truth becomes our own, interweaving itself among all the thoughts and activities of our life, nay, entering the life itself, to become in a real sense the strength and vitality of it.[11]

For people who do not experience the Bible this way, the 'theological' Bible can be hard to understand. But history always requires openness and imagination. And even in non-theological terms, the Bible's sacred status is crucial to its impact in culture. It is what sets the Bible apart from its nearest rival for influence in Australia – the works of William Shakespeare. The comparison is clarifying. Like the Bible, Shakespeare has been a staple text since the arrival of Europeans, widely read over several generations. His words and phrases have become part of ordinary language. His plots and characters have infiltrated common culture. His insights into human nature have also been mulled over and valued. Many Australians have learned passages by heart and some have been changed by it.

But here's the rub: Shakespeare's plays have not been treated as works of divine inspiration. This means they have not been routinely read in a devotional manner, as a means of hearing God's voice or as a guide to eternal salvation. It means readers have not tried to bend their lives to Shakespeare's teaching, or taken on his stories as a framework for understanding the universe. It also means Shakespeare's plays have not been so widely distributed or so zealously promoted. His influence in Australia is a distant second to the theological Bible's.

WHEN IT COMES TO THE LIFE OF FAITH, THERE ARE EVIDENTLY changes afoot. Census data shows that Australians' adherence to non-Christian religions has been growing steadily. The proportion of people willing to identify with 'no religion' at all has been increasing fast since the 1980s: as the first option listed in the 2016 census, it proved the choice of almost 30 per cent of Australians. However, as late as 2009, roughly two-thirds of people still identified more with Christianity than with any of these alternatives.[12] According to a Nielsen poll, 58 per cent of those Christian-identifying people – about one-third of Australians overall – considered the Bible to be the Word of God, as opposed to a book 'written by men and not the Word of God'.[13] It is a remarkable result at a time when fewer than 15 per cent of adults go to church once a month or more. Could it really be that one in every five or six Australians rarely if ever attends church, but retains at least a residual belief in the Bible as a sacred word?

Of course, such data does not tell us what people *mean* by 'the Bible is the Word of God'. Christians have usually agreed that the Bible bears witness to the drama of redemption – both in the history of ancient Israel and the life, death and resurrection of Jesus Christ. But what is the nature and extent of its authority? How it should it be interpreted? What is its relationship to tradition, reason, experience? What exactly does it teach on various topics? Even regular church-goers hold significantly different views. Indeed, differences among Christians on these points have defined the recent history of the faith, and had substantial consequences for the relationship between the churches and wider society. At the very least, though, recent Australian surveys of both churchgoers and the wider population indicate that the theological Bible cannot be consigned to the past. In the early twenty-first century – and all the more so in earlier periods – the Bible's significance is bound up with its sacred qualities.

The Bible still matters, then, because of its role in the life of faith.

It has enduring importance to Australia not only because it is part of what connects us to other people and places, and because of its dynamic relationship to culture: people strive to follow its teaching, and in some way take on its vision of the world. As such, the Bible has an intriguing place in the history of Australians' subjectivity and emotions. (How many, like Christiana Blomfield, resolved to study the Bible, struggling against 'selfish feelings' and asking 'for assistance from the Almighty to do His will'?[14] Or, like Mary Hassell, heard the Bible preached and 'felt the blessing of forgiveness from a compassionate Saviour flow into her heart' – such that she later, when alone, wept in the new conviction of sins forgiven?[15])

As a transformative religious text, the theological Bible has also influenced a dynamic Christian citizenship. It has informed a posture of altruistic engagement towards wider society, which, in turn, has been brought to bear on a whole host of social movements and organisations – from trade unions to savings banks, political parties to environmental groups. 'Working out its Divine mission in a living Christianity', as Jefferis said, the Bible has furnished Australians with 'the power to face danger and conquer difficulty, and by the might of self-sacrifice to regenerate the world'.[16]

THE BIBLE'S PLACE IN AUSTRALIAN LIFE HAS BEEN DIVERSE and changing, sometimes surprising and very often debated. But since its introduction in the late eighteenth century, its influence has been far-reaching. Its imprint is extensive and intricate in areas from politics to the arts, the environment to social relations. The relative importance of the globalising Bible, the cultural Bible and the theological Bible has fluctuated in Australian history, but all suggest that the Bible is well and truly under Australian skin.

PART 1

COLONIAL FOUNDATIONS

'Where the deuce is Sydney Cove Port Jackson?' joked the surgeon George Worgan on arriving there in 1788. The answer, he wrote to his brother back in England, was a good ten weeks' voyage beyond the Cape of Good Hope. Earlier in the summer, the fleet had stopped over at the Cape to stock up on provisions. They had collected everything they expected to need in forming a new colony: bulls, cows, mares, colts, sheep, hogs, goats, fowls 'and other living Creatures by Pairs', as well as a vast number of plants, seeds and other garden articles such as orange, lime, lemon, quince apple, pear trees – 'in a Word, every Vegetable Production that the Cape afforded'. Worgan quipped that each ship steered away for New South Wales 'like another Noah's Ark'.[1]

Worgan was not an especially devoted Christian. A musician's son with a romantic bent, he was more interested in bushwalking and fine music than biblical religion. He has the distinction of bringing the first piano to Australia. But the Bible was part of Worgan's cultural baggage too. His casual reference to Noah suggests its place in his thought and imagination. Whatever his personal beliefs, the Bible was a familiar text. It shaped the way he looked at the world around him.

The European colonists of Australia came from the only region of the world that was majority Christian at the time. They carried the Bible with them, wrapped up with particularly European histories of interpretation. This European Bible was a changing, controversial thing: by the late eighteenth century, it had been the focus of debate for almost 300 years. From the Reformation to the scientific revolution to the high point of the Enlightenment, the Bible's influence among Europeans had been repeatedly unsettled and transformed.

The question is: how did this hotly contested European Bible influence colonial settlement in Australia? How did the early colonists understand the Bible, its status and meaning? What role did the Bible play in cultivating a society of immigrants in an unfamiliar land? And what was its role in the contact of European and Indigenous cultures? The answers have mattered a great deal to Australia. Their legacies reverberate into the twenty-first century.

CHAPTER 1

IN THE BEGINNING?

For as long as Europeans had read the Bible, it had shaped their ideas of the Great South Land. Way back in the fifth century, St Augustine, one of most important theologians of the Western church, had speculated on whether there were Antipodes – 'that is to say, men on the opposite side of the earth, where the sun rises when it sets to us'. He thought not: descendants of the first man, the biblical Adam, could not possibly have 'taken ship and traversed the whole wide ocean, and crossed from this side of the world to the other'.[1] Europeans still went looking, all the while speculating on the kind of land they might find and who might inhabit it.

In 1522, more than 1000 years after Augustine, Magellan's expedition achieved the first circumnavigation of the globe. There was almost certainly a Bible on board ship, as the expedition made its way from Spain to South America and across the Pacific Ocean to the Philippine islands and the Malay Archipelago. Voyage records depict Magellan explaining Christianity to the people of Cebu, advancing 'arguments to induce them to accept the faith' and arranging a mass baptism.[2] Journeys like his had long-term consequences for the spread of Christianity through South-east Asia and the Pacific.

The Australian continent itself continued to elude Europeans. The navigator Pedro Fernandez de Quiros thought he had found it in 1605; arriving in present-day Vanuatu, he assumed the largest island was the South Land he was seeking. He promptly hoisted an 'emblem of the Holy Cross – on which Jesus Christ's person was crucified and whereon He gave his life for the ransom and remedy of the human race'. He claimed possession of the land, naming it *Austrialia del Espiritu Santo*, 'land of the Holy Spirit'. Europeans like Quiros imagined Australia with the mind of faith. They wove stories of discovery and Christian expansion into one grand narrative – anticipating the spread of Christendom to the Great South Land.

The first foreigners to succeed where Quiros had failed were traders more than missionaries. Muslim seafarers from Macassar, in southern Sulawesi, made regular visits to northern Australia, setting up annual camps in Arnhem Land, interacting with the local Yolngu and harvesting trepang, or sea cucumber, for trade as far away as China. Beginning with Janzsoon in 1606, Dutch voyagers visited the coast, charting long sections of the continent's north, west and south. Similarly, English, Spanish and French explorers ventured into Australian waters, carrying their own cultures and beliefs – and possibly hard-copy Bibles.

In September 1770, the English navigator James Cook arrived at the island of Savu, near Timor, having just sailed up the east coast of Australia in the *Endeavour*. Two and a half centuries had passed since Magellan, and Europeans had made their presence felt in many parts of South-east Asia. By then the Dutch, in particular, were entrenched at Batavia (now Jakarta). Seeking wealth, they had drawn much of Indonesia into a web of unequal exchange. They had also established new places of worship and stationed chaplains among their own employees. Cook noted that the people of Savu 'speake a Language peculiar to themselves into which the Dutch have caused the New-Testament to be Translated'. '[L]etters and writing' had been introduced among them too, he observed, and 'by this means several hundreds of them have been converted to Christianity'.[3] The remark reveals a new phase in the Bible's career in the region, and the spread of the New Testament to within a few days' sail of Australia.

Cook's own voyages dramatically extended these developments. They confirmed a connection between the European Bible and the processes of imperialism and globalisation, inaugurated a British sphere of influence in the Pacific, and opened the way to trade, missionary activity and the formal colonisation of eastern Australia.[4] They also pointed to some of the huge changes that had occurred back in Europe over the previous two and a half centuries, which would have major consequences for Australia.

COOK'S *ENDEAVOUR* BIBLE IS A LARGE VOLUME, WEIGHING nearly four kilograms, bound in leather and embossed with gold writing. Thanks to Gutenberg's invention, it was mechanically printed, on the rag paper in use at the time. A handwritten note inside the cover explains that it accompanied Cook on all three of his Pacific voyages, and was then kept by his widow Elizabeth. After her death in 1835 it was passed down among her relatives. Eventually donated to the Australian Museum, it is now held by the State Library of New South Wales, Sydney.

Turning the first page, one sees signs of the great *changes* that had unsettled the European Bible over the previous two and a half centuries. The title page identifies it as a 1765 Oxford edition of the King James Version: 'The Holy Bible, containing the Old and New Testaments, newly translated out of the original tongues, and with the former translations diligently compared and revised, by His Majesty's Special Command'. A few pages further on, the book of Genesis begins in English: 'In the beginning God created the heavens and the earth'. These features underline that Cook's Bible was not just a timeless old book, but a product of the English Reformation.

When Magellan had left Europe in 1519, no English Bible existed in print. The standard text of the Western church was the Latin Vulgate, a version prepared by the scholar Jerome more than a millennium previously. Other versions existed, within the reach of the rich and well educated, including translations of the Vulgate into certain European languages, and new critical editions like Erasmus' Greek New Testament. But the Vulgate was the common version of public worship, the text used to illuminate the Catholic liturgy, and the undisputed reference for Western scriptural theology.

All this changed in the heat of the Reformation. In September 1522, the monk Martin Luther published a translation of the New Testament into contemporary German. Luther had been in rebellion against the Catholic Church for five years by then, but his Bible took the conflict to a whole new level. It epitomised his rejection of the Pope's authority and came to symbolise the reformers' catch-cry of 'Scripture alone'. His Bible challenged many established doctrines with its new translations of key terms and verses. (Luther famously rendered Romans 3:28 as 'we reckon a man to be justified by faith *alone*'.) Most radically, Luther placed the Bible in the hands of ordinary people – along with an encouragement to read and understand it for themselves. It marked a turning point, eventually felt in most parts of the world.

The first English translator of the Reformation era was William Tyndale. Influenced by Luther and himself a gifted linguist, Tyndale sought refuge in Germany, where he began turning the Greek and Hebrew into crisp and memorable English. Some of the phrases he coined in the 1520s are still in common use: 'the signs of the times', 'the powers that be', 'fight the good fight', 'it is a sure thing'. All these and more originate in his English New Testament. Tyndale's goal, however, was more subversive. He declared: 'I defy the Pope and all his laws! If God spares my life ere many years, I will cause the boy that drives the plow to know more of the Scriptures than the Pope himself!'

Copies of Tyndale's Bible were printed in the new Protestant cities of northern Europe, pushed into bales of cloth and smuggled back to England. There they were read in great secrecy or burned on discovery. (Only one copy of the first edition survived. It is now among the greatest treasures of the British Library in London.) Tyndale remained abroad, but was eventually caught, imprisoned, and in 1536 executed for heresy. His work nevertheless survived to provide a foundation for many more English editions. Within a few years of his death, a vernacular Bible was authorised by Henry VIII for reading in English churches. This 'Great Bible' (1539) incorporated large chunks of Tyndale's original translation, and helped make the Bible familiar even to illiterate English speakers. Decades later, the translators of the King James Version similarly retained many of Tyndale's phrases: 'In the beginning was the word'; 'For God so loved the world'; 'Give us this day our daily bread'.[5] Cook's *Endeavour* Bible included these words.

Cook's Bible embodied broadly Protestant ideas about God's word. At the same time, it hinted at the challenges posed by the vernacular Bible. If there were many competing translations, who decided what the Bible actually said? And if anyone could read it, who decided what it taught? Should 'laymen and silly old women' be allowed to interpret Scripture, Luther's adversaries had asked?[6] And what if people read the Bible in ways that threatened the whole social and political order? What if they used it to instigate rebellions and found republics in the place of monarchies?

As the poet John Dryden rhymed in the decades after England's civil war:

> The book thus put in every vulgar hand
> Which each presumed he best could understand
> The common rule was made the common prey
> And at the mercy of the rabble lay.

The King James Bible was meant to rein in such conflict and confusion; to stem the tide of competing translations and provide a common reference point. As the name suggests, too, it was the product of a church and crown establishment. Its alternative name, 'the Authorised Version', points to its status as the sole standard for public worship.

The illustrations of Cook's handsome edition give a similar impression. Most of the etchings depict Bible characters and their well-known stories. But some depict the rites and ministries of the Church of England, including infant baptism, Holy Communion, the visitation of the sick. A few combine Bible verses with scenes from recent monarchical history. For instance, the foiled gunpowder plot against James I accompanies Psalm 9:16 – 'The Wicked is snared in the Work of his own Hands'. Cook's Bible was a political as well as a religious thing; it subtly expressed a particular vision of the nation, its politics and history. Later, in Australia, such politics would rise to the surface as colonists fought over the Bible and the society they were building.

THERE IS ONE MORE CLUE TO THE EUROPEAN BIBLE AND ITS characteristics in Cook's era. It is a chronology stretching from the beginning of the world to the life of Jesus Christ, developed by the Irish scholar and Archbishop James Ussher in the mid-seventeenth century. An index at the back of Cook's Bible gives the relevant dates; they are also printed inside the margin at the top of each page. The date of creation, for example, is given as the year 4004 before Christ. The Great Flood survived by Noah is said to have happened in 2348 BC. To many readers now, such dates seem absurd, even a religious denial of science. But Cook lived prior to the discovery of an old earth. Ussher's dating of Genesis roughly corresponded with the calculations of scientific giants Johannes Kepler and Isaac Newton. In Cook's time, an idea of creation about 4000 years before Christ was still the consensus of European science.

This chronology reminds us of the great shifts between Cook's time and ours. It warns us against projecting our own assumptions and worldviews into the minds of people in the past. It also alerts us to the ingrained habits of thought that defined the European Bible. In particular, it highlights the historic European habit of calibrating knowledge about the world with the text of the Bible. This was a crucial legacy of the theological Bible. If Scripture was God's revelation about himself, humanity and the world, it was the unrivalled starting point for knowledge, the framework for understanding the world and its workings. It meant the Bible was a tool not only for private and public devotion, but for social and political thought, for science, geography, and scholarship of all kinds.

In practice, European theology encompassed several specific methods for reading and interpreting the Bible. History has also shown that changes in the *ways* people read Scripture often went along with changes in understandings of the world. During Cook's lifetime, new theories and findings in the observable world prompted new questions of the Bible.

WHEN COOK RETURNED TO ENGLAND, HAVING CLAIMED eastern Australia for its King, he returned to a society steeped in the Scriptures. It can be hard for twenty-first-century people to grasp the extent of the Bible's ubiquity – but in the late eighteenth century, roughly 250 years after Tyndale, the Bible was by far the most widely available book in English, the central product of the British printing industry. It circulated as a whole volume, in individual Testaments, and in its separate books. It was also extracted, abridged and interpreted in a host of aids, guides, compendia and other commonplace books – a reminder that the Bible was a very flexible thing. Not only that, the sermon was the dominant literary genre of the day, easily eclipsing the popular novel. (Present estimates suggest that for every page of secular fiction published in Britain in the eighteenth century, there were about fifteen pages of sermons or other explicitly religious material![7]) Church services were also the most common form of community gathering, which meant many people had a thoroughgoing familiarity with the Scriptures.

The published version of Cook's *Endeavour* journals proved a bestseller. Offering a fascinating account of the Pacific and its many societies and peoples, they prompted a range of responses, from the sceptical to the evangelical. For some, Cook's voyages magnified a question they were already asking: What should Europeans make of places and people not directly mentioned in the Bible? Was there only one true revelation for all humanity? What was the nature of religion, morality, society and politics?

For others, reading Cook galvanised a vast missionary vision. This response was especially common among people buoyed by the rising tide of evangelical religion. For them, Cook's voyages highlighted the extent of the non-Christian world and prompted fresh efforts to convey the gospel to the nations. John Newton, for example, was a former slave captain turned evangelical minister and hymn writer, now most famous as the author of 'Amazing Grace'. Engrossed by Cook's account, he responded with a prayer: 'May I be suitably affected with the case of the countless thousands of my fellow creatures, who know thee not, nor have opportunities of knowing thee'.[8] (He went on to mentor the first clergyman to the colony of New South Wales – advising him, praying for him and encouraging him in regular letters – dubbing him, in the process, the Apostle to the South Seas.) The shoemaker William Carey read Cook and had his attention awakened to missions. In 1792, he responded with his famous *Enquiry into the Obligations of Christians to use means for the Conversion of the Heathens.* Carey co-founded a missionary society and soon departed for India, where he spent most of the rest of his life in Bible translation.

These responses to Cook's voyages reflected beliefs and mentalities which European colonists would soon convey to Australia. When it was eventually decided to send a fleet to the place Cook had named and claimed as New South Wales, the colonists hauled hard-copy Bibles ashore with them, along with the swirling history of the Bible in Europe, from the Reformation to the Enlightenment. The British arrived with diverse ways of reading Scripture, with unresolved debates about its status and meaning.

Dry land: the European Bible at Sydney Cove

The first hard-copy Bibles in Australia arrived in the luggage of Richard Johnson, the sensitive young chaplain to the British colony of New South Wales. He was a Church of England clergyman, and a protégé of some of the leading evangelicals of his day. He joined the First Fleet with his new wife Mary – whom he described as 'about half a Baptist and Half a Methodist' – and hundreds of copies of the Bible. There was his own, of course – a very plain, unillustrated King James. There was also a *Book of Common Prayer* which he likely used in his private as well as public devotions. Both these books survive today, among the historical treasures of St Philip's Anglican Church, Sydney. Both show signs of frequent use and repair. Apart from several worn pages, the Bible is missing its original cover and title piece – presumably damaged by fire when the colony's first church burned down. As for the Prayer Book, the marriage service is spattered with ink and the page with the order for Communion is torn from turning.

Apart from these personal volumes, Johnson brought out a cargo of books provided by the Society for the Propagation of the Gospel. These were the first religious works circulated in the colony, evidently chosen with the convicts in mind. The consignment included 100 full Bibles, 400 New Testaments, 500 Psalters, and 200 copies of the Sermon on the Mount. There were also 200 church catechism books, 100 Prayer Books and 100 copies of Osterwald's *Necessity for reading the Scriptures*. Various other devotional, moral and educational pamphlets also contained scriptural texts, and helped to spread reformist ideas and values associated with the Bible. These included *Dissuasives from Stealing*, *Exhortations to Chastity*, an *Exercise Against Lying* and a *Caution to Swearers*.[9]

Evangelicals and the theological Bible

Johnson believed the Bible was a sacred book, 'our only sure and infallible guide, given by inspiration of God', containing 'all that is needful to make us wise unto salvation'. He was committed to reading it himself and urged others to do the same. As chaplain, he did his best to make sure that people did not mistake the essential message of sin and forgiveness, faith and salvation. As he told the convicts during the 1790s:

> From this book we may learn the malignity of sin … [and] the just and certain condemnation due to our disobedience. It shews us, likewise, the way of our recovery. How perfectly the mediation of Christ is suited … to display the justice of God, in harmony with his mercy, and thereby to give peace to the consciences of convinced sinners.

> Thus it is said, 'God so loved the world, that he gave his only begotten Son that whosoever believeth in him should not perish, but have everlasting life' (John 3:16). 'He that believeth in him is not condemned … his faith is counted to him for righteousness' (Romans 4). … My friends, search the scriptures, and you will find that this is the tenor of the whole Bible.[10]

Johnson was an evangelical, one of the many thousands of eighteenth-century Protestants swept up by a vibrant, transatlantic movement that transformed religious life in Britain, its empire and beyond. Within a generation of Cook's voyages, the influence of evangelical revivals in Britain and North America, combined with Continental pietism, burst into an unprecedented movement to carry the gospel to all peoples of the world. Within a few years of the foundation of New South Wales, English evangelicals formed several new groups to express and promote their beliefs around the world. One in particular, the British and Foreign Bible Society (BFBS), pursued an extraordinary goal: 'to make these Holy

Writings known, in every nation and in every tongue' and 'to render them the actual possession of every individual on the face of the whole earth'.[11] Along with missionary organisations and churches, the BFBS played a major role in the spread of the 'the good book' and its message throughout Australia and the South Pacific.

Sceptics and the cultural Bible

Other European colonists did not share the evangelicals' high view of the Bible. To the chagrin of the clergy, many did not accept or aspire to the same standards of personal conduct either. For all kinds of reasons, they were sceptical of Christian claims that the Bible revealed divine truth for the whole world, and casual about its moral teaching. Among the common sailors, soldiers and convicts, there were people with a more contingent view of the world. Some were also openly anticlerical and suspicious of the church. (Some even alluded to the Bible to express their contempt for the clergy: in 1815, the vessel *Hebe* conveyed Australia's first Wesleyan missionary, Samuel Leigh, to Sydney. In the course of the voyage, the ship was buffeted by such a hellish storm that most of its livestock died and many of its stores got washed away. 'I expected nothing else', pronounced one of the crew, 'after taking Jonah on board'.[12])

Among the officers, there were better educated men influenced by Enlightenment thought. Like some of Cook's readers, they doubted or even denied the Bible's status as the unique and universal Word of God. In 1799, the Irish evangelical missionary William Henry visited Sydney from Tahiti. During a stay of several months, he formed the view that many of the military officers were deists or atheists. 'I have had several controversies with some of them, but have been obliged to lay aside the Bible, as its authority was of no consequence with them, and reason with them from the principles of philosophy in vindicating some of the great truths of Christianity.'[13]

Even if most officers did not live up to the clergy's ideals of Christian faith and conduct, they still carried the Bible to Australia in the ways they thought and spoke. We see this in many of their early accounts of New South Wales – such as Surgeon Worgan's quip about Noah's ark, and his references to the Indigenous Eora as 'Adamites' and 'Evites', 'naked and not ashamed' as in the Garden of Eden. The use of biblical phrases and allusions shows that the Bible was a common reference for literate types, if not for matters of philosophy then at least for stories about the world. The difference was that they tended to draw on a cultural, more than a theological, version of the Bible.

The good order of society

Admiral Arthur Phillip, the first governor of New South Wales, was a 'trusty and beloved servant' of the British crown. He represented a state that, in its formal arrangements, assumed a national church as a basis for national life. By the late eighteenth century, there was a widening gap between theory and practice: religion did not unify perfectly, either in politics or society. It was increasingly difficult to deny that there was more than one focus for religious loyalty, and more than one way of interpreting the Bible. But the established churches of the realm were still major and meaningful partners of the crown, and until as late as the 1820s, their members had unique access to various political and social institutions.

Phillip's own attitude was one of detached regard for the Church of England, into which he had been baptised. Neither a vital believer nor a doctrinaire atheist, he recognised the role of the church in promoting morality, public order and civil life. In New South Wales, his official instructions were to 'by all proper methods enforce a due observance of Religion and good order among all the inhabitants' and to 'take such steps for the celebration of publick Worship' as circumstances allowed. From an official point of view New South Wales was not primarily a religious settlement, but the church was to play a civilising, stabilising role in colonial society.

Similar expectations congealed around the Bible. Even before the fleet had set sail, Phillip had told Johnson to begin his preaching to convicts with 'more moral subjects'. When they arrived, Phillip outlined his own expectations by quoting the Bible. It was good for couples to get married, he lectured the convicts, and they should all work hard and not be idle. 'Those who would not work should not eat', he pronounced (Thessalonians 3:10).[14]

A few days later, on a warm but cloudy Sunday morning, the troops and the convicts gathered again for a collective encounter with the Bible. Under a great tree, Johnson led them in divine service – confirming the Bible's place in public ritual and inaugurating a practice that became a regular feature of colonial life. Following the *Book of Common Prayer*, the liturgy involved numerous quotes from Scripture. Longer passages from the Old and New Testaments were read, and Johnson took the opportunity to address them. The event is commemorated today by a modest monument, on the corner of Hunter and Bligh streets in Sydney, bearing the biblical text of Australia's first sermon: 'What shall I render unto the Lord for all his benefits towards me?' (Psalm 116:12).

WHAT EMERGES FROM ALL THIS IS AN INFLUENTIAL BUT contested Bible – one conveyed to Australia by Europeans with varied beliefs, enveloped in all kinds of agendas and interpretations. One implication is that the story of the Bible in Australia does not follow a simply trajectory of decline from a religious past to a secular present. From the outset, it has followed a fluctuating path of negotiation and transformation. This distinguishes the story of the Bible in Australia from the story of the Bible in Europe, and even from certain other settler societies such as the United States of America. It is illustrated first, and most colourfully, by the Bible's career in convict society.

Original sin: the Bible in convict society

Old Susannah Watson had a difficult life. As a young mother in the slums of Nottingham, she had lived with grinding poverty, hunger and illness. Unable to see her children starve, she had turned to stealing. Caught and convicted, she was sentenced to fourteen years' transportation, arriving in Australia in 1829. Separated from her family and suffering the worst of the convict system, Susannah's life experiences ultimately resonated with her reading of the Bible. During the 1870s, she wrote to her daughter about her efforts to bear patiently with a bad leg 'for Jesus sake, who has borne so much for me'. She also recalled 'how good God has been to me all my life long. Though he sends trouble and affliction, he cheers us with the life of his presence and gives us a hope of heaven through the merits of our precious Redeemer'.[15] She died at the age of 83, looking forward to an eternal reunion and trusting in Christ.

A convict colony might seem an unlikely beginning for the Bible in Australia: it is certainly a stark contrast with the Pilgrim Fathers who colonised Massachusetts. It would also be easy to think that the convicts themselves had little to do with the Bible.

By the high standards of the colonial clergy, they certainly seemed an irreligious bunch. But there were some, like Susannah Watson, who embraced the suffering saviour, Jesus Christ. Many more, in the period of transportation, had some use for the Bible. Its ideas, imagery and stories circulated in the common imagination of the time. Whatever their personal beliefs, convicts encountered it and made use of it, in ways that suggest its surprising relevance.

In the first place, the Bible was part of popular culture. We see this in the descriptions convicts wrote about the experience of transportation. Echoing the Genesis story of Adam and Eve's expulsion from Eden, some described themselves as 'exiles' or 'banished sinners', and their new surrounds as a 'solitary waste of the creation'.[16] Linus Miller, a New Yorker transported to Van Diemen's Land for his role in a rebellion against the British in Canada, dubbed it 'the land of Nod', a biblical place east of Eden. 'Hell' became a common description for places like Macquarie Harbour, a settlement specifically for convicts who re-offended while under sentence.[17]

The Bible was also a major element of visual culture, as we see in the many biblical tattoos recorded among convicts. By the 1830s and 1840s, perhaps a quarter of convicts arriving in Australia had tattoos – we know because they were recorded along with other identifying physical details. Biblical images and quotations were very common. A number of convicts tried in Scotland were tattooed with 'crosses, images of the fall, crucifixion and apocalypse'.[18] Crosses appeared in as many as 40 per cent of the Irish convicts' tattoos. Among the English, they were almost as popular as images of anchors and women. The meaning of the anchor symbol, too, probably drew its meaning from the Bible. Hebrews 6:19 speaks of the 'hope we have as an anchor of the soul, both sure and steadfast'. Numerous English pubs of the period were called Hope & Anchor, while anchor tattoos were often accompanied by a person's initials, symbolising hope and constancy.

CONVICTS MADE USE OF BIBLICAL SYMBOLISM IN INTRIGUING, even subversive ways. While several convicts were tattooed with Adam and Eve scenes, including serpents and trees, William Brown was tattooed with a tree and two naked men – a suggestion, perhaps, of homosexuality?[19] William Shemmett was tattooed with scenes including Christ on the cross together with a centurion and Mary Magdalene. His body was also inscribed with the text of Luke 18:13 – 'God have mercy on me a sinner'. Taken from Jesus' parable about the Pharisee and the publican, the phrase admitted guilt and expressed a need for forgiveness. At the same time it raised a rebuke to those confident of their own righteousness and who looked down on everybody else. Shemmett drew on the Bible to embrace the identity of sinner in ways that also cast his gaolers as Pharisees and suggested resistance to their moral authority.[20]

In at least a few cases, convict tattoos expressed Christian faith. Cornelius Hickey's tattoo comprised a crucifix, an anchor and the initial H. According to Hamish Maxwell-Stuart, it could be plausibly read as 'I have hope in salvation through Christ's sacrifice on the cross'.[21] Eliza Roberts was tattooed with a crucifix and the letters I.N.R.I., a Latin abbreviation of 'Jesus of Nazareth the King of the Jews' (Matthew 27:37).[22] George Isherwood had 'a well-executed representation of the crucifix' and, in capitals, the words of a famous hymn by Isaac Watts:

SEE FROM HIS HEAD HIS HANDS HIS FEET

SORROW AND LOVE FLOW MINGLED DOWN

DID ERE SUCH LOVE AND SORROW MEET
OR THORNS COMPOSE SO RICH A CROWN.[23]

Convicts also encountered the Bible through the institutions and ministrations of the colonial church. From the outset of penal settlement in Australia, virtually all convicts had some interaction with one of the major Christian denominations – initially just Anglican, but later also Catholic, Presbyterian, Methodist and others. They participated in church rituals for the baptism of children, marriage and burial, and received pastoral visits from various clergy. Johnson, for example, took great pleasure in going door to door, talking with the convicts in their huts. One of the first Catholic chaplains, John Joseph Therry, maintained a long and demanding pastoral ministry to the large minority of Irish convicts. (Therry's unofficial predecessor, Father Jeremiah O'Flynn, had spread the Word in a different way, going around Sydney singing about the crucified Christ – 'sweet are the nails and sweet the wood' – and other biblically inspired hymns.[24])

On most Sundays, convicts also attended religious services where they heard the Bible read, preached and prayed. In early 1790s Sydney, when church attendance was effectively voluntary, between a quarter and half of all convicts went along.[25] Later, church attendance was more or less compulsory – a new development evidently resented by those who burned Johnson's first church to the ground.

Church sermons were arguably the most important genre for presenting the Bible to convicts. It seems likely that a lot of preaching included exhortation to more moral conduct and encouragement to accept proper authority, as well as stern warnings about the fate of the unredeemed. But this does not necessarily mean that sermons had a 'denigrating function', or that the Bible was a mere tool for 'dragooning convicts into submission', as some scholars have suggested.[26] When delivered with appropriate compassion and humility, and when accompanied by the message of the cross of Christ, such preaching could have a liberating effect on its hearers. One Sunday in 1838, the convict blacksmith at Macquarie Harbour, Thomas Warwick, heard chaplain William Schofield preach on 'the sufferings of Christ and particularly him being scourged and that he died to save the vilest of the vile'. The very next day, Warwick was flogged himself – for 'having two iron wedges in his possession', presumably stolen from the government forge. The association of his own sufferings with the torments of Christ made such a deep impression on Warwick that he afterwards resolved to join the Wesleyans.[27]

THE BIBLE WAS ALSO MADE AVAILABLE TO CONVICTS IN WAYS specific to their situation as transportees. The assumption was that they needed reform and redemption, and that the Bible, and Christianity more broadly, would be instrumental in achieving it. In the 1820s and 1830s, Bibles and New Testaments were routinely distributed among convicts about to set sail for the colonies. Ships' surgeons usually conducted divine service at sea, and some of the more devout doctors took the opportunity to urge the Scriptures upon their congregations. On one remarkable voyage, Dr Colin Arnott Browning provided religious instruction three times a day, and by journey's end happily reported that 156 of the 200 convicts had converted (in token of their gratitude, the group made donations totalling £8 8s to the Bible Society).[28] On another trip, surgeon Peter Cunningham was impressed to find convict passenger William Jones reading the Bible of his own choice:

I never passed his berth without observing him earnestly
toiling away with a pair of huge spectacles arched over his
nose, or else the Bible lying close to his hip, ready to be
snatched up on the instant. Indeed, so earnest was he in his
religious exercises that he could not even attend muster, on
Sunday, without the Bible in his hand and his fore-finger
stuck between the leaves, to mark the passage he had been
reading.[29]

Convicts like Jones may have read the Bible to entertain themselves. Containing stories about love, war, betrayal and friendship,
tales of invasion, slavery, rescue and redemption – not to mention
a vast cast of characters including spies, warriors, prostitutes and
musicians, kings, queens, cops and robbers, even a giant fish and
a talking donkey – the Bible could definitely relieve some of the
tedium. The moral effect was less certain, however. During a stay
in the ship's hospital, Jones stole money from the medical crew. His
accomplice dobbed him in for failing to pass on a fair share – and
denounced him, in the process, as 'in reality the greatest ruffian in
all Wales'.[30]

Once they had a Bible in hand, convicts did a lot with it besides
read. During the voyage out, some convicts made a point of looking after the volume they had been given, apparently in the hope
of winning some favour on disembarking. (Other Christian books
were a different matter: walking the ship one sunny morning, surgeon Cunningham came across a group of convict women 'unpa-
pering their curls' – and found the floor littered with the shreds of
religious tracts.[31]) At other times, colonial clergymen despaired of
convicts 'destroying' Bibles and Testaments to make cards for gambling, or else using the pages to roll cigarettes.[32]

Once on land, the Bible was valuable to some convicts as a

tradable commodity. In 1789, Richard Johnson complained that he had 'distributed many books … but I fear this has done them little good. One sold his Bible for a glass of liquor, others tear them up for waste paper – this discourages me greatly'.[33] In the early 1820s, John Thomas Bigge, a royal commissioner sent to investigate the effectiveness of the convict transportation system, similarly found that:

> Several of the newly arrived convicts have received presents of Bibles and prayer books from the surgeons of the different convict ships … I have observed, however, that in the first marches to the different stations in the country, they lose and sometimes sell them for the purchase of bread and liquor.[34]

Small comfort, perhaps, that for such a transaction to succeed there must have been a willing buyer.

In very literal ways, too, convicts used the Bible to facilitate their escapes. London burglar Thomas Stacey arrived in New South Wales in 1832. After a series of unsuccessful attempts to abscond, he and the five other men in his chain gang escaped and turned to bushranging in the Bathurst area. Eventually caught and convicted, Stacey was sent to Norfolk Island where he continued to defy the penal authorities, suffering floggings for disobedience and being absent. In 1846, Stacey tried to convey two saws concealed in the pages of a Bible to a prisoner confined in the new gaol. For his efforts, he was given nine months in solitary confinement.[35]

Grimly, the Bible was formally offered to convicts one last time at the gallows. Wherever possible, those facing execution were attended by a priest or parson who urged repentance and offered consolation, often in the words of a Psalm. Some prisoners were apparently impervious to such efforts. William Riddell was the son of devout Scottish Dissenters and had read the Bible so frequently, as a youth, that he had memorised dozens of chapters. By the time he was convicted of receiving stolen sheep, he had also read Paine's *Age of Reason*, as well as works by Palmer, Voltaire and Volney – and given up his faith. Asked to state his religion upon his arrival in Sydney, Riddell astonished the colonial secretary with the answer 'none'. Convicted of murder on circumstantial evidence and against all protests of innocence, he was sentenced to hang in March 1829. Both the Presbyterian JD Lang and the evangelical Anglican William Cowper 'laboured earnestly' to bring the condemned man to a proper frame of mind. But asked again what he believed about a person's future state, Riddell was unwavering in his reply: 'I shall know the grand secret on Monday'.[36]

Riddell was unusual in refusing all spiritual consolation: many more of the condemned found some truth or comfort in the Bible. Many included statements of piety and penitence in their final declarations – no less heartfelt for its being expected of them. Several also faced their final moments with the gospel accounts of Jesus' death clearly in mind. In 1834, for example, a group of Catholic convicts condemned for mutiny stood on the scaffold repeating Jesus' own last words over and over, 'Into thy hands I commend my spirit' (Luke 23:46), and praying that the Lord would receive their souls.[37] When the murderer John Hawes prepared for the noose, he made a more subversive reference to the dying Christ. Replicating Jesus' last act of forgiving his persecutors, Hawes suggested that he, too, was more sinned against than sinning:

Take warning by my fate, But I would sooner be hanged here this morning than return to Moreton Bay. Starvation and ill usage there have brought me to this untimely end. It is not my natural disposition to commit an inhuman act. *I forgive all my oppressors.*[38]

Whatever conclusions we may draw about the convicts' spiritual beliefs, it is clear that the Bible had a significant career among them. They encountered the Scriptures in all kinds of ways, some quite independent of the church and clergy. Most observers denounced the convicts as ignorant of the Bible's contents, and few remarked positively on their fidelity to its teaching. But of all books, the Bible was the one they knew, and some of the more literate convicts had an impressive knowledge of it, too. According to the Reverend John Merewether, the better educated men transported in the 1840s were 'wonderful talkers' who 'hate hard work [and] can quote scripture enough to dazzle the clergyman'![39]

CHAPTER 2

INDIGENOUS ENCOUNTERS

Boorong belonged to the place where eels lie down. She was born there sometime in the mid-1770s, a daughter to Maugoran, a Burrumattagal elder, and Goorooberra, meaning 'firestick'. It was rich and nourishing country, home to many animals and edible plants. The higher ground had tall trees and an understorey of grasses, the result of careful management by regular burning. The river there was still tidal, but its salt water met a fresh stream. It was usually good for fishing, but when the eels came to breed, the Burramattagal and neighbouring clans gathered for a feast. They sang songs on the sandy shore, in a country alive with ancient meaning. For Boorong and her people, this was an inspirited land, the source of identity, sustenance and being.

When Boorong was about twelve years old, Europeans set up camp a few miles downriver at Sydney. Within months, they had crossed into her country with axes, hoes, guns and seeds. They established a second settlement, with a military base, and began farming in their own manner. Their invasion soon forced an angry Maugoran to relocate his people to the north side of the river. It marked the beginning of the destruction of Burramattagal society – one that intensified when smallpox tore through the region in autumn 1789. In less than three months, half to two-thirds of the local population caught the disease and died. Mass death, like dispossession, challenged the very foundations of Indigenous being.

It plunged communities and cosmologies into crisis. It altered the basic possibilities for Boorong's life.

In the midst of this devastating disruption, Boorong became the first Indigenous Australian to have a substantial encounter with the Bible. In April 1789, some of Governor Phillip's men found her sick with smallpox and took her to Sydney for attention. She was nursed there by Arabanoo, an Eora captive at government house. She was afterwards 'received as an inmate, with great kindness, in the family of Mrs Johnson, the clergyman's wife'.[1] Boorong remained with the Johnsons for about eighteen months before returning to the bush – an intense cross-cultural experience which included an introduction to the Bible.

Boorong observed the habits of the foreigners around her. She saw Johnson and some convicts farming; she saw Mary washing clothes, caring for her baby, keeping house. Boorong routinely heard the couple speaking their own language. From time to time, she likely saw them making marks on paper, somehow capturing their sounds and meanings in writing. Boorong would certainly have noticed the Johnson's attentiveness to an object her people came to call 'buk'. The chaplain studied it when he could, and often took it out with him. On Sundays, Boorong and other young Eora often went along and watched him read and preach from it to the crowd.[2] (Afterwards, one officer wrote, they were often seen to 'take a book, and with much success imitate the clergyman in his manner – for better and readier mimics can nowhere be found'.[3])

As long as she lived with the Johnsons, Boorong was urged to do more than observe them. The chaplain encouraged her to wear clothes, to speak English and to make herself useful around the house. He taught her the Lord's Prayer and tried to convey an idea of 'a supreme being etc' – hoping, as he put it, to see 'these poor heathen brought to the Knowledge of Christianity'. Johnson also 'took pains' to instruct Boorong in reading, presumably using the Bible as a text for lessons, introducing to her an alphabet, a language and a new kind of literacy, as well as a broadly Christian understanding of the world and how to live in it.[4]

In 1790, other First Fleet officers were absorbed in an effort to set up a proper channel of communication with the locals, and to conciliate them to the Europeans' arrival. They prevailed on Boorong to act as their translator and go-between. Her new language skills meant she got caught up further in the fraught interactions of black and white.[5] Politics are never far from the Bible.

Boorong proved a reluctant advocate for the colonists, and eventually left the Johnsons' house. In October 1790, she returned to the bush neither converted to Christianity nor convinced of the colonists' way of life. She continued to visit the Johnsons occasionally for at least five years after that, but in Mary's words she did so 'quite naked' and 'evidently preferred [her] own way of life'.[6]

By 1797 Boorong was married to Bennelong, the famous Wangal man who, more than anyone else, sought to manage the initial contact between black and white. Like Boorong, Bennelong had closely examined and then rejected white society. By the late 1790s, he had gathered a group of about 100 Indigenous survivors, including some of Boorong's brothers and people from various Sydney tribes. The group was usually observed west of Kissing Point, on the north side of the Parramatta River – just across from the place where the eels lie down.[7] Bennelong and Boorong made it their home for about fifteen years. They were buried there together, around 1813, on the estate of the ex-convict brewer James Squire.

OVER 60 000 YEARS, INDIGENOUS PEOPLES GRADUALLY OCCUPIED every habitable region of Australia, including what is now Tasmania and the Torres Strait Islands. In the process, they forged hundreds of distinct clans and language groups, each with their own traditions, practices and intimate relationships to particular sites. They developed ways of managing their environments to meet their basic needs, and to ensure ample opportunities for ceremonial and artistic life. This diverse population totalled between about 400 000 and 1.5 million people when the first European colonists arrived.

What was it like for Indigenous Australians to encounter the Bible? How, in the past 230 years, have Christianity and its Scriptures affected Aboriginal peoples and societies? These are endlessly complex and recurring questions. There is no one-size-fits all answer, nor even an agreed way of figuring one out. But Boorong's experience draws our attention to some issues of lasting importance, to do with the broad context and character of the Bible's introduction to Australia, that resonate even now.

Most basically, the Bible reached Indigenous Australians in the midst of European colonisation. It arrived with the British flag and an influx of white settlers on to Aboriginal land. By contrast, in parts of Aotearoa New Zealand and various Polynesian islands, missionary activity was years in advance of more overtly imperial ventures. There were always imbalances of power, but the European propagation of the Bible in the South Pacific did not always involve an immediate, wholesale challenge to local sovereignty and society. In Australia, however, settler colonialism meant the impact of Europeans was rapid and profound.

From an Aboriginal point of view, the arrival of European settlers typically involved dispossession from traditional lands, the scourge of new diseases, and the fracturing of families, clans and societies. The actual course of colonisation varied, but this was the basic context in which many Indigenous Australians first encountered the Bible. Some, like Boorong, were exposed to it in the midst of initial invasion. Many more, like her son Dickey, encountered it in the aftermath. This is significant in the history of Aboriginal missions: in several parts of the country, whole generations were damaged and displaced by whites before any word of Christian salvation arrived.

This context matters for the *kind* of Bible Indigenous people encountered. First, the Bible came in a European imperial guise, wrapped up in colonial thought and culture. Various interpretations of the Bible played into the ways the colonists thought about the land they claimed and occupied. In complex ways, the Scriptures also influenced their perceptions of Aboriginal people as 'heathen', 'degraded' and 'uncivilised'. In time, competing European attitudes and approaches to the Bible would fuel a raging debate about Indigenous people within the British empire.

The Bible also arrived with the cultural products of its long history in Europe, including the form of the book, print technology, and the English of the King James Bible. It often came with an alphabetic kind of literacy, too, and certain habits of reading and communication. Its cultural products and trappings also extended to the realm of imagination, such as a new kind of sacred geography, including hell below and heaven above. At the same time, Europeans brought an idea of being defined less by place than by time. The colonists typically thought in linear terms of a past creation, a present age and a future end. Their assumptions of progress had deep roots in Christian theology, and new energy from the ideas of the Enlightenment. To Aboriginal people – who made meaning in cyclical ways, in relation to journeys and sites – all this represented a radically different cast of mind.

Third, the Bible arrived laden with certain expectations about how it would work on Indigenous societies. Some of these were theological, to do with the life of faith and eternal salvation.

Others involved the Bible as an agent of civilisation. During the early nineteenth century, these were hotly debated – which came first? How were they advanced? What was the relationship of Christianisation to civilisation? The two impulses were rarely separated completely, and they informed both broad groups that exposed Aboriginal Australians to the Bible: colonial governments and missionary societies. Under government auspices, Indigenous Australians typically encountered the Bible as the part of a wider effort to conciliate and civilise – it was a means to the end of successful colonial settlement. Missionaries usually emphasised the theological Bible – its message was 'the power of God unto salvation to everyone that believeth' (Romans 1:16). But even if Christianisation came first, even if eternal salvation was the ultimate end, European missionaries still carried expectations about how local practices should change, how Indigenous communities should be 'civilised'.

The missionary element

Dickey Bennelong was born sometime around 1802, the only known child of Boorong and Bennelong. He presumably grew up within their Kissing Point community. He was ten or eleven years old when his parents died. After that, Dickey may have moved north-west: in 1816, colonists associated him with the Richmond tribe. That year Dickey was enrolled at the Parramatta Native Institution, established by Governor Macquarie in 1814 in a period of renewed frontier violence. Dickey entered after one of Macquarie's 'friendly meetings with the natives', possibly by consent. Other children are known to have been forcibly removed from their families in a terrible prefiguring of the Stolen Generations.

Dickey stayed five years, receiving instruction in mechanical arts and agriculture. Presumably he also acquired some skill in reading and writing, and some familiarity with the Bible.

Towards the end of 1821, Dickey was adopted out of the Institution by a newly arrived Wesleyan minister. Twenty-one-year-old William Walker was an eccentric man by some accounts: an earnest evangelical and a charismatic and intelligent preacher. Employed by the Wesleyan Methodist Missionary Society (WMMS), he was the first designated missionary to the 'black natives' of New South Wales.[8] Walker apparently developed a considerable rapport with Dickey. He rejoiced when, after three months, Dickey had 'learned to read his Bible' and accepted the gospel of Jesus Christ.

Dickey Bennelong was attentive to Walker. He went along to class and prayer meetings. When the missionary fell ill, Dickey prayed for him: 'You *murray bajul* [very poorly] Mr Walker, you cannot pray with me but I prayed before you came, that God make you well'.[9] He also showed great feeling for 'the condition of his countrymen'. Walker noted, 'in one instance to my knowledge (and the practice, I think, was frequent), he collected the young natives of his own tribe, to whom he gave an exhortation, which he concluded with prayer'.[10] On another occasion, Dickey attempted to convert an old man, telling him:

> You must love God – you must settle, then Mr Walker can
> preach to you, else I shall go to heaven and you will go to hell
> – the fire burn you, you will ask me for water and I would not
> give you a drop.[11]

Dickey's short sermon reveals a remarkable fact: Bennelong and Boorong's son was the first Indigenous Australian evangelist. It also gives a rare insight into the message he had absorbed from his mentor: a fire and brimstone version of the gospel, mixed with an assumption that his people had to 'settle' to become Christians. His 'drop of water' reference is also intriguing: it echoes Jesus' parable of the rich man and Lazarus, in Luke chapter 16.

On 27 September 1822, at his own 'earnest request', Dickey Bennelong was 'outwardly initiated into the Church of God' through baptism. The event was witnessed by an unusually large congregation at Parramatta Wesleyan chapel. 'Many of his brethren' were present, the newspaper said – meaning 'brethren' in a racial rather than a properly theological sense.

Walker gave Dickey the baptismal name Thomas Walker Coke, in honour of the Wesleyan missionary hero.[12] He also preached from the Book of Acts chapter 10, which recounts the spread of the gospel beyond ethnic Jews and proclaims the radical inclusiveness of Christianity: 'Can any man forbid water, that these should not be baptized, which have received the Holy Ghost as well as we?'[13] For Walker, and probably Dickey too, his conversion and baptism was fresh proof that God did not confine his work to the Jews, or the British, or indeed to any national group that saw itself as a divinely chosen. The Word was for everyone, including the Aboriginal people of Australia.

THE MISSIONARY IMPULSE IS PART OF A MUCH LONGER history of Christian expansion, which can be traced back through two millennia to the apostolic era. The New Testament relates Jesus' injunction to his disciples: 'Go ye into all the world, and preach the gospel to every creature' (Mark 16:15). Christians have spread their faith in various ways through the centuries. During the sixteenth century, the challenge of the Reformation fired fresh Catholic missionary zeal – aimed first at the reconversion of

Protestants, and then at the wider world. Work often expanded along the lines of the Spanish, Portuguese and French empires.

When Europeans began colonising Australia, this burst of Catholic missionary activity had begun to decline.[14] Protestant activism was rising with the emergence of the Dutch and the British as maritime powers. Another factor was the growth of a dynamic, gospel-sharing movement – evangelicalism – nourished by a biblical faith and piety. One of the chief expressions of evangelical religion was activism for the conversion of others. William Carey famously expressed this outlook in the early 1790s: Christians should pray for the gospel to spread to all people, and exert themselves 'in the use of means for obtaining' that end – for example by giving money, forming societies and dispatching missionaries overseas. In justification, Carey liked to quote from Paul, in Romans chapter 10:

> There is no difference between the Jew and the Greek; for
> the same Lord over all, is rich unto all that call upon him.
> For whosoever shall call on the name of the Lord shall be
> saved. How then shall they call on him, in whom they have
> not believed? and how shall they believe in him of whom they
> have not heard? and how shall they hear without a Preacher?
> and how shall they preach except they be sent?[15]

For all that, European Christians were slow to establish missions among Indigenous Australians. Established groups like the Society for the Propagation of the Gospel focused on the spiritual needs of convicts and free settlers, while the emerging evangelical movement directed its first energies to India, Africa and the Pacific islands. Missionary-minded individuals instead conveyed their faith in personal ways, as Richard and Mary Johnson attempted with Boorong. Samuel Clode was a missionary to the Pacific based for a short period in Sydney, who reportedly 'spent much of his time among the natives'.[16] In Victoria, an unnamed old shepherd read his Bible to a Wotjobaluk youth known as Nathanael Pepper. Pepper later learned to read the New Testament for himself and converted to Christianity – the first success of the Moravian mission at Ebenezer.[17]

Other devout Christians looked for opportunities within the activities of the state. In 1814, William and Elizabeth Shelley took the job of managing the Native Institution at Parramatta, making Bible reading, hymn singing, prayer and worship part of the routine. They may have looked for personal conversions, but the Institution's governing purpose was to 'conciliate' the local people to the presence of Europeans, and to aid their transformation into useful subjects of the Crown. In Tasmania, from 1829, George Augustus Robinson led a government-sponsored 'friendly mission'. By then, large-scale dispossession and disease, as well as outright war and violence, had reduced the island's entire Indigenous population to fewer than 200 people. Robinson persuaded the survivors to accompany him to a refuge on Flinders Island, in Bass Strait, where they were schooled in the Bible and encouraged to wear clothes, keep the Sabbath, live in houses, and practise European farming. Having secured the Tasmanian island for the colonists, Governor Arthur told staff on Flinders Island: 'The Bible is the most effectual mode of introducing civilisation'.[18]

Such collaborations shared characteristics with wider evangelical action of the time. As in the campaign to end slavery, evangelicals sought to use the instruments of policy and government to achieve their moral and religious vision. More immediately, this approach provided opportunities to 'do something for the poor natives'. The danger was that it all but dissolved any meaningful distinction between imperial attempts to 'conciliate and civilise', and evangelical efforts to foster spiritual transformation.

By the time William Walker reached Sydney to establish his mission, more than thirty years had passed since the first incursions of the British. He soon confronted an array of challenges that became all too familiar to his successors. The worst was that promising converts kept dying before they could have a significant influence. The greatest loss was Dickey Bennelong, who became sick and died a mere four months after his baptism. The same fate befell Jemmy, another young convert. 'No man ever loved his son with a more ardent affection than I did these youths', Walker lamented. 'These Providential occurrences have greatly impeded the prosperity of the work of God among the poor blacks'.[19] Walker himself struggled on for a few more years, until his relationship with his overseers broke down and the WMMS suspended the mission.[20]

From this inauspicious beginning, Christian missions were eventually established throughout Australia. By the 1960s, approximately 200 institutions with strong religious affiliations had been formed to service and convert the Indigenous population.[21] Some, like Walker's, lasted only a few short years. Others flourished for a time as the locus of a resilient Indigenous community. Still others were taken into government hands and re-organised as secular ventures. By the 1910s, virtually every church-run mission in New South Wales and Victoria had closed or been changed into a state reserve.[22] During the twentieth century, the church focused its work mainly on the centre, north and west of Australia.

Missions were diverse institutions, run by men and women of different personalities, affiliations, theologies, languages and ethnicities. Many had their roots in some form of British Christianity – especially Anglican, Methodist, Congregational and Presbyterian. Others were staffed by Irish nuns, Italian Passionists,

Spanish Benedictines, German Lutherans or Moravians. Germans in fact had a disproportionate influence. Their missionaries were typically men from a poor background, barely twenty, newly married, with no experience in leading a community, and outside Germany for the first time. But they conducted eight of the first sixteen missions to Aboriginal people, and shouldered 'an inordinately large share of the mission effort' right through to the First World War period.[23]

Missions also had a variety of supporters and stakeholders. Some of the most important ventures were essentially private undertakings – such as William Ridley's pioneering work among the Kamilaroi and Daniel and Janet Matthews' Maloga mission by the Murray. Many others drew on local donations and grants from their parent bodies, which in turn raised funds from a vast network of supporters in Britain, Germany and elsewhere. A number also received government support – a grant of land, perhaps, or a contribution towards salaries. Missions were not simply extensions or agents of government native policy, however. At times they were merely tolerated, or undermined and even banned, according to state priorities.[24]

Overall, Christian missionaries only ever made up a small proportion of all Europeans in contact with Indigenous Australians. Their immediate impact in comparison with other colonists and government agents was small. By their own standards, moreover, their early efforts largely failed. Baptisms were few, deaths were many, and the number of Indigenous clergy ordained before 1910 could be counted on one hand.[25] Compared to the mass conversions reported among Pacific islanders and the embrace of Christianity by the Māori, the impact of nineteenth-century missions in Australia seemed very small.

Missions were nevertheless important as places of intense

encounter with the Bible.[26] As missionaries worked to bring Christianity to Indigenous communities, they made reading, hearing and learning from the Bible part of the rhythm of mission life. At Poonindie mission in South Australia, residents gathered for the reading of Scripture, prayer and a hymn first thing every morning and again at sundown. A simple exposition was given daily, and there was also study at the school and worship on Sundays. At Hermannsburg mission in Central Australia, the Bible loomed so large in the lives of the Aranda people that 'they referred to everything associated with Christianity – church buildings, church sermons and meetings, as well as the Bible – as *pepe* (paper)'.[27]

Missions were also places where Indigenous people began to evaluate and interpret the Scriptures for themselves. The scope of their opportunities for interpretation were usually constrained: it was typically the missionaries who decided which passages to emphasise, the kind of access people would have to them, the interpretative gloss or framework that would accompany them, and the range of acceptable readings. But even within these substantial limits, Indigenous people retained a degree of agency. They grappled with what they heard, and made judgments and responses. Ultimately, missionaries could not entirely control their interactions with the Bible.

As early as the 1830s, Indigenous people began to articulate a perspective drawn from an understanding of the Bible. Thomas Brune came from Bruny Island, off the south-east coast of Tasmania. Sometime in the early 1820s, he was 'took' and placed in the Orphan School in Hobart. During a few years there, 'I was taught to read the Bible and I understood it and I was taught to cipher an I was taught to learn the geography and the grammar and the catechism all them did I learn'.[28] Then he was removed again – this time to the Aboriginal refuge on Flinders Island. This settlement brought together the surviving members of various Tasmanian clans and language groups, under the protection of a white superintendent and a number of staff. By 1835, the schools typically provided religious instruction in a rote, catechetical form. It was common for young people like Brune to copy out passages from the English Bible.

Brune was good at reading and writing, and apparently accepted Christianity along the lines taught. He became a teacher at the school, a regular lay preacher, a writer and editor of the *Aboriginal or Flinders Island Chronicle*. Several of Brune's sermons and journalistic writings survive, providing an insight into his interaction with the English Bible.[29] They also reflect the unfolding tragedy of the settlement on Flinders Island:

My friends will you thank the Commandant for all that
he done for you in bringing you out of the bush when you
knew not God and knew not who made the trees that where
before you when you were living in the woods yes my friends
you should thank the Commandant yes you should thank
the Commandant. There is many of you dying my friends
we must all die and we ought to pray to God before we get
to heaven yes my friends if we don't we must have eternal
punishment …

Let us hope … that something may be done for us poor people
they are dying away the Bible says that some of all shall be
saved but I am much afraid none of us will be alive by and by
as then as nothing but sickness among us. Why don't the black
fellows pray to the king to get us away from this place.[30]

The spectre of death haunted Wourraddy, too. He was a much older Bruny Island man, who had accompanied Robinson on his 'friendly missions' before moving to Flinders Island. Wourraddy did not learn to read or write, but he absorbed certain ideas from conversations and sermons. Addressing the 'weekly meeting for prayer and mutual instruction' in April 1838, he drew on the New Testament to suggest how people from different clans and languages might respond to the shared experience of colonisation:

> The white men have killed us all; they shot a great
> many. We are now only a few people here and we ought
> to be fond of one another. We ought to love God. God
> made everything, the salt water, the horse, the bullock,
> the opossum, the wallaby, the kangaroo and wombat.
> Love him and you go to him by and bye.[31]

For some Indigenous converts, the Bible was a resource for processing the devastation of European invasion. For others, it was a focus for disagreements about the claims of Christianity and its impact in their community. At Raukkan (Point McLeay) in South Australia, the stern George Taplin urged the Ngarrindjeri to turn to God for forgiveness and salvation, and to abandon their own culture and practice in favour of agricultural settlement and European habits. In early 1860, eight months after the mission's foundation, a boy named Waukerri began avoiding his ceremonial obligations and contravening certain Ngarrindjeri customs. Waukerri's older brother was angered by this, but Taplin took it as a sign of his receptivity to the gospel, defending Waukerri by proclaiming that 'there is only one God, Jehovah, and only one Bible'. The older brother replied with a challenge:

'Well, how do you know that Bible is Jehovah's book?
Did he give it to you? Did he tell you it? Did not whitefellow
make it?'

'No, Jehovah gave it to my fathers long time ago.'

'Well, and our God tell my father these customs long
time ago and so we must do them.'

'Yes, but your God is a devil, he is not Jehovah …
we know that your God is *brupe* a devil.'

'No, no, we must do what he tells us.'

'You do not believe what I say.'

'No, we don't.'[32]

Taplin kept up his campaign. He promoted the Bible as the Word
of the one true God and, at the same time, opposed virtually every
aspect of Ngarrindjeri culture as the work of the devil. By 1863,
Waukerri was routinely wearing clothes, washing his hair, reading
the Bible and explaining it to others. The boy died of consumption
in November 1864, but, in the next two decades, more than forty
others received Christian baptism from Taplin.[33]

Questions about the authority of the Bible did not go away.
Neither did questions about the gospel and its relationship to Aboriginal culture. Throughout the nineteenth and twentieth centuries,
European missionaries came to varied conclusions. Some were far
more positive towards Indigenous ways than Taplin had been. Virtually all – Taplin included – recognised that white society itself
was not perfectly or thoroughly Christian. Even where missionaries confused Christianity with aspects of European culture, they
were still among the harshest critics of settler conduct.

Indigenous people forged answers of their own to the question
of gospel and culture, making sense of the Bible in light of their
own experiences and understandings. Some took up the Bible as a

resource for making sense of colonisation, for articulating a revised Indigenous identity, for critiquing white society according to its own sacred texts and standards. In time, Indigenous pastors and theologians would lead a wholesale reassessment of the relationship of the Bible and culture. As Djinyini Gondarra put it in the 1990s, 'God has given us the vision for the Aboriginal Church to think and theologise the gospel in the language and culture of the people'.[34] This was in fact one of the great keys: translating the text into Indigenous languages, and the creation of vernacular Bibles, opened a new frontier.

Translating the text

Sometime during the 1810s, an Awabakal boy was taken from his ancestral country, around Lake Macquarie in New South Wales, and assigned as a servant to a military captain in Sydney. Given the name M'Gill, he spent the next several years working for British officers. He became fluent in English and familiar with white ways. He also acquired specific skills as an interpreter, guide and 'bush constable' tracking runaway convicts.

When M'Gill's master moved to Newcastle, in Awabakal country, in late 1824, M'Gill re-established contact with his clan. He was in his mid-twenties by then, well past the usual age of initiation. He immersed himself in tribal learning and, in autumn 1826, travelled to the mountains to undergo a transformative ceremony. The Awabakal elders tested him and instructed him in the exclusive spiritual knowledge of men. A *karakul* or medicine man knocked out his front tooth. He came back from the mountains as Biraban, meaning 'eaglehawk', a fully initiated man. Biraban cemented his adult membership of the clan by marrying

Ti-Pah-ma-ah, with whom he had at least one child.

Biraban returned to a community on the cusp of change. In the early 1820s, the Awabakal were still able to fish and hunt on their own lands, and to maintain their spiritual connections to country. But British colonists were already flooding through the port at Newcastle and along the Hunter River valley to the north, into neighbouring Wonnarua land. On a smaller scale, they were also beginning to encroach on the area around the nearby Lake Macquarie: several pastoralists took up land in Awabakal territory from the mid-1820s. Biraban's knowledge of Europeans and his skills as a cultural mediator would soon be put to use.

In 1825, the London Missionary Society commissioned Lancelot Threlkeld to work among Indigenous Australians. Threlkeld was a London-born circus actor turned evangelical missionary. He arrived in New South Wales after a period in the Society Islands, an experienced missionary mourning the death of his wife. Remarrying, he went first to Newcastle and then to a place the locals called Bahtahbah, on the north-eastern shore of Lake Macquarie.

Biraban and Threlkeld forged a remarkable partnership. Probably at the prompting of his old master, a trustee of the LMS mission, Biraban began teaching Threlkeld his language and educating him about Awabakal beliefs and practices. As Threlkeld later remarked, Biraban was 'my daily companion for many years, and to his intelligence I am principally indebted for much of my knowledge respecting the structure of the language'.[35] Over the next seventeen years, Biraban and Threlkeld collaborated to document Awabakal language and culture. They became involved in an exchange of sacred knowledge and made path-breaking translations of the Bible. The major results were an *Australian Grammar* (1834), a *Spelling Book* (1836) and translations of the Gospels of Luke and Mark, now considered landmarks in Aboriginal studies.

They also included a set of morning and evening prayers, a draft of at least the first five chapters of Matthew and several Old Testament stories. Collectively, these materials have an unrivalled place in the Australian history of translation. They underpin Biraban's reputation as one of the outstanding Indigenous men of his generation and the saviour of his language.

Biraban's interaction with the Bible is unparalleled in early colonial Australia. It depended a great deal on his personal intelligence, his sacred and linguistic knowledge and his cross-cultural experience.[36] But why was the Bible even part of the linguistic encounter between Indigenous people and colonists? Why was there any thought of translating the Bible at all? Why, at a time when very few colonists made any serious attempt to learn Indigenous languages, did some take on the huge task of translating it?

The answer is not simply that the Bible is a sacred text. Otherwise we might expect to find translation projects associated with other world religions at some point in Australian history.[37] It has to do with particular Christian ideas about God's word, as a word possible to translate. By the Bible's own account, God has spoken 'in many times and in various ways' – through the prophets and especially through Jesus (Hebrews 1:1–2). According to the New Testament, Jesus was not merely a messenger of the divine word, but as John's Gospel insists, himself the Word (John 1:1–18). An idea of God's word as living, dynamic and embodied has stimulated European thinkers for centuries.

Crucially, the Bible preserves a distinction between God's word and any one language. In contrast to the Qur'an, for example, which Muslims hold to be the eternal word of God, perfectly revealed to the Prophet Mohammed in Arabic, Christians have usually recognised the Bible as irreducibly multilingual, in both form and content. As colonial believers were aware, its composite texts were originally written in Hebrew, Aramaic and Greek. And while Muslims consider the Qur'an miraculously inimitable – such that any translation is merely an approximation of its meaning, not the Qur'an itself[38] – Christians have usually held that God's word can be authentically expressed in new languages.

Translation is also shaped by Christian ideas about human language. The Bible accounts for the diversity of tongues in the famous story of the Tower of Babel (Genesis 11), in which God acts in judgment against human pride by confusing the builders' language and making them incomprehensible to one another. In the New Testament, however, the diversity of human languages is divinely endorsed. On the Day of Pentecost, the Holy Spirit gives Jesus' disciples the ability to speak in numerous tongues (Acts 2). In the book of Revelation, the speaking of many languages appears to be part of God's intention for humanity (Revelation 7:9–10).

HISTORICALLY, THERE HAVE BEEN MAJOR FLUCTUATIONS IN church attitudes to translation. Some versions, such as the fourth-century Latin Vulgate, have had a hegemonic place within a particular tradition of Christianity. When Protestant reformers sought to wrench the Bible from the control of the Catholic Church, the Council of Trent reaffirmed the Vulgate's supreme position over and against new versions. The breakaway churches pursued new translations all the same: between the Luther Bible (1522) and the King James Bible (1611), virtually every major European confession and language acquired at least one translation. But even Protestants have not been uniformly enthusiastic about new vernacular scriptures. As the risks of theological and political instability came to the fore, the project of biblical translation ground to a halt. During the seventeenth century, liturgies solidified, catechisms hardened and a new canon of vernacular Bibles emerged.[39]

When missionaries began arriving in Australia, the push to translation was again on the rise. This was only partly because of developments in textual scholarship. Much of the impetus came from a vast new missionary enterprise. Some European believers imagined the spread of vernacular Bibles to all peoples on earth. They combined Bible translation with missionary expansion on a global scale.

Missionaries in Australia were slow to pursue substantial Bible translation. William Walker set the tone when he baulked at the difficulty and diversity of local languages, and settled on English as 'the medium … through which the truths of religion must be conveyed'.[40] English was appealing, and certainly easier for many missionaries – but several still made an effort to learn Indigenous languages. Walker's assistant, John Harper, was probably the first to try Bible translation: he travelled to Wellington Valley, in central western New South Wales, in 1824 to scope out possibilities for a second Wesleyan mission.[41] After eight months Harper claimed to have mastered the Wiradjuri language and translated the first chapter of Genesis.[42]

In New South Wales, the exceptional missions that prioritised language and translation work included Threlkeld's, in Awabakal country, and the CMS (Anglican) mission at Wellington Valley. The CMS venture began in 1832, six years after Harper's departure from the area. It was staffed by the fractious William Watson, Johann Handt and James Günther. They set about learning the Wiradjuri language and developing a vocabulary of over 2000 words. They also translated the first three chapters of Genesis, the Ten Commandments, parts of Matthew and Luke, and the Lord's Prayer.[43] To the north, in the 1850s, the Presbyterian William Ridley pursued an itinerant ministry among the Kamilaroi. He devoted himself to 'acquiring their language and gaining all possible information concerning them, then declaring plainly unto them in their own tongue the way of salvation of Jesus Christ'.[44] Ridley's booklet *Gurre Kamilaroi: or Kamilaroi Sayings* was published in 1856, and contained vernacular renditions of Bible stories.[45]

In Victoria, missionary-minded Europeans followed the pastoralists who overran the country in the 1830s and 1840s. Several of them learned local languages – such as the Moravians at Ebenezer, in Wotjobalak country, and the Cornish Methodist Francis Tuckfield at Buntingdale, on the Barwon River. Tuckfield translated the Commandments, the Lord's Prayer and parts of Genesis into Wathawarrung – a language spoken from Airey's Inlet to the Werribee River and inland to Ballarat and Beaufort. Tuckfield also compiled a large vocabulary and a list of more than 200 sentences, including *Kanam-tjarring-bulang kinkinbil dirdabil murrupo-nhuk baap mamam-nhuk*: 'The Great Spirit and His Son love the blacks'.[46]

William Thomas, a Wesleyan, was an assistant under the short-lived Port Phillip Protectorate. He has been judged 'more successful than any other first generation settler in attempting to comprehend and sustain Aboriginal society' in Victoria.[47] Thomas travelled from place to place with Indigenous communities, all the while living 'in the presence of God, his Heavenly Father'. He began each day with Bible reading and closed it with prayer, and regularly recommitted himself to the Lord's purposes.[48] Thomas held divine service twice every Sunday, and soon learned to preach in the Boonwurrung tongue. With the help of clan head Budgery Tom, he translated Psalm 121, the Lord's Prayer and the first chapter of Genesis. He also translated the creed, the 'Old Hundredth' hymn and a call to confession and repentance.[49]

In South Australia, an English effort at Bible translation was led by the indefatigable George Taplin. Despite his hostility to Ngarrindjeri culture, he set about learning the local language. 'The old people like me to sit in the wurley and let them correct me', he noted in his journal. 'They never seem to get weary of telling me. It is the only way of getting divine truth to their minds, and I pray that God will bless it.'[50] Within a few years Taplin had translated school primers and portions of Scripture. In 1864, the South Australian Auxiliary of the BFBS published *Tungarar Jehovald; Extracts from the Holy Scriptures in the language of the tribes inhabiting the lakes and lower Murray and called Ngarrindjeri (Narrinyeri)*. It included the opening of Genesis, the chapters containing the Ten Commandments from Exodus, the Sermon on the Mount from Matthew and the narrative of Jesus' death and resurrection from John.[51]

The most substantial translation work in colonial Australia was initiated by German-speaking missionaries – especially Lutherans and Moravians. Vernacular Bible translation was central to both these denominations at the formative period of the Reformation. In the nineteenth century, their representatives in Australia often arrived with poor English and so were more inclined to learn and use local languages. Intellectually, they were influenced by wider currents that emphasised the importance of language to culture. Their mental universe made 'far more room for the exploration of meaning and ideas than the Anglophone discourse of "science"'.[52] Such missionaries devoted themselves to Aboriginal languages as a means to understanding 'the soul of a people'.

In central Australia, for example, Lutherans Johannes Reuther and Carl Strehlow made extensive studies of the vocabulary, grammar, culture and mythology of the Dieri and Aranda peoples. Their output included major ethnographies and the first complete New Testament in an Indigenous Australian language: *Testamento Marra: Jesuni Christuni apantjani jaura ninala karitjimalkana wonti Dieri jaurani*, published in 1897. Strehlow went on to Hermannsburg, where he worked with Moses Tjalkabota, Nathaniel Rauwirarka and Jacobus to translate the New Testament into Aranda. It was completed in 1919, and parts were eventually published as *Ewangelia Lukaka* (1925) and *Ewangelia Taramatara* (1928).[53]

All told, Bible translation occurred in a smattering of locations and communities across colonial Australia. But in comparison with nineteenth-century India, New Zealand and various nations in the South Seas, its scope and scale was modest indeed. Why didn't these beginnings develop into something more extensive and lasting? The main reason is that translation work was caught up with the politics of forging settler societies. Like missionary work in general, it was often compromised by the agenda to civilise as well as Christianise.

Thomas Wilkinson was a catechist to the settlement of Tasmanian survivors on Flinders Island. In mid-1833, he began translating the book of Genesis. When he was four chapters in, he proudly informed Governor Arthur that the people 'seemed to understand his translation … and showed an interest in what they heard'. Arthur was a Christian who believed that 'scriptural religion should be the grand object of attention in the education of the Aborigines'. But he dismissed Wilkinson's translation as imprudent, deeming it counterproductive to translate the Bible for what he deemed an 'uncivilised' society.[54]

Lutheran pastors Clamor Schürmann and Christian Teichelmann set up the first Aboriginal school in Adelaide in 1839. Their missionary society had instructed them to focus on spiritual work, rather than on remaking Indigenous societies along European lines. They learned the local language and resolved to use it. One result was *Outlines of a Grammar, Vocabulary, and Phraseology, of the Aboriginal Language of South Australia, Spoken by the Natives in and for Some Distance around Adelaide*, published in 1841. They also translated hymns, prayers, Bible stories and the Ten Commandments. In 1842, however, the school came under the financial control of a group of prominent colonists – several of whom were respectable churchgoing Anglicans. The new committee insisted on English as the language of instruction, claiming that the students would be civilised sooner if their own tongues were put aside. The missionary staff did not like it, but they had little choice: the committee's view reflected the emerging trend of government policy.[55]

In other cases, too, where missionaries took steps to utilise Australian languages, they were prevented by government policies that gravely endangered those languages. At Cape Bedford in Queensland, during the 1890s, Lutheran missionaries were pressured to abandon teaching in Guugu-Yimidhirr. At Aurukun, in the 1930s, Presbyterian missionaries were prevented from using the Wik languages in their school – again because government policy mandated the use of English.[56]

These examples highlight the politics of missionary language and translation work. On the one hand, Christian conversion was rarely seen as an end in itself. For colonial governments and many churchgoing settlers, Christianity was to aid civilisation in the sense of pacifying resistance. Missions were to draw Indigenous people into defined locations where they would not compete with expanding settlement. They were to teach skills – such as English fluency – that would make Indigenous people useful to settlers.[57]

Missionaries themselves did not always maintain their distance from this agenda: their aims often converged with those of state and settler. Sometimes, however, they opposed such interests.

The priority to share the Scriptures – like the insistence on the human worth and dignity of Indigenous people – could bring them into conflict with other settlers. Threlkeld, for instance, recognised that 'if it could be proved that the Aborigines of NSW were only a species of wild beast, there could be no guilt attributed to those who shot them off or poisoned them'. In rejection of such racism, he devoted himself to language work as 'a convincing proof that they have an equal share of intellectual power with others of the human race'.[58] In the midst of conflict over land and hardening notions of race, language and translation work was as contested as the idea of common humanity.

Beyond the arguments about settlement and racial difference, translation work was also constrained by the practical devastation of colonisation itself. As Europeans occupied more of the country, the size of the Indigenous population visibly declined. Some colonists boldly declared that the blacks were dying out – a view initially buttressed by appeals to Providence, and increasingly reinforced by social scientific ideas of 'survival of the fittest'.[59] Evangelical thought was not immune to the influence of such discourses. In the face of creeping pessimism about the long-term future of the Aboriginal 'race', local support for missions apparently waned. Some missionaries persisted with their efforts to rescue at least a 'remnant' for salvation. A very few – like Reuther and Strehlow – focused on the radical work of Bible translation. In this sense translators stood head and shoulders above other colonists: they not only assumed the equal humanity of Indigenous people, they imagined their long-term survival as linguistically distinct communities.

Overall, the colonial effort to translate the Bible made little progress in producing Indigenous Scriptures. In 1904, when the British and Foreign Bible Society celebrated its centenary, it claimed a global distribution of no fewer than 186 680 000 copies of the Bible, complete or in part, in 378 different languages and dialects.[60] Australian languages, however, were barely among them. Threlkeld and Biraban's translation of Luke, Taplin's Ngarrindjeri selections, and the Dieri New Testament had found their way into print – but the official catalogue of BFBS editions was not very far from the mark when it listed the number of Australian Scriptures as 'nothing'.

> OUR FATHER ON TOP SKY.
> Thy name be feared.
> Thou art our boss.
> Men-women will listen to Thee this place earth
> as the good souls of men-women listen to Thee on top sky.
> Give us tucker till this sun goes down.
> We did wrong; make us good.
> We have good hearts to them who did us wrong.
> Watch us against bad place.
> Thy hands be stretched out to guard us from bad.[61]

What happens to the Bible when it is translated into new languages? How does the Bible change and what are the consequences? After all, translation is not just a matter of pouring an old word into a new container and passing it on unchanged. The word flows into new channels and absorbs new things, specific to the language of its new expression. Translation alters the range of possible meanings and interpretations. It unsettles the old with a new incarnation.

The desire to convey a living word drives the project of translation. But the process involves many interpretive choices, risks and challenges. How much should translators accommodate their text to the conceptual world of the intended readers? Is the aim the closest possible word-by-word equivalence? Literary quality? The communication of a certain meaning? Is translation always possible at all? Missionary linguists have usually been acutely aware of such issues. Threlkeld and Biraban negotiated them over several years, and in the process, they gave the Bible a new life of its own.

Looking over some of the manuscripts, it is obvious that translation is hard. On every page of Threlkeld and Biraban's Gospel of Mark, there are words crossed out or corrected, spaces left and filled in, notes and questions scrawled into the margins.[62] Sometimes words in English leap from the page – words for things so foreign to Awabakal belief and experience that Threlkeld judged them untranslatable. In chapter 10, for instance, it is still a camel that passes through the eye of a needle. Chapter 12 introduces a man who plants a vineyard, makes a hedge, presses wine and builds a tower – all in a single verse.[63] In the space of just two verses in chapter 15, the Awabakal text is punctuated with the undigested English for soldier, pretorium, crown and purple.[64]

Sometimes, missionary translators were prepared to be inventive, to reimagine a text in a changed cultural setting. Psalm 23, 'The Lord is my shepherd', derives from a pastoral society readily able to think of God as a shepherd, the world as a pasture and people as sheep. This was not the world of the Awabakal, however. To convey the Psalm's core idea of taking care of something, Threlkeld and Biraban opted for *wirrilli*, from *wirrilliko* – 'for to wind up as a ball of string which the blacks do to their long fishing lines, and opossum fur cords, to take care of them, to preserve them'. They wove Awabakal culture and experience into the very text of Scripture. (A century and a half later in the Northern Territory, the translators of the Kriol Bible drew on the experience of recent generations in the cattle industry to present God as a 'good one stockman who always minds about me': *YAWEI, yu jis laik det brabli gudwan stakmen/Yu oldei maindimbat mi.*)

The stakes were higher and the challenges deeper in translating more conceptual terms. Threlkeld found no direct equivalents for words such as heaven, hallowed, glory, eternal. He also learned that Biraban's language, like many other Australian languages, made no distinction between knowing and believing. Of course, the distinction only needs to be made where there are rival systems of knowing. The Awabakal language expressed a seamless world. But as the stress on 'belief' itself suggests, Christianity has always existed in pluralist settings. Conversion involves deep conviction, not just intellectual assent or understanding: 'Believe on the Lord Jesus Christ, and thou shalt be saved' (Acts 16:31); 'To those who believed in his name, he gave the right to become children of God' (John 1:12). Translating such texts posed a great challenge in Australia. Threlkeld and Biraban debated the possibilities at length. In the end, they opted not to introduce a new term for belief, but to use the Awabakal *ngurrulliko*, meaning 'to know, to perceive by the ear', as distinct from knowing by sight or by touch.[65]

Perhaps translators' largest challenge was to name their god. What words should they use to locate the biblical deity in their readers' spiritual world? Some missionaries were inflexible and simply stuck with their own vocabulary. Threlkeld was more willing to seek common ground and to build his Christian case from there. He quickly ruled out using the English term 'God' – not least because Biraban's people were already familiar with it from hearing the settlers swearing! As he learned more from Biraban about Awabakal spirit worlds, he wondered if the powerful figure Koun might lend his name for God. Threlkeld eventually decided not, because Koun seemed too different to the biblical God. Threlkeld opted instead for Hebrew-derived words *Eloi* and *Yehoa* (Jehovah).[66]

Naming God *Koun* had seemed a step too far, but Threlkeld agreed to a bold experiment with 'Holy Spirit'. After prolonged discussions, he and Biraban combined two Awabakal terms to make *marai yirri yirri*. As language historian Anne Keary has explained, *yirri yirri* meant 'sacred, reverend, holy, not to be regarded but with awe'. It also had the more concrete meaning of an initiation site, 'the place marked out for mystic rites, not to be profaned by common use'. As such, *yirri yirri* was not a generic term for holy: it invoked a specifically male spiritual domain. A line in the 1834 *Grammar* illustrates the point: 'Why do not the women go with the men? Because it is a sacred concern … *Yanoa yirri yirri ka ke*.'

The use of *yirri yirri* for holy gave a new cast to the message. It shows how translation could push the text beyond a missionary's theological comfort zone. It points to a loosening of missionary control, a transfer of interpretive authority. For Threlkeld, using *yirri yirri* meant a narrowing of his message. He too thought of God as male, and his own tradition limited certain roles and offices to men. But as a linguist Threlkeld may have appreciated the grammatical gender of the Spirit in Hebrew (female) and Greek (neuter). His theology certainly affirmed that women as well as men could relate directly to God. The gift of the Spirit was not restricted to initiated men. But rather than introduce another new term, Threlkeld accepted *yirri yirri* – and not only for Holy Spirit but for every instance of holy or sacred in the Gospels. At Biraban's prompting, he even translated the concept of prayer as 'speaking in a sacred way', *wi-ya-li ta yirri yirri*.[67]

For Biraban, translation provided an opportunity to assert and explain his own conception of the sacred. At a time when

Awabakal sacred sites and practices were under intense pressure from the encroachment of white colonists, this was no small thing. Translation also positioned Biraban as a primary interpreter of Christianity and its texts to the Awabakal community. Though he did not actually convert, he mediated the message to others as a source of sacred knowledge. In 1837, Threlkeld was astonished to meet Hunter River people who recognised him as 'the person of whom M'Gill the Aborigine had spoken' and 'appeared to be apprised of my pursuits'. A year later, Threlkeld spoke to another group about 'Death, judgement and a Righteous God' only to be told 'O yes! M'gill had informed them before!' From such experiences, Threlkeld concluded that 'the Christian knowledge which has been communicated to M'gill and other Aborigines has been the subject of discussion amongst the remnant of the tribes forty miles distant'.[68]

For both Threlkeld and Biraban, translation afforded a different kind of interaction between Awabakal and European. But it did not completely decolonise the Bible, or prove sufficient for the challenges of the colonial situation. In his report for 1837, Threlkeld catalogued a catastrophic loss of life among the Awabakal. Quoting the Old Testament book of Job, he lamented that:

He who 'increaseth the Nation', or 'destroyeth, that there shall be no inhabitant,' has visited the land, and the Measles, the hooping cough, and the influenza, have stretched the Black victims in hundreds on the Earth.[69]

Threlkeld was forced to abandon the mission house at Lake Macquarie, where sixty Awabakal lay buried. By 1842, when the mission finally closed, Biraban's wife was among the dead. Biraban also told Threlkeld, *'wonni bountoa tea unnung tatte ammoun-ba'*,

'My child there is dead'.[70] Biraban himself died at Newcastle on 14 April 1846.[71]

Threlkeld persisted with his language work, but by the late 1850s he feared that 'the native Blacks are so rapidly becoming extinct, the language must of necessity become utterly lost to posterity unless preserved by the press'.[72] When he died in 1859, his translations still had not been published. His life's work had produced no conversions, supported no ongoing Christian community, and could barely be read by anyone.

A living word

Once, after a shooting star appeared in the sky, a British officer saw Boorong 'greatly agitated and prophesying much evil to befall the white men and their habitations'.[73] Whatever Boorong might have meant by this, it seems the prophesy was not borne out. In the decades after the First Fleet arrived, no great evil befell the whites. Their numbers continued to rise. Their habitations continued to spread and multiply. Two hundred and thirty years later, Burramattagal country has become Parramatta – a city with skyscrapers, shopping malls and hundreds of thousands of people within greater western Sydney. Biraban's homeland has become part of greater Newcastle: the area around the lake is especially popular with sea-changers and holiday makers.

Both Parramatta and Newcastle are still home to communities of Indigenous Australians. Across Australia as a whole, Aboriginal and Torres Strait Islander peoples make up about 3 per cent of the population. Their adaptability and resilience is evident in all kinds of ways – not least, in recent generations, in successful campaigns to win recognition of native title over at least 15 per cent of the landmass of Australia. At the same time, the damage done in the past continues to shape the injustices of the present. Of the 250 Indigenous languages spoken across Australia in 1800, for example, only eighteen remain robust today. Another eighty or so languages exist in a highly vulnerable form, perhaps spoken fluently by only a small number of older people. The rest of Australia's Indigenous languages have been reduced to fragments or effectively wiped out, along with the specific cultural knowledge and identity they carried.[74] Boorong's mother tongue was one of them.[75]

Language extinction is not unique to Australia, but it has been happening faster here than virtually anywhere else in the world. Along with the devastation of speaking communities, this is one of the major legacies of colonisation. It continues to matter to the wellbeing of Indigenous Australians, as Phyllis Darcy, an Awabakal descendant, has explained:

> Language is very important to us; it is our connection to our ancestors and for those of us who still use our language can connect with the ancestors of the past. We belong to the land; without the land we are nothing. Our life blood comes from the land and what is of the land. Language holds secrets to the connection of the land.[76]

In recent years, several Indigenous communities have taken up the task of salvaging and reviving what they can of their language – scouring the archives for word lists, making recordings, compiling dictionaries, writing songs and curriculum resources. Not all missionary sources have survived into the present, but where they have, they have often proved vital to the task.[77] A century and a half after Threlkeld and Biraban, their grammars and translations have provided the foundation for a concerted revival of the Awabakal language. Similarly, the Indigenous language revival in South Australia is almost entirely underpinned by German missionary sources – a legacy of Lutheran and Moravian work among the Dieri, Aranda, Kaurna and Ngarrindjerri.[78]

Language revival from missionary texts and vernacular Bibles is not unique to Australia, either. In the United States, for instance, the Myaamia of Oklahoma and the Wampanoag of Massachusetts have recovered their languages with the help of seventeenth-century Bibles. What stands out, in Australia, is that missionaries did more to learn local languages than virtually any other group of colonists. Their limitations and failures were often considerable, and they played their own part in undermining Indigenous cultures. But they and their Indigenous collaborators left an important legacy nevertheless. In their drive to communicate the Word of God in a language that Indigenous communities could understand on the deepest level, they documented and described tongues that, in most cases, have since become extinct. Bible translations and related texts now form the only or most significant record of those languages. Without them, it would be much more difficult – sometimes impossible – to recover anything of those tongues.[79] The Bible, in the vernacular, is a living word yet.

CHAPTER 3

GOD'S IMMIGRANTS?

Downstream from London, at Gravesend, the barque *Fortitude* stood at anchor. It was an early autumn day in 1848 and the main deck was packed with people. Having stowed their luggage, numerous emigrants gathered with friends and relatives to worship one last time in sight of the English shore, before setting sail for Australia. The ship's bell rang, an opening Psalm was sung and prayers were said. Then the clergyman John Dunmore Lang stepped up to the capstan and addressed them: 'Fellow-countrymen and Christian friends, it is … the eve of your departure from this land of your fathers to the far-distant land of your adoption'. He assured them they could be confident in their decision to depart: 'Divine Providence is, for the wisest and most beneficent purposes, now saying to many of the very best men in our country, as to Father Abraham of old, "Get ye up out of your country and from your father's house, unto a land that I will show you. And I will make of you there a great nation"' (Genesis 12:1–2).[1]

MIGRATION IS ALWAYS AN ACT OF FAITH, WHEN FREELY undertaken. It expresses at least a shy hope for the future, for a fresh beginning and new opportunities. It was relatively uncommon during the first forty years of white settlement in Australia. But from the 1830s, concerns about overpopulation in Britain plus a shortage of labour in the colonies prompted governments to adopt pro-migration policies, and significant numbers opted for Australia and New Zealand. By 1850 free settlers made up 40 per cent of Australia's non-Indigenous population. During the gold rushes, hundreds of thousands more people flooded to the colonies – primarily from Britain but also from continental Europe, the Americas, and Asia – especially China. By 1860, the settler population had surged to 1.15 million. Immigration drove most colonial growth until the early 1870s.[2]

Free migrants changed both their own horizons and the face of settler Australia; the immigration boom amounted to a second beginning for colonial Australia. Free migrants established whole new colonies, such as the Swan River settlement, Western Australia, in 1829 – a collaboration between private investors and the Colonial Office. It aimed to recreate the best of rural England but it took decades, and the introduction of convict labour, for the colony to find its feet. In South Australia, the new colony was to be marked by religious, political and commercial freedom. Determined to avoid the convict stain of the east and the planning mistakes of the west, its founders adopted principles of 'systematic colonisation'. The first Britons arrived in 1836 and quickly flourished.

In the older, penal colonies of New South Wales and Tasmania, free migrants spurred expansion and transformation. Some settled in the emerging urban centres while others helped forge new rural settlements. Along with the locally born and convicts who had obtained their freedom, free migrants debated the occupation and ownership of land, the provision of care for the sick and needy, the interests of capital and labour, the scope of political participation. In these colonies, the boom in free arrivals put convictism into a new perspective and tempered its influence.

Isabella Wyly's family was reduced to poverty during the Irish famine of the 1840s. The calamity forced her to migrate to Adelaide, orphaned and alone, with a respectable reference but no money. Arriving in 1851, she found work as a draper's assistant. It was a good job, but the eighteen-year-old nevertheless wrote home about how new and distant she felt, echoing the ideas of Hebrews 13: 'I [k]new no one, nor had I a friend to take my hand, but thank God I had Him who Never has forsaking'. Isabella eventually married her employer, an Irish Wesleyan. She proved an energetic businesswoman and soon prospered: 'Everything seems to go well with me as it went ill with me atome', she reflected. Over a long life, she helped many in her extended family to migrate and had ten children of her own, always maintaining her belief in 'the care of Him who will never forsake, tho all friends may'.[3]

Around the same time, Stephen Doust gave his son David some advice for making his way in New South Wales: 'The way to git on is to git the Bible open before you and read a verse and pray over it, and read it again and pray and let six verses last an hour in that way till you feel it is yours and heaven comed down on earth and you are filled with a power that will carry you above and through all'.[4] For Doust, a Primitive Methodist, the Bible had a power that spanned the whole globe. Like Wyly and other free migrants, he expected the Word to travel with him. After all, the Bible told a purportedly universal story. Christians carried it to the colonies in hard copy, and in their deepest attitudes about life, God and the world. Doust was one of those who read it frequently and literally, expecting that its power would transform everyday life as he established a new home.

WHAT DID FREE MIGRATION MEAN FOR THE BIBLE IN Australia? How did the Bible inform the forging of colonial culture and society? Not every immigrant was as devout as Doust and Wyly, but the British arrivals of the 1830s–1870s tended to be more deeply immersed in Christianity and its scriptures than the convicts and men of the officer class had been. More of them had been influenced by the evangelical revival, more attended church, more were confident readers. Some, like the Presbyterian Scots who migrated to the Western District of Victoria, were so steeped in the Scriptures that 'most of them had little need to refer to it, for they could recite chapter after chapter by heart'.[5] More generally, the influx of free people accelerated the growth of denominational Christianity, especially in its mainstream Anglican, Catholic, Presbyterian and Methodist expressions. In this way, free British migration extended the presence of the theological Bible in settler culture and society.

At the same time, this migration boom bolstered small communities of Jews, Muslims and adherents of Buddhism, Taoism and Confucianism – a reminder that religious life in Australia is shaped not only by empire but by the wider experience of globalisation. Even within the Christian tradition, free migrants made colonial religion more diverse: millenarian sects such as the Christian Israelites flourished, and many smaller or non-British denominations founded their first Australian congregations.[6] This meant the Bible was subject to a growing range of readings, complicating its place in colonial culture.[7] This mattered to the ways colonists made sense of an unfamiliar land, and related to its Indigenous peoples.

People and place

John Dunmore Lang was nearly fifty when he farewelled the *Fortitude* and its passengers to Australia. A Presbyterian clergyman originally from Scotland, but resident for more than twenty-five years in New South Wales, he addressed the group with a few words from Scripture and a few from his own experience. Back in his early twenties, his departure for Australia had aroused the usual feelings of affection for his country and sadness at leaving it.[8] At the same time, his young heart had soared with optimism: 'How gallantly the ship rises over the waves, carrying in her bosom an insignificant fragment of Britain's supplementary population, but a great empire, perhaps, in embryo'.[9] Even then, Lang had seen migration to the colonies as part of a divine plan to build the nation.

Lang had gone on to an extraordinary career in New South Wales, eventually spanning more than half a century from his arrival in 1823 to his death in 1878. He was active not only in founding and leading the Presbyterian church, but as an educator, newspaper proprietor, and member of parliament. He travelled extensively within the colony and back and forth from Britain, and published widely on subjects ranging from Polynesian history to geology to convict transportation. An activist evangelical whose political and ecclesiastical views became progressively radical, he is best known today as one of the earliest advocates of an independent Australian republic.

Free migration was one of Lang's deepest and most long-standing concerns.[10] Convinced that 'the benefit likely to accrue to the colony' from the introduction of a virtuous, industrious British population was 'incalculably great', he gave speeches, wrote books, and used the press to promote his vision.[11] He lobbied the Imperial government to adopt a plan for large-scale Protestant colonisation, and eventually acted unilaterally to charter and supply several ships – including the *Fortitude* – from his private resources.[12] Overall, he personally arranged for more than 1000 people to migrate to

Australia. As many as 10 000 more may have been influenced by his writings to do so.

The Bible was a major source for Lang's ideas; his writings on migration are steeped in references to Scripture.[13] He wrote his first major book, *An Historical and Statistical Account of NSW*, published in London in 1834, in part to persuade potential immigrants of the opportunities awaiting them. The title page bore a quotation from the Old Testament account of Israel's settlement of Canaan: 'We have seen the land, and, behold, it is very good' (Judges 18:9). The chapter on the colony's pastoral expansion reminded readers that Abraham himself had 'waxed great and went forward, and grew until he became very great, for he had possession of flocks, and possession of herds, and great store of servants' (Genesis 26:13). The chapter on agriculture, in turn, elevated the subject to new heights by presenting the colony as a Promised Land:

> The Lord thy God bringeth thee into a good land – a land of wheat and barley, and vines and fig trees, and pomegranates; a land of oil-olive and honey; a land wherein thou shalt eat bread without scarceness; thou shalt not lack any thing in it; a land whose stones are iron and out of whose hills thou mayest dig brass (Deuteronomy 8:8–9).[14]

Lang's position expressed a deeper theology. He argued that Britain should adopt a 'grand, national, systematic plan of emigration' because 'God made the earth to be inhabited' (Isaiah 45:18). It seemed marvellous to him that 'the Divine injunction to "replenish the earth and subdue it" (Genesis 1:28) … can now be obeyed even in regard to the peopling of so remote a country as Australia'. He expected those who took up the divine call to migrate would experience the promise of the prophet Hosea – becoming:

> [as] numerous in these regions as the sands of the sea which cannot be measured or numbered, that in the place in which it hath been said 'Ye are not my people' it will yet be said 'Ye are the sons of the living God' (Hosea 1:10).[15]

Lang had particular – even idiosyncratic – ideas about how God was forging a new, chosen nation in Australia. But he was not alone in drawing on the Bible to interpret and promote immigration. The founders of South Australia, for example, were primarily Protestant non-conformists with a specific vision of Christian civilisation.[16] They too expected migration to fit an heroic, biblical pattern, and drew on the Bible to describe the destination. The first edition of the *South Australian Record* compared the arrival of European colonists to the 'awful emigration of Noah, and the promise that painted his horizon, and that of Moses'.[17] The land itself was compared to ancient Judea, certain to yield 'seed for the sower and bread for the eater' (Isaiah 55:10). Such language played a part in attracting Protestant evangelicals in particular to South Australia; they were substantially over-represented there, with consequences for its church–state relations, as well as its enduring religious demography.

Lang was not alone, either, in assuming that divine providence was at work. When he spoke on the deck of the *Fortitude* that day, he thought of the biblical God calling free migrants, as God had called Abraham, to a new future in a new country. Many other British evangelicals of his era thought in similar terms – of an immanent God, active in the world according to His purposes. But even the less devout commonly believed in a providence of sorts. As the historian of popular religion Phillip Gregory found,

'Providence' was in fact the most common metaphysical term in early colonial Australia.[18] The settlers believed their experiences occurred with the order and action of a divine will, force or person. Many ordinary people assumed a benign providence would ensure things eventually turned out well. They maintained a quiet confidence that can be roughly translated as 'She'll be right, mate'.[19]

However they understood it, virtually every Briton in Australia believed that time and history flowed with some external purpose. Such assumptions were crucial to the foundation of settler societies. Especially when framed by the biblical language of Christian publishers and migration promoters, they helped cast migration as a positively moral, even godly undertaking. Not only did God go with them and not forsake them, as Isabella Wyly liked to remind herself, free migrants were part of a much bigger unfolding of divine activity in the world. Further still, it readily seemed the good plan of providence for British immigrants to colonise Australia.

In *A Mother's Offering to Her Children* (1841), the first children's book published in New South Wales, the characters Emma and Mrs Saville had a revealing exchange:

How favoured the place seems, Mamma; as if Providence
had designed it for a Settlement.

It might indeed have been so ordained, my dear: you know
nothing happens without God's knowledge: the party
might have been under His especial providence when they
selected it.[20]

This was fiction, but it reflects the attitudes of real-life colonists. In 1839, the founders of South Australia claimed to be 'multiplying the British nation' in co-operation with 'the schemes of

Providence': 'We are rocking the cradle of great empires … and causing Christian civilisation to "cover the earth as the waters cover the sea"' (Habakkuk 2:14).[21] In New South Wales, the geologist William B Clarke was similarly confident that God was guiding the nation's development. As he pursued his studies on colonial coal deposits, he saw a connection between mining, imperial expansion and 'the spread of scriptural truth'. It was no accident, he said in 1846, that 'depositaries of fossil fuel' were found to exist 'wherever the Anglo-Saxon race have established themselves': it was part of God's plan for Britain, its empire, and ultimately for the globe. He argued for more research into coal as a step towards extending 'the boundaries of civilisation, arts and manufacturers' – and, with the spread of the British empire, the spread of Christianity throughout the world.[22]

THE BIBLE ALSO PROVIDED A SUITE OF STORIES ABOUT PEOPLE in relation to the land they travelled and settled. Beginning with Adam and Eve's expulsion from the Garden of Eden, it offered numerous accounts of people leaving their homeland for some other destination. Lang, as we saw, took up the famous narratives about Abraham's departure from his home to found a great nation, and the ancient Hebrews' journey through the wilderness to the Promised Land of Canaan. Other influential stories included the exile to Babylon and return to Jerusalem, and, more apocalyptically, the prophesies of a new heaven and a new earth – including a heavenly Jerusalem. Reinforced by the key texts of popular Protestantism – Milton's *Paradise Lost*, Bunyan's *Pilgrim's Progress*, the *Book of Common Prayer* – these biblical narratives shaped the way many colonists imagined their surrounds in Australia. References surface in settler letters, diaries and accounts of journeys and expeditions, as well as the descriptive writings of the colonies' early historians and promoters.

Some, like surveyor Thomas Mitchell, saw certain regions as a new Eden – a Paradise just as it 'fell from the hand of the Creator', in which he was the 'only Adam'.[23] Others imagined a land like Goshen, where Abraham had enjoyed abundance. To Barron Field, in 1822, the Bathurst Plains appeared 'the promised land of Australia'.[24] In the eyes of the young pastoralist William Broddribb, the Monaro similarly seemed a 'land of promise' where sheep, cattle and horses would 'do remarkably well and ... get very fat'.[25] Or as Lang told the *Fortitude* migrants, the area around Moreton Bay resembled 'that glorious and pleasant land which the Lord gave to Israel of old – it is a land of hills and valleys, of rivers and streams of water ... literally a land flowing with milk and honey', just like the biblical Canaan.[26]

European explorers in challenging situations were far less confident of God's blessing. In 1862, John McDouall Stuart was almost blind and weak with scurvy, having all but crossed the continent from south to north on his third attempt. He contemplated his physical decline in words echoing the Psalms of lament and complaint: 'I hope the Almighty will have compassion on me, and soon send me some relief'.[27] Ernest Giles, who travelled the central south and west in the 1870s, evoked a 'fearful waste, this howling wilderness, this country vast and desert idle' – like the writer of Deuteronomy.[28] Twice he compared his physical sufferings to those experienced by the Egyptians during the plagues: 'We are eaten alive by flies, ants, and mosquitoes, and our existence here cannot be deemed a happy one. Whatever could have obfuscated the brains of Moses, when he omitted to inflict Pharaoh with such exquisite torturers as ants, I cannot imagine'.[29] For George Grey, a more orthodox Christian who made exploratory journeys in the south-west of the continent, the only way to deal with diffi-cult country, sometimes, was to sit down and compose his mind by actually reading the Bible. Relying on 'the goodness of God' and the 'merits of our redeemer', he accepted that God could either rescue him from trouble or allow him to die of starvation.[30] He sur-vived the ordeal, and later served as Governor of South Australia, New Zealand and the Cape Colony (South Africa).

The Bible helped colonists make sense of the unfamiliar world they encountered. Was this cursed ground to be struggled against? A promised land to be enjoyed? A wasteland of trial and testing? A wilderness to be cultivated and ultimately transformed? While colonists also drew on classical literature, historical example, and even popular plays and novels such as Defoe's *Robinson Crusoe,* biblical narratives helped them find meaning in migration and in the land they encountered. The Bible nourished notions of place and providence that went to the heart of the emotional and psycho-logical history of white settlement in Australia. It mattered to what it *felt* like for Britons to come to grips with a new environment. The Bible was a central part of the culture they brought to nature.

This matters, because the stories colonists told themselves had political consequences. They usually erased the presence of Indig-enous people, and reinforced the European idea that the land was theirs to settle. At the grave expense of Indigenous Australians, colonists often interpreted the Bible to justify British expansion. Not only that, their discourses informed the ways colonists actually used the land, and their assumptions about their relationship to the physical environment. This was to have long-term implications for Australian ecology and society.

In 1841, about one hundred miles south of Swan River, Western Australia, a family of English colonists struggled to come to terms with the bush around them. The middle-aged John

Wollaston had given up parish work in Cambridgeshire in favour of a pioneering life with his wife Mary Amelia and their near-adult children. 'I have always entertained a wish to see a Country in a state of primitive nature', he wrote a few months after arriving. 'Now that wish has been granted, but the impression on my mind has been *very* different to what I anticipated':

> Nothing can be more depressing than the loneliness of the Bush away from any Settlement … such an awful silence prevails, except when broken by the horrid screech of the great black or white Cockatoo, that I have been almost tempted to shed tears at the desolateness of the scene, had I not called to mind the ubiquity of the God of Nature who can make 'a wilderness like Eden and a desert like the Garden of the Lord' – can cause 'joy and gladness to be found therein, thanksgiving and the voice of melody' (Isaiah 51:3).[31]

The Reverend Wollaston and his sons threw themselves into the tasks of clearing land, fencing new fields, sowing and reaping crops. They found the soil mixed, the climate changeable, and the trees themselves a challenging barrier: 'they turn the edge of the axe [and] we can only subdue them by sawing and burning'. The Wollastons persisted and by winter 1843 saw signs of desirable change: 'in the place of a thick and gloomy wilderness', there was 'a beautiful green level of springing corn … an inexpressible relief to the eye, and no less so *to the mind*'.[32]

It was theoretically possible for the Wollastons to adopt local methods of procuring food, and to provide for themselves as the Kaniyang people had for millennia in that region. To some extent, they did. The family hunted kangaroo, opossum, bandicoot, emu and fish. They reported that cockatoos, crows and 'the Bronze winged Pigeon' made excellent eating. The clergyman was only half joking when he suggested his friends in England visit the zoo to form 'some idea … of our repast'.[33] But neither they nor any other early colonist seriously contemplated adopting local methods of raising food, wholesale. They arrived with axes, saws, hoes and seeds, intending to farm in their own familiar ways. This was partly a matter of putting food on the table, but their agricultural method was also an art, a cultural practice, rooted in the colonists' worldview and imagination.[34]

The Bible was a deep source of European attitudes to sowing and reaping. The most influential verse was the one Lang quoted briefly in promoting migration, from the Genesis account of God blessing the first man and woman:

> Be fruitful, and multiply, and replenish the earth, and subdue
> it: and have dominion over the fish of the sea, and over the
> fowl of the air, and over every living thing that moveth upon
> the earth (Genesis 1:28).

Debate still rages over the role this text has played in fostering an exploitative attitude towards nature from which Western societies, in particular, have yet to recover. In colonial Australia, it was the root of two of the Bible's most significant cultural products. One was the notion of agriculture as 'improvement' and progress. The other was the legal concept of 'waste' land, so critical to the doctrine of *terra nullius*.

'Improvement' was one of the most potent ideas to circulate among colonists. It recurs through Wollaston's journals, and many other sources of his day, illuminating how, exactly, the Bible influenced their interaction with the land they claimed.[35] When Wollaston referred to his new surrounds as being in 'a state of primitive nature', for example, he was expressing the widely shared European view that nature needed to be 'subdued' through agriculture. The wilderness needed cultivating to the point of complete transformation. Then, and only then, would 'joy and gladness be found therein'.

'Wilderness' was the most common biblical term colonists used to describe their surrounds in Australia. Even as Wollaston sighed with relief at the sight of his corn field, people in the more established colony of New South Wales used similar language to express confidence in progress. In 1819, the barrister and explorer William Wentworth wrote of 'what is now one vast and mournful wilderness becoming the smiling seat of industry and the social arts … covered with bleating flocks, lowing herds and waving corn'. The country's transformation would fulfil 'the gracious intentions of its all-bounteous Author', he declared.[36] In 1826, the settler and agricultural writer James Atkinson promised that the colony's 'untenanted wastes … shall be covered by productive flocks and herds and enlivened by the presence and industry of civilized men'.[37] By 1841, soldier Edward Macarthur could write of 'thousands of industrious families … who were changing the face of the country'. Free settlers were turning 'the wilderness of yesterday into the scene of improvement and order that was now to be seen'.[38]

These perspectives had biblical roots in the mandate to 'subdue the earth', but they were not the text of Scripture straightforwardly applied. They illustrate how the Bible was refracted through European culture and reshaped according to wider intellectual currents of the day. Specifically, what God seemed to say in Genesis was bound up with Enlightenment assumptions of improvement and progress. By the time Britons colonised Australia, it had become axiomatic that unruly environments should be ordered by human industry, 'improved' and made 'productive'.[39] Again, this view was influenced by Scripture – but it was in the secularised sense of 'improving the earth' that the Bible most influenced colonial land use.

THE LEGAL NOTION OF *TERRA NULLIUS* WAS ANOTHER CRUCIAL cultural product of the Bible's long, thick history in Europe. It too involved a particular interpretation of the Genesis mandate to replenish and subdue the earth, as a divine endorsement of broadly agricultural land use. As the English philosopher John Locke had famously argued in the late seventeenth century, God had given the world 'in common to all mankind' but also commanded 'man' to labour. Whoever 'in obedience to this command of God, subdued, tilled and sowed' any part of the world thus transformed nature into their own private property, Locke claimed. Not only that, land 'left wholly to nature, that hath no improvement of pasturage, tillage, or planting,' should be considered 'waste'. Such waste land was not property, Locke argued, and until it was improved, it belonged to no one – it was *terra nullius*.[40]

Locke had justified his theory of property in part by appealing to the Bible. At the same time, he had not attempted to account for what the whole of Scripture might say on the topic, or to relate his arguments to the Christian gospel. In this sense, he had not offered a properly Christian theology of land use and ownership. Rather, he exemplified a practice common to intellectuals in societies that had long upheld the theological Bible – that of calibrating new knowledge and ideas with the text of Scripture. It was a secularising practice that, at the same time, confirmed the Bible's importance to those societies' cultural and intellectual products.

As European colonists overran more of Australia, dispossessing its Indigenous inhabitants, they cited Locke's idea that their own labour was the critical factor that transformed nature into property. 'It may be questioned by some feather-bed philanthropist whether we have any right to take the country from the blacks', spat the Victorian pastoralist Robert von Steiglitz, 'but I believe the general rule is that, if the people cultivate or graze the land they have claim to it. These creatures did neither.'[41] Or as a contributor to the *Sydney Herald* put it, along similar lines, Aboriginal people 'bestowed no labour upon the land and that – and *that only* – it is which gives property in it'.[42] These arguments involved a crude interpretation of the Bible, mediated by Locke's theories, that remained legally influential in Australia for roughly two centuries. *Terra nullius* was finally thrown out as a fiction by the High Court's *Mabo* decision.

On the frontier

Trugananner saw the worst of the whites. Her mother was killed by sailors, her uncle shot by a soldier, her sister abducted and sexually abused by sealers, and Paraweena, her betrothed, was murdered by timber-getters.[43] Tragically, her family's experience was not unusual among Indigenous Tasmanians. As Protector George Robinson wrote in 1830:

> The children have witnessed the massacre of their parents and their relations carried away into captivity by these merciless invaders, their country has been taken from them, and the kangaroo, their chief subsistence, have been slaughtered wholesale for the sake of paltry lucre. Can we wonder then at the hatred they bear to the white inhabitants? … We should make some atonement for the misery we have entailed upon the original proprietors of this land.[44]

The dynamics of the frontier varied. In New South Wales, the spread of European settlement was fitful and uneven. Intermittent conflict was protracted over at least half a century. In Tasmania, the violence was more concentrated and intense. By the end of the notorious 'black war' of the 1820s, roughly 450 colonists had been killed or wounded, and the entire Indigenous population had been reduced to just 200 survivors.[45] In the Port Phillip region of Victoria, the destruction was perhaps swiftest of all. In 1835, land-hungry pastoralists and speculators from Tasmania established a camp on the banks of the Yarra River. The settlement was formally authorised by government a year later. The announcement prompted an extraordinary land grab, unique in world history. In the space of a single generation, about 4000 Europeans and 20 million sheep occupied over 400 million hectares of Aboriginal land.[46] For the local Kulin, the results were devastating. In just seventeen years, the Indigenous population fell by 80 per cent. By 1853, there were just 1907 Aboriginal people alive in all of Victoria, once the most densely populated part of Australia.[47]

Some writers have suggested that frontier atrocities could not have been widespread, because the colonisers were a British and ostensibly Christian people. But in reality, people who knew the Bible, even believed it, were among those who harmed Aboriginal people or profited directly from frontier violence. The staunch Presbyterian Niel Black migrated from Scotland to Victoria in 1839. He journeyed west from Melbourne, searching for a sheep run where he might establish himself. As he travelled, he heard appalling advice from other settlers. For a European to secure land, the 'natives' had to be 'brought into subjection', 'tamed' with 'a few doses of lead'. They might try to steal stock or spear sheep, but the majority could be 'easily kept at bay ... once a few are shot'.[48]

Black drew his own conclusions about the frontier: 'Great

numbers of the poor creatures have wantonly fallen victims to settlers … [who] do not care a single straw about taking the life of a native'. Black could not stand the thought of committing such murder himself, so he purchased an established estate in what is now Corangamite Shire. The original inhabitants had been 'very troublesome', he wrote, but a previous superintendent had 'managed' that by committing an outright massacre on the site. Up to forty men, women and children had been killed, and the 'poor creatures' who remained were 'terror stricken', noted Black. He did not expect any more 'trouble' from them.[49]

One Sunday night, as Black settled in, he heard his dogs barking furiously outside. 'Never doubting that some of the natives … were about to steal our sheep', he and a young relative, Donald, got up and armed themselves with guns. Hearing sounds in the garden, Donald ran to the spot and got ready to pull the trigger. 'Had he got sight of any object in the shape of a man, I think he would not have stood much on ceremony', Black later confessed. 'If a black fellow had met him he would have done what till then he did not think himself capable of.'[50]

On the frontiers of settlement, the conventions and commitments of Christian gentlemen often came unstuck. Niel Black was shaken by the realisation, but evidently knowledge of the Bible was no guarantee of moral conduct. Scripture did not stop everyone from profiteering from dispossession, or prevent them from entertaining or even committing outright violence.[51] In a sense, the frontier produced terrible examples of the Bible's own teaching on the human condition – that no person is righteous, not even one, and that even Christians deceive themselves if they claim to be without sin (Romans 3:10; 1 John 1:8).

At the same time, in some instances, the Bible nurtured more of a conscience. Young Horatio Ellerman had been a belligerent pastoralist on the Victorian frontier, responsible for the shooting death of at least one Kulin woman in the mid-1840s. When he converted to Christianity, says historian Felicity Jensz, he 'put down his gun and picked up his Bible'. Its teaching restrained his worst impulses, and he eventually abandoned pastoralism altogether in favour of the Presbyterian ministry.[52] Just as courageously, a few bold Christians were moved to expose and denounce actual massacres of Indigenous people, with missionaries reporting atrocities at Pinjara, Western Australia, in 1834, at Waterloo Creek in New South Wales, in 1838, and later at Forrest River in Western Australia.[53] The Myall Creek case of 1838, first exposed to the public by the evangelical journalist Edward Hall, shows that such Christians acted on particular ideas drawn from the theological Bible.

In June 1838, a party of eleven colonists slaughtered at least twenty-eight unarmed Wirrayaraay people at Myall Creek, New South Wales. Appalled by the crime and by the Supreme Court's initial failure to reach a guilty verdict, Baptist minister John Saunders preached a blistering sermon on Isaiah 26:21 – 'Behold the Lord cometh out of his place to punish the inhabitants of the earth for their iniquity: the earth also shall disclose her blood, and shall no more cover her slain'. He denounced the way the colonists had 'robbed' Aboriginal people 'without any sanction': 'we descended as invaders upon his territory and took possession of the soil … From these their hunting grounds, they have been individually and collectively dispossessed'. Not only that, he went on, colonists had killed them 'wholesale, in cold blood': 'The spot of blood is upon us, the blood of the poor and the defenceless, the blood of the men we wronged before we slew … We are guilty here'.[54] After a re-trial, seven of the perpetrators were found guilty and sentenced to death – a highly unusual outcome in the history of frontier justice. The judge, Catholic John Plunkett, drew on Psalm 36:1 when he pronounced: 'The crime had been witnessed in heaven and could not be concealed … You had not the fear of God before your eyes, but were moved and seduced by the instigations of the devil'.[55]

Plunkett, like Saunders, had a moral vision rooted in an understanding of the theological Bible — especially in the idea of God's concern for the poor and oppressed and his righteous judgment against injustice. This idea is pervasive in the text of Scripture — surfacing in the story of the Hebrews' slavery in Egypt, in Psalms and the Prophets, and various other passages. In the hands of humanitarians like Saunders, it enabled a devastating condemnation of the colonists' worst conduct. The idea that God heard the cries of the suffering, and would act to punish those who did evil, gave a biblical shape to humanitarian defences of Indigenous people.

Even more significant was the biblical idea that all people were ultimately part of a single human family. Saunders referred to it when he pronounced that 'the New Hollander is a man and a brother'. John Dunmore Lang drew on it too, in a sermon he preached later the same year: 'they are bone of our bone and flesh of our flesh — formed originally after the image of God, like ourselves'. On this basis, Lang went on to argue, the colonists' mistreatment of their Aboriginal 'brethren' was nothing less than a 'national sin', for which the Lord was rightly punishing them with severe drought.[56]

IN THE EARLY TWENTY-FIRST CENTURY, COMMON HUMANITY is widely enough assumed that it can be easy to forget its biblical sources. But as the historian of race Colin Kidd points out, not every culture and society has assumed the unity of peoples. It was part of the biblical inheritance that informed European thought and society. Specifically, it stemmed from the Bible's depiction of human beings in the image and likeness of God, and its nomination of Adam and Eve as the common forebears of all people (Genesis chapters 1–2). It was further reinforced by the words of Paul in the New Testament: God 'hath made of one blood all nations of men for to dwell on all the face of the earth' (Acts 17:26). This was a widely quoted text among Christian humanitarians in Australia and the wider empire.

Of course, the idea of common humanity has been contested, even in societies heavily influenced by the Bible. Especially when European interests came into conflict with the claims of others – over land, for instance – it has often been challenged or put aside. But as Kidd shows, this biblical notion nevertheless constrained the development of alternative European theories of race. In colonial Australia, it provided the deepest and most important basis for condemning settler rapacity and upholding the rights of Indigenous people. With the authority of God's own word, 'one blood' was the primary foundation for humanitarian thought and action.

Reforming colonialism

During the 1830s and 1840s, humanitarians built an empire-wide campaign for a more Christian form of colonisation. In Britain, many who had campaigned to abolish slavery turned their attention to the plight of Indigenous populations. Evangelical politicians established a Parliamentary Select Committee which collected evidence, largely from ministers and missionaries, of the abuse, exploitation, dispossession and impoverishment of Indigenous people in British territories. In 1837, their *Report ... on Aboriginal Tribes in British settlements* placed a panoply of wrongs before the public. It roundly condemned 'the work of spoilation and death' being perpetrated in Britain's name.[57]

In advocating reform, humanitarians sought to make colonisation more moral. They expected this to involve 'the propagation of Christianity together with the preservation ... of the civil rights of the natives'.[58] In practice, one element concerned the moral and religious improvement of British settler populations. Surely properly Christian colonists would treat the local people better? The campaign to end convict transportation was fired by such a vision. So were Christian schemes to bolster the right kind of free migration. Lang, for example, encouraged 'virtuous, industrious' small farmers to migrate to Australia, hoping they would counter the effects of large-scale squatting – which, for Aboriginal people, had been 'literally ... tantamount to a sentence of confiscation, banishment and death'.[59] His ideal immigrants were Protestant Christians who would seek the physical and spiritual good of their Indigenous brethren. 'Infallibly', he believed, they would join in denouncing atrocities like Myall Creek and help 'originate a healthy state of public opinion' on race relations.[60]

Similar ideas circulated in South Australia. Colonisation 'by industrious and virtuous settlers' would help prevent violence and illegal land-grabbing, explained a promotional book of 1839:

Far from being an invasion of the right of the Aborigines, [it] is a necessary preliminary to the displacement of lawless squatters, the abandoned sailors, the runaway convicts, the pirates, the worse-than savages, that now infest the coast and island along that extensive portion of New Holland, and perpetrate against the defenceless natives crimes against which humanity revolts.

Its promoters thought Christian colonisation would enable land to change hands fairly. Looking to the new colony's founding documents, journalist James Stephens certainly expected South Australia to be free of 'bloodshed, violence and injustice'.[61]

Humanitarians advocated extending Christian missions to Indigenous people, believing that the gospel was an immeasurably valuable thing which the British might share with colonised populations. For all the loss of land and life, the spread of Christianity would secure them an unsurpassable, eternal benefit. Apart from whether Indigenous peoples themselves agreed this was an adequate exchange, it was a deeply patronising idea that traded on the notion of the unenlightened heathen native. At the same time, it was a radical idea relative to other colonial attitudes of the day: it assumed that Indigenous peoples could relate to God on the same basis as Europeans.

Most radically, Christian humanitarians also affirmed that Indigenous peoples had 'an incontrovertible right to their own soil'. This view ran counter to the actual practice of many settlers, and challenged prevailing assumptions of 'terra nullius'. It is clear in the Select Committee *Report* of 1837, which historian Henry Reynolds judged a landmark expression of a minority tradition of law that finally bore fruit in the *Mabo* decision.[62] It is also clear in John Saunders' Myall Creek sermon, which explicitly denounced the fiction that Aboriginal people had 'no notion of property':

> It is not just to say that … we could not rob them of that
> which they did not possess; for accurate information shews
> that each tribe had its distinct locality, and each superior
> person in the tribe a portion of this district.[63]

This view had a practical impact. In Aotearoa New Zealand, it provided some impetus for the 1840 Treaty of Waitangi, which intended to outline terms of partnership between Māori and Pākehā, including on the possession and sale of land.[64] In New South Wales and Tasmania, where huge areas had already been taken over by settlers, a small handful of Christian leaders raised the possibility of making reparations.[65] In Victoria, John Batman read the mood and sought to gain ownership of the land by means of a treaty – though for various reasons, it did not work either as a legal agreement or to protect the Kulin.[66] In South Australia, the idea of a treaty was woven into the legal documents that governed the process of British settlement: whatever land was actually occupied or enjoyed by the 'Aboriginal Natives' of South Australia was to remain theirs by right, unless the British acquired it by means of formal bargains or treaties.[67] (The colony's Resident Commissioner was even instructed to retain evidence of his 'faithful fulfilment' of any agreements he made of that nature.) Similar provisions to preserve Aboriginal land rights were incorporated into the *South Australia Amendment Act* of 1838.

OVERALL, HUMANITARIANS STOPPED WELL SHORT OF SAYING that European colonialism should end. No Briton of the era could imagine that. Their efforts to mitigate its effects were rarely concerned with structural justice. They did not listen to Indigenous people as well as they could have. Their exertions usually bore the marks of white paternalism. But within these serious limits, they held out the possibility of a less destructive form of colonialism – including at least a partial recognition of Indigenous rights to country. For all its considerable shortcomings, Christian humanitarianism was the most radical, most powerful critique of colonialism advanced among whites. It illustrates how the Bible, interpreted in certain ways, could provide a platform for criticising the worst of settler behaviour and nurture a vision for a more humane interaction with Indigenous Australians. In other words, the humanitarians' example shows that the Bible was more than the root of a special kind of hubris. The idea that the British nation played some part in extending God's blessings to the world certainly buttressed the colonial project, and fostered the conceit that the British could, at least in theory, colonise properly. But it also provided a mechanism for criticising settler rapacity as sin, and for calling the settler community to a standard higher than self-interest. Uniquely at that time, it supplied a moral standard beyond the law, and afforded a critique of *terra nullius*.

Even at its peak, the humanitarian movement faced challenges that constrained its impact. Its core idea of common humanity was contested, on the one hand, by people like the Reverend Hull, who attempted to justify inequality with contrary arguments from Scripture. Weren't Indigenous Australians descended from Noah's son Ham, the father of Canaan, he who was cursed to serve his brothers? Wasn't it the design of Providence that 'the inferior races must pass away before the superior races', as Hull pronounced in 1846?[68] Such views were not typical of Christian clergy in the post-slavery era, and do not appear to have won acceptance among policy makers of Hull's day. But this interpretation of Aboriginal dispossession and decline continued to circulate, with a kind of divine authority, into the late twentieth century.

On the other hand, the idea of one blood came under fire from the new 'science' of race.[69] In new, scientific ways of thinking, the non-European 'savages' had not fallen or declined from an earlier state of equality with other peoples: they had been savage from the outset, and did not possess even the capacity for civilisation.

(The fashionable new study of phrenology, for instance, claimed to explain differences between 'races' according to the contours of skulls.) Some Europeans also began to question whether there *was* a single human family at all, or whether the different peoples of the world might spring from multiple origins. This view contradicted Christian theology, which depended on single, common humanity for its doctrines of creation and salvation to make any sense. Yet it gained considerable traction from the mid-nineteenth century, undermining the old European consensus on common origins and dealing a severe blow to evangelical humanitarianism.

In this context, humanitarian efforts to 'protect the civil rights of the natives' ultimately failed. Even in South Australia, the idea of obtaining land by treaty was dropped in favour of asserting Crown possession of legal wastes. The humanitarian experiment there had lasted a mere seven years, in which time not a single treaty had been made.[70] In the other colonies, where humanitarians had always struggled for influence in land policy, their clout was further constrained by the shift in power from London to colonial legislatures. With the advent of self-government, colonists got control over land policy and native affairs – and humanitarian interests were effectively sidelined. In Australia, as in many other parts of the world, Christianity has rarely been sufficient, in itself, to prevent acts of racial oppression when whites have had tempting opportunities to obtain wealth or power.[71]

STILL, THE IDEA OF ONE BLOOD DID NOT GO AWAY. WHEN other colonists explicitly denounced Aboriginal people as less than human, humanitarians clung to the biblical principle of a single human family. When Aboriginal people were treated as disposable and subjected to violence, humanitarians affirmed both the sinfulness of such behaviour and the essential dignity of their Aboriginal 'brethren'. And when others explained the decline of the Indigenous population as the workings of providence, or the operation of natural laws, Christian humanitarians continued to imagine a future for Indigenous communities.[72]

Missionary supporter Septimus Lloyd Chase put that faith – and its implications – into words in the late 1850s, when many others expected the eventual extinction of Victoria's Indigenous population:

> They are dead in sins, as we know; and they are dying from off
> the earth, as we too certainly bear witness: but 'prophesy now
> to these dry bones, and say to the wind, Come from the four
> winds, O breath, and breathe upon these slain' (Ezekiel 37:4–5).

Chase's reading of the Bible made it clear that Aboriginal people should not and would not be wiped out by colonists. His theology led him to hope, apparently against the odds, for their present survival and eternal future. In the meantime, he argued, it was incumbent on a so-called Christian society to show mercy, not to oppress. He liked to quote Proverbs 14:31 – 'He that despiseth them reproacheth his maker; but he that honoreth God, hath mercy on them'. He also insisted, with the New Testament, that the colonists should 'Honor all men' (1 Peter 2:17). For Chase, the practical corollary of biblical hope was that 'the Aborigines of this country are worthy of more love than has yet been bestowed upon them'.[73]

SIMILAR IDEAS SURFACED IN WESTERN AUSTRALIA, AS THE frontier expanded through the 1880s. There, missionary John Gribble clashed with pastoralists in the Gascoyne region over their treatment of the Yamatji. The settlers had 'one desire', alleged Gribble

– 'to deal with the natives in their own way. They want to be "a law unto themselves" [Romans 2:14] and cannot tolerate the advent of one who comes with the Gospel of "Peace and Goodwill" to the poor black man'. Gribble was an experienced if idiosyncratic missionary, connected to a wider imperial network of Christian humanitarians.[74] He opposed 'the injustice and wrong-doing of interested and unprincipled white men', and made use of the press to put his case. His 1886 pamphlet *Dark Deeds in a Sunny Land* detailed a system of exploitation 'bordering on slavery': Indigenous men were being run down by whites and forced into labour, and then chased and chained up for weeks if they tried to escape. Gribble also drew attention to the 'assignment of native females against their will for purposes of immorality' – that is, their sexual slavery.[75]

For his trouble, Gribble was abandoned by his church, boycotted by powerful settlers and thwarted by a corrupt magistracy – a clear example of the colonial church, in alliance with the state, acting against the interests of Indigenous Australians. Forced out of Western Australia, Gribble returned to New South Wales and opened a new mission.[76] He shook the dust off his feet as he went, paraphrasing the judgment of Isaiah 30:10: 'Truly this colony is filled with violence, the priests prophesy smooth things, and the people desire to have it'. The experience proved to him the truth of John 3:19: 'Men love darkness rather than light because their deeds are evil'.

Less public Christians than Gribble also used the Bible to urge the more humane treatment of Indigenous West Australians. Lillie Mathews was a young Irish Protestant living in Melbourne during the early 1880s. Her fiancé Alick Crawford wrote to her regularly from Western Australia, where he managed a remote sheep station. Their correspondence positively drips with love and affection, but at times Alick's letters upset his girlfriend: he was involved in 'nigger hunts', as he called them, shooting on and terrorising the local population. Lillie replied to Alick, urging him not to neglect his 'study of God's word' and to remember the biblical precepts of his Methodist upbringing:

> I do wish you had not so much to do with the blacks. It is a dreadful thing to be continually hunting down one's fellow creatures, for they are our fellow creatures and have precious and immortal souls. Oh my darling, keep your hands free from your fellow creature's blood. For you to need to fire on them makes me feel miserable. It seems dreadful when really in your heart you cannot blame them for taking the sheep … in God's sight they are precious, Christ died for them as well as us, and for this reason we should protect them as far as lies in our power …[77]

She wrote again a month later:

> The whites will have a deal to be answerable for someday I fear, so-called Christians. … we should strive to 'do unto others as we would have them do to us'.

People like Lillie Matthews embraced the Bible as part of the life of faith. Like Christians in every age, they reflected on the world in light of what they believed God to be doing and saying. Their theological readings were not free of culture, nor did they lead to uniform conclusions. But as we see with Lillie Matthews, they were conditioned by the ways readers understood the Christian gospel: 'Christ died for them as well as us'. And crucially for colonialism, these theological readings sometimes came into conflict with older, more culturally embedded appropriations of the Bible – as when the impulses of evangelical humanitarianism ran counter to the doctrine of *terra nullius*. Even in the hands of colonists, Scripture offered critical resources to challenge the received wisdom of colonialism.

If there was an overall idea of biblical colonisation that characterised Christian humanitarians in Australia, it combined a desire to make a good land productive with a determination to secure a future for Indigenous people. In the moving words of Edward Parker, a devout Methodist who worked as an Assistant Protector of Aborigines in Victoria in the 1840s:

> … let every Christian man … rise, and say with one voice, to the government, the legislature and the nation; – occupy the land, – till its broad wastes, – extract its riches, – develop its resources, – if you will; – but in the name of God and humanity, SAVE THE PEOPLE.[78]

PART 2

THE GREAT AGE
OF THE BIBLE

Isaac Livermore travelled mainly on foot, with a good-sized box of Bibles on his back, another on his front and a leather bag containing his favourite samples in his hand. He was already in his fifties when he started, around 1855, but he travelled the length and breadth of Tasmania for at least a decade that way, spreading the good news. His genial disposition made him welcome wherever he went – from shepherds' huts to the halls of the wealthy. He was evidently good company, too – sharing 'a word in season' or, when the occasion arose, giving a recitation or performing a temperance song. Most years, Livermore succeeded in his primary aim – distributing thousands of Bibles and New Testaments to settlers who did not have one. By 1860, he happily reported that 'scarcely a family could be found without at least one copy of the sacred volume'.[1]

Mr Livermore was a Bible colporteur, paid by the Tasmanian Bible Society to distribute its books. He was one of hundreds of such people, employed the world over, to convey cheap Bibles door to door. Behind these colporteurs was an enthusiastic network of Christians committed to spreading the Word, and allied to *them* was one of the century's emerging technological marvels – a vast industrial Bible publishing and distribution industry.[2] Combining new means of paper making, printing and transportation, this industry made the mass-produced Bible a new and defining object of modernity, alongside the ballot box, the newspaper and the steam train.

The scale of the enterprise was staggering. From 1804 to 1904, the British and Foreign Bible Society circulated 186 *million* Scriptures in more than 370 languages around the world, at an eventual dispatch rate of one every five seconds. At the same time, the university presses of Oxford and Cambridge each printed the King James Bible for the British market. Producing more than one million copies a year by the 1850s, even this was not enough to stave off competition from unofficial, pirated and imported editions. Across the Atlantic, literally tens of millions more English-language Bibles were produced and sold by the American Bible Society,[3] by firms dealing in more lavishly illustrated or annotated versions,[4] and by various printers of the Catholic versions. This unprecedented work made the Bible available to more people in more places and in more languages than at any previous point in history. It established the nineteenth century as 'the great age of the Bible'. And in Australia, where it coincided with a significant period of institution-building, it left a lasting imprint on society and culture.

CHAPTER 4

SPREADING THE WORD

The Quaker missionary James Backhouse was unimpressed with Maitland, when he visited the Hunter region of New South Wales the mid-1830s. He had been told to expect 'a large proportion of the inhabitants of this place, drunken with rum and prosperity'. Stepping off the steamship from Newcastle, he judged that description 'not without ground'.[1]

Two decades of European expansion had made the traditional country of the Wonnarua into the principal agricultural and grazing district of New South Wales – devastating the Indigenous population in the process.[2] When some of the locals had resisted, the colonial government had sent in military forces, providing a stark lesson in terror.[3] By the time Backhouse travelled through, most of the survivors had been forced into dependence on the invaders. Their former livelihoods destroyed, many earned 'a scanty and precarious subsistence, chiefly by begging' in the larger towns.[4]

Maitland itself had grown from a timber-getters' camp into a permanent settlement with all the attributes of a busy gateway town. It had a lock-up, several inns and a considerable number of houses. A rudimentary building on Stockade Hill served as a schoolhouse and place of Anglican worship; the large Irish Catholic community met in a new, neat chapel on the main street of town. In the mid-1830s, most of Maitland's settler population still were or had been convicts. (If only they had attended to 'the convictions of the Holy

Spirit, as the witness in their own minds against sin', Backhouse lamented. They might have been 'led to repentance and faith in Christ, and through him ... become of the number of his reconciled and obedient children, free from the bondage of Satan'.[5]) But the character of the community was changing. In Maitland and places like it, the infrastructure of settled respectability was already being laid down.

The half-century that followed – from the 1830s to the 1880s – saw the wholesale renovation of settler Australia. The population boomed, its wealth increased, its territory expanded and both its technology and state took new forms. Many knew they were building something for the future. The prevailing mood was optimistic; there was an expectation of progress; the settlers looked for the dawn of a 'glad, confident morning'.[6]

In a regional centre like Maitland, the surviving Indigenous population was further marginalised as Europeans pursued their own success. New townships developed. New public institutions emerged. New churches opened to accommodate a range of denominations. In 1842, Caroline Chisholm opened an immigrants' home to assist female arrivals: it grew into a benevolent asylum and eventually a hospital. Other colonists founded temperance unions, sports clubs and Benefit Societies. The wealthiest landowners began electing members to a district council. The advent of colonial self-government in 1856 saw local men enter the New South Wales parliament. In March 1857, a crowd of thousands gathered to celebrate the opening of a railway line from Newcastle to Maitland.[7] A procession of clergymen, firefighters, and representatives of all manner of community organisations was graciously overseen by Governor and Lady Denison, and written up in great detail by the *Maitland Mercury*.[8] It was a spectacle of settler progress and respectability unimaginable in Backhouse's time.

HOW WAS THE BIBLE BOUND UP WITH THESE CHANGES? How did it become the staple text of colonial Australian life? To answer this, we need to look outwards to the globalising Bible. This was the Bible that travelled most easily along the channels of empire, connecting people in the Australian colonies to other places and communities. During the busy decades of the mid-nineteenth century, flows of free migration, the transplanting of institutions, and the circulation of ideas all assisted in spreading the Bible. So did the expansion of the British and Foreign Bible Society and the wider 'cultural infrastructure' of evangelicalism. The Bible Society began as the project of philanthropists and politicians, but soon developed a wide network of voluntary auxiliaries in which women did much of the work of fundraising and administration.[9] Allied to the new technologies of industrial book production, this movement and its work had a substantial effect in the Australian colonies.

At the same time, colporteurs like Isaac Livermore were grappling with the challenge of distance, while in larger settlements and major towns, a burgeoning print culture and patterns of church development helped propagate the Bible. As settler governments adopted new policies – especially on worship and schooling – they helped reposition the Bible as a tool of Christian citizenship in a plural, post-penal society. On the goldfields, Chinese Christians fleeing the Taiping rebellion evangelised with Chinese Bibles. Among Indigenous Australians, a small cohort of Aboriginal evangelists brought the Word to their own societies. Together, this unprecedented work made the Bible ubiquitous, familiar and influential in a critical era of change for Australia.

THE REVEREND GEORGE KEYLOCK RUSDEN AND HIS FAMILY arrived in New South Wales in 1834. They were better educated, and from a higher social class, than the average free migrant of the time, but they were not unusual in their efforts to cultivate a Christian society. The clergyman had a Masters degree from Cambridge and a deep interest in Asian languages, mythology and culture. Ordained to the Anglican ministry, he had lived the settled life of a schoolmaster at Leith Hill Place, Surrey, until, at the age of fifty, he followed his eldest son to the colonies.

Settling into the parish of East Maitland, in the Hunter Valley, Rusden devoted himself to the work of the church and its school. As well as preaching, teaching, and providing pastoral care, he gave help and advice to many people around him, acting as an informal employment agent and financial advisor to Protestants and Catholics alike. He also took up a range of wider causes, helping to found the community's first savings bank and Mechanics Institute. To all this, the clergyman brought faith and deep piety. He believed in a God who is 'the giver of all grace', who won salvation for people by 'the precious blood of Christ'. He felt deep thankfulness of heart for 'the love of our Redeemer … who hath procured for us, by his powerful atonement and intercession, a happiness unspeakable'. He looked forward to 'an inheritance imperishable', an 'immortal bliss and glory … as much beyond our *hopes* as above our *merits*'.[10] Rusden found his gospel in the pages of the Bible – a 'surer authority, even than our own senses … the revealed Word of Him who made them'. Throughout his life, he urged others to look to the Scriptures for their faith too, commending the Book of Life to all comers as both indispensable and richly satisfying.

The other pillar of the family was Mrs Anne Rusden. Descended from a distinguished clerical family, she was well educated and highly accomplished in her own right. In New South Wales, she involved herself in both church and school, as well as philanthropic work in the wider community. 'Whenever any trial is sent to a neighbour,' she once explained, 'I feel it an especial call upon me ... to strive to give sympathy if not consolation'.[11] Her own busy home fostered familiarity with the Bible and a thoughtful piety. It was a place of creativity and curiosity, too, as the Rusdens encouraged their children in foreign languages, painting, arts and handicrafts, as well as serious reading in history, geography, orientalism and the classics.[12]

The Rusdens' activities were buoyed by a much wider effort to Christianise settler society. From family prayer and Bible reading to public preaching; from providing pastoral care to supporting Christian charities and publishing societies, they were part of a multi-pronged effort to promote the theological Bible in colonial life. Within their particular community, they helped make the middle decades of the nineteenth century 'the great age of the Bible'.

Christianising settler society

The Rusdens arrived in New South Wales on the cusp of a period of dramatic church growth, as governments and settlers alike lent their energies to creating a more Christian society. The change began under a liberal Irishman, Sir Richard Bourke, Governor of New South Wales. He sought to lay 'the foundations of the Christian religion' by offering state aid to the four largest denominations – Anglican, Catholic, Presbyterian and Methodist. This meant putting an end to formal Anglican privilege, which concerned Rusden, among others. But Bourke recognised that the colony had a mixed population, including English, Irish and Scots. Anglicanism could not claim the allegiance of them all, but broadly Trinitarian Christianity could yet bring its communities together. Hoping to see 'people of these different persuasions … united together in one bond of peace' (a phrase he borrowed from Ephesians 4:3), Bourke promoted Christianity, in its most common denominational expressions, as a basis of citizenship.[13]

Bourke's *Church Act* (1836) turned out to be one of the most important pieces of legislation in nineteenth-century Australia. It provided grants for new churches and clergymen wherever the settlers raised an initial minimum themselves. Signalling a new partnership between subject and government, it stimulated a massive expansion of church infrastructure. In Maitland, Reverend Rusden had initially ministered in a rudimentary old schoolhouse: the *Church Act* enabled the construction of St Peter's Church, and the Bishop travelled up from Sydney to set the foundation.[14]

VIRTUALLY EVERYWHERE THE CHURCH ACTS OPERATED, colonists built places of worship. Their impact is still visible, on adjacent corners of many country towns. The same policy was soon rolled out in Tasmania and Western Australia, establishing mainstream Trinitiarian Christianity at the core of colonial religious life. It probably put the brakes on the emergence of new, specifically Australian denominations and fringe movements too: until as late as the 1960s, more than 80 per cent of Australians identified with one of the four denominations supported by the Church Acts.[15]

For all the support of the state, the colonial churches were not simply an arm of government. Even under the Church Acts, colonists had to make voluntary donations to qualify for aid. And even when the state did not contribute funds, church growth was still spectacular. In South Australia, for example, many colonists came from dissenting traditions of Protestantism, which treasured independence from the state in the name of freedom of religion and conscience. The colony's architect, George Fife Angas, a Baptist, summed up the prevailing sentiment: 'Bible Truth should be given unfettered and without state aid'.[16] Churches began there under their own steam – though for a few years during the depression of the 1840s, the colonial legislature *did* step in and grant aid. When this was overturned again in 1851, South Australia became the first part of the British Empire to abolish state aid to religion. By 1895, the colony had 908 churches just in Adelaide.[17] In most other colonies, state aid to religion was abolished in during the 1860s – yet church expansion went on. In New South Wales between 1870 and 1890, the number of church buildings and clergy more than doubled among Anglicans, Presbyterians and Congregationalists, and almost doubled among Methodists as well.[18]

When the English writer Anthony Trollope toured the south-east of Australia in the 1870s, he was struck to find a visibly Christianised settler society. 'Wherever there is a community there arises a church, or more commonly churches … the people are fond of building churches.'[19] Not only that, 'Religious teaching and the exercise of religious worship are held as being essential to civilisation and general well-being … the feeling is stronger there [in the Australian colonies] than it is at home'.[20] Such comments do not fit well with the stereotype of a godless ex-convict community, happiest to keep the church at a distance. But Trollope was correct. Through the middle decades of the century, weekly attendance rates actually increased.[21] The Sunday school movement, entering its golden age, attracted close to a literal majority of colonial children. In South Australia, the proportion of four- to fifteen-year-olds attending reached an extraordinary 70 per cent in the 1870s.

THE CHURCH BOOM EXPOSED LARGE SECTIONS OF THE community to the theological Bible. Whatever people's reason for attending, whatever meaning they drew from their participation, it brought them into contact with Christian ideas and teaching. After all, the Bible was the common property of all the Christian churches. They all spread the Bible as the Word of God, with the weight of divine authority, allied to a particular vision of the world and how best to live in it. Church participation involved a distinctly religious kind of socialisation.

A closer look at colonial sermons brings the scale of this exposure into focus. Until as late as the 1920s and the advent of radio, church preaching was the most common form of public speech in Australia. Hearing a sermon was an ordinary part of life.[22] Using the term 'sermon-event' for the experience of a congregation hearing a preacher, historian Michael Gladwin has estimated that in a single year – 1851 – the Anglican clergy alone produced 16744 sermon-events among the colonial population.[23] Several thousand more would have been created by ministers of other denominations, travelling evangelists, visiting missionaries and lay preachers, and for special occasions. Across Australia during the 1850s, an annual figure above 30000 is virtually certain. The subsequent growth of the colonial churches plus the increase in visiting preachers from overseas probably pushed the number of sermon-events to at least 60000 a year by the end of the 1880s. Conservatively estimated, a total of at least *two million* sermons were preached in Australia in the sixty years from 1830 to 1890.[24]

Sermons provided their hearers with a substantial encounter with the Bible. Individual hearers might doubt, question or even reject a preacher's contentions. But in most cases, oratory from the pulpit provided 'the ethics, meaning and framework' of life for those who heard it.[25] Enabled by the dramatic expansion of church infrastructure and buttressed by high rates of church participation, sermons were influential in propagating the theological Bible. With churchgoing more generally, they fostered familiarity with the Bible among generations of Australians, and helped weave biblical language, narratives and ideas into the settler imagination.

The specific ways people encountered the Bible at church depended in part on their denominational affiliation.[26] For Catholics, the Bible was one of several legitimate points of religious reference, a text to be used in approved translations and understood according to the authoritative interpretations of the Church. Churchgoers absorbed it primarily through the words of the Missal, the choral mass, as well as the catechisms taught to children. Private Bible reading was deemed a fraught activity. Stereotype editions of the Douay-Rheims version were distributed from some parish offices and sold by colonial booksellers from the early 1830s, accompanied by printed warnings about the dangers of reading the Bible unguided: the Holy Scriptures are 'hard to be understood, and wrested by many to their own destruction' (2 Peter 3:16); and 'not of private interpretation' (2 Peter 1:20). According to notes printed at the back, non-Catholic versions had been 'corrupted by Heretics' and definitely were not to be trusted.[27]

For Protestants, the Bible was the sole authority in matters of faith and doctrine, which meant that the traditions and teachings of the church were subject to Scripture. In more radical forms, it extended to the right of private judgment: believers were free to interpret the Bible according to the dictates of their own conscience. Affirming *sola scriptura*, Protestant services tended to emphasise the reading and preaching of the Word rather than the sacrament. Among children, formal catechising was not universal, but the rote learning of Bible verses was prevalent in Sunday schools.

But even Protestants did not absorb the Bible solely through reading, preaching and recitation. Anglicans and Presbyterians typically sang metrical versions of the Psalms, while Methodists revelled in the musical legacy of their co-founder Charles Wesley, author of literally thousands of hymns including 'And Can It Be' and 'Hark! The Herald Angels Sing'. From the 1870s, the songs of American gospel singer and composer Ira Sankey, among other revivalists, were also widely sung in Australia.[28] Such music instilled biblical concepts and phrases deep in the faithful and, in the best-known cases, helped circulate them in popular culture.

Colonial Anglicans made up a third group that itself ranged from evangelical Protestant to Tractarian. They were diverse in the respective weight they gave to private conscience and church tradition regarding the Bible. But they all belonged to a church whose Articles of Religion defined it as explicitly scriptural, upholding the Old and New Testaments as 'containing everything necessary to salvation'.[29] Anglicans gloried in the densely biblical liturgy of their *Book of Common Prayer*.[30] Bible reading, like other endeavours, was approached rationally and with order, and commended to congregations as a path to true faith.[31] As the Reverend Rusden once explained from the pulpit of St Peter's East Maitland, a person had to 'exercise their reason, as given to them by God', and diligently 'search the Scriptures' (John 5:39) as the Saviour had said. These differences between the churches ran far deeper than preference or taste. They were rooted in the Reformations of sixteenth-century Europe and England, which had basically cast Catholics as people of the Church, Protestants as people of the Book, and Anglicanism as a middle way. They were matters of identity and conviction that could unite and divide whole sections of the population. From one point of view, the Bible certainly exposed denominational differences. Until well into the twentieth century, it was a major fault line for Catholic/Non-Catholic sectarianism. From another point of view, however, the Bible provided a rallying point for people from different denominations, especially Anglicans and various other Protestants who otherwise differed on matters of church government, membership, relations with the state, and many finer points of doctrine. It was a major focus for a pan-denominational colonial Protestantism.

The colonial churches had substantial allies in the family, the press, and para-church Bible organisations. Each of these institutions helped extend – and complicate – the place of the Bible in Australia through the middle decades of the nineteenth century. Family Bible reading, for instance, became more widespread. As the ratio of settler women to men improved from one to eight, among convicts, to something approaching parity by the time of federation, more marriages occurred and more families took shape. At the same time, an emerging ideology of domesticity imagined the family home as both a refuge from the public world and the centre of moral and spiritual goodness. This new way of thinking positioned settler wives and mothers as 'angels of the house', agents of both religion and civilisation.

In this context, family Bible reading was a mark of an increasingly settled European society. Protestant families commonly read the Bible together at least on Sundays, if not daily. The Rusden family read and prayed together every day, presumably guided in part by the Prayer Book. Christiana Blomfield, a well-to-do evangelical who settled near Maitland in the 1820s, invited her children to discuss their ideas about particular passages as part of their general education:

They come to me for an hour of a morning, when they read
a portion of the Scripture, which I explain to the best of my

ability, and I encourage them to make remarks on what
they read. This hour is considered quite a recreation, and
I endeavour to make it a pleasure to them.[32]

Family Bible reading involved reading the same book intensively, aloud, in a small group. As such, the practice – and even the object – was bound up with family relationships, experiences and identities. The writer Mary Gilmore recalled reading her family Bible in the 1870s – a huge tome handed down through at least six generations. Despite its age and advanced state of disrepair, the family regularly undid the flannel and silk wrapping to read it. As a little girl, she had received her first lessons from it while sitting on her grandfather's knee.[33]

The print media fostered familiarity with the Bible too. Newspapers carried articles on state aid, sectarian politics and the hot topic of education. Many colonial editors also considered missionary meetings, charitable appeals and Sunday school anniversaries to be newsworthy. It is not difficult to find the annual reports of colonial Bible Societies reprinted verbatim. The reportage of actual sermons was widespread too: it increased over the course of the century, rising sharply in the later decades, in rough parallel with both the expansion of the press and estimated rates of churchgoing.[34]

Newspapers also helped weave the language of the Bible into public discourse. Journalists often employed biblical phrases and allusions in their general reportage. Articles on religious topics often included quotes direct from the Bible, sometimes running to several verses. Some articles even instructed their readers to go and consult the Scriptures in more detail. Louisa Lawson's feminist paper *The Dawn* was hardly a religious publication, but in 1896 it offered a prize to the reader who submitted 'the Best Verse from the Bible advocating a wife's right to control of property'. The winner suggested the very last verse of Proverbs: 'Give her of the fruit of her hands'. (The prize, of course, was 'a well-bound Bible'.[35])

Colonial newspapers also provided a new kind of encounter with the Bible. Hearing a sermon is an ephemeral experience, while readers can go over a text again. But compared to encountering the Bible at church, or through family reading, the dissemination of the Bible through newspapers was less direct, less authoritative, more fragmented and partial, less devotional and less embedded in personal relationships. The press made the Bible part of public discourse, but in a detached, impersonal way.

RELIGIOUS PUBLISHING SOCIETIES WERE FURTHER ALLIES. These included longstanding organisations like the Anglican Societies for the Propagation of the Gospel and the Promotion of Christian Knowledge, as well as newer evangelical bodies that embraced publishing and book distribution as a key missionary strategy. The Religious Tract Society (RTS), for instance, established in England in 1799, aimed to 'diffuse divine truth' as widely as possible among a mass of readers whose 'respective attainments, condition and character demanded … different modes of address'. The RTS developed an extraordinary catalogue of tracts, short books and periodicals, ranging from illustrated Bible passages and simple outlines of the gospel, to discussions of natural science.

Religious tracts were initially channelled to the colonies by sympathetic clergymen. In 1823, the Australian Religious Tract Society formed in Sydney.[36] By 1828, it had distributed approximately 80 000 items — more than two for every colonist in New South Wales. By its thirtieth year, total distribution had risen more than tenfold to 831 000 items. By its Australian jubilee in 1873, it had distributed just over 3.1 *million* tracts, books and periodicals.[37]

It is difficult to know exactly how much these tracts were read, but their huge circulation helped cement Christian concepts in common literate culture and contributed to the population's basic religious knowledge. If British studies are any guide, they also presented information on historical, geographical, political and scientific topics through a Christian frame.[38]

The Bible Society concentrated its efforts on publishing and distributing the Bible itself. Established in England in 1804, it had an auxiliary in Sydney from March 1817. Now known as Bible Society Australia, it is the oldest continuously operating voluntary association in the country. The Sydney group was followed by a Van Diemen's Land Auxiliary in 1819, and others in Melbourne, Geelong and Adelaide during the early 1840s. In 1856, a visiting agent from Britain found thirteen active Bible Society affiliates across Australia, with a cumulative distribution of at least 100 000 Scriptures.[39]

Bible Society work in Australia flourished in the 1850s, 1860s and 1870s. In Maitland, for instance, the Reverend Rusden helped form a Hunter River group in 1858. Within a decade it had a subscriber list of over 520 local colonists: promoting the Bible – and being *seen* to promote the Bible – was a popular cause. By 1875, the Sydney Auxiliary claimed thirty-two 'vigorous' branches, in addition to several flourishing independent New South Wales auxiliaries. There were eleven active groups in Victoria, including six in the Geelong district.[40] In Queensland, Bible Society branches and depots stretched all the way from Warwick to Cooktown, and there were dozens more in Tasmania and South Australia. In the west, where the settler population was smaller and more thinly scattered, individual Christians acted as agents of Bible Society work.[41] An auxiliary was finally established in Perth in 1884; its first order was for more than 2500 Bibles in eleven languages, for distribution through nine depots from Albany in the south to

Roeburn in the mid-north.[42] Circulation figures are difficult to track through this period, due to the growing number of groups and inconsistent reporting. But the Sydney Auxiliary alone distributed a total more than 328 000 Scriptures between 1860 and the mid-1890s.[43] It is likely that over one million Bibles and Testaments were circulated by Bible Society affiliates in Australia before the end of the nineteenth century, when the settler population itself reached four million.

The work of distribution was remarkably successful: by the 1860s, the Bible was widely available, with just a few exceptions. One was among the urban poor of the colonies' burgeoning cities. To many middle-class observers, this group seemed to fall sadly short of the standards of Christian knowledge and respectability. Bible societies, like other Christian groups, directed missionary attention to the cities, aiming to engage the poor with the text of Scripture. In Melbourne, Sydney and Brisbane, this work was done primarily by women, along lines first developed in overseas missionary contexts, particularly India. A designated 'Bible Woman' would go visiting door to door, talking with other women, urging them to accept a Bible and where possible reading a passage with them. In 1866, for example, Mrs Adair was appointed to visit private homes, hospitals, asylums and prisons in South Brisbane. Having done similar work in Belfast, she maintained it for seven years in Queensland. She was succeeded by Mrs Mellish, who had been a Bible Woman in England. By 1879, the team also included Miss Chapman, who worked in the Spring Hill, Fortitude Valley and New Farm districts, and Mrs Cherry, who worked in Red Hill, Kelvin Grove, Paddington and the streets off Petrie Terrace. Mrs Cherry pursued this ministry for at least ten years, eventually receiving an honorarium of one pound a week. A report noted her zeal for the physical and spiritual welfare of other people:

Wherever her help is needed, either in the pure Bible reading work, or the kindred tasks included in the Christian ministry of comforting the sick and troubled, watching by the dying, helping the poor to the means of relief, and drawing back the straying to the Christians [sic] churches, she is ever ready to do her utmost.[44]

Many other women threw their support into similar ventures. They raised funds, collected donations, and literally carried Bibles through the cities. In the 1870s, the ladies of Redfern Congregational Church, Sydney, made fortnightly or even weekly visits through their neighbourhood, distributing Christian literature. This period also saw numerous *new* women's groups formed with the 'chief aim of … disseminating the Word of God among the working classes'. These included the North-East Adelaide Bible Woman's Mission, the West Adelaide Bible and Mothers Domestic Mission, the Darlinghurst and Surry Hills Ladies' Branch Bible Association (Sydney), and the Geelong Bible-Woman's Agency.[45] Beyond the doors of the church, women did most of the work of propagating the Bible in urban Australia.

In rural and remote areas, men did more of the initial work of distributing Scripture, focusing on colonists who lived far from churches and schools, and thus 'placed to a sad extent beyond the reach of Bible influences'.[46] The idea of a godless frontier, a zone of spiritual need beyond the edge of settled European civility, had real potency right through the nineteenth century. And as historian of secularism David Hilliard pointed out, it had a genuine basis: at each census, well into the twentieth century, 'the highest proportion of self-declared agnostics, atheists and freethinkers lived in the outback, in mining towns and on the goldfields'.[47]

Beginning in 1852, colporteur James Robinson and another

man spent several months rowing a boat down the Hawkesbury and Macdonald rivers in New South Wales, calling at every house and hut within a few miles of each bank. At one spot, they found 'no less than seven Protestant families located on small farms of their own, without a Bible or Testament amongst them; no church, no school and no man to care for their souls'.[48] (Each of them 'eagerly purchased copies of the Word of God', the society reported, and 'heaped kindness on those devoted men who had … brought it to their doors'.[49]) In Tasmania, Bible Society members were shocked to hear that the magistrate for the Huon district once neglected to take a Bible to an inquest to swear in the witnesses. When he asked to borrow one from the owner of the house where the jury was sitting, none could be found there, nor among any of the neighbouring settlers. He had to send for seven or eight miles and wait four hours before a Bible could be obtained.[50] The society promptly dispatched Mr Livermore as colporteur, who within a few years had overcome the scarcity of Bibles in remote regions. Such colporteurs produced accounts of long, exhausting journeys, navigating rough terrain and generally risking their lives to distribute God's word in the back country. These became staples of Bible Society publicity: a Christian variation on the 'heroic bushman' theme.

Missionary frontiers

Spreading the Bible often occurred in step with certain social ideals. For example, among the urban poor, middle-class Bible women typically encouraged mothers to play a key role in training their children in morals and religion. Among the scattered settlers of the bush, colporteurs and travelling clergy laboured to institute regular habits of religious observance, with the Bible at the centre of workplaces and households. In this sense, Bible distribution was a settling enterprise. Yet the activist evangelicals who promoted the Bible most zealously aimed at far more than improving settler society. They sought to bring a living word of salvation to all, that all might taste the Word of life and believe. This vision extended beyond British colonists to non-Europeans, and in some important cases involved non-European agents and evangelists. Even as British settler society consolidated its position in Australia, the Bible crossed cultural boundaries and became the text of marginalised communities.

Bible Societies in Australia had always tried to make the Bible available to people who did not read English. In the five years to 1823, the Sydney Bible depository and lending library accumulated Scriptures in more than twenty different languages. The Bible Society still has some of them today: a Welsh Bible, an Assam Bible, a Hindi Bible inscribed in Elizabeth Macquarie's hand, and a Bible given to her husband, Governor Lachlan Macquarie, by the Tsar of Russia and donated for the use of Russian sailors passing through Sydney.[51] The Sydney Bible Society also made Bibles available in Irish and Scottish Gaelic – a full Scots translation having been published for the first time in 1801. It is unclear if Bible distribution in languages other than English kept pace with the flow of free migration through the 1830s and 1840s, but the gold rushes of the 1850s spurred a major new work of distribution, especially among miners from China.[52]

The gold rushes prompted most colonial churches to establish pastoral ministries on the diggings. Evangelicals, and especially Methodists, treated the gold regions as mission fields and rejoiced in several localised instances of Christian revival. Chinese diggers – who numbered at least 35 000 by 1861 – were the focus of specific ventures aimed at Christian conversion. In the terms Bible Societies used at the time, the arrival of so many Chinese people seemed a providential opportunity to ensure that 'these poor idolaters' were 'furnished with an adequate supply of scriptures in their own language'.[53]

White supporters of the Chinese ministry usually displayed the European cultural prejudices of the era, alongside the genuine conviction that the Chinese could receive the same salvation as Europeans. However, the practical work among Chinese diggers was often led by Chinese Christians. A number of these early missionaries came from Hong Kong, or sought a safer field of work during the Taiping rebellion. Chu A Luk and How A Low commenced work at Castlemaine in 1855, visiting the encampments, reading the Scriptures to Chinese diggers and speaking to groups and individuals. They distributed New Testaments in Chinese, and entered into an evangelical commentary and explanation of them.[54] Subsequent missionaries included Lo Sam Yuen, based in Ballarat, Leong On Tong and James Moy Ling, who ministered in the Chinese chapel on Little Bourke Street, Melbourne, and Joseph Tear Tack, who was born in China, converted in Bendigo and ordained to Methodist work in New South Wales. A Methodist ministry to the Chinese of Perth and Fremantle was established in the 1890s, under Paul Soong Quong.

These ventures were encouraged and resourced by colonial Bible societies, in the wider context of Bible translation and distribution work among the Chinese. The BFBS had printed the world's first full Chinese translation of the Bible just a generation previously, in the 1820s.[55] A revised version, not based on a classical, literary style, was one of its main priorities in the late 1840s and early 1850s. Bible Society branches in places like Melbourne, Geelong, Bendigo, Castlemaine, Sydney and Moreton Bay channeled several thousand of these Chinese Bibles to the colonies during the 1850s and 1860s.[56]

MOSES TJALKABOTA WAS BORN AT LAPRAPUNTJA, IN WESTERN Aranda country, central Australia, sometime around 1869, the son of law man Tjita and his wife Aranaljika. Very early in his child-hood, Tjalkabota's people got news that whites were coming, along with their strange animals – horses and sheep. 'We thought that white men were black men who had died and then returned as spir-its to the place where they had died long ago.' These white people set up a mission a few miles west, at Ntaria (Hermannsburg), and began learning the local language. When they gave Tjita trousers and a shirt, the Aranda people said 'This is a different skin'. Tjita also reported that their leader, Mr Kempe, had a lot of books and did a lot of writing.

Tjalkabota began attending the school set up by the missionar-ies, coming and going according to his family and community obli-gations. 'First we learnt the Commandments, and songs. The first song was *Jesuai, nauna pitjai* [Jesus come to us]', he later remem-bered. Tjalkabota avidly absorbed the new teaching and was soon sharing it with his peers. On a walking trip with his relative Rau-erkara, Tjalkabota taught him *Jesuai, nauna pitjai* and the Psalm 'The Lord is my shepherd'. 'I taught him the Commandments too. We were there about two weeks.'

Tjalkabota's desire to keep studying with the missionaries eventually brought him into conflict with his parents and other elders. About 1891 they urged him to leave Hermannsburg: 'Boy, if you continue here, your head will implode, and you will dry up. Then the wind will blow you away to the sand hills like a dried-up cicada, and we will be unable to find you'. But when his parents returned to Laprapuntja, he stayed working at the mission, receiving baptism and the Christian name Moses in December 1890.

'When I was about to be baptised, I felt a change in my heart', Moses later explained.

> I rejected a lot of the old men's ideas. I thought like this: 'These old men, and also my father, they are speaking their own words, not like the missionaries'. I said to them 'Our teachers are more correct when they say God is in heaven'.

He also came to a different view of creation, rainmaking and what happens after death. He argued with his father Tjita and other elders about the power of *tjurunga*, the Aranda's sacred objects. At one point he told his father 'You are ignorant, you don't understand'. Tjita replied: 'I am more knowledgeable than you. I am an *iliara* [fully initiated man] … You received good clothes, I received many *tjurunga* decorations'. Neither Tjita nor many other old men were willing to become Christians like Tjalkabota. When missionaries told them the *tjurunga* were 'wrong', they answered: 'I want my very own *tjurunga*. This is more precious'; 'My *tjurunga* are invaluable. I cannot give them up.'[57]

Moses, however, became an assistant at the Hermannsburg school and helped instruct classes for baptism. In time, and despite the onset of blindness, he developed an extensive ministry as a Christian evangelist and teacher. He had a prodigious memory and could recite whole chapters of Scripture.[58] Missionary Freidrich Albrecht recalled listening 'with rapt attention to some of his addresses. To him the New Testament just lives, and he knows how to make it live again before his hearers'.[59]

Most of Moses Tjalkabota's preaching was directed to the younger Aranda growing up in the colonised world of cattle and sheep stations.[60] He spoke to stock workers and their families at Deep Well, Alice Well, Horseshoe Bend, Idracowra, Jay Creek, Alice Springs, Undoolya, Arltunga and other locations. Peter Bullah remembered hearing Tjalkabota preach: 'One day an old man came to Henbury [cattle] station, old blind Moses. He taught us the Word of God. Many people heard God's word at that place'. On one memorable visit Moses stayed for five weeks, later giving an outline of his Bible teaching:

> I began with the Commandments. Then I started on the Old Testament with the story of creation. I told them everything as far as Adam. They had a real keen desire for the Word of God. 'Moses teach us and admonish us with the real word of God' and that is what I did … I taught the people the gospel. On [the last Sunday] I taught them about Jesus' Sermon on the Mount, the beatitudes.[61]

Through all this, Blind Moses maintained a significant connection to culture. Even after his Christian baptism, he underwent full initiation as an Aranda man, and later ensured that his sons did too. He also worked to record the customs, beliefs and culture of his people, acting as one of missionary Carl Strehlow's primary ethnographic informants.[62] Not only that, Tjalkabota's own Christian practice was steeped in Aranda ways. He taught the Christian message to others with the same methods that young Aranda initiates were instructed about their *tjurunga*. He told the story of the Bible with pictures, and taught hymns, the Commandments, and prayers by rote.[63] Unlike most European missionaries, he did not attempt to change the way people lived, the food they ate or their dress. In the recollections he dictated to missionary FW Albrecht in the 1950s, he presented his evangelising as a series of serious intellectual discussions with others. And in recounting his missionary journeys, he paid keen attention to country – describing in detail the routes he took, naming the places he passed by, where he slept along the way, and the things he 'saw'. As such, Moses' recollections 'conform to Arrernte [Aranda] cultural forms rather than any Lutheran missionary template'.[64]

Indigenous evangelists were a major feature of the global expansion of Christianity in the nineteenth century. In Africa and especially the South Pacific, they vastly outnumbered missionaries from Britain, playing a leading part in religious change. Most of the early missionaries who successfully evangelised the Torres Strait Islands during the 1870s and 1880s, for example, were converts from the Loyalty Islands, in New Caledonia, or Samoa. Associated with the London Missionary Society, whose British staff played a superintending role, these Islander missionaries established chapels and schools, and even commenced local translations of the Bible. On Mabuiag Island in the Torres Strait, the Samoan missionary Isaia translated the four gospels, the catechism, and a number of hymns into Kala Lagaw Ya. In collaboration with local men Tom Nabua, Peter Papi and Ned Waria, he also rendered the Bible translations made by missionaries into related dialects into the Mabuiag tongue.[65] Samoan missionaries led most of the churches and schools in the Strait until at least the First World War, when the influence of Anglicanism became stronger.[66]

The mainland Australian story is very different. After the disappointments and failures of the early colonial missions, the second half of the nineteenth century saw a new wave of work among Aboriginal peoples. This included the formation of several Presbyterian stations (managed by Moravian missionaries) in Victoria and Queensland, Lutheran missions in central Australia, Anglican missions in Queensland and Western Australia, and a few independent missions established by individual Christian couples.[67] Most were in areas remote from white settlement.

Beginning with the conversion, in 1860, of the Wotjobaluk man Nathanael Pepper at Ebenezer Moravian mission, in Victoria's Wimmera region, several of these missions eventually gave rise to communities of Indigenous believers.[68] The scope of Indigenous evangelism, however, is difficult to determine. Australian missionary sources make relatively little mention of Indigenous evangelists, and very few of the evangelists themselves left memoirs like Moses Tjalkabota.[69] It seems likely that Indigenous ministry did not occur in nineteenth-century Australia on anything like the mass scale of other locations.

That said, it is also clear that a number of early Christian converts sought to share their new understanding with their communities – beginning with Dickey Bennelong in 1820s Sydney, Thomas Brune on Flinders Island in the 1830s, and Jane Marshall, one of the new believers at William Watson's mission at Apsley, near Wellington, New South Wales. In the 1840s, Watson wrote of how Jane came 'unrequested ... almost every morning to repeat a hymn and six or eight verses of Holy Scripture'. She also read the New Testament with her husband Jemmy, who had not converted, and frequently entered conversation with the other women.[70]

From the 1860s, converts at the newer missions began to spread the Word among their own people. James Ngunaitponi, a Ngarrindjeri man, was the first adult Christian at George Taplin's mission at Point McLeay, South Australia. Born at Piwingang, a Murray River lagoon, about 1830, he came to Christian faith in 1862 through the gentle teaching of an itinerant missionary, James Reid of the Free Church of Scotland. He accompanied Reid as an interpreter for a couple of years, also learning to read and write. After Reid was tragically drowned, Ngunaitponi settled at Point

McLeay. Taplin quickly recognised him as 'indeed a true follower of Jesus', who was already 'accustomed to converse with natives to try to induce them to come to Jesus'.[71] The two men prayed and translated passages of the Bible together, and Taplin encouraged Ngunaitponi to act as a 'Scripture reader' in the lakeside camps, supplying him with a boat and paying him a wage for the task. In 1871, Ngunaitponi was appointed the first Ngarrindjeri church deacon, assisting Taplin to administer the sacrament. Over the next several years, he continued to make lengthy tours along the Coorong and to outlying Ngarrindjeri camps, walking 200 kilometres or more to spread the message of the Bible.[72] He made some of these trips in the company of another Indigenous evangelist, James Wanganeen of Poonindie Mission, and the young Point McLeay man, William Kropinyeri.[73] He died a respected leader of his people in 1907. One of his sons, David Unaipon, who also preached, became so famous he graces the $50 note.[74]

Emma Timbery was the leading figure at La Perouse mission, Sydney. Born at Liverpool, about 1842, into a Dharawal-speaking community, she apparently moved to the city during her teens.[75] Sometime after her marriage she settled at La Perouse Aboriginal settlement, converting to Christianity in the early 1890s. Working closely with whites, from whom she learned to read a little, Emma became vice-president of the La Perouse Aborigines' Christian Endeavour Society. Through Christian work, she and the young missionary Retta Dixon became 'friends and comrades'. The two women often travelled together to other Aboriginal settlements along the New South Wales South Coast, spreading the Word.[76]

In several cases, Indigenous evangelists greatly enabled European missionary ventures, and were critical both to the success of the missionary station and the ministry of sharing the Scriptures. James and Angelina Noble are a relatively well-known example:

they worked closely with John Brown Gribble in north Queensland, before establishing a new mission at Forrest River on the Cambridge Gulf, Western Australia.[77] Johannes Pingilina, a Dieri speaker, was among the first group baptised at the Lutheran mission at Coopers Creek in 1879. A champion shearer, literate in his own tongue, he possessed outstanding linguistic abilities. In the mid-1880s, he travelled to Cape York, Queensland, in the company of missionaries. He learned the local languages, and was soon acting as the missionaries' translator and language teacher. He also shared the work of evangelism and teaching, though his efforts were meanly appreciated. By June 1888, Pingilina was asking why all the other mission staff were getting paid while he was not. The missionary Meyer agreed to put £5 a year in a trust for him. On the eve of his wedding, Pingilina wrote (in Dieri) to ask for it, explaining 'the work he was doing among the local people, the difficulty of spreading the gospel of love among people who dismissed it as mere talk, affirming his commitment to the faith'. It is unclear from the historical record if he was ever paid or what happened to him.[78]

As Pingilina's story suggests, the work of Indigenous evangelists was often constrained by the realities of white paternalism and prejudice. European missionaries rarely treated Aboriginal Christians as true partners in ministry, usually designating them as perennial 'assistants' instead. Few mission organisations acknowledged the value of their work with formal support, let alone equal pay. And in all but a handful of cases, before the early twentieth century, the settler churches failed to ordain Indigenous Australians, thus withholding status and security from even the most devoted and gifted Christian leaders among them. Even in the face of these considerable obstacles, though, the work of Indigenous evangelists was critical to spreading the Bible in Aboriginal communities. It marked a key crossing of cultural boundaries. It demonstrated that the Bible was not simply a white man's book: it did not travel solely along the paths of empire. It could be shared within Indigenous communities, by Indigenous people, in ways that shed some of its European freight.

CHAPTER 5

SEEKING THE GOOD SOCIETY

Bessie Harrison Lee had an unfortunate early childhood in Victoria. Her mother died when she was still very young, and her father, a butcher, arranged for her to be cared for by other relatives. Their at times terrifying behaviour instilled in her an intense dislike of alcohol abuse. Eventually settling with a kind uncle and his wife on the diggings at Enoch Point, in the late 1860s, Bessie grew up with little formal schooling, almost entirely isolated from other children. With few companions, she read voraciously. 'I don't think Aunt was very well acquainted with the Bible', Bessie later recalled, 'but both she and my uncle liked to see me reading my own little book, and enjoyed listening every Sunday morning to my small stock of dear old hymns'.

Aged about nine, Bessie received a real fright from reading Milton's depiction of hell in *Paradise Lost*. She found many of the words incomprehensible, but 'there came to me through its pages the awful knowledge that I was a lost creature':

> It seemed to slowly dawn upon me that beyond this life
> there were two places: one place for the redeemed, and that
> was where mother had gone; the other for the lost, where
> murderers and evil-doers were going … and I, – I was in the
> lost state.

She suffered for days with 'a heart like lead and a head like fire'. Then:

> As I was washing the breakfast things one morning … my
> eyes wandered to a side table where lay my little black-covered
> Bible. I threw the tea-towel across my shoulder and went to it.
> I did not know what I wanted, or what to look for … To me
> the Bible was a beautiful story book … I did not know that
> in its pages was to be found the only way of escape from the
> wrath to come …
>
> As the pages opened I looked down and read the words: 'Be of
> good cheer, thy sins are forgiven thee' (Matthew 9:2). A great
> flood of light and radiance and soft beautiful sunshine seemed
> to burst upon me. I knelt down on the floor and folding my
> arms on the table and laying my head upon them, I whispered
> … 'Thank you Lord thank you' and from that moment I was
> saved, and lost all fear of death and hell forever.[1]

From then on, the Bible had new life and meaning for her. She read it frequently and literally, absorbed in 'the beauty of the scriptures' and delighting in its vision of 'love to God and love to man'.

The Bible brought Bessie Lee joy, relieved her terror, and spurred her to prayer and worship. She read it intensely, devotionally, and took it to heart. But as she grew older, the Bible was about more than the inner life, or even the world to come: it nourished a posture of transformative engagement towards the society around her. After marrying a railway worker, with whom she settled in Melbourne, Bessie began attending church, taking Bible classes and visiting the poor and sick. As her activities widened to include Sunday school teaching and temperance activism, her reading of the New Testament encouraged her to further social service. She became an activist and popular speaker, well known in Australia, New Zealand and North America, with a ministry eventually spanning temperance evangelism, the campaign for female suffrage, and labour rights for factory women.[2] For Lee, among many others, the Bible anchored a vision for wider society.

THE TASK OF BUILDING THE GOOD SOCIETY WAS A PRE-occupying one in Bessie Harrison Lee's time. The colonies were feeling the ripple effects of what has been called the 'age of reform' and the 'age of improvement' in British life. They also continued to shape the institutions of their own communities as they transitioned from penal settlement to civil society. The process enlivened causes from temperance to education to suffrage to workers' rights. It encompassed issues including the nature of the state, the character of good citizenship, and the emerging institutions of social and political life. It engaged individuals, governments, churches and many other groups, with consequences still visible in Australia today.

In all this, the Bible was not just a relic of the old world, which an increasingly confident colonial community discarded and left behind. It was actively woven into the fabric of settler families, movements and societies. In fact, during the second half of the nineteenth century, people in Australia encountered the Bible more often and more substantially than in any other period. The hard copy became readily available, ubiquitous in both the cities and the bush. Biblical ideas and teachings were widely promoted by churches, then approaching the height of their influence. Scriptural stories, phrases and ideas circulated in printed materials and in public conversation. In other words, it was in the context of peak

Christian socialisation, when levels of biblical literacy were at an historic high, that colonists debated the good society. The Bible was a shared point of reference, a part of common life.

Crucially, the Bible was still more than a storehouse of public rhetoric, or even of shared basic assumptions. In the hands of activist believers, it anchored and conditioned the broad contours of what historian Alan Atkinson has called the 'dynamic altruism' of religion.[3] As a religious text, after all, the Bible had authority in the lives of believers. Christians typically tried to bend their lives to God's word – to live in step with its ethics, pursuing its vision of 'life to the full' (John 10:10). Concerned as much with the love of neighbour as personal devotion to Jesus, this was both a public and a private matter. It readily produced transformative engagement with society and its members.

In the 1880s, the well-known Australian Congregationalist James Jefferis offered this account of the Bible's role in Christian citizenship:

> There is a power in the Bible itself … The Bible, working out its Divine mission in a living Christianity, furnishes the one power to face danger and conquer difficulty, and by the might of self-sacrifice to regenerate the world.[4]

These phrases suggest a living faith, expressed in selfless citizenship, rooted in a devotional embrace of the Scriptures. They describe a dynamic that greatly influenced modernising Australia. This is not to suggest that Christians (then or now) had a monopoly on public-spiritedness. Many Australian Christians and their churches fell well short of the ideals of love, humility and self-sacrifice. At their worst, their behaviour could be profoundly destructive. This has been painfully apparent in recent decades, with the failures of the institutional church to protect children from abuse at the hands of its leaders and clergy.

But one reason why the Bible mattered – and continues to matter – is its role in fostering active concern for the common good. In modernising Australia, where more people were influenced by Christianity than any other tradition of moral or religious thinking, Christian teaching encouraged a self-giving spirit of social service.[5] This has had lasting consequences, apparent in emerging institutions from charities to newspapers to the education system.

The challenge of need

On a winter Sunday morning in August 1801, the first public charity in Australia commenced with Divine service. 'The church was pretty well attended', recalled Rowland Hassall, who with his wife Elizabeth had travelled from Parramatta to Sydney to be present. After the reading of prayers, colonial chaplain Samuel Marsden preached on a text particularly apt for opening an orphanage: 'When my father and my mother forsake me, then the Lord will take me up' (Psalm 27:10). According to Hassall, Marsden's sermon included 'a true description of the parents of the children of this colony' and emphasised 'the children's exposedness to ruin'. Marsden hoped that, under the auspices of the asylum, children would be instructed 'in the knowledge of Christ, whome to know is life eternal'.

Afterwards, Marsden led the way to the Orphan House – a mansion formerly owned by naval officer and magistrate William Kent, standing near the present north-eastern corner of George and Bridge Streets.[6] Hassall remarked, 'we was highly delighted with seeing the girls in the greatest order feasting on excilent rost pork and Plumb puddin and seemed very Happy in their new situation'.

He thought the establishment did 'much credit' to its management committee, which included Marsden as treasurer, two colonial surgeons, and 'the two first ladies in rank in the colony', Anna King, wife of the governor; and Elizabeth Paterson, wife of the lieutenant governor.[7]

Less than a fortnight later, Marsden made his first visit to the Orphanage residents. There were thirty-one girls, initially, aged between about seven and fourteen. Not all of them were technically orphans, but they had all been judged to need rescuing. 'I made a beginning to instruct them in the principles of Christianity, sang a hymn, and went to prayer with them', Marsden reported to an English friend.[8] He exalted, 'New South Wales while I was performing this duty appeared more like a Christian Country than it had ever done since I first entered it'.[9]

CHARITY IS FREQUENTLY CITED AS AN EXAMPLE OF THE Christian contribution to the common good. Apologists and historians often remind us that responding with compassion to the needy was both a hallmark of early Christian thought and a radical departure from classical ways of thinking. It is certainly true that Christians played a leading role in the Australian colonies' burgeoning organisations for relieving poverty. As with the Female Orphanage, they often acted in partnership with the state, combining government subsidies with voluntary subscriptions and personal donations.[10] Their efforts were also shaped by historical and ideological factors, which could include concerns about female sexuality, the moral instruction of children, and transforming the poor into useful workers. But amid such complexity, it remains clear that Christians brought their religious beliefs to bear on the issue of want and poverty. They provided considerable practical aid, and established institutions that remain part of Australia's social landscape today.

Several examples emerge from the early British settlement at Sydney. The NSW Society for Promoting Christian Knowledge and Benevolence was created by a devout group of colonists, including three former London Missionary Society (LMS) missionaries to the South Pacific and several other evangelical Christians. Its initial aims of 1813 were 'Relieving the Distressed, and enforcing the sacred duties of Religion and Virtue in New South Wales'; 'Protecting the natives of the neighbouring Islands by using legal and prudent means, from fraud and oppression'; and 'Promoting the Great missionary cause' particularly in Tahiti and its region.[11] These wide intentions highlight the scope as well as the seamlessness of Christian humanitarianism in that period. At the Governor's behest, however, the Society's aims were soon constrained to focus on relieving distress and promoting piety in New South Wales. In its first five years, the Society spent just under £1000 in relieving more than 600 people with food, rent aid, clothes, extras for hospital patients and burial funds. In 1818, the group was reorganised to become the NSW Benevolent Society — now the oldest charity in Australia. If this seems a step towards a more secular, utilitarian vision, it nevertheless retained religious elements.[12]

In April 1817, well-off Christian colonists established a savings bank in Sydney. The idea was to give poorer people an alternative to 'dissipating' their money 'in spirituous liquor or gambling' — and thus to protect them from remaining 'poor, vicious and unmarried'. The founders hoped that, by encouraging people to save, the bank would foster habits of economy, industry and even matrimony.[13] If this seems a strange idea for a bank, it drew on perceptions of thrift, industry and prudence as 'Christian virtues' — accompaniments to personal godliness and domestic tranquillity, as well as to economic enterprise and development. The bank itself is now known as Westpac, the oldest bank in Australia.

A generation later again, as the colony's social and economic life continued to grow, Bible-believers kept forging new organisations. Thomas Holt migrated to Sydney in 1842 after reading JD Lang's *Historical and Statistical Account of New South Wales*. Believing he was required to 'be not slothful in business' but 'fervent in spirit, serving the Lord' (Romans 12.11), he proved a very unslothful businessman.[14] Dealing mainly in wool, but with many other investments and ventures, he became extremely rich. He also came to play a leading role in several charitable and commercial bodies.

One of these was the Australian Mutual Provident Society, now known as AMP. Established in 1849, its initial rationale was to enable working people to band together to provide themselves with life insurance. At a time when there was no state welfare system, this was an early and important Australian expression of an evolving British model for supporting labouring families. The AMP's early directors and chairmen included Holt, newspaper proprietor John Fairfax and the merchant David Jones — all regular and devout readers of the Bible, who held positions of responsibility in Sydney's churches. The early AMP mirrored 'that Protestant view that people must accept responsibility for their own well-being and that individual responsibility was a form of godliness'.[15] As a *mutual* organisation, it also embodied 'bear ye one another's burdens' (Galatians 6:2). By 1881, nearly one in four people in New South Wales were members of a mutual or friendly society.[16] They came in both Catholic and Protestant varieties, with both the Oddfellows (Protestant) and the Hibernian Society (Catholic) drawing their motto from 1 Corinthians 13:13 — 'faith, hope and charity'.

Such ventures were replicated throughout the Australian

colonies, as Christians concerned themselves with community welfare. Bishop Charles Perry and Mrs Frances Perry in Melbourne, for instance, took the lead in establishing hospitals, orphan asylums, and institutions for the elderly and people with disabilities.[17] Similarly, in Hobart, the non-conformists Henry and Sarah Hopkins liberally supported the Ragged School, Benevolent Society, City Mission and the Hobart High School, as well as the Bible Society, the LMS and various Protestant churches. Sarah directed her personal energies to home and church, while Henry also served as a trustee of the savings bank and as chairman of both the Van Diemen's Land Bank and the Tasmanian Insurance Company. According to Hopkins' biographer, he regarded money as 'a trust and a stewardship' – a view based on Jesus' teaching about wealth in Luke chapter 16.[18] In Sydney, the Presbyterian philanthropist Ann Goodlet gave decades of active leadership to the Benevolent Society, the NSW Institution for the Deaf and Dumb and the Blind, the Queen's Jubilee Fund and the Sydney Female Refuge Society. Her husband John, a successful merchant, gave generously to his church and charitable organisations, including the Thirlmere Home for chronic consumptives at Picton, the Sydney Hospital, the Royal Hospital for Women at Paddington, and the Sydney City Mission.[19] Clergy and Christian businessmen were outdone only by churchgoing women in the practical work of colonial charity.

THE BIBLE DID NOT PRODUCE A SINGLE, AGREED IDEA OF how best to deal with want and poverty. This is obvious from the range of interventions and institutions conducted by colonial Christians – from hospitals, homes and asylums to financial bodies to various mutual organisations – and later again to trade unions (see chapter 7). This raises an important point about the character of Christian citizenship: 'its energy was not all channelled in the one direction … It was rather implicated in the passionate trial of options'.[20] In that very 'trial of options', though, is something significant: the Bible nourished a posture of concern towards the needy. Among other impulses and agendas, various efforts to address poverty were shaped by biblical ideas. Marsden mentioned one such idea at the opening of the orphanage. As his sermon explained, the biblical God himself took up the orphan, the poor, the distressed and needy. Or in the language of the Benevolent Society's annual reports, the task was to care for the needy along the lines implied by Jesus. Echoing his teaching in Luke chapter 14, its Second Annual Report (1820) described the Society's intention:

> To lessen the sum of human misery, by imparting to the aged,
> the blind, the paralytic, the sick, and the distressed, some
> small relief to aid in the mitigation of their bodily sufferings,
> and at the same time to direct their minds to the true source of
> all consolation, our holy Religion.[21]

At the same time, the Bible urged such concerns on believers as the mark of the true Christian. The ageing Marsden explained the logic in a sermon for the Benevolent Society during the 1830s. His text was Matthew 25:35–40, including Jesus' famous words: 'Inasmuch as ye have done it unto one of the least of these my brethren, ye have done it unto me'. Marsden argued that since 'God is love and every one of us … is created anew after his Image', love must be 'the distinguishing feature of the real Christian'. Such love went beyond acts of private devotion to an active concern for one's fellow citizens. Or as a Christian newspaper in Melbourne put it in 1850, with reference to the Good Samaritan (Luke 10):

> The Christian is taught to regard every man, with whom he
> has any kind of intercourse ... as coming within the scope
> of the commandment 'Thou shalt love they neighbour as
> thyself'.[22]

Tragically, Australian churches have often fallen well short of these ideals. In practice, colonial Christians could be selective, even punitively discriminatory. Marsden himself is a prime example: the same man who preached on love for all showed a gradual hardness towards some classes of convict and eventually abdicated from any serious effort to benefit Aboriginal people.[23] Christian shortcomings were also evident in distinctions made between the deserving and undeserving poor, and in the relatively limited efforts to extend relief to Indigenous Australians and non-European migrants, such the Chinese. In most cases, too, colonial Christian charity stopped well short of addressing structural injustice. The influence of the Bible was insufficient to guarantee either the right conduct of believers or the effective care of the needy.

That said, the Bible did help lift the colonists' sights above the horizon of immediate self-interest. Its teaching informed the dynamic altruism of religion and enlarged the colonists' moral imagination. This matters not only in terms of the actual aid provided, which in some cases must have been critical to survival. It matters because of its lasting institutional legacies. Not only have several originally Christian charities persisted into the present, a habit of co-operation between Christian groups and the state has defined the Australian way of providing welfare services. The relationship between these welfare partners has been subject to considerable change, particularly with the cultural shifts of the 1960s and government moves towards contracting out social services more recently. But in the early twenty-first century, Christian organisations are still over-represented in delivering charity and welfare in Australia, compared to both the United States and the United Kingdom.[24]

Finally, biblical ideas have continued to sustain the ethical thinking and action of numerous Australians, including some who may not personally identify as practising Christians. According to Geoffrey Robertson, the international human rights lawyer, there are three enduring philosophic bases for the widely shared idea of human dignity, which he outlined to the ABC's *Q&A* program in September 2015. The first is Jesus' Parable of the Good Samaritan, which means that 'we don't pass by when someone is bleeding to death'. The second is Portia's speech about the quality of mercy in Shakespeare's *Merchant of Venice*. Mercy is 'an attribute to God himself', says Portia, in step with Bible passages like Psalm 136. The third is Immanuel Kant's imperative to treat others as you would have them treat you.[25] This, too, can be traced back to the Bible, and particularly to the teaching of Jesus: 'in everything, do to others what you would have them do to you' (Matthew 7:12). These ideas are not the exclusive property of the Christian tradition, but their influence in Australia has been largely bound up with Christianity and the reception of its Scriptures.

A free press

It was not unusual, during the 1860s, for the arrival of a clipper ship to send colonial journalists into a spin. The population was hungry for news from abroad, and each clipper carried British newspapers current at the time of their departure ten to fourteen weeks before. Melbourne's major dailies, the *Argus* and the *Age*, were in stiff competition with one another, and with many smaller papers, to be the first to report the incoming stories. At Queenscliff, on the west head of Port Phillip Bay, the *Argus* correspondent used a whale boat to meet each steamer even before it entered the bay. Once back at the pier, a waiting buggy would drive him at breakneck speed to the nearby telegraph station so he could transmit the main points back to Melbourne. There was only one telegraph wire then, and, determined to hold it for the scoop, the correspondent would hand the operator a copy of the Bible before leaving for the heads, with orders to telegraph it to the *Argus*, Melbourne. This meant nobody else could use the telegraph wire until he returned and filed his story. The *Argus* office knew that when the Book of Genesis began to arrive, the European mail was not far behind.[26]

The Bible played more than a cameo role in the development of the press in Australia. Even before the first issue of the *Sydney Gazette* was published in March 1803, the Bible and its particular history in Europe had influenced deep (if sometimes competing) assumptions about freedom of conscience, expression and proper authority. More tangibly, in the 1820s, when the colonies' first non-government newspapers appeared, the Bible informed debates about press freedom. Several early editors had an almost sacred sense of their role and responsibility, which they expressed with scriptural language. For Edward Smith Hall, for instance, journalism was a vocation shaped by Scripture – viewed, in his case, through the lens of evangelical Protestantism.

Hall was one of Australia's first journalists and an outspoken advocate for freedom of the press. Describing himself as a 'Bible Christian', among other things,[27] he believed in 'the greater portions' of both the Old and New Testaments, and studied them to the point of giving away all his other religious books so he could concentrate better on the Bible.[28] Hall's faith prompted his involvement in a great range of community causes. In his native London, he had devoted himself to religious and social work, winning the notice and approval of William Wilberforce. Within a few years of arriving in Sydney, he had helped found the Society for Promoting Christian Knowledge and Benevolence and the Sydney Auxiliary of the British and Foreign Bible Society. The son of a banker, he also served as cashier and secretary of the first bank of New South Wales.[29]

Hall's calling, however, was to journalism and in 1826 he founded the *Monitor,* one of the most important independent papers in early Sydney. Hall's personal reading of the Scriptures shaped his vision for it. He declared that newspaper editors were 'pastors of the public liberty', responsible for 'preaching' upon important information 'in season and out of season till the people believe it'.[30] (His reference is to the New Testament text of 2 Timothy 4:2 – 'Preach the word; be instant in season, out of season; reprove, rebuke, exhort with all long suffering and doctrine'.) And since 'the Christianity of the New Testament' was 'purely democratical', Hall said, people of power and influence should be held accountable for their public acts, not least by the news media.[31]

Hall practised what he preached, perhaps to excess: his fierce criticism of Governor Darling, whom he considered oppressive, landed him in prison for libel. But even from gaol, Hall petitioned the Colonial Office in London for greater journalistic freedom. After his release, he continued to hound Darling, eventually rejoicing in both the Governor's return to England and the easing of restrictions on colonial publishing. Hall strenuously promoted representative government and trial by common jury, and was a lifelong advocate for 'Liberal Principles and Free Institutions, Rational Liberty and Equal Justice'.[32]

Not every colonial Australian journalist was as fascinated by the Bible as Hall, or as directly inspired by it. But as restrictions were lifted and the colonial press began to flourish, Christians played a prominent part in the industry.[33] Anglican clergymen were among the most prolific early journalists, but lay and ordained people of all denominations contributed as writers, editors and newspaper owners.[34] In New South Wales, for example, the Wesleyan minister Ralph Mansfield founded the *Australian Magazine, or Quarterly Register* (1821–22) and afterwards edited the *Sydney Gazette*. The 'red hot Presbyterian' JD Lang established three separate, if short-lived, newspapers to forward his particular views on colonial events and politics. He also published several books, contributed articles to other titles, and helped two other pioneer newspaper proprietors to immigrate – William Kerr of the *Port Phillip Patriot* and James Swan of the *Moreton Bay Courier*.[35] In 1841, the committed Anglican Charles Kemp and Congregationalist John Fairfax took the helm of the *Sydney Morning Herald*. This widely circulating daily soon involved several members of Pitt Street Congregational Church. For more than thirty years, it was edited by Protestant ministers: Mansfield (1840–54) and then Congregationalist John West (1854–73).[36]

In other colonies, too, people well versed in the Scriptures fostered a publishing industry of wide civic importance. In South Australia, the Wesleyan John Stephens won public acclaim for championing independent journalism.[37] In Queensland an Independent minister, the Reverend G Wight, was involved with the *Daily Guardian*, and Charles and William Buzacott oversaw a chain of provincial papers. In Victoria, the main man behind the *Age*, David Syme, had trained for the Congregational ministry. He lost enthusiasm for a 'doctrine of Salvation by faith' and became an influential exemplar of Victorian liberalism, but the religious texts and cultures of his early adulthood nevertheless left their mark on him.[38]

In Australia, the movement away from state publishing

monopolies towards independent journalism was significantly shaped by Christian citizenship, in turn informed by applying particular understandings of the Bible to public life. There were other approaches, of course: Governor Darling, for instance, was a churchgoing Anglican who envisaged a society led by an alliance of squire and parson. Many others of his ilk similarly resisted liberal challenges to the ideal of rural aristocracy. But non-conformists like Hall and West, and the Presbyterian Lang, were among the most effective advocates for making government more accountable to the people. Their religious insistence on the right of independent judgment, the necessity for religious freedom from state interference, and the equality implied by the notion of 'the priesthood of all believers' was a fertile source for reformist thinking.

In other ways, too, colonial Christians directed the emerging institution of the press to the common good. Throughout the nineteenth century, as the dispossession of Aboriginal people continued apace, humanitarians both in Britain and Australia utilised the print media to both expose white violence and seek better treatment for Indigenous people. Hall's *Monitor*, for instance, was the first to publish news of the Myall Creek massacre of 10 June 1838.[39] He maintained an editorial line sympathetic to the victims throughout the trials, as did JD Lang's *Colonist*. *The Sydney Morning Herald* reflected the view of most settlers in supporting the white defendants, describing Aboriginal people as a 'whole gang of black animals'. But in 1841, after it was purchased by Kemp and Fairfax, and the Reverend William B Clarke engaged as features editor, it adopted a contrary, humanitarian editorial line on Aboriginal matters.[40] In the hands of the more devout Christian editors, and through the contributions of Christian missionaries, from Lancelot Threlkeld to John Gribble, the press was a major vehicle for seeking positive change.

Schooling for citizenship

The Reverend Rusden, the clergyman from Maitland, could not agree with his son George William about school education. They had a lot else in common, including an active Christian commitment to social welfare and some basic assumptions about the culture of the book, and the place of the written word in communicating knowledge, ideas and faiths.[41] They even agreed, in general terms, on the importance of Christian doctrine in cultivating moral citizens – not least in a former convict colony! But when it came to creating schools for colonial children, the clergyman and his son advocated different systems.

In mid-nineteenth-century Australia, few people could agree on the proper approach to schooling. It was the most longstanding and contested issue in colonial political life. The protracted debate reflected the high stakes: education was bound up with the kind of society being envisaged, affirmed and created. Discussion was especially intense in light of emerging ideas about childhood, including a preoccupation with 'the rising generation' as the key to the future of the community and its progress in 'civilisation'.[42] It was complicated, too, by wider considerations of church and state – an age-old issue which was taking on new dimensions. Schooling also exposed contested ideas about the Bible: who should interpret it? What did it mean? What access should students should have to it? No wonder it took more than half a century to establish a lasting framework for primary education in Australia.

By the 1830s, the Reverend Rusden had decades of experience as a parson-teacher himself. He saw education as the proper responsibility of an established Anglican church, as it had been for centuries in England. The church catered both for the poor and for paying pupils, with the primary aim of inculcating right doctrine. The parish school he oversaw at St Peter's East Maitland, for example, encouraged both male and female students:

> To write out and learn by heart many parts of the scriptures; such as our Saviour's Sermon on the Mount, His parables and miracles &c. All these were regularly and carefully explained … and [students were] thoroughly examined in them from time to time. We laid the foundation deep and broad and strong, to bear the hope that was to reach as high as heaven.[43]

Schools like the Anglican one Rusden oversaw in Maitland emerged in many parts of New South Wales, along with a few run as private commercial ventures, and schools connected to the other major denominations. The church schools were initially subsidised by the state but without interference. There was no set curriculum and the content and quality of teaching varied greatly. Together, however, denominational schools made up the first system of colonial education. They did the lion's share of educating young people, and played a substantial role in transmitting the Bible.

To the younger George William Rusden, by the 1840s it was clear that denominational schooling had serious limitations. It was expensive and unwieldy, and could not hope to educate anything like the majority of children. Especially in rural areas, where the population was scattered and denominationally mixed, it seemed more practical to establish one school that catered for everyone. Such schools could be funded by government, and conducted on a common Christian basis. In making education more accessible and avoiding dogmatic divisions between churches, they could secure good Christian citizens to the state.

From 1848, George William Rusden worked as the paid agent of the government's new system of national education. He rode thousands of miles, holding meetings and giving talks outlining its principles to parents.[44] As he was careful to explain, these early government schools were not un-Christian. In fact, they actively continued the work of placing the Bible before their students. Church representatives still had weekly access to teach the children of their own denomination, including by reading the Bible 'either in the Protestant authorised or Douay versions'.[45] In addition, the list of books recommended for use in general lessons included the two-volume *Scripture Lessons (Old and New Testaments)*, *Sacred Poetry* and *Lessons on the Truth of Christianity*.[46] The general curriculum also included religious teaching calculated to avoid differences among Christians – in favour of that '*common* faith in which all are agreed … Eternal Life, the gift of God, through the Saviour of the World'.[47]

Many church leaders were wary of government-run education. Its Catholic opponents considered common Christianity a Protestant fiction which relied on an artificial division between faith and doctrine. Even worse, it allowed students to read portions of Scripture for themselves, unguided by traditional Church teaching. Supporters of the old Anglican establishment felt an ordinary teacher could not teach a generic Christianity with any benefit. As the Reverend Rusden claimed: 'It is impossible [for non-denominational schemes] to secure steady adherence to the great doctrines of the Gospel … teachers [bring] in damnable heresies under the pretence of pursing a liberal course of religious instruction'.[48] And then, in the eyes of some non-conformist Protestants, any religious instruction in government schools represented a dangerous state interference in religious matters – a threat to freedom of belief and conscience to be avoided at all costs. The influence of this view in South Australia, especially, led to a distinctively secular system of schooling there.

In the midst of these contrary views, a growing proportion of lay people, as well as some Protestant clergy, supported government education. Common Christianity resonated with those fatigued by sectarian division. It also reflected a new religious sensibility which placed less emphasis on forms and rituals, and more on personal conduct and relationships.[49] James Jefferis summed this sentiment up when he said Christianity was 'not a doctrine but a life': what mattered most was 'the spirit of love after the manner and example of Christ'.[50]

The government system of national schools institutionalised a Christianity that emphasised ethics and social peace. According to its architects, it was grounded in Jesus' teaching 'to love even their enemies, to bless those that cursed them, and to pray for those that persecuted them'. It was also informed by specific New Testament verses to be displayed in every national school classroom:

We ought to shew ourselves followers of Christ who, when he was reviled, reviled not again (1 Peter 2:23).

Christians should endeavour, as the Apostle Paul commands them, to live peaceably with all men (Romans 12:18).[51]

In this view, the Bible was a spur to tolerance in the face of denominational diversity, a foundation for right living more than a foundation for right thinking.

THE PUBLIC INSTRUCTION ACTS PASSED IN MOST COLONIES during the 1870s and 1880s established a third approach, now commonly called 'free, compulsory and secular education'.[52] They put an end to all state aid for religious schools in favour of a single, centralised government system. This had major consequences for church primary schools, as well as for the Bible's place in state classrooms. Their main feature was not an anti-religous triumph, however, but the new centrality of the state. Agnostic and secularist critiques of Christianity had some influence, particularly in Victoria. But even there, as JS Gregory found, education reform was primarily inspired by a determination to make the state the focus of citizenship.[53]

Many ordinary Protestants greeted the new system as an acceptable end to a long period of active adjustment by the churches to the colonial situation.[54] There were even several evangelicals among its architects and advocates. Samuel Grimes, for example, a member of South Brisbane Baptist Church, had a decisive influence on Queensland's 1873 legislation.[55] James Greenwood, one-time minister of Bathurst Street Baptist church in Sydney, led the movement away from denominational education and played a key role in framing the *Public Education Act* for NSW.[56] These examples confound binary assumptions of 'religion verses secularism' and 'church versus state'. There were myriad views among Christians, not least on the role of government in relation to faith. And when it came to the specifics of secular education, actual policies and practices varied from colony to colony, as they still do from state to state. This was nowhere clearer than in the changing place of the Bible in formal education.

Victoria went the furthest in removing religion from the new curriculum. Standard texts were quickly revised to exclude references to Christianity in favour of more generic references to a Creator. To give some examples from the fifth *Royal Reader*: a poem on 'The Nativity' was exchanged for an 'Address to the deity'. A prose extract on 'Paul at Athens', presumably from the Book of Acts, was deleted in favour of an extract on 'The Wonder of Cotton

Manufacture' and a poem 'To a Waterfowl' to make up the space. Tennyson's poem 'Late, Late, So Late', an exploration of a parable in Matthew's Gospel, and Sir Walter Scott's famous 'Dies Irae' were also replaced.[57]

Across the border in New South Wales, the Reverend Rusden's son-in-law, Canon Selwyn, was deeply troubled:

> They [in Victoria] have carried matters to such a pitch that the Bible … has been cast out as an unclean thing, unfit so much as to be mentioned, and the very name of God himself has been eliminated and banished out of every book that is permitted to enter their schools.[58]

The root problem, as Selwyn saw it, was that the role and authority properly belonging to God was being assumed by the state: 'Their one aim and object is to inculcate the doctrine that the people is supreme; parliament is supreme; whatever parliament decrees must be right. Everything they say depends on human law; no one need trouble themselves about any law of God'. ('Marriage' he added as an example, was in this view 'nothing but a civil contract. It is quite open to be abolished altogether if only a sufficient number of members of the Upper House or Lower House determine that it should be so'.)

In Selwyn's own colony, however, secular education had different implications. In both New South Wales and Western Australia, the term was explicitly defined 'to include general religious teaching as distinguished from dogmatical or polemical theology'. In addition, church representatives had access to students of their own denomination, whose parents wished them to receive 'special religious instruction' (SRI). As Henry Parkes explained, 'It was never the intention of the framers of this Bill to exclude such a knowledge of the Bible as all divisions of the Christian church must possess, or a knowledge of the great truths of Revelation'.[59] Secular, on this view, meant rejecting sectarian division in favour of common Christianity as a basis for citizenship.

Tasmania and Queensland left the meaning of 'secular' undefined. Practically, the former allowed church representatives to provide weekly SRI. In 1910, Queensland voters passed a referendum that had previously failed in Victoria and South Australia – to substantially increase Bible teaching as part of the general curriculum. Church representatives were given weekly access to state schools and classroom teachers were authorised to give Bible lessons of a 'common Christian' kind.[60] Even in Victoria, the interpretation of secular education softened in time. During the 1890s, parliament resolved to reintroduce 'the name of our Lord and Saviour' to the standard readers. The minister of public instruction also introduced the *School Paper*, which combined non-denominational Christian elements with moral teaching.[61] Such variations underline the fluidity of secular education. The new government system was frequently compatible with common Christianity and allowed some scope for teaching from the Bible.

The Public Instruction Acts had one more major consequence for the Bible in elementary classrooms. Though the new system was more or less accepted by most Protestants in Australia, it was rejected by the Catholic hierarchy. Any lingering possibility of Catholic support for a unified, common system had finally evaporated in 1864, when Pope Pius' *Syllabus of Errors* unequivocally denounced 'liberalism in general and state education in particular'. The Catholic church responded to the end of state aid by developing an entirely independent system of education. Staffed by religious, imported from all over Catholic Christendom, the Catholic parish school became one of the most significant and enduring features of the social and educational landscape, at times educating as many as one in four or five Australian children.[62]

EVEN THE BRIEFEST SURVEY OF HISTORY – OR OF CURRENT affairs – makes it obvious that the Bible does not produce a single, agreed idea of the good society. This is because Christianity is internally diverse, in its interpretation and theology. It is also because issues of class, gender and race usually inform the ways believers live out their faith in public. Even within fairly homogenous groups – even within a single family, such as the Rusdens – Christian citizenship could involve numerous, sometimes competing, visions of the good society. Such diversity challenges a simplistic idea of Australia as a society founded on the Bible, in any straightforward or homogenous way. At the same time, it underscores the importance of the Bible and its reception in Australian life. In 'the great age of the Bible', numerous colonial Christians applied their faith, and their particular understandings of Scripture, to the emerging institutions of settler society. Dealing with poverty, developing the press, and forging a system of public education, all involved contests and compromises to do with the Bible. That trial of options produced institutions – and even ideas – still important in Australian life. At the same time, yet another kind of Christian citizenship was emerging among those largely excluded from the benefits of the good society. Among the small but growing number of Indigenous Australian Christians, the Bible nourished radical hopes for the future, and bolstered campaigns for structural justice.

Radical hope

Simon Wonga, a Woiwurrung man, was born near Healesville, Victoria, sometime in the 1820s. His father Billibellary, the leader or *ngurangaeta* of his clan, was one of the signatories to John Batman's 'treaty' of 1835, an event young Wonga may have witnessed.[63] Billibellary was open to dialogue with white society, and sent his eldest son to the first school opened by missionaries. He also articulated his people's claims to land, a claim his son repeated, with some limited success, in the 1850s and 1860s. Within a few years of Billibellary's death in 1846, Wonga was widely recognised as the new *ngurangaeta*. He also continued to associate with Europeans, forging a particularly useful friendship with William Thomas, an Assistant Protector of Aborigines, and an extraordinarily humane and self-sacrificing Wesleyan.[64]

In 1859, Wonga took a small group of Taungurong men from the Goulburn River to see Thomas, acting as their interpreter and mediator: 'I bring my friends Goulburn Blacks, they want a block of land in their country where they may sit down plant corn potatoes etc etc, and work like white man'.[65] This clear statement of hope for an Aboriginal future within the constraints of settler society was well received: Thomas sent the group on to the appropriate administrators, who granted 1820 hectares to the Taungurong on the junction of the Acheron and Goulbourn rivers. Thomas described the group's journey there with the biblical language of entering the land of promise: they 'wended their way to their Goshen' (see Genesis 45:10).[66]

Encouraged by this precedent, Wonga returned to Thomas in 1860 to ask for land for his own people. He chose a site in his traditional country, on the Yarra flats near Healesville. Under the new government policy of reserving land for Indigenous Victorians to live on, this site became Coranderrk Aboriginal settlement. Wonga's people settled there in March 1863. They were soon joined by dozens of Taungurong refugees, who had been forced from their earlier grant by greedy neighbouring pastoralists. The Coranderrk community set about clearing and fencing the land, building houses and planting crops: in short, forging a new Aboriginal way of being within radically changed conditions.[67]

Earlier in the 1860s, the white manager of Coranderrk, John Green, had described his friend Wonga as 'almost a Christian'.[68] By 1865, Wonga had become 'a decided Christian', well acquainted with the Scriptures. According to one press report, he recognised the Bible's authority 'both for principle and practice; and all his speeches, when he enters into any discussion, are pervaded by references to it. It is impossible to be in his company without perceiving that he is a man of superior natural ability, possessed of more than ordinary penetration, and soundness of judgement'.[69]

Around the same time, Wonga made a speech to the Coranderrk community on the occasion of Green's birthday. He recalled how:

Mr Green told me plenty of good words from the Bible and they made me very glad. … I now know plenty of good words from the Bible. I am very glad. Mr Green and all the Yarra blacks and me went through the mountain. We had no bread for four or five days. We did all this to let you Goulburn blacks know about the good word. Now you have all come to the Yarra, I am glad.[70]

Wonga, it seems, had come to envisage Coranderrk as an Aboriginal Christian community.[71]

THE SUBSEQUENT STORY OF CORANDERRK IS ONE OF THE most important, and painful, in Australian history. Wonga's resilient band of men and women negotiated the challenge of white invasion, appropriating elements of the Europeans' technologies and traditions to forge a new life in colonial conditions. Uniquely, among Indigenous Victorians of this era, their designated reserve was in country traditionally significant to their people. Uniquely, again, they were managed there by a couple, John and Mary Green, who 'passionately identified with the plight of the downtrodden'.[72] The Greens were missionary-minded Christians who devoted their lives to the welfare of Indigenous Victorians.[73] At Coranderrk, as John put it himself, 'my method of managing the blacks is to allow them to rule themselves as much as possible. When there is any strife among them this is always settled at a kind of court, at which I preside'. In anthropologist and historian Diane Barwick's judgment, Green was the only one of a succession of managers across the six Victorian reserves who ever entrusted full responsibility for discipline to the residents. The practice stemmed from the Greens' radical Christian conviction that Wonga and his people were free and independent men and women.

Building on their earlier efforts to share Christianity and alphabetic literacy with Aboriginal people, the Greens ran Coranderrk as a missionary settlement. Church services were prominent in the daily routine; and just as the school was central to activities, the Bible was central to the curriculum. In September 1865, Green invited his friend, the minister Robert Hamilton, to conduct the first baptisms. Twenty-seven adults underwent this initiation into Christian community. By the time the Greens left, in 1874, Coranderrk had become a large farm and village with a schoolhouse, bakery and butcher – a valuable piece of land.[74] Thirty-seven children and thirty young adults could read and write in English, yet the traditional authority of the *ngurangaeta* and senior men remained largely in place. As in so many other cases, this kind of literacy proved a critical skill: it enabled the residents to read the newspapers, and thus to keep abreast of the plans of colonial administrators – and to protest against them.[75]

The hard-won success of the Coranderrk community attracted the interest of covetous settlers. In the early 1870s, neighbouring landholders began lobbying the Board for the Protection of Aborigines (BPA) to sell Coranderrk into private hands – ostensibly so this already valuable land could be used 'more productively'. They approached the BPA chairman on the quiet, seeking to break up the settlement for cheap lease or purchase by whites. By 1874, the BPA was seriously considering closing the Coranderrk reserve, selling its land, and exiling its people to a colder and less fertile site on the Murray. The situation forced Green's outraged resignation in protest: the Board's refusal to reinstate him added to the community's grievances.

Simon Wonga died in 1875, in the very midst of this crisis. He was succeeded as leader by his cousin William Barak. Barak spent his life searching for a sustainable Aboriginal existence in a colonised society. Like Wonga, he embraced those elements of European society and belief that enabled his people to survive. And at a time when Indigenous life was under extraordinary pressure, he found in Christianity a vision of society that encompassed Aboriginal people. As explained and modelled by John and Mary Green, Christianity regarded all peoples as God's valuable children. It also affirmed a higher authority than white government to which Barak and his people could appeal.[76]

Such an appeal became urgent as the settlement's very existence was threatened by settler ill-will and greed. Breaking up the reserve would mean fresh eviction from all that remained of the residents' once extensive ancestral country.[77] Barak led a number of deputations from Coranderrk to officials in Melbourne, making the trek several times over a period of ten years. William Thomas was long dead, so Barak and others forged an alliance with the Presbyterian humanitarian, Ann Fraser Bon – an imperious but devoutly religious philanthropist with a longstanding interest in the welfare of Indigenous people. (For decades, Bon herself worked to prevent the closure of Coranderrk station, and supported Indigenous activists in their opposition to BPA policy.[78]) Coranderrk residents also wrote letters to the editors of Melbourne newspapers, to the BPA itself, to government officials and to humanitarian supporters. Eventually, their campaign forced the Victorian government to conduct two major inquiries. In 1884, Chief Secretary Graham Berry finally gazetted Coranderrk Station as a 'permanent reservation'.

This victory did not mean, however, that the residents' troubles were finished. In 1886, new legislation increased the Indigenous community's vulnerability to eviction. The 'Half-Caste Act', as it was known, forced many people of mixed parentage out of Coranderrk, breaking up the settlement's families and depleting its population. Some of these exiles joined other Kulin refugees who had already fled across the New South Wales border.[79]

Those who remained, including Barak, continued to fight the Board of Protection and its policies. Barak declared: 'Me no leave it: Yarra, my father's country. There's no mountains for me on the Murray'. He also said: 'We don't want any Board nor inspecting Captain Page over us – only one man, that is Mr Green, and the station to be under the Chief Secretary. Then we will show the country that we can work it and make it pay, and I know it will'.[80]

In a letter to the *Argus* in 1889, Barak grounded his argument for just treatment and permanent tenure directly in the text of Scripture:

Why don't those white fellows that want to break this station
go and try to break some of the squatters' stations? … White
fellows would not like us to come down to take their land
from them and move them out of their homes. We are in
Christian land and ought to love one another with brotherly
love [Romans 12:10].[81]

Barak's biblical arguments fell on deaf ears. His vision of an inclusive Christian community, marked by brotherly love and structural
justice, was too radical, too humbling and challenging, for white
society to heed. Despite the permanent reservation made in 1884,
half of Coranderrk was alienated by an Act of Parliament in 1893.[82]
Having outlived all his children, and successive wives, Barak spent
his final years recording aspects of his traditional culture in a series
of paintings. He died bereft, his radical hope quashed, in 1903.

CHAPTER 6

RE-EVALUATING THE TEXT

Richard had a book open and was making notes as he read. Polly walked over, and bent to drop a kiss on the top of his head. She was staggered by what she saw. It was his Bible, and opposite the third verse of the first chapter of Genesis – 'And God said, Let there be light: and there was light' – he had written: 'Three days before the sun!' Her heart seemed to shrivel, to grow small in her breast, at the thought of her husband being guilty of such impiety. She looked again, but there it was: his beautiful writing, reduced to its tiniest, wound round the narrow margins.

'Richard, do you think that … is … is right?' Polly asked in a low voice.

He raised his head. 'Eh? – what, Pollykin?'

'I mean, do you think you ought … that it is right to do what you are doing?'

The smile, half-tender, half-quizzical that she loved, broke over her husband's face. He held out his hand. 'Polly, my dear, don't worry. You know I wouldn't do anything I believed to be wrong? It's Saint Paul, you know, who says: "we can do nothing against the Truth but for the Truth" [2 Corinthians 13:8]. And you may depend on it, Polly, the All-Wise would never have given us the brains He has, if He had not intended us to use them. Now I have long felt sure that the Bible is not wholly what it claims to be – direct inspiration'.[1]

Henry Handel Richardson – as Ethel Florence Richardson was better known – wrote this scene in *The Fortunes of Richard Mahony*, a classic of Australian literature. It is the saga of an Irish immigrant to gold-rush Victoria, and his younger, locally born wife, as their respectable, sane and comfortable life goes through a slow and traumatic decline. The title character is a restless soul, forever searching for some satisfaction, some meaning in life. Over the course of the novel he abandons the Protestant orthodoxies of his youth, revises his view of the Bible, and embraces a kind of spiritualism without giving up religious concerns entirely. Mahony says, at one point, that he had no wish 'to decry the authority of the Book of Books … Without it, one would be rudderless indeed – a castaway in a cockleshell boat on a furious sea'. But he 'could no longer concede the tenets of election and damnation' – these were 'the last hampering relics of bigotry and ritual'. He believed 'God was a God of mercy, not the blind, jealous Jahveh of the Jews, or the inhuman Sabbatarian of a narrow Protestantism. And He might be worshipped anywhere or anyhow: in any temple built to His name – in the wilderness under the open sky – in silent prayer, or according to any creed'.

Richardson wrote in the early decades of the twentieth century, looking back on her own experience and her observations of her parents' generation. She reflected, in fiction, the great crisis of religious certainty that unsettled so many people in the second half of the nineteenth century. Her novels were monuments, of a kind, to yet another aspect of 'the great age of the Bible': heady doubt about its authority, inspiration and interpretation.

The Word reconsidered

Critical readings of the theological Bible were not new in the nineteenth century. Already contested in Europe, the Bible had been subject to debate and re-evaluation from the outset of its career in Australia. The period between the 1860s and 1890s was, however, very significant. In these decades theories emerged that challenged common assumptions about Scripture. The new ideas circulated widely, involving not only the intellectual elite, or those beyond the margins of respectability. There was an unprecedented willingness among the middle classes – among people like Richardson, her father Walter and her character Mahony – to consider that the Bible was not what they had assumed it to be. By the 1880s, it could be *respectable* to entertain doubts about Christian revelation in a way it certainly had not been even fifty years previously.

The re-evaluation of the theological Bible was an event in popular culture. It was shaped by broader patterns in the transmission of ideas – indeed by many of the same technologies and industries that had enabled the mass circulation of the Bible and related materials. These included a booming industrial print trade, the proliferation of newspapers, and the prominence of public lectures and debates as a form of rational recreation, even popular entertainment. It was shaped, too, by the actual movements of people – from the migrations of ordinary folk who had imbibed certain ideas at home and brought them (sometimes with hardcopy books as well) to the colonies, to tours of visiting speakers from overseas.

In Australia, as in Britain, debates about the theological Bible were exhilarating for some, and profoundly unsettling for others. They complicated the Bible's reception, as well as its influence and authority, in settler culture and society. At the same time, debates about the Bible ensured that it remained front and centre of public conversation. In the 1880s, Australians were engaged with issues of Scripture and theology as never before or since.[2]

WHAT WAS IT, EXACTLY, THAT PREOCCUPIED THE INQUIRING public of the day? When Richard Mahony looked around his study, he saw evidence of two broad sets of concerns. First, 'the great cork-slabs on which hundreds of moths and butterflies made dazzling spots of colour; the sheets of pink blotting-paper between which his collection of native plants lay pressed; the glass case filled with geological specimens'. This was the stuff of nature, the stuff of enthusiasm for geology and biology and other new fields of science. Next, Mahony's eyes lighted on 'his Bible, the margins of which round Genesis were black with his handwriting; a pile of books on the new marvel Spiritualism; Colenso's *Pentateuch*; the big black volumes of Swedenborg's *Arcana Coelestia*; Locke on Miracles'. This was the stuff of Scripture, the stuff of unorthodox spirituality and the higher criticism of the Bible.

Science and nature

Western science, like the Bible, was part of the intellectual freight of British expansion. It became entangled with the story of Australia in the age of exploration, from Janzsoon and Dampier to Cook, Banks and the colonists who followed them. Crucially, the kind of science the British brought to Australia was bound up with the long, thick European history of the Bible.[3] Scientific investigation and biblical interpretation were entangled in a variety of ways, but in the late eighteenth and early nineteenth centuries, most practical scientists in Britain and its colonies worked within the framework of 'natural theology'. The basic idea was that God revealed himself in two 'books' – the book of Scripture and the book of nature. Or more poetically, in the famous opening verses of Psalm 19:

> The heavens declare the glory of God;
> the skies proclaim the work of his hands.
> Day after day they pour forth speech;
> night after night they reveal knowledge.

There was a range of views about how, exactly, the two 'books' might relate, as well as a small but growing number of people who were prepared to remain silent on God when they discussed the workings of nature. But scientific research was typically seen as a pursuit that led people to the knowledge and contemplation of God.

THE CHRISTIAN CLERGY WERE AMONG THE BEST-EDUCATED people in early European Australia, and played a leading role in colonial science. They helped form numerous institutions of learning, interpreted new scientific ideas to the wider population, and undertook research to accumulate actual scientific knowledge.[4] The first chaplain, Richard Johnson, sent plant specimens to Joseph Banks. The Reverend WB Clarke was the leading practical geologist, as well as a very influential science communicator. From 1856, William Scott, another Church of England minister, was government astronomer at Sydney. And in botany, found historian

Lionel Gilbert, Anglican ministers made 'a greater contribution …
than any other group of amateurs during the nineteenth century'.[5]

In the middle decades of the nineteenth century, as European
readings of the book of nature changed in some revolutionary
ways, European ideas about the book of Scripture were also radically reshaped. On par with the medieval discovery that the earth
revolved around the sun, the discovery of an old earth, as well as
new theories about the mutability of species, challenged the old
ways people understood the universe and their place in it.

To get a sense of this revolution in perspective, it helps to
recall some broad assumptions that late eighteenth- and early
nineteenth-century Britons held. First, nearly everyone assumed
the earth had been created by God roughly 6000 years previously. It was also widely believed that the earth's features had
been shaped primarily by catastrophes – such as Noah's Flood
(Genesis 6), commonly thought to be responsible for all the animal
fossils geologists were finding. By 1788, a few individuals were
beginning to articulate other ideas (James Hutton, a Scot, observed
acutely the landscape around him, and speculated that it had been
formed by a long, continuous and fairly uniform geological cycle.[6])
But it would still be at least four decades before geology became a
properly inductive science, and the idea of an old earth began to
enter the mainstream.

Second, most ordinary Britons believed plants and animals
had always existed in their present state. As the poet Milton had so
vividly suggested in his interpretation of Genesis in *Paradise Lost*:

> The earth obeyed, and straight
> Op'ning her fertile womb, teem'd at a birth
> Innumerous living creatures, perfect forms,
> Limb'd and full-grown …[7]

Third, humans were thought to be distinct from animals, because humans alone bore the imprint of the divine image. Humans, too, were assumed to be descended from common parents – the biblical Adam and Eve. As such, observable variations between peoples were the result of subsequent experiences and activities, not of original difference. Rooted in prevailing interpretations of the book of Genesis, such notions of a recent, unified and unique human family were widespread among colonists until at least the mid-nineteenth century.

THE REVEREND WB CLARKE STEPPED OFF A SHIP IN SYDNEY in 1839 with several scientific books in his luggage. One of them was Charles Lyell's *Principles of Geology* (1830–33), an influential new text that disposed of Noah's Flood as a primary and universal geological cause. Drawing on the work of Scottish geologist James Hutton (1726–97), Lyell offered an extended theory of the slow transformation of the earth's crust. Clarke was impressed, and eventually gave up his own earlier catastrophist view, which had centred on Noah's Deluge.[8] The stratification of Australian rocks, the nature of the colony's mineral and fossil deposits, would preoccupy Clarke for the next forty years.

The other leading scientist in 1840s New South Wales, William S Macleay, corresponded with Clarke about the findings of contemporary science, and how they might relate to the creation account in Genesis. 'I do not believe that vegetation preceded the appearance of the sun and every kind of aquatic animal', he admitted in 1842. 'My interpretation of the Bible is that the sun existed before the fourth day, but the creator at the epoch made it to regulate the day and year as they at present exist'. Macleay did not think 'the statements of Moses inconsistent with the truth', but he also renounced the Bible as a scientific book, saying he had as much confidence in [Moses'] opinion on the binomial theorem as I have in his dictum on geology'.[9]

By the late 1840s and 1850s, such conversations were moving well beyond the colonial scientific elite; the relationship between the new science and Genesis was becoming a topic of popular discussion. By 1859, when Charles Darwin's *Origin of Species* was published, the idea of an old earth, forged gradually over perhaps millions of years, was becoming common currency. It opened the door wide to a whole host of further possibilities. As controversial speculative works like the anonymous *Vestiges of the Natural History of Creation* had not shied away from asking: perhaps in biology, too, there had been time for slow transmutation? Perhaps humanity itself was of more ancient date? Could human life, and all animal life, have emerged from much simpler organisms?

Copies of the *Origin of Species* were available in Australia within four months of its publication in Britain. It was not an immediate sensation, but it began circulating among the more scientifically interested. Macleay had read it by May 1860, and described his qualms to a friend in London:

> This question is no less What am I? What is man? a created
> being under the direct government of the Creator, or only an
> accidental sprout of some primordial type that was the common
> progenitor of both animals and vegetables ... I am myself so
> far a Pantheist that I see God in everything. But then I believe
> in his special Providence, and that he is the constant and active
> sole Creator and all-wise Administrator of the Universe.[10]

Three years later, Macleay still saw no reason to revise his views. 'I am utterly opposed to Darwin's ... theory,' he wrote to Clarke.

No one, he judged, had done greater harm to Genesis than Darwin, Darwin's expositor TH Huxley, and Lyell.

For his part, the Reverend Clarke devoured the *Origin* and was soon offering to lend his copy to others. Fascinated especially by Darwin's geological chapters, he wrote enthusiastically to the author with corrections from his own researches. (Darwin wrote back, delighted.) Clarke's openness set him apart: most other colonial scientists reacted coolly, particularly on theological grounds, and remained generally opposed to Darwinism until as late as the 1880s.[11] But even in 1867, Clarke was telling the newly formed NSW Royal Society that its members should take a long and liberal view of new interpretations of nature, like Darwin's. A flood of light was streaming in from every scientific quarter, he said, and there was room for limitless investigation of the physical world. 'We ought not to be accused of nervousness as to the fate of the Scriptures, if we would wait for further evidence or for a wider range of experiment.' The task of colonial scientists was not to rush to judgment, but to pursue the patient observation of the physical world. In that way, said Clarke, they might add 'one grain to the enduring pyramid which is now in the course of erection – as to the testimony of Nature to the truth of Revelation'.[12]

Clarke was confident that, in the end, the book of nature and the book of Scripture would reveal one and the same Creator. But others were not as relaxed. Macleay's questions about the Bible, science and humanity did not go away. Intensified by Lyell's *Geological Evidence for the Antiquity of Man* (1863), and Darwin's *Descent of Man* (1871), such questions were, by the 1870s and 1880s, the focus of intense public deliberation. How, if at all, could the two 'books' be read in harmony with one another? Was it true, as some felt, that the new science demanded a parting of ways?

Where would the restless search for truth lead Richard Mahony's generation? And what kind of Bible would remain in its wake?

Critiquing Scripture

Even as the new science posed questions about the origins of the world, on another front, the origins and authorship of Genesis itself were opened to radical revision. Perhaps Moses did *not* write Genesis, as commonly believed? Perhaps it was a composite text, gradually cobbled together from multiple documents and traditions? To what extent was the Old Testament's depiction of events historically accurate anyway? One of the books on Richard Mahony's desk helped circulate such ideas among colonial readers: John William Colenso's *The Pentateuch and the Book of Joshua Critically Examined* (1862). Colenso was a Church of England bishop in the missionary diocese of Natal, southern Africa. From his knowledge of geology, he had come to the view that Noah's Flood could not have been a universal deluge in the manner Genesis seemed to suggest. From conversations with his Zulu informants, with whom he worked on a translation of the Bible, he had also learned that the hare does not chew its cud – contra Deuteronomy 14:7. Prompted to investigate more closely, Colenso abandoned a literalist understanding of the Pentateuch. His book radically revised its key narratives, including the exodus to the Promised Land. Colenso maintained that the story, whoever wrote it, still imparted 'revelations of the Divine Will and Character' – but it could not be regarded as 'historically true', since events could not possibly have occurred in the manner depicted.[13]

Colenso's book caused a sensation everywhere it was read. In Australia, the controversy played out primarily in the newspapers

– which both reported the latest ideas and offered colonial readers a forum for expressing their own views and opinions. In January 1863, for example, the Melbourne *Argus* published an approving extract of Colenso's book from the *London Examiner*. It ignited a reaction among readers of its main rival, *The Age* – several of whom wrote long replies to the editor. Over the rest of the decade, Victorian newspapers since digitised in the National Library's *Trove* database carried almost 700 articles referring to Bishop Colenso, including scores that gave substantial treatment to his arguments and to various counter-claims. Across Australia as a whole, the number of press articles on Colenso in the 1860s exceeded 2800 – suggesting an extraordinary level of public interest in new and controversial views of the Old Testament and its interpretation.

When the tools of higher criticism were trained on the New Testament, similarly unsettling ideas emerged about the historical Jesus. Where the gospels really authored by the four evangelists? Did Jesus' miracles actually happen? Perhaps Jesus was better understood as a first-century Jewish teacher, a perfect man, a moral exemplar, rather than as a divine saviour or even as the founder of a religion? Along these lines, popular European works such as David Strauss' *Life of Jesus* and Ernest Renan's *Life of Jesus* were readily available from colonial booksellers. They were also discussed in Australian newspapers – though not as widely as Colenso – as part of a popular reconsideration of the central figure of Christianity, the nature of religion, and the interpretation of Scripture. To critics, Renan's *Life* appeared 'a distillation of all the heresies of which the German higher critics had been guilty'. But short, popular and sentimental, it intrigued many with its depiction of Jesus as an amiable carpenter from Galilee, whose achievement was not to defeat sin, conquer death, or bring salvation to the world, but to inspire high ideals and cause his fellow men to make a great step towards divinity.

Some colonists, engaged by these ideas, also ventured into print – adding local voices to the international criticism of the Bible in this period. Edward William Cole was a labourer's son who had left England with little education and twenty pounds, at the age of eighteen. Eventually settling in Melbourne during the 1850s, he ran an evening pie stall in Russell Street and spent his days researching in the public library. Sympathetic to the idea that the positive ethical teaching of religion was beneficial, but sceptical of the divine origin and miraculous powers of figures like Jesus, Cole produced a manuscript, *The Real Place in History of Jesus and Paul*. When publishers in Sydney and Melbourne unanimously rejected it, he produced the book cheaply himself (1867), opening a market bookstall to sell it. A second edition followed, bound with additional pamphlets Cole had written on religion. He eventually prospered as the proprietor of what became Cole's Book Arcade – by the 1880s one of the world's largest bookshops, stocking more than one million items and attracting visitors including Rudyard Kipling and Mark Twain.[14]

Richard Davis Hanson, the Chief Justice of South Australia, wrote from the other end of the social and academic spectrum. Raised in a family of London dissenters, and for many years staunchly evangelical himself, Hanson followed developments in science and especially biblical scholarship more closely than virtually any other colonist. By 1860, his views of Scripture had changed to the point that members of the South Australian Bible Society refused to re-elect him as President. In 1865, he argued in *Law in Nature and other Papers* that Scripture should not be exempt from critical inquiry – attracting the praise of Bishop Colenso, whose work had influenced him. A few years later, *The Jesus of History*

(1869) was published anonymously in London. Hanson's presentation of Jesus as a human figure, without miracles or divinity, was far more measured and scholarly than Renan's. He followed this work with an 'original, penetrating and rationalistic' study of *The apostle Paul and the Preaching of Christianity in the primitive church* (1875). This time, Hanson was prepared to identify himself as author – suggesting that the social pressure against heterodox ideas had begun to relax in the colonies.[15]

Grappling with new ideas

People in Australia caught wind of this new thinking through all manner of printed materials. 'Nearly everybody can read', remarked the visiting English writer Richard Twopenny in the 1870s, 'and nearly everybody has the leisure to do so'. Colonial newspapers were entering their golden age: there were almost 600 titles in circulation by the 1880s. Even more remarkably, Twopenny guessed that the proportion of people who could afford to subscribe to one was 'ten times as large as in England' – rightly dubbing Australia 'the land of newspapers'.[16] This mattered because, by 1890, the newspaper was 'the dominant medium of civil society – recording, interpreting and disseminating public opinion'.[17] Reading the paper was becoming the main 'private, and yet mass, ritual which set the tone for many men (if not women) at the start of each day' – to some extent replacing morning prayer.[18] In spreading knowledge, and forging new means of knowing, newspapers were crucial to the way Australians received new ideas.

At the same time, a rising tide of books, journals, pamphlets and almanacs surged into the colonies. The quantity of books imported to New South Wales and Victoria in 1871, for instance, meant that every person there might have bought several small volumes. By 1884, the Australian colonies were the principal overseas market for British publishers.[19] Such materials were also made available through a burgeoning suite of lending libraries and discussion clubs, print shops and bookstores: reading was a primary pastime for colonial Australians.

The spoken word, too, played a crucial role in the spread of new ideas. People flocked to public debates and lectures, as a veritable train of freethinkers, spiritualists, theosophists, revivalists and other speakers sought to make their mark in colonial cities. To the Melbourne judge George Higinbotham, it seemed that anyone, in the 1870s and early 1880s, who claimed to be able to communicate on religion and philosophy, could:

> secure a numerous, earnest and attentive audience of
> thoughtful men – provided only that his hearers were not
> invited to assemble within the walls of a Christian church, and
> that the preacher has not founded his teaching upon the lines
> of any of the Christian creeds![20]

Altogether, the popular critical discussion of the Bible was a literate, predominately urban phenomenon. In the later decades of the nineteenth century, its primary centre was Melbourne, followed by Adelaide. The former was only a generation or two old, but it was quickly emerging as Australasia's premier city. Melbourne had 'a general sense of movement, of progress, of conscious power', wrote the journalist Francis Adams.[21] Its middle-class intelligentsia, hungry for big ideas, readily embraced the ferment surrounding the Christian Scriptures.

LIKE SO MANY OTHER FREETHINKERS OF THE PERIOD, Henry Keylock Rusden came from a devout Protestant background: he was the youngest son of the Maitland clergyman and brother of the national education advocate. Growing up, he had been encouraged to apply his mind to the Bible, and to be thoughtful in matters of religion. 'It is right', his father had once preached, 'that [a person] should enquire whether such a revelation, which claims his allegiance, does really come from God; and therefore have reason and a moral sense been given to him, to try and test it'. (According to Henry's father, the key was to actually open the Bible up and 'search the Scriptures', as Jesus himself had said.[22])

Henry became familiar with the text, but did not embrace it in the way other family members hoped and expected. He left home at fifteen, worked various jobs in the Riverina and then followed the gold rushes from New South Wales to Victoria. Settling in Melbourne as a public servant in 1853, he revelled in the vibrant, open culture of that burgeoning international city. An autodidact who relished an argument, he threw himself into the fray. By the late 1860s, he had emerged as an active public critic of Christianity. In the 1870s, he freely described himself as 'an atheist in theology'.[23]

Over many years, Henry Rusden railed against Christian orthodoxy and disputed the integrity of Scripture. He attended public lectures on biblical topics and used the question time at the end to share sceptical opinions, later re-working some of his notes into pamphlets for a wider readership. He also helped to found the Eclectic Society (1867) and the Sunday Free Discussion Society (1870) – two irreverent and enquiring groups that contributed to the emerging infrastructure of scepticism and unorthodox spirituality in Melbourne. Rusden also took his arguments directly to the press, writing occasional letters to the papers and publishing several essays. In a pamphlet on 'Christ in the Sepulchre', for example, he argued that the gospels were 'utterly unworthy of credit or respect' because they contradicted themselves, and other parts of Scripture, on the point of how many days Jesus had been buried.[24] In *The Power of the Pulpit* (1877), 'a lay sermon dedicated to the people and clergy of Victoria', he cited a range of New Testament passages to argue that the colonial clergy had utterly betrayed their calling.[25] Provocatively, this pamphlet carried the biblical epigraph 'The truth shall make you free' (John 7:32).

Henry Rusden represented one end of a spectrum of responses to the Bible, as it was examined and critiqued in the later decades of the century. At the other were people like temperance activist Bessie Harrison Lee, who lived in Melbourne with her husband from 1880 – mainly in Richmond, a poor, working-class area in the inner city. She attended church, taught Sunday school, and went to hear visiting evangelists and temperance preachers – inhabiting a vibrant Christian world apparently untouched by the religious issues that others found so captivating. Accepting the assurances of the Bible itself that the Word of God would stand forever, she devoted herself to the Christ she found in its pages and to what she saw as his work in the world. For Lee, that seemed a large enough task – given the continuing problems of widespread alcohol abuse, and the harm to women and children which so often followed. Her example reminds us that the story of the restless urban middle class certainly was not everybody's.

Between Rusden and Lee, there were many different responses to the re-evaluation of the theological Bible. Some Melbournians encountered and absorbed new ideas within their existing religious frameworks, and remained largely untroubled in their beliefs. It was possible, after all, for a person to subscribe to one of the denominational papers, to attend a full program of events featuring Christian speakers, and to learn about topical issues from titles produced by evangelical Christian publishers. The Australian Religious Tract Society, for example, reported issuing nearly 26 000 books, 82 750 tracts, and 41 000 periodicals just in 1872.[26] The local impact of its work has not yet been studied, but if British studies are any guide, religious tracts were among the most widely available sources on contemporary science and Bible history.[27] For their many readers and consumers, there was no great crisis of faith, no urgent conflict between religion, science and criticism.[28]

For others, the intellectual issues of the day were not so easy to avoid or absorb. Sensing that something was up, they did not want their ministers to stay silent on the new science, or on new interpretations of the gospels. As a reader complained to the *Argus* in 1868, people had to be *shown* how to harmonise Moses with Lyell and the doctrines of St Paul with the doctrines of Darwin – and it was frustrating that so many ministers stayed silent. (The writer went on to outline some of the troubling books he had been reading – prompting many earnest replies from other readers.[29])

Of course, quite a few colonial clergy attempted to give just such a demonstration. As early as 1839, the leading Congregational minister in Adelaide, Thomas Stow, gave a public address on 'The amicable relations and reciprocal services of Revelation and Science'.[30] Such addresses became increasingly common through the 1860s, 1870s and 1880s. Responding, perhaps, to the complaint in the *Argus*, the evangelical Anglican Bishop of Melbourne, Charles Perry, offered a lecture on 'Science and the Bible'. 'In my opinion … there is no quarrel between them', he said; a harmony 'must always subsist'. Such harmony 'may not be in all cases discernible', however, which meant people needed to be careful, and patient, in their evaluations of both science and Scripture. On the one hand, new hypotheses were just that – fluid theories rather than settled, conclusive findings. It was not wise to rush to conclusions about the implications of emerging science. On the other hand, certain popular understandings of Scripture should not be held above critique. Citing the example of Galileo's discovery of a heliocentric universe, Perry declared: 'I have no difficulty in admitting … that Science … in many instances … has … necessitated modifications both of the received text and interpretation of the Bible'.[31]

Perry's recognition of the Bible as a complex, composite text transmitted, in very human ways, from its original languages to the English of the King James, was nevertheless conservative. As historian David Hilliard notes, he saw Christianity as a body of revealed and objective truth which would stand the test of modern scholarship and the changed intellectual climate.[32] Ultimately, Perry's encouragement to his audience was to 'read constantly, day by day, the Bible itself … and pray that God will, by His Holy Spirit, enable you to inwardly digest' it.

It is difficult to know how many were satisfied by Perry's approach, but there were certainly a number who became impatient with the re-statement of traditional doctrine. Arriving in Melbourne in 1877, Perry's successor James Moorhouse recognised 'great unsettlement of belief, wide spreading distress, and deep social discontent'. He wondered if Melbourne's churches were marked, not by outright unbelief, but by 'the absence of any belief strong and quick enough to serve as a stimulus to self-sacrifice'.[33] Whatever allowances might be made for a more sophisticated view of biblical inspiration, there seemed a need for some theological adjustment.

Moorhouse relished the task of engaging publicly in areas of new knowledge. According to Hilliard, the underlying theme of his many lectures and sermons was that 'orthodox Christianity, if slightly adjusted, could accommodate contemporary thought'. He argued that God's revelation through Jesus Christ was 'final and complete' – but that the church's understanding of Christ's revelation could grow and develop. He defended the doctrine of the trinity and the uniqueness of Christ as saviour. He described the miracles of the Bible as both possible and probable. But unlike more conservative Protestants, Moorhouse believed that articles of faith could be 'altered and gradually conformed to the demands of increasing knowledge', and he accepted the findings of moderate biblical criticism.[34] Moorhouse's articles in the press, his public addresses, and his famous exchanges with sceptics such as Marcus Clarke won him many admirers, and helped foster a more liberal Protestantism in the city of Melbourne.

For some, Moorhouse's gently reforming, intellectual Anglicanism still did not go far enough. My great-great-grandfather, William Miers, grew up in a loosely Methodist family in the gold region around Ballarat. He moved to Moonee Ponds, Melbourne, some time after his marriage in the mid-1870s, and built a comfortable and respectable life as a commercial traveller for the grocery firm Robert Harper and Co, selling herbs and spices. At one point, he served as President of the Commercial Travellers' Association of Victoria. In the late 1880s, when Miers was in his late forties, he purchased and read popular works of New Testament criticism, such as *A Study in Primitive Christianity* by the New York Unitarian Lewis Janes. I still have his copy, bearing the stamp of 'O. H. Bamford, Little Collins Street, Melbourne, importer of books on Spiritualism, Free Thought, Physiology etc, 20 Jul 87'.

Turning the pages, now yellowing, the margins are frequently annotated and many passages are underlined. Miers seems to have been absorbed by the various historical sources for Jesus, and receptive to the idea that Jesus was a remarkable historical figure, but neither unique nor divine. Miers underlined the statement that we should 'let him live in our hearts and minds a heroic, manly character, not too saintly to be human'. Christianity, he apparently agreed, was 'like all other religions of the world, a human institution, a natural growth out of pre-existing conditions' (Miers underlined this, and added 'Hear!'). His own comment, written after a chapter on the social teaching of Jesus, was 'Yes [let us try to be men as he], and let us cease building churches in the name of Jesus to maintain armies of persons who are as unlike Jesus, as Jesus was unlike the Pharisees'.

The idea of a Jesus without dogmatic religion, a Jesus free of the clerical control of the churches, found a ready audience – especially among educated people from Protestant backgrounds with a confident sense of human progress and development. In his controversial 1883 lecture, 'Science and Religion', Justice Higinbotham observed that 'adult laymen … think that the teaching of Christ's ministers … may possibly be of use to women and children, but it has nothing whatever to do with them'. The solution, he proposed, was for laymen to abandon 'the religion of the Christian churches', with their creeds and ecclesiastical systems, in favour of 'the religion of Christ'.[35]

A similar notion buoyed the formation, in 1885, of the Australian Church by the sacked Presbyterian Charles Strong.

> The Australian church is a society held together by a common Religious Spirit of trust and hope towards God as our Father, and of love towards man as our brother, and not by dogmatic creed or an unchanging ecclesiastical form. It recognises the principle of development, and seeks to reinterpret Christianity in the light of present-day knowledge and experience.[36]

A Jesus freed from the clergy also surfaced in the more stinging attacks of the Wesleyan lay preacher turned freethinker Joseph Symes, who railed against the hypocrisy of rich and respectable churches in lectures, pamphlets, and his freethought newspaper the *Liberator*.

The great age at its end

The wave of religious unsettlement peaked in the 1880s. In that decade, sixteen distinct freethought societies were formed in Australia's towns and cities, and secularist lecturers regularly drew big crowds.[37] It was a time of tense excitement, historians agree, and many among the thinking classes found themselves in a kind of mental distress.[38] Surveying the mood, some commentators predicted the end of Christian creed and dogma; others, the end of substantive religion itself. In 1899 it seemed to AG Stephens, editor of *The Bulletin*, that 'our fathers, or their fathers, or some of them, had the kernel of religion; we in Australia have little more than the husk, and we shall have less and less as the years go by'.[39]

Such predictions turned out to be premature. In New South Wales, 0.4 per cent of the population had answered 'no religion' or 'other persuasion' in the census of 1851; by 1901, that proportion had risen to 2 per cent.[40] But the organised secularist movement did not retain its initial vigour much beyond the 1880s – either in New South Wales or anywhere else. Several freethought groups folded during the economic depression of the early 1890s, others faded in the federation period.[41] At the same time, in Victoria, churchgoing was reported at an historic high of 60 per cent.[42] Nationally, a stable proportion of people – around 96 per cent – identified as Christian from the mid-nineteenth century until the early 1920s.[43]

If the crisis of religious unsettlement did not lead to a mass exodus from the churches, or even to a cooling of Christian affiliation at the census, what *was* its contemporary impact? Most basically, it made the Bible the central, preoccupying text of the age – both within and beyond the churches, among people of faith and doubt. In capturing the attention of those who may not have interacted with the text in a devotional way, debate helped extend the Bible's visibility in popular culture. (The Bible's visibility expanded in this period more literally, too, as the Salvation Army and other groups hosted crowd-pleasing lantern shows, featuring slides illustrating Scripture verses, Bible scenes, Christian stories and popular hymns. From 1892, the Salvos also made use of the new marvel of moving images, bringing Bible stories to life for mass audiences.[44])

Second, among those who *were* entranced by the new thinking, it became harder to keep believing precisely as before. Middle-class audiences confronted the idea that 'there was an alternative explanation to the world, different from that which they had inherited'. As Owen Chadwick explained, it was enough to impress on them that 'the Bible is not what it was thought, that we cannot therefore be so confident over the precise expressions of religion'.[45] One of the major casualties was the popular literalist approach to Scripture.

A number of Christian apologists rose to the task of public re-interpretation. Some utilised the insights of older Christian thinking – for example by emphasising that the 'six days' of creation were periods of indeterminate length, as Augustine, Origen and other fathers of the Christian church had realised.[46] The challenge of evolutionary ideas about the origin of species was sharper, however, and responses took longer to develop. As historian Walter Phillips has shown, most colonial Protestants were ultimately willing to concede some kind of change over time, while continuing to insist on the uniqueness of humanity. By the 1890s, when the broad outlines of Darwin's theory had been finally accepted by most scientists, most Protestant churches in Australia had also significantly accommodated evolutionary thinking.[47] Conservative responses, so pronounced in the United States from the early decades of the twentieth century, cropped up mainly in Queensland and among the smaller sects – but they never defined the majority of Australian evangelicals, let alone the broad sweep of Australian Protestantism.[48]

In meeting the challenge posed by higher criticism, several scholars showed the colonial faithful how to be both Christian and modern.[49] Among local Methodists, for example, William Binnington Boyce challenged the anti-supernaturalistic trends in German biblical studies in a major work, *Higher Criticism and the Bible* (1881). Evangelical Anglicans usually followed the lead of their bishops in accepting the 'reverent criticism' offered by British New Testament scholars Lightfoot, Westcott and Hort. And in Dr Andrew Harper, Melbourne Presbyterians boasted a world-ranking oriental linguist and Old Testament scholar. Harper's critical approach to the Bible made him a controversial figure, but by the end of the century, his insistence that the religious revelation of Scripture did not depend upon the historical infallibility of biblical statements had become widely acceptable.[50]

Of course, literalist interpretations of Scripture did not collapse completely. A century and a half after Darwin, a significant minority – around 24 per cent – of regular churchgoers in Australia continue to prefer a literal approach to Scripture over the alternatives.[51] But in the late nineteenth century, assumptions about the Bible as direct verbal revelation, infallible in every detail, to be read and understood at face value, were dethroned from 'default' status in many people's minds.

In step with a cooling of popular literalism, some adjusted their idea of the scope of the Bible's authority. As early as the 1820s, one of the colonies' first science writers, the Reverend Charles Wilton, explained that 'the Bible was designed not to teach geology but Religion – not the structure of the earth but the way to heaven'.[52] Or as the Reverend J Stephen Hart told a Church Congress in Melbourne in 1906, there was no use trying to construct detailed harmonies between Genesis and geology, for Genesis and geology represented two different genres – and who indeed would 'want to think that Moses was made mechanically to write in the style of Sir Charles Lyell'.[53] Taking a different tack again, Walter Richardson came to the conclusion that the Bible 'contains the words of God but not *all* the word of God.' As he wrote inside a copy he gave his novelist daughter, 'the book is poetry, allegory and tradition'.[54]

AS ATTITUDES AND BELIEFS ABOUT THE BIBLE CHANGED, SO did its place in the life of faith. Of course, the devotional Bible was not displaced within the church: the Catholic hierarchy resisted the inroads of higher criticism and materialist science, and many colonial Protestants continued to treasure the Scriptures as the Word of God that makes 'wise unto salvation through faith in Christ Jesus'. Habits of family prayer and Bible reading may have experienced a slight decline, but from 1880 newly available Bible reading guides produced by the Scripture Union in Britain rapidly accumulated several thousand Australian subscribers. By 1886, Victoria had 8000 Scripture Union members in 150 branches, New South Wales had 10 000 members in 170 groups, and a start had been made in South Australia and Tasmania as well. Another decade later, the Scripture Union in Victoria reached a peak membership of 20 000 people – all of whom received notes guiding the individual reader through a four-year course covering the whole Bible, with the goal of encouraging a 'decision for Christ' and nurturing 'those who have eternal life in him'.[55] Interestingly, female subscribers outnumbered male ones by approximately two to one.[56] It seems that women and girls not only made up the majority of churchgoers in this period, they were becoming the popular custodians of the devotional Bible as well.

In parallel with this largely female, evangelical core of devotional Bible readers, another section of the colonial population sought a new kind of spirituality which upheld the Bible as one among several valuable texts, a guide less to religious truth than to ethical conduct. New religious movements such as Spiritualism and Theosophy attracted a considerable level of interest in the colonies, including that of Henry Handel Richardson's father Walter, and her character Richard Mahony. Most adherents continued to identify formally as Christians at the census, but these movements went well beyond Christian orthodoxy. In various ways, they attempted to combine the best of Christianity, as they saw it, with certain discoveries of science and the insights of other religions.[57]

The main relevance of the Bible for these movements lay in the ethical idealism of the gospels. Dr EF Hughes, a former Wesleyan clergyman who visited Victoria in 1875 as a Spiritualist lecturer, explained he had 'relinquished the ministerial office under pressure of the conviction that the Bible was not infallible.' He found its account of creation 'irreconcilable with the demonstrations of modern science' – and when a man's creed and his conscience were at odds, he argued, it was his creed that should give way:

In looking round upon society – that of the colony, that of the world at large – what was it that society most needed? Was it a firmer belief in the Trinity; in plenary inspiration … in the Fall; in the incarnation; in the atonement; in salvation by faith alone; or the validity of the sacraments and the sanctity of the Sabbath? No!

Was is not rather in the perpetual, the personal, the emergent, the unconditional, the uncompromising obligation to observe the practical moralities, to cultivate righteous being and righteous doing, truthfulness, honesty, purity, sobriety, love to one another, kindness and mutual help?[58]

Quoting the book of Proverbs, Hughes concluded: 'For righteousness exalteth a nation!'

There were a few, like Henry Rusden and Marcus Clarke, who sought to articulate a non-religious basis for moral conduct – and not a few more who perceived certain parts of the Old Testament as morally objectionable. But in general, there was little sense that disbelief could be a basis for social life.[59] Many of those who doubted the truth of historical Christianity accepted a civic version, and continued to uphold the New Testament as a primary source of moral teaching and inspiration. According to Charles Strong, minister of the Australian Church, it was the ideal taught by Christ which defined true spirituality and made sense of the otherwise diffuse body of texts called Scripture:

> The unity of the New Testament is to be found in the … development of Israel's religion towards the worship of God as the Father of all men, whose prevailing characteristic is the Righteousness of Love.[60]

Finally, for all the debate surrounding the Bible as God's Word – or perhaps precisely because of it – the cultural Bible approached its peak. This was an idea of the Bible as a bedrock of British spirit and culture, and it gained strength through the second half of the nineteenth century and into Australia's early federation era. One factor in its rise was a growing popular appreciation of the Bible's historical-cultural production. As European archaeologists and biblical scholars brought more and more of the Bible's textual history to light, 'the English Bible' became a regular subject for public discussion. By the latter decades of the century, lectures on the history of Bible translation were routine events in Australia's major cities. Literally thousands of newspaper articles were also published on the general subject between the 1870s and the 1910s – with a peak around the time the Revised Version of the New Testament was published in 1881. The Englishness of the English Bible had never been more visible. It also helped that the cultural Bible was not the sole property of devout believers. It appealed to doubters and agnostics as well as churchgoing Christians. It existed alongside, without relying on, the theological Bible's sacred qualities. 'Take the Bible as a whole,' pronounced the famous English agnostic Thomas Huxley in 1870, and 'make the severest deductions which fair criticism can dictate for shortcomings and positive errors':

> There still remains in this old literature a vast residuum of
> moral beauty and grandeur. And then consider the great
> historical fact that, for three centuries this book has been
> woven into the life of all that is best and noblest in English
> history … it has become the national epic of Britain …
> familiar to noble and simple from John O'Groat's house to
> Land's End.[61]

As Huxley's widely quoted line about 'the national epic of Britain' indicates, the cultural Bible was ultimately buoyed by a rising tide of nationalism. In fact, the whole notion of the cultural Bible was crystallised into a single phrase during the imperial reign of Queen Victoria. Whether or not the exchange actually occurred, the Queen was reported to have received an African envoy and presented him with a Bible, remarking 'That is the secret of England's greatness'. In 1863, the story was immortalised in a large painting by Thomas Jones Barker, and exhibited in a frame itself depicting an open Bible and a verse from Psalm 119: 'Thy word is a lamp unto my feet, and a light unto my path. I love thy commandments above gold; yea, above fine gold'. As a slogan – or a cliché – asserting the Bible's importance to British imperial culture, 'the secret of England's greatness' became a great favourite of Protestant preachers in Australia.

As a meme, the secret of England's greatness probably peaked in 1887, the year of Queen Victoria's Jubilee. In the colonies, it was widely parroted in Protestant pulpits, buttressed by sermons on how 'Righteousness exalteth the nation, but sin is a reproach to any people' (Proverbs 14:34). At a time when most colonists saw themselves as essentially British, and many imagined their new society as an improvement on the one they had left behind in Britain, the Bible's ostensibly British qualities lent it wide appeal. For all the uncertainty about the theological Bible, the apotheosis of the cultural one underscored its enduring potency in Australian culture.

PART 3

BIBLE AND NATION

We must not kiss in the gardens,
We must not sing in the street,
We must not jump with a joyous shout
When a long-lost friend we meet.

We must not race by the sea-shore,
We must not sit on the sand,
We must not laugh on a New Year Night,
For this is the Wowsers' land.[1]

'Wowser', like 'Bible-basher', was a term coined in Australia in the heady years around federation, to deride those who pursued a social vision that critics such as poet Henry Lawson did not like. Applied especially to clergymen, temperance activists and other straight-laced Protestant types, it gives little insight into what such moral reformers actually wanted for their communities – but the rise of the term points to an intense contest over the nature and future of Australian society. What would the colonies become? What kind of society would this be? Who got to sum up the character and behaviour of an 'authentic' Australian? Wowser terminology suggests that these were partly questions of morality – if only people could agree on the ethical aspirations of a modernising Australia.

In the critical period spanning the late nineteenth century to the war of 1914–18, artists and activists alike put forward visions of the 'real Australia' in an effort to define the national character. Colonists also invested great energy into creating the Commonwealth – not just as a new political structure, but as a vehicle for building a better society. With the outbreak of the Great War, the population faced a crisis widely regarded as a national test – which in turn proved a watershed in the Australian experience and imagination.

Through it all, the Bible retained a central place in common culture: its vocabulary, teaching and imagery were widely familiar to people, and pervasive in popular culture. Though it was not universally believed, or subject to agreed interpretations, all kinds of people drew on the Bible in their efforts to shape a national culture and polity. From the theological character of nationhood itself, to the proper application of Scripture in social life and politics, the task of nation-building brought into play a wide spectrum of ideas about the Bible.

ADVANCING AUSTRALIA FAIR

Robert Hammond turned twenty in 1890 – just as his prosperous hometown of Melbourne plunged into a severe economic crisis. After a boom that had lasted decades, and made Melbourne the jewel in Britain's Australasian crown, the city sank into a depression felt more deeply there than in most other parts of the world. By 1893, 28 per cent of the city's trade unionists were unemployed, and probably more than a third of breadwinners overall. About one in ten houses were repossessed from defaulting owners, and several of the major banks were forced to close completely for a time.[1] In the absence of government relief, charities in Victoria and across Australia were overwhelmed by the needs of the newly destitute. Citizens on all sides questioned the causes of such calamity, and how best to secure something like the good society.

Though Hammond remained relatively unscathed himself, the 1890s were significant in shaping the course of his life. He had graduated from Melbourne Church of England Grammar School in 1888, both muscular enough to play football for Essendon and Christian enough to spend his time teaching Sunday school and giving open-air stump sermons. He was also smart enough to silence his hecklers with devastating repartee. Once, a man interrupted a temperance speech he was giving by shouting, 'You're talking through your hat – you've never even been drunk!'

Hammond replied: 'True, and I've never laid an egg – but I know a rotten one when I smell it!'[2]

Hammond's Christian faith was galvanised by a mission led by visiting Irish evangelist George C Grubb, who inspired 'hordes of Melbournians to yield to the Lord' in 1891.[3] Within a few years he presented himself for Anglican ordination, ministering in various locations in Victoria before moving to Sydney in 1899. The worst of the depression was over by then, but poverty continued to plague the unskilled and the underemployed, as well as the aged, the sick, the orphaned and widowed. Hammond served in a series of inner-city parishes home to many poor labourers and their dependants. From 1904 to 1911, he also led the Mission Zone Fund, an Anglican agency that offered both the gospel and charitable relief to the communities of Waterloo, Woolloomooloo, Surry Hills, Darlington and Redfern. Then as rector of St Barnabas, Broadway, from 1918, he transformed a struggling church into a major centre of evangelism and practical poor relief – eventually including a soup kitchen, an employment service, and a network of crisis accommodation. During the depression of the 1930s, the ageing cleric offered a lifeline to dozens of homeless families by establishing one of Australia's most successful land settlement schemes. His impact had much to do with his ready sympathy for the down and out, and his warm-hearted insistence that no failure was final – God offered a second chance to everyone.[4]

HAMMOND'S MINISTRY SIGNALS THE RANGE OF ISSUES THAT confronted turn-of-the-century society – from the welfare of poor families to relations between capital and labour to the tragedy of substance abuse and addiction. These issues weren't entirely new, but they were intensely felt – especially in the midst of economic crisis. Crucially, too, the relatively recent advent of self-government and the extension of the male franchise suggested new possibilities for politics in meeting the challenges of the times. Social reformers of all kinds had to negotiate the interaction of citizen and state, law and morality, in their efforts to secure the good society.

Diverse reformers drew inspiration from their particular understandings of the Bible, as we see in the campaigns for temperance, female suffrage, and workers' rights. Some found in the Bible a vision of the godly nation, marked by its members' moral uprightness. Some recognised a scriptural imperative to seek a more just society. Sometimes these views stood in tension, sometimes they overlapped powerfully. The spectrum of interpretations was complicated further by different attitudes to the law and its role in creating the kind of community that activists desired. For all these complexities, though, the Bible proved a deep well of reformist thinking on both the left and the right. Competing understandings and applications of the text shaped the struggle to influence and improve turn-of-the-century Australia.

Temperance and moral reform

Soon after settling in Sydney, Hammond went to Dymocks Book Arcade on George Street and purchased a Temperance Bible Commentary. The particular book he chose offered 'criticism and exposition in regard to all passages in Holy Writ bearing on "wine" and "strong drink" or illustrating the principles of the temperance reformation'.[5] Running to more than 500 pages, it was a tangible expression of a certain Christian moral reformism that held, almost as an article of faith, that intoxicating drink was an unmitigated evil – 'poisonous to the body, seductive to the soul, and corrupting to the circumstances of man'.[6] Hammond thought much the same himself. Sensitive to the problems of alcoholism and its effects, especially on working men and their families, he became an active proponent of total prohibition. Over a long career, he personally persuaded thousands to give up the drink and to regularly read the Bible. He also served for decades as president of the Australasian Temperance Society and of the New South Wales Alliance, revelling light-heartedly in the derogatory epithet 'wowser'.

Temperance was a key battleground for earnest Christians seeking to reform society. While Henry Lawson and his ilk wanted to 'go with the drinking fighters/with the laughing rakes and carls', many so-called wowsers – who were usually but not exclusively evangelical Protestants – sought nothing less than the complete prohibition of alcohol. Without ever achieving that, as some states in America did, Australian temperance advocates successfully prompted every colony to put some form of 'local option' in place by the 1890s. (Local option laws gave certain residents of an area, usually ratepayers, the right to vote on liquor licences.) Activists also persuaded every colony except Western Australia to close pubs on Sundays. It was not until the crisis of the Great War, however, that they succeeded in their campaign for six o'clock closing on other days – inadvertently inspiring the now legendary practice of 'the six o'clock swill'.[7]

The proponents of legislative intervention on temperance are easily characterised as meddling middle-class puritans, or power-seeking churchmen interfering in properly personal matters. But in the tradition of evangelical humanitarianism, their campaigns often went beyond social control to express a kind of altruism. In Hammond's case, a commitment to temperance went hand-in-hand with a commitment to the renovation of the whole person – the thoroughgoing conversion of damaged drinking men.

For many of those associated with the Women's Christian Temperance Union (WCTU), too, the campaign reflected a constellation of concerns to do with preserving the home and the family from the effects of intoxicant abuse, typically by men. In their eyes, as we'll see, temperance reform was necessary to protect the community and its most vulnerable members.

BEYOND THAT, SOME OF THE POTENCY OF SUCH MORAL reformism stemmed from an assumption about the nation as a community that flourished or suffered according to its fidelity to God's moral laws. Drawing on the archetype of biblical Israel, this way of thinking understood the nation as a community divinely constituted, chosen and called. More than the sum of its individual members, the nation was a single moral entity that could itself sin and deserve punishment, display true penitence and be restored. In its cruder versions, a nation's godly behaviour correlated with divine blessing, and immorality with punishment by God. As such, a lot hinged on the conduct of its citizens and the content of its laws. For 'righteousness exalteth a nation: but sin is a reproach to any people' (Proverbs 14:34).

From this perspective, it was easy to believe that collective morality went hand-in-hand with national flourishing. As one cleric told the New South Wales Premier Henry Parkes, 'the greatness of the British Empire was founded on observance of the Sabbath'.[8] On the other hand, if righteousness had made the nation great, then any departure from Christian standards was a serious problem: it represented a catastrophic abandonment of Divine Providence, precipitating national decay.[9] If the Bible was the secret of national greatness, then righteousness had to be maintained for the good of all.

Such thinking was common across greater Britain, including Australia, until the mid-twentieth century.[10] It influenced local debates on temperance, Sabbath observance, adultery, divorce, prostitution, sodomy, gambling and blasphemy, among other topics.[11] But even evangelicals could disagree on the proper role of the law. While some saw legislation as the road to a Christian nation, others saw it as a denial of that precious liberty which also came from God. Every Sunday, John Fairfax sat in Sydney's Pitt Street Congregational Church, and read these words painted high over the altar: 'Where the Spirit of the Lord is, there is liberty' (2 Corinthians 3:17). Like many other dissenting Protestants, who placed a high value on freedom of conscience, he could not accept that enforcing morality through legislation was consistent with such a verse.[12]

These differences on law and morality played out in various proposals for legislative reform. Consider the effort, in 1880s New South Wales, to extend the grounds of divorce. On one side, the Anglican Bishop Barry used his Synod charge of 1886 to condemn the Bill as another serious step towards secularising that old English law, 'of which "Christianity" (we used to be told) "was part and parcel"'.[13] On the other side, the Bill's main advocate, former Chief Justice Alfred Stephen, argued that Jesus' teaching was an ethical ideal – and that to impose it on everyone without considering specific circumstances would lack compassion. Stephen also contended that the English law based on the Reformation settlement actually permitted divorce for cruelty, unresolved bitterness, intemperance and marital violence. In this, he enjoyed support from the NSW Presbyterian Assembly, which affirmed that the Westminster Confession similarly allowed divorce for adultery and desertion – drunkenness, crime and cruelty being tantamount to desertion. In 1892, the NSW Divorce Extension Bill passed into law. It was not a victory for secularism, so much as a victory for a certain view of Christian ethics in relation to the law. As even Bishop Barry realised: 'If the Bill is carried, it will be mainly by Christian hands and on motives of compassion and philanthropy'.[14] Even in the heyday of the wowser, efforts to build the godly society were complicated by contested applications of the Bible.

Women want the vote

Mrs Margaret Hampson was the religious sensation of 1883. She was originally from Liverpool, England, where she had spent years involved in temperance and evangelism work before her husband died and she migrated to New Zealand. As a middle-aged widow, she had conducted successful missions in Auckland, Dunedin and on the goldfields, before proceeding across the Tasman for a tour of the Australian colonies. Supported by an interdenominational committee, a spate of prayer meetings, and a vigorous advertising campaign, she visited Melbourne, Adelaide, Sydney, Hobart, Launceston, Ballarat, Bendigo and Geelong during 1883–84. People flocked to hear her – with the crowd at Sydney's Exhibition Building rising to as many as 8000 a night by the end of her campaign. A sceptical observer called it a 'festival of religious emotion' for the two-thirds of the audience who were already evangelical Christians, but the power of curiosity was also a significant motive: 'a woman orator with an intercolonial reputation … a vast crowd and perhaps some religious excitement'.[15]

In Melbourne, Bessie Harrison Lee hesitated to go and hear Mrs Hampson preach. Lee had read the Bible from end to end herself and taken it quite literally. She implicitly believed in giving away one dress if she had two, and even gave away her husband's clothes if there was urgent need. Bessie's literalism had also led her to strong views about a woman's subordinate position in the home, and to opinions 'strongly antagonistic to women's public work for God'. Yet Lee had also imbibed the teaching of Jesus in the Sermon on the Mount: 'Judge not, lest ye be judged' and 'with what measure ye mete, it shall be measured to you again'.[16] She eventually went to hear Mrs Hampson, and was so thoroughly impressed by her manner and message that she simply 'could not believe that this Spirit-filled woman was working in direct opposition to the Spirit's commands'.

Mrs Hampson's example prompted a number of Christian temperance women to consider a more public activism. For Lee, reconciling this new experience of women's public ministry and her understanding of the Bible was a struggle of some difficulty. It began when she was invited by her minister to join the team of Sunday school teachers. In the hope of 'leading them to Christ' she accepted, conceiving of her role as simply 'talking to the children of the One she loved … never dreaming that she was either teaching or preaching'. She was subsequently asked to give a Bible talk to a meeting of the Young Women's Christian Association, where she attended a Wednesday night Scripture class. It proved a rather terrifying ordeal, but it went off so well that she began receiving invitations to preach to Sunday congregations, which included both women and men. All these she immediately refused, wondering how clergymen could ask her to do what Paul had forbidden! But those very clergymen directed her back to the gospels:

Have you ever read the parable of the talents, Mrs Lee? What excuse will you give God for neglecting the talent with which He has evidently endowed you? When the woman of Samaria brought the whole village to Jesus did He rebuke her? No.

> Wouldn't you like to bring a whole village to Christ, Mrs
> Lee? And what about Mary, whom Jesus sent as a messenger
> specially to men after his resurrection. Will you not go when
> He bids you, and tell the people He is risen?[17]

After long prayer and struggle, Lee said 'Yes, Lord'. She did not put aside the Bible she had always read, or consider it any less the inspired and authoritative word of God, but came to read it differently. Burning to promote the kingdom of God, she placed greater weight on the teaching and example of Jesus. Finally convinced in her conscience, and with a new sense that God was in fact calling her to preach, Bessie Lee embarked on a public career, advocating for temperance, promoting a nobler form of marriage, and arguing for female suffrage. (Many years later, after her husband's death, she moved to New Zealand where she became a foundation member of the United Labour Party. Appointed a 'world missionary' of the Women's Christian Temperance Union, she remained an activist, on the international stage, until her death in 1950.)

Bessie Lee's story shows the importance of the theological Bible to the activism of Australian temperance women. She was one of many Australian reformers who emerged from the ranks of the WCTU, whose values and beliefs were shaped by a deep devotional encounter with Scripture. These women included Elizabeth Nicholls, Serena Lake, Rosetta Birks, Mary Coulton, Jessie Rooke, Elizabeth Brentnall and Margaret Ogg. Another, Mary Lee, was an Anglican turned Methodist who contributed energetically to a range of philanthropic causes and initiated the South Australian Women's Suffrage League. Seeing all her work as part of a Christian endeavour, Mary Lee made 'frequent and natural references' to the Scriptures in her advocacy. It was not unusual to show either strong faith or a command of biblical sources, but as historian

Helen Jones has remarked, it 'clearly identifies a main source of her exceptional strength of character'.[18]

EMERGING FROM THE AMERICAN WEST IN THE 1870S, THE WCTU was established in each Australian colony during the 1880s. It appealed especially to devout middle-class Christians – women often of modest education and means, with a distinctly evangelical faith.[19] Its Victorian members adopted Zechariah 4:6 as their motto: 'Not by might, nor by power, but by my spirit saith the Lord of Hosts'.[20] And as the movement grew, it expressed and enabled new kinds of citizenship – nourished, in complex ways, by the theological Bible.

The WCTU sought to banish the 'demon drink' with all the zeal of a religious cause. As historian Anthea Hyslop has found, members believed that they had been summoned by God to assist in 'His great scheme for the redemption of the world ... for His sake we unite to remove the stumbling-blocks of the liquor traffic out of the way of our brothers and sisters'.[21] Members also knew that, while 'they might rescue individual drunkards through their own efforts', it would take state intervention to defeat the liquor traffic itself. In 1885, for example, around a quarter of the adult female population of Victoria – some 45 000 women – signed a petition asking the government to introduce 'local option' to protect their sex from 'ill-usage', which often accompanied men's drinking.[22] Such petitioning was a feature of temperance activism, but realising that the legislative process could be influenced most directly through the ballot box, the WCTU quickly developed an interest in votes for women. Not only, then, did the WCTU itself provide one of the earliest and most substantial bridges between 'home and church on the one hand, and social and political action among middle class women on the other', but within a few years of its foundation, it had begun working for female suffrage in every colony of Australia.[23]

In historian Pat Grimshaw's judgment, the WCTU was 'outstanding' among the organisations that pursued the women's franchise in Australia. It was not synonymous with the suffrage movement, but the WCTU was crucially aligned with women's rights and its impact was significant in every state. In South Australia, for example, the WCTU gathered 7000 of the 11 000 signatures on the petition to the House of Assembly for female enfranchisement. Soon after, in 1894, the Bill was passed: one of evangelicalism's most conspicuous victories.[24] In Western Australia and Tasmania, the work of the WCTU was a 'predominant' factor in the early success of the suffrage movement (wth enfranchisement achieved in 1899 and 1903 respectively). In New South Wales, Queensland and Victoria, too, it mobilised thousands of members whose grounding in evangelical Protestantism – along with their temperance work – lent 'particular determination and skills' to the overall campaign. As Grimshaw concludes, 'it would be hard to envisage the relatively early passage of the franchise in Australia without the organisation's close involvement'.[25] It was a movement of Christian women which redefined the dimensions of citizenship, with lasting importance for the nation.

Of course, the WCTU did not have a monopoly on the suffrage cause. At the other end of the spectrum were unconventional radicals like Henrietta Dugdale – the first president of the Victorian Women's Suffrage Society, and a member of the Eclectic Association. (In 1885, Dugdale addressed the latter on 'male bias' – arguing that all religions were oppressive, most particularly to women, because they had been devised by men.[26]) Louisa Lawson, founder of the feminist newspaper *The Dawn*, was always sensitive to religion. As a child growing up around Mudgee, in New South

Wales, she had regularly attended a Methodist chapel. She continued going as an adult, until a narrow-minded preacher, and the grief of losing a child, apparently turned her off. She embraced a kind of mystical pantheism instead, and joined a spiritualist group. Upon moving to Sydney in 1883, she joined the Progressive Spiritualist Lyceum and sent two of her children, Henry and Gertrude, to its Sunday school. (Another of her sons, Peter, developed an intense interest in biblical religion which, at some points of his life, amounted to a mania. In his more settled later years, he attempted to teach himself New Testament Greek as well as Hebrew, as part of his study of the Bible.[27])

Louisa Lawson founded her paper in 1888 and threw herself into the women's cause. Within a year she was running a successful printing and publishing business, employing ten women, including some as printers. She fought the NSW Typographical Association for the freedom to do so, and became a formidable advocate of numerous feminist reforms.[28] In 1891, she was elected to the first council of the NSW Womanhood Suffrage League – but it was mainly through her writing and the Dawn Club that she advanced women's claims. Some of her arguments shared the same general logic as the temperance feminists': women needed the vote 'to redeem the world from bad laws passed by wicked men'.[29]

In her activism, Louisa like many others found certain biblical ideas and phrases a powerful resource. Her inaugural address to the Dawn Club, for instance, borrowed from an apocalyptic passage in the book of Revelation to present the feminist vision in vast terms. The desire to see 'brother and sister standing shoulder to shoulder and heart to heart in the fight for right, truth and justice, for better laws, for better protection to our sons and daughters, for better and purer homes' was nothing less than a vision of 'a new heaven and a new earth', she proclaimed.[30] In a long editorial of

1892, Lawson marshalled detailed evidence from the Scriptures for the equality of women. While 'no sophistry is more plausible than that which flies to the Bible as the source of women's subjection,' she admitted, 'the spirit of its teaching is directly contrariwise'. She went on to highlight that, in Genesis, men *and* women bear the image of God. She also cited the examples of Miriam and Deborah as leaders of Old Testament Israel, Jesus' own consistent refusal to consign women to a position of inferiority, and Paul's command that husbands love their wives as their own flesh. She concluded in the famous words of Galatians 3:28: 'There is neither Jew nor Greek, there is neither bond nor free, there is neither male and female, all are one in Christ Jesus'.[31]

Clearly, the Bible was not the concern solely of evangelical, temperance types – and even wowsers drew on it to imagine much more than a narrowly sober society. Many WCTU women, for instance, sought a world in which women, as well as men, shaped the laws of the land to secure a safer, purer and more just society. In the hands of people like Louisa Lawson, too, whose politics tended towards socialism, and whose relationship to orthodox Christianity was complicated to say the least, the Bible could provide a language – a vision – for something like heaven on earth. The Bible was a repository of inspiration for varied readers, nourishing high ideals for a better nation and society. And as the common property of a broad coalition of activists, it indirectly nourished the successful campaign for female suffrage.

Workers, writers and the challenge of wealth

One Sunday evening in October 1893, a procession of several hundred unemployed men marched through the streets of Sydney.

They carried a rough wooden cross with an effigy of a man smeared with blood. It was inscribed on the front 'Humanity Crucified', and on the back, 'Murdered by the rich'. When the group reached Market Street, they were confronted by police who confiscated the crucifix, prompting the crowd to retrace its steps back up York Street. Entering the Methodist Centenary Hall, the men found a service in progress. As they filed in, one of their number, Thomas Dodd, raised his voice in prayer:

> Oh, Almighty God, our Heavenly Father. We beseech Thee to look down upon this suffering people who are starving in our midst. During the past month 10 men have died of starvation. Oh Lord! we believe that this has been done through the terrible 'sweating' that is going on amongst us. Large numbers of the clergy are shareholders in these sweating dens. Oh Lord, we beseech Thee to look down upon us and help us, and grant that those clergy who have the education and ability may meet together to devise some scheme for removing this terrible evil. Oh Lord! look down and curse the sweater …

At that point, the choir struck up a vigorous tune, making it impossible for Dodd to continue. He and the other protesters nevertheless kept their places until the end of the service, when the Reverend Rainsford Bavin came over to address them. The preacher admitted that the church was terribly to blame: 'They had not lived up to their religion. There had been a large amount of hollow pretension, and the results of it were coming down on their own heads'. He was deeply moved by the men's presence – for 'God loved these men and wanted to save them, and to make use of the church in doing it'. He hoped the church would act just as Christ would before these men.[32]

LIKE ALCOHOLISM AND THE PERILOUS SITUATION OF WOMEN, the condition of the working poor was an acute social and moral problem in the decades either side of 1900. Unsurprisingly the issue made its way into the work of writers, artists and other social commentators, several of whom were involved in the labour movement in this difficult period. Henry Lawson was among those who recognised the desperation of the unemployed and the injustice of their situation. He questioned how workers could be so downtrodden in a reputedly righteous nation. In light of Jesus' teaching that 'Ye cannot serve God and mammon' (Matthew 6:24), he wondered:

> … would the avarice of wealthy men endure
> Were all the windows level with the faces of the Poor?
> Ah! Mammon's slaves, your knees shall knock, your hearts in
>   terror beat,
> When God demands a reason for the sorrows of the street!

Lawson was not a Christian in any conventional sense, but he considered the Bible 'one of the truest books ever written, a book of life and human nature by men who knew it'.[33] Its truth did not lie in its revelation of God, he judged, but in its record of human character and experience: 'We're freethinkers and atheists who found the Bible true'. He also professed an 'immense liking and respect' for Jesus – whom he saw as 'the champion of the underdog; of the prostitute, the gambler, the drunkard, the prisoner and the poor'. In the gospels, Lawson found a portrait of the ideal man, if not of God incarnate. In his 1898 poem 'Christ of the Never', for example, he presented Jesus as the bushman's friend, the true spokesman of the spirit of mateship. He saw a central place for such a Jesus in the new national culture he and other artists sought to create.[34]

Novelist Joseph Furphy had a broadly similar idea of Jesus as the working man's friend. Writing in *The Bulletin* in the mid-1890s, he pronounced that the New Testament, 'rightly read', would become 'the textbook of ideal socialism'. 'In the interest of moral progress, the Bible must be read; and in the interests of honest interpretation, the parson must go.'[35] Furphy was anti-clerical, even irreverent, yet in his own words, he was equally 'bushman and bookworm'. The Bible, along with the works of Shakespeare, was among his most constant companions. In 1883, a drought ruined his livelihood as a bullock driver, and he went to work at his brother's iron foundry in rural Victoria. He also spent more time on his writing, which he hoped would be a means of 'forwarding the New Order'. In 1897, when Furphy got to Sydney to discuss the publication of his first novel, an anonymous wit described him as a man:

Who never drinks and never bets
And loves his wife and pays his debts,
And feels content with what he gets.[36]

As for the novel itself, *Such Is Life*, Furphy described its temper as 'democratic' and its bias as 'offensively Australian'. Purporting to be the diary of 'Tom Collins', it was a fiction spun from Furphy's own experiences among the rural workers of southern New South Wales and Victoria during the 1880s and 1890s. Marked by Furphy's acute ear for idiom, it drew on a number of biblical phrases and ideas to express a moral vision for humanity in Australia: 'I acknowledge no aristocracy except one of service and self-sacrifice, in which he that is chief shall be servant, and he that is greatest of all, servant of all' (alluding to Matthew 20:26).[37] Jesus' teaching is presented as a practical, workable code for life on the wallaby track.

BOHEMIAN WRITERS WERE NOT THE ONLY ONES PREPARED TO suggest more socialist readings of the New Testament – to both critique the contemporary exploitation of workers, and imagine a radically different kind of 'righteous nation'. In August 1889, *The Bulletin*'s cartoonist Livingstone Hopkins drew an exhausted working man, drab coat in hand, returning home to his wife and children. He finds the woman lying on the floor, obviously ill and probably dying. There is little he can do. The children are already crying. Hopkins presented the scene as a comment on the London dock strike. Captioned 'The Secret of England's Greatness: 5d an hour', the idea was that the nation's wealth derived from the oppression of its labouring men and women, not from any kind of Christian righteousness.

Similar ideas recurred through the workers' press, where journalists took issue with the notion that 'Britain owes its success in arms and in prosperity to the Bible'. Was the empire's pre-eminence really connected to observing the Sabbath, or temperance, or any other such moral law, one Adelaide paper asked? How much was actually due to 'the accidental success of the pirate Drake'?[38] A writer for the *Daily Herald* went further. After hearing a sermon on 'the righteousness that exalteth a nation' on a visit to a suburban church, he noted that the speaker had 'quite omitted to refer to the small matter that it was perhaps owing to the navy and military equipment that Britain had been able to rob weaker nations of their home and land'.[39] He added: 'There used to be an old commandment about "Thou shalt not covet thy neighbour's" (Exodus 20:17) – but perhaps the nation forgot this when it was on the lookout for fresh land'.[40]

Like Lawson's allusion to Jesus's teaching on mammon, the reporter's reference to the Ten Commandments is revealing. This was very much a debate about the implications of the Bible for national life and morality. It can be easy to miss this, because some of the most vocal anti-wowsers made a sport of lampooning the clergy, and satirised the allied version of the cultural Bible. But even the radicals who rejected the conventions of Victorian-era morality, and especially the discourse of national righteousness, envisioned an alternative kind of moral reform informed by the Bible.

During the latter decades of the nineteenth century, in fact, a second major stream of biblically derived ideas entered the main current of national public culture. Manning Clark had a phrase for it, 'the image of Christ'. He used that term in his own idiosyncratic ways, but it helpfully points to an appropriation of the Bible that drew mainly on the person and teaching of Jesus Christ. Centred on the New Testament, and particularly the gospels, this way of thinking emphasised relations between people, rather than between God and a chosen nation. It was concerned with a godly society, indeed the creation of heaven on earth – but its vision of godliness was defined not by the Old Testament, but by the Sermon on the Mount. At the same time, it tended to avoid the miraculous aspects of Jesus' ministry, and did not assume divine intervention in human affairs. In the broadest terms, it relied on a reading of the Scriptures more attuned to ethical elements. In that way, it suited both a practical culture and more sceptical times.

WILLIAM GUTHRIE SPENCE WAS A GENIAL SCOTTISH MINER who became arguably Australia's greatest ever union organiser. With superb negotiating abilities and rare skill in organising widely dispersed workers into coherent movements, he played a crucial part in developing the Amalgamated Miners Union and the Amalgamated Shearers' Union. He was the founding secretary of the Australian Workers Union, and then its president for nearly twenty years.[41] Elected to the NSW Parliament in the late 1890s, Spence went on to serve in the new Commonwealth legislature, including in the cabinets of Labor Prime Ministers Andrew Fisher and Billy Hughes.

Born in 1846, Spence did not have a formal education, but his mother taught him to read using the Bible. He developed a vibrant Christian faith, and as an adult took an active part in his local Presbyterian church, serving as secretary and Sunday school superintendent in the early 1880s. He later joined the Primitive Methodists and, like so many other labour activists of this period, became a regular lay preacher. For such labour men, as for many temperance women, church work helped hone the skills, the zeal and the vision for a new and better Australia.

Spence's faith and politics were thickly intertwined, with the Bible as a basic reference point. His understanding of the gospels, in particular, led him to criticise the churches for failing to challenge the sins of the wealthy, and for telling believers 'to be content with the lot Providence has given them' when there were people going without. (He took a rather different view to those Christians who, earlier in the nineteenth century, had founded the first savings bank – once declaring that Jesus 'did not say anything in favour of thrift'.) As he explained to a meeting of socialists in 1892:

> The aim of 'new unionism' is a grand one, a noble one …
> If asked to give a short definition … I should say it is an
> effort to give practical effect to the teachings of the founder
> of Christianity, by making it easy and natural, for men to act
> justly, truthfully and honestly … If I understand anything
> of the teachings of the founder of Christianity, it is that he
> came to bring heaven upon earth – to set up the kingdom of

> heaven on earth … an ideal state where we can escape from
> all the ills and sorrows that we experience here …

A bit further on Spence added:

> I don't want to preach to you, but I will ask you, in reading
> His life – and I suppose all of you have read it – did it ever
> strike you that it is possible to live as he did … He went
> about doing good.[42]

The gospels were assumed knowledge for Australian socialists in the 1890s. In fact, in this period, the ideals of organised labour were deeply infused with a dynamic vision of Christ. 'Honest Jim' McGowen, a boilermaker, was an experienced unionist first elected to the NSW Parliament in 1891. For decades, he attended the evangelical Anglican church of St Paul's, Redfern, whose socially aware minister, FB Boyce, promoted temperance reform, the introduction of age pensions, and the care of the poor. McGowen served as a lay preacher, church warden and parish councillor. He superintended the Sunday School for thirty-five years, even while Premier, openly revering the Jesus of the gospels in the various facets of his life. In numerous speeches, McGowen declared that the Nazarene Carpenter was his role model, and that Jesus' teachings were the foundation of his view that government could and should make society more humane.[43]

Other leaders, notably including coal miner and prime minister Andrew Fisher, shared a similar outlook, as did activists beyond the white, male mainstream of organised labour. Jean Beadle was a long-time campaigner in the Western Australian women's labour movement. Interpreting the gospel in a collectivist way, she 'saw parallels between the Kingdom of God and the movement's aim of righteousness, truth and brotherhood'.[44] Bill Ferguson was a leading Indigenous unionist who fought for the rights of workers and Aboriginal people in the NSW shearing industry. He joined the Labor Party in 1915 and promptly re-formed the local branch where he was living at Gulargambone, between Coonamble and Gilgandra in the central west of New South Wales. A 'sincere and active' Christian, he settled his family in Dubbo in 1933, and was appointed as an elder of the Presbyterian church there. In 1937 he called a public meeting in Dubbo to launch the Aborigines Progressive Association. From this platform, he publicised specific cases of gross injustice, and called for the abolition of the NSW Aborigines Protection Board as well as full citizen rights for Aboriginal people. He was often heard to quote the Bible: 'Thou shalt not muzzle the ox when he treadeth out the corn' (Deuteronomy 25:4); and 'The labourer is worthy of his hire' (Luke 10:7).[45] For such activists, the labour movement was a way of enacting the values of Christ. They looked to the unions, and eventually to the state, to create a fairer, more brotherly society.

AUSTRALIAN SOCIETY HAS CONTINUED TO GRAPPLE WITH issues of wealth and poverty, capital and labour – not least during the depression of the 1930s and in the face of growing inequality today. Jesus' teaching has also continued to influence both personal reflection and public debate. Like the gospel-quoting unionists of the turn-of-the-century labour movement, advocates for the poor have continued to find in the Scriptures a vision for a fairer Australia.[46] At the same time, Jesus' teaching has continued to pose troubling questions about wealth. Can a nation in which the poor are oppressed or ignored consider itself righteous, or Christian? How hard is it for a rich man to enter God's kingdom?

Australia's iconic bush outfitter, RM Williams, certainly felt the challenge on his journey from rags to riches – and halfway back again. Over the course of his life, he thought deeply about the Bible but never made peace with its teaching, its saviour, and perhaps not even with himself.

Williams was born into a working family in rural South Australia in 1908. His mother was a pious Catholic who attended mass every Sunday; his father waited outside, holding the reins. His schooling failed to teach him to read, but when he left home, and then went bush, his mother packed a Bible with his clothes. Williams wandered and worked in remote areas through the late 1920s and early 1930s. He travelled across central Australia as the cameleer for a 'born again' expedition leader. Around the fire, he shared stories with Aboriginal people, white bushmen and 'Afghan' cameleers. Taking on whatever odd jobs he could, he sank wells around the Flinders Ranges. He also married and had a couple of children, without going anywhere near a church. He described himself as a rebel against 'dogmas which had a big influence on my mother's life, certainly on mine in turn'.[47]

Through all those years, Williams kept the Bible that his mother had put in his pack. Sometimes, in sheer boredom, he looked over the pages which someone had marked. Williams later identified this practice as the beginning of his 'long journey towards literacy': 'I spelled out these passages and I remembered many of them through life … these early steps represented a great advance on not being able to remember a single address or not having read a single book'.[48]

In 1932, Williams and an old itinerant swaggie, Dollar Mick, made themselves a pair of boots. They cut each one from a single piece of leather and blocked them while wet to the shape of the foot. Williams was soon plaiting leather belts and making saddles for sale too. The business grew, and over the next few years he made some very profitable investments: 'I slowly climbed from the lowest level of unemployed humanity to a position of financial strength'.

At the peak of his wealth, Williams bought an Adelaide mansion, hired servants, and took up playing polo. He lived the life of high society and travelled around the world. But 'when I had done this, my conscience bothered me. "What shall it profit a man if he gain the whole world and lose his own soul?" "How hard it is for them that trust in riches to enter into the Kingdom of God!"' Jesus' words pierced him to the bone.

Williams' solution was to leave his life of wealth, his marriage and the city, and return to a simple existence – this time in rural Queensland. He reflected: 'I have at times climbed out of the pit where muddy boots are the mark of a man, but inevitably the long arm of Conscience reaches out and claims me as a working man. I am a son of Martha'.[49] He kept thinking about the Bible, its teaching and its Jesus, without ever coming to a firm conclusion. His autobiography, published in 1984, contained some astonishingly candid remarks:

'Render unto Caesar the things that are Caesar's and unto God the things that are God's' [Matthew 22:21] is a humble recipe for life, perhaps, but one that offers something better than a scramble for wealth. I cannot claim to render in either category willingly, nor do I feel satisfied that I have been a good steward.

If the man Jesus were to step inside my door, or come knocking, would I know him? … Would I welcome him? I might. What would he say to me, looking through my façade of respectability into my soul? If it were what he said to the rich young man – 'Sell all that thou hast and give it to the poor and thou shalt have treasure in Heaven, and come, follow me' [Luke 18:22] – I would not recognise him or abide by his words … I am torn by the tragedy of it all. How do I follow him? How would I know God if I saw him?[50]

The challenges Williams felt so keenly have not been resolved. In twenty-first-century Australia, the quest continues for 'something better than a scramble for wealth'. Structural inequality remains significant and, by some measures, the gap between rich and poor has been growing. Yet from grassroots social justice movements to the halls of parliament, many still seek a fairer society and a more expansive human flourishing than market economics dictates. In this, activists have a diverse tradition of biblical thought to draw on. As the various reform movements of the 1890s show, the Bible inspired multiple visions of a better Australia. Utilised by so-called wowsers, female suffragists and labour activists in the broad tradition of Christian socialism, it contributed to powerful movements that shaped the nation.

CHAPTER 8

POLITICS AND THE BIBLE

Clash! Clash! Clang! Boom! The sound of cathedral bells and a royal salute burst through the air. On the streets of Melbourne a huge crowd began cheering and waving. People craned their necks for a glimpse of the parade. His Royal Highness the Duke of Cornwall and York – the future King George V – was on his way to Exhibition Hall to open the first Commonwealth Parliament of Australia.

Inside the building, another 12 000 people stood solemnly, waiting. There were representatives from across the empire and hundreds of guests from each of the Australian states. Once the royal party arrived and the first members of parliament filed in, proceedings commenced with the 'Old Hundredth', a song based on a Psalm from the Bible:

> All people that on earth do dwell,
> Sing to the Lord with cheerful voice.
> Him serve with fear, His praise forth tell;
> Come ye before Him and rejoice.

A hush fell over the crowd and the Governor General, Lord Hopetoun, delivered the prayers: for their Majesties the King and Queen, and for the new Federal Parliament of Australia. According to the Melbourne *Age*, 'his Excellency bowed his head at the last syllable' and the multitude joined in the Lord's Prayer.[1]

The words 'rolled in muffled tones through the building', the *Age* correspondent said, 'and the religious portion of the ceremony was concluded'. The Bible, however, had a further part to play. After a speech by the Duke and a message of congratulation from the King, the first members of the House of Representatives and the Senate were duly sworn in. The Governor General read out the oath and the members followed him, Bibles in hand.[2] The ceremony finished with the Hallelujah Chorus from Handel's *Messiah* – 'For the Lord God omnipotent reigneth' – then the national anthem and an eruption of cheers.

More than a century later, Australians rarely reflect on the event of federation. It evokes no memory of struggle for the colonies' independence from Britain, no settler civil war or political revolution. The inauguration of the Commonwealth was an orderly occurrence on 1 January 1901, the culmination of a series of conventions and referenda. The anniversary is not marked by a designated holiday: the day is instead devoted to New Year's celebrations. The anniversary of the first Commonwealth parliament on 9 May similarly passes without comment every year.

When Australians *do* think about federation, a few figures from school history lessons probably come to mind: the white-whiskered Father of Federation, Henry Parkes; the intense young visionary Alfred Deakin; the suave lawyer Edmund Barton, who became the first Prime Minister. Federation is dimly remembered as a matter for men, one of talk and administration rather than national feeling. Historians increasingly paint a different picture, but Australians are certainly not used to thinking about federation as a religious undertaking.

The opening of the first federal parliament invites a closer look. The proceedings suggest a society comfortable with Christianity in public, even in the political square. They also hint at the

Bible's influence on an emerging national polity – in ritual, sentiment and ideas.

Imagining a federation

The Bible was a deep well for federating thought and imagination in Australia. As early as the 1850s, decades before it became a mainstream concern, individual church leaders turned to the Scriptures to suggest the way to federation. The Presbyterian John Dunmore Lang applied the model of Old Testament Israel under the leadership of Moses to colonial Australia, to argue for 'free and independent' Provinces of a remarkably democratic kind. Around the same time, his Congregational counterpart John West canvassed both theoretical arguments and practical possibilities for the union of the colonies.[3] These two were among the earliest and most important initial advocates of federation.

A generation later, another Congregationalist, James Jefferis, drew on the Bible to offer a dazzling vision of a federated nation. Jefferis was a Bristol carpenter's son with Dissenting inclinations, a concern for the poor, and a happy willingness to reconcile scientific discovery with religious belief. He arrived in Adelaide in 1859 and had long pastorates there and in Sydney. A popular preacher and a prolific contributor to the press, Jefferis promoted the cause of federation for nearly four decades.

At a time when levels of biblical literacy were high, Jefferis helped weave scriptural images and ideas into popular ideas of nation. In the centenary year of 1888, for instance, he compared the Australian colonists to Old Testament Israel:

> ... brought across the watery wilderness to this land of promise
> – a land of favourable climate and fertile soil, with lofty
> mountains and deep cleft valleys, with rivers and streams and
> subterranean waters, a land of inexhaustible wealth, with corn
> like that of Egypt, with grapes like that of Eschol.[4]

Settled in a promised land, the colonists, like Israel, were called to godly nationhood. Their particular task, said Jefferis, was to construct a 'great Commonwealth ... welded together in the strength of an empire which realises the Divine ideal of justice and freedom'.[5]

By the late 1890s, the population was learning to think of Australia as a single home for a single community. The practical process of unification was making headway through the federal conventions. And numerous clergy lent their support publicly, taking up the theme in sermons, lectures and articles for the press. As the *Sydney Morning Herald* observed in April 1898, ministers 'concede first place to *no-one* in the intensity of their interest in matters pertaining to federation'.[6] According to historian Alan Atkinson, no other pro-federation organisation or movement was so large or far-reaching as the churches.[7]

ALFRED DEAKIN WAS BORN IN MELBOURNE ON THE CUSP OF the gold rushes. As a young man in the 1870s, he embraced the city's heady opportunities for spiritual inquiry and experimentation. He also studied law, dabbled in journalism, and eventually found his way into politics. A liberal member of the Victorian Parliament and then a leading advocate of federation, he went on to become the first Attorney General and second Prime Minister of Australia.

Deakin attended every official federation conference and convention. He played a significant part in designing and shaping the Commonwealth Constitution. Especially in 1898–99, when the proposed Constitution was put to the popular test, he lent his considerable gifts to the campaign for success. Launching the 'Yes' campaign in Victoria, ahead of the referendum, Deakin gave a stirring address. It climaxed with a poem expressing the widespread idea that God wanted Australia to federate:

> From all division let our land be free,
> For God has made her one: complete she lies
> Within the unbroken circle of the skies,
> And round her indivisible the sea
> Breaks on her single shore; while only we,
> Her foster children, bound with sacred ties
> Of one dear blood, one storied enterprise,
> Are negligent of her integrity –
> Her seamless garment, at great Mammon's nod,
> With hands unfilial we have basely rent,
> With petty variance our souls are spent,
> And ancient kinship under foot is trod:
> O let us rise, united, penitent,
> And be one people – mighty, serving God![8]

This sonnet, by the local idealist William Gay, was popular in the period immediately before federation.[9] Drawing on the Bible, it presented colonial unity as the divine will for Australia. To divide the people was to deny their destiny, a blasphemous repudiation of God's goal for them. (After all, even Christ's executioners had respected the seamlessness of *his* garment![10]) In this light, federation was a profoundly moral undertaking. It required the colonists to turn away from greed and division, to humble themselves, and to unite in the service of God.

A BIBLICALLY LITERATE POPULATION READILY UNDERSTOOD federation in religious terms.[11] Among leaders of the cause, Henry Parkes prayed 'that the Almighty may guide the young Commonwealth on the high road'; 'that her people may be abundantly blessed … that their influence beyond may be a blessing to all'.[12] Alfred Deakin hoped that federation 'might be the means of creating and fostering throughout all Australia a Christ-like citizenship'.[13] Even the worldly Edmund Barton declared that 'God means to give us this federation'![14]

Among ordinary people, too, religious ideas and impulses pulled in a federal direction. As Alan Atkinson put it in his award-winning account of *The Europeans in Australia*, 'It is impossible to understand the federation period in Australia without taking account of religion … Religious feeling made federation possible'.[15] A Mr Shoobridge from Glenora, Tasmania, echoed the language of the gospels when he explained that 'we must lay aside differences that lead to estrangement and quarrels, and be prepared to treat each other in a friendly and brotherly spirit. When this is done on a large scale it must tend to promote peace and goodwill … for the good of all within the Commonwealth'.[16] A Sydney woman interviewed by the *Evening News* supported federation as a means to 'rise to a higher platform than self-interest'. To her the 'federal spirit' was a spirit of sacrifice for the greater good – a spirit of mutual charity and forbearance, even social justice.[17] Mr Murnane, a school teacher from York in Western Australia, quoted directly from Jesus:

> We have it by divine command
> 'A house divided cannot stand'
> Australia rich, united, free
> Is what we hope and long to see.[18]

The Bible stretched like a canopy above the forest of federal feeling. This is not to imply that the Bible somehow 'caused' federation, nor that inspiration sprang simply or directly from the pages of Scripture. Edmund Barton's example shows that a person could use religious rhetoric to promote federation without believing God had anything much to do with it. (Australia's first prime minister had a distinctly secular view of government and no serious personal faith to speak of.[19]) Alfred Deakin considered Jesus 'the central figure of humanity' and valued the Bible as 'by far the greatest book of religious revelation', but his own lifelong search for truth ranged across all the world's major faiths as well as philosophy both ancient and modern.[20]

Yet the Bible played a key role in nourishing the cause. It equipped Europeans in Australia with a set of stories about a people becoming a nation; it provided a moral language, an enlarging sensibility, and a sense of higher significance. In January 1901, when the new Commonwealth was finally inaugurated, Jefferis welcomed it as the beginning of an era of justice, righteousness and blessing.[21]

THE NATIONALISM NOURISHED BY THE BIBLE LEFT A VERY tangible trace on the federal Constitution: a statement noting that the people 'agreed to unite in one indissoluble Federal Commonwealth … humbly relying on the blessing of Almighty God'. This last phrase was a late edition to the text of the Preamble. Early drafts, initially prepared by lawyers, made no reference at all to the divine will or person. But in response to petitions from colonial legislatures and a veritable deluge of signatures from ordinary people, an Adelaide lawyer, Paddy Glynn, championed the issue at the last convention. Glynn had grown up in the Catholic tradition and developed a mind attuned to the various intellectual trends of his century. He perceived both a Christian and a classical consensus around the idea of a Divine Mind guiding the destiny of states and peoples. Recognising a popular 'spirit of reverence for the Unseen [which] pervades all the relations of our civil life', he thought it important to formally register the feeling of 'the breath of a Divine Being'.[22]

Glynn's first proposal, 'invoking Divine Providence', was voted down at the Adelaide session. Barton thought it nonsense, not least because he imagined the nation differently. He thought of the people as individual voters who dealt with the Almighty one to one – and who could ever understand or sum up such private dealings? It could not be known if they invoked providence or not as they filled in their ballot papers. But Glynn had something altogether different in mind. He thought of 'the people' as a single being, 'moved by spiritual impulse towards one mighty destiny'. It was an old idea, at odds with the new trend towards both a more individualistic and private idea of religion. But it still had real appeal and potency.[23]

Federation underscores the importance of civic Protestant nationalism in Australian public life and feeling in the decades either side of 1901.[24] Although cast in an Old Testament mould, mainly by Protestant hands, its key ideas were readily secularised and accepted by people of varied theological commitments – from Jefferis to Deakin to Patrick Glynn. We hear it in Gay's poem, which describes the barriers to federation in essentially moral rather than practical or political terms. We see it in the widespread notion that federation would be achieved only in humility, penitence and obedience to the call of God. And we meet it in every suggestion that creating a Commonwealth accorded with God's plan not only to bless Australia but to forward his purposes in the wider world. In contrast to Barton's view, Glynn's motion relied on a popular idea of the nation rooted in the old assumptions of civic Protestantism. The motion was eventually carried in a revised form – as convention delegates deferred to 'the great demonstration of public opinion' in favour of acknowledging God.[25] The resulting clause may well have have tipped the balance towards 'Yes' in the final referenda to adopt the Constitution.

Religion and the early Commonwealth

The federation of the colonies presented an immense new canvas on which to build the good society. Six states stretched across a continent of 7.5 million square kilometres, plus the island of Tasmania. The population included an uncounted number of Indigenous people and 3.8 million new Australians. Some doubted if it could work: could such an extended government nurture effective democracy or a truly civil society? Sydney feminist Rose Scott believed that the good society was better realised on a much smaller scale. Others of the substantial minority that voted 'No' to federation probably held similar views.[26] But for many white Australians, the possibility of a collective movement towards a higher form of life, of a new community stretching shore to shore, was intensely appealing. This significant stream of popular sentiment was summed up in the very term 'Commonwealth'.

Realising the good society became a captivating enterprise in the decade and a half from 1901. These were years 'stirred by the hope that a youthful Australia might yet be in the vanguard of political and economic progress'.[27] There were questions about the precise role of the state in promoting social welfare. As much as anything else, building the good society was an experiment in democratic processes and practical politics. There were also questions about how appropriate a religious presence was in the legislative sphere. The debates and decisions reached on this issue illuminate the Bible's place and influence in Australian politics.

AT THE TIME OF FEDERATION, AUSTRALIANS HELD VARIOUS ideas about the proper relationship of church and state. Some looked forward to a national government as an instrument of religious discipline. In the midst of state debates about observing the Sabbath, the liquor trade, divorce and other issues, some Christians hoped federation would bring new political opportunities to bolster 'the righteousness that exalteth the nation'. Other Australians were concerned by precisely the same prospect. They campaigned for, and eventually achieved, a prohibition against the establishment of a state religion and the imposition of religious observance. The vast majority of these were fervent Christians, typically from one of the smaller Protestant sects or denominations.

Seventh Day Adventists were among the most vocal advocates for separating church and state. Their efforts were motivated by a particular understanding of the Bible and the value they accorded religious freedom. Founded in the 1830s, the sect had spread quickly from the north-eastern United States: it was active in Australia by the mid-1880s. Adventists upheld the Bible as their sole source of belief, as interpreted by themselves. They adhered strictly to the Sabbath as it fell on a Saturday, as in the Old Testament and for modern Jews. In the midst of colonial debates about observing the Sabbath, Adventists worried about the imposition of a Christian Sunday on the whole of Australia. They also identified a trend — both in the United States and Australia — towards blurring church and state boundaries. 'While we believe that both the church and the state are ordained by God for the good of man, we also hold that they are ordained for entirely separate lines of work.'[28] For most of the 1890s, Australian Adventists opposed any reference to religion in the new Constitution, as a means of preserving religious liberties and especially freedom of conscience. Their numbers were small but their print materials circulated widely, informing popular attitudes to church–state relations.[29]

At the constitutional conventions, the debate was couched in less overtly religious terms. The move to formally prevent the Commonwealth from establishing a single religion for all citizens was led by the lawyer Henry Bournes Higgins. Higgins was the son of an Irish Wesleyan minister, raised in an atmosphere of evangelical piety and familiar with the Christian Scriptures. He was on the cusp of adulthood when his family migrated to Melbourne in 1870. He had enrolled at the university and proved an outstanding student. Higgins' reading there introduced him to the great intellectual issues of the day, and prompted him to examine the foundations of his family faith. His anguished doubts prompted a shift away from his father's Methodist convictions. He discarded a belief in hell and other doctrines and became reticent about religion. Yet Higgins' agnosticism was not complete and never atheistic: his biographer judged that he 'retained some sort of religious faith'. One contemporary later recalled that he had never met anyone 'so aloof from religion in any sense of creed, whose life lay so deep in the things of the spirit'.[30]

When Glynn succeeded in introducing 'Almighty God' into the constitutional preamble, Higgins insisted on an amendment which became section 116:

The Commonwealth shall not make any law for establishing any religion, or for imposing any religious observance, or for

prohibiting the free exercise of any religion, and no religious
test shall be required as a qualification for any office or public
trust under the Commonwealth.

In proposing this section, Higgins was well aware of the First
Amendment to the US Constitution, which prevents Congress
from making any law respecting an establishment of religion. The
delegates went on to debate the section with frequent reference to
the US precedent – another example of how Australian discussions
about religion do not occur in a vacuum, but in a global swirl of
experiences and ideas. The final wording clearly echoed the US
provision, but did not exactly repeat it. Did the framers of the Constitution intend to separate church and state in the same sense as
the United States? What did section 116 mean for the Bible in
national politics?

These questions have attracted different views among Australian judges, academics and political commentators.[31] In the longer
context of colonial church–state relations, it is likely that the new
Constitution was *not* meant to exclude all religion from federal
institutions, and still less to prevent public or political expressions
of faith. It rejected sectarian division while tacitly accepting and
even assuming a place for religion in civil life.[32] The religion of
the federal parliament was to be 'undogmatic, unsectarian and
unsacredotal', as historian Richard Ely comments.[33] But in the tradition of common Christianity, less concerned with doctrine than
ethical conduct, the door was open to religious faith. In this, the
Constitution embodied a particularly Australian secularity – one
quite distinct from the stricter, more exclusionary secularism that
had a few advocates then, but has become more common in the
twenty-first century.[34]

THE BIBLE HAD A VISIBLE INFLUENCE IN POST-FEDERATION politics. Even if the framers of the Constitution *did* intend to exclude all religion from new national institutions, this possibility was immediately set aside in the early Commonwealth. The procedures of the new parliament accepted the Lord's Prayer as a reflection of popular religious sentiment. They also included legacies of the Bible's longer history in English history and politics. Certain debates in the early federal parliament reflected the residual influence of Christian theological categories. Indirectly, too, the Bible had a substantial impact on some of the Commonwealth's emerging social policies.[35]

At the time of federation, prayer in parliament was not the norm in Australia. It had been usual in England since the 1560s, but in the colonies it extended only to the legislatures of Queensland and Western Australia. During the federal conventions, Alexander Peacock explained that the Victorian Upper House also opened its sessions with the Lord's Prayer. At this, Deakin interjected: 'And nearly all the members know it now!'[36]

Whether or not to have prayer in the Commonwealth parliament was one of its members' first decisions. Some of the strongest arguments for omitting it stemmed from a certain reading of the Bible. In the House, Prime Minister Barton suggested the possibility of leaving it aside. 'A very high teacher … told us to pray in our closet', he said.[37] His reference was to Jesus' teaching in the Sermon on the Mount: 'When thou prayest, enter into thy closet, and when thou hast shut thy door, pray to thy Father which is in secret' (Matthew 6:6). In the Senate, South Australian Gregor McGregor, a devout Presbyterian, pointed to section 116: 'Did they mean that parliament was not to impose religious observances anywhere else but here?'[38] His argument, too, drew on the teaching of Jesus – particularly the parable of the Pharisee and the publican in Luke chapter 18. Real religion 'is in the heart', McGregor argued: it does not need to be paraded 'either in parliament house, the theatre, or at the street corners'. It was real religion, not religion 'on the coat sleeve', that would make senators 'behave as brothers towards each other and as Christians in all things'.[39]

These arguments considered parliamentary prayer in individual terms, as an expression of each politician's own religious state. Seen from this point of view, most federal politicians had no qualms about it – the Lord's Prayer seemed suitably unsectarian, acceptable to Protestants, Catholics, and perhaps also Jews, Unitarians, and agnostics. At the same time, prayer in parliament could also express something more collective, the posture of a nation. According to the *Sydney Morning Herald*, it provided 'a regular expression of the statement in the preamble … that *we as a people* humbly rely on the blessing of Almighty God'.[40] This way of thinking was widespread, rooted in a particular kind of religious nationalism. Barton probably recognised this as he weighed up the issue. He ultimately advised the doubters to conquer their personal scruples, because prayer in parliament was 'the course least offensive to the religious susceptibilities of the public'.[41]

In the century since, parliamentary prayer has spread in Australia. The practice was introduced in South Australia during the crisis of the First World War, and in Tasmania and New South Wales during the 1930s depression. In recent years, there have been moves to abandon it again, but these have stalled partly because of popular support for their retention.[42] In 2014, a straw poll by Fairfax media found that two-thirds of Australians did not want parliament to put an end to the Lord's Prayer.[43] For now, at least, that famous excerpt from the New Testament still sounds the first note of each sitting day.

AT THE OPENING OF THE FIRST COMMONWEALTH PARLIAMENT, members were sworn in with an oath on the Bible:

> I do swear that I will be faithful and bear true allegiance
> to His Majesty King Edward the Seventh, His heirs and
> successors according to law. SO HELP ME GOD!

Like prayer in parliament, the practice remains common today. There is no stipulation about the specific text on which oaths must be made, but since 1901, most federal politicians have chosen the Bible – typically using a personal copy or a family heirloom. Unlike prayers in parliament, oaths can only be personal. What does it mean for a politician to swear one, or to make an affirmation instead? Affirmations use similar language and have the same legal force as oaths, but omit the phrase about God and the use of a holy book. Since 1901, a growing minority of Australian politicians have chosen this alternative: two senators in 1901, and as many as one in four representatives and two in five senators in 2010.[44] This trend is not a straightforward sign of declining religious faith, however. Historically at least, many people have refused to swear on the Bible precisely because they say the Bible tells them not to. Michael Tate, a Catholic Labor senator for Tasmania, explained it this way in the mid-1980s:

> It is quite clear from [the] Sermon on the Mount … that
> Christians should not invoke an oath to bolster their
> undertakings or truthfulness. A plain yes or no is all that is
> required of a Christian. I refuse to take the oath precisely
> because of my understanding of that injunction.[45]

Parliamentary affirmations suggest the surprising relevance of the European Bible to Australia today. The idea that all you need to say is 'Yes' if you mean yes, 'No' if you mean no, stems from Jesus' teaching in Matthew 5:34–37. It was as a concession to Quakers and others, as a protection to their religious consciences on precisely this point, that affirmations first emerged in 1690s England as an alternative to oaths. After a general right to affirm, rather than swear an oath, became British law in 1888, affirmations were incorporated in parliamentary procedures in Australia as well. Thus the Bible, as interpreted in European history, made a direct contribution to Australia's parliamentary practice – including to those elements that enable the free expression of *un*belief.

A social laboratory?

Australian experiments in the good society became famous in the years around federation. Australia, with New Zealand, could boast a number of world-leading innovations. These included an eight-hour day, a minimum wage, and a new national system of compulsory arbitration for labour disputes between management and workers. From 1902, women who were British subjects could vote in federal elections; by 1908, they could also vote in every Australian state. The Commonwealth introduced pensions for the aged (1908) and the invalid (1910), and a maternity allowance (1912). Investigators flocked from Britain, Germany, France and the United States to see 'the social laboratory of the world' in progress.

In actual fact, the early federation was not an entirely inclusive or equitable place. There were still plenty of poor whites to keep the charities busy, and non-British minorities were excluded from social welfare benefits. Indigenous Australians continued to bear the heaviest burden of all, restricted under the protection system and thought by most whites to be a dying race. Beyond these groups, however, many congratulated themselves on progress: compared to the old world, surely things were better in Australia.

For its part, the new Commonwealth government sought to lay down the planks for a prosperous nation. Some of the policies it forged helped define modern Australia. Its immigration and economic settlements, in particular, remained in place for decades. The debates around these issues show the Bible's complex influence – on both the new national polity and the society it governed.

THE FIRST SUBSTANTIVE PIECE OF COMMONWEALTH LEGISLATION was the *Immigration Restriction Act*. It enjoyed almost universal support among decision makers and the wider settler population. Its essence was to exclude non-Europeans from the nation – creating and preserving a 'white Australia'. With few exceptions, it operated to exclude even European immigrants who were not British. It also involved reducing the size of Australia's existing Chinese population, and the mass deportation of Melanesians from Queensland. It remained strictly in place until after the Second World War, and was finally dismantled only in the late 1960s.

At the time, White Australia was justified in all kinds of ways, many of them ostensibly altruistic. The new nation saw itself as a leader in social progress, on its way to solving the great problems of injustice and inequality – at least for its own citizens. It was described as necessary for everything from upholding working conditions to enabling racial purity and preserving superior British cultural and political traditions. Some even argued for preserving a Christian population.

The Australian churches generally absorbed and reflected the conventional wisdom of the day – with some exceptions. James

Jefferis castigated the policy as 'high treason against God and man'.[46] The Anglican Synod of South Australia passed resolutions condemning its effects as 'unwise, unjust and unchristian'. The South Sea Islanders employed in the sugar cane industry – many of whom had become Christians – lamented the destruction of their communities. And various Chinese congregations – which had continued to grow in size and vitality since the gold rush period – watched their numbers fall and dwindle. Pastors including Cheong Cheok Hong and his son James Cheong in Melbourne, James Ken Yee in the Hunter region of New South Wales, and Soo Hoo Ten and John Young Wai in Sydney, persisted all the same – sometimes speaking out against white racism and the challenges it posed to their ministries and communities. However, most Christian clergy did *not* lend either their moral authority or their powers of persuasion to the critique of white Australia. The settler churches did not show collective leadership in shaping public opinion as they had with the issue of federation, initially offering no effective opposition to the racist heresies of the day.

What does such widespread consensus on restricting immigration suggest about the Bible's influence and interpretation in Australia? The question deserves deeper study, but it seems probable that the broad popular acceptance of White Australia reflected the influence of ideas bequeathed by Christianity, but since cut adrift from the close reading of Scripture. Certain appropriations of Old Testament narratives of nation, for instance, served to buttress an idea of Australia as white, British and Christian, and enabled a benevolent gloss on the policy. With the residual assumptions of civic Protestantism, the Anglican Bishop of Bathurst put it this way in 1919:

> Australians … believe it is at once a duty and an opportunity
> for them to bear witness and to let their light shine as a
> distinctively European civilisation in the far orient, and that

they can make their noblest contribution to the developing
life of the orient itself, as well as the peace and happiness
of the whole world, in the form and manner of a white
community.[47]

When the policy *was* explicitly evaluated with reference to Scripture, it quickly looked very shaky. This was increasingly clear from
the 1940s, when Alan Walker, among other people of Christian
conviction, began to advance scriptural arguments against immigration restriction and 'white' nationalism. But even in the policy's
first decade, when very few white Australians mounted sustained
critiques, the Bible was a primary resource for refuting it. An interesting example is Edward Cole – the same sceptical Melbourne
bookseller who, in the 1870s and 1880s, had attacked the theological Bible and many orthodox Christian doctrines. In 1903, Cole
published a collection of essays on *The White Australia Question*.
He sought to prove that the policy was both impossible and unde-
sirable, in part by refuting it from the Bible:

> 'We will not allow any Asiatics or other Coloured People to
> settle in any part of Australia.' So say many Australians.
>
> 'God hath made of one blood all nations of men for to dwell
> on the face of the earth.' 'Do unto others as ye would they
> should do unto you.' These just and humanitarian doctrines
> were taught by two Asiatic, coloured men, Jesus and Paul.[48]

Cole reminded his readers that, by the standards of the policy, Jesus
himself would not be allowed in to Australia – 'Yes! the man who
taught men to love one another, that the foreigner is our neighbour,
and to do as we would be done by'. He argued not from personal

faith, but from his reading of Scripture and especially its principle of 'the oneness of man'.

IF WHITE AUSTRALIA UNITED THE EARLY FEDERAL PARLIAMENT, trade policy divided it. What was the Commonwealth's proper economic stance towards the other nations? The issue was difficult because the two largest states were committed to contrary policies: New South Wales to free trade; Victoria and several smaller states to protection. A number of the early federal elections were fought on the question. Governments were formed and reformed on the floor of the house, depending on which side won the support of the Labor members. The debate was prolonged and nation-shaping. Intellectual historian Greg Melleuish has shown that it essentially turned on 'differing ethical conceptions of the world, different ideas about moral order, which had their foundations in religious understandings'. Specifically, the debate involved arguments that re-worked, in more secular forms, much older theological ideas about providence, sin and human nature.[49] These, in turn, had emerged from the long European history of the theological Bible and its interpretation.

The resolution of these two views – in favour of protection – was achieved in 1909. This outcome was the result of a brilliant Deakin-ite compromise: the Commonwealth would grant protection only to those industries which paid their workers a fair and reasonable wage.[50] It fell to Henry Bournes Higgins, by then President of the Commonwealth Court of Conciliation and Arbitration, to define a 'fair and reasonable' wage. In the famous *Harvester* judgment of 1907 he said it must be enough to support a working man, his wife and three children at a standard of 'reasonable and frugal comfort'. It was a wage determined by the 'normal needs of the average employee, regarded as a human being living in a civilised community' –

not by what an employer could afford. 'Normal needs', in turn, were defined as a minimum standard 'sufficient to secure to the workman food, shelter, clothing, frugal comfort, provision for evil days'. The *Harvester* judgment also provided for double time on Sundays and Good Friday, Eight Hours Day, Christmas and New Year's Day.[51]

The living wage was a major foundation of the Australian welfare system – an internationally distinctive system dubbed 'the wage-earners' welfare state'.[52] Higgins' thinking about the living wage was profoundly shaped by Catholic social teaching on money, wages and labour – teaching which itself expressed long, deep reflection on the theological Bible.[53] Though opposed to religious establishment, he was open to and appreciative of religious responses to social questions. Sometime before 1896, in the midst of unprecedented economic and industrial crises, Higgins read the Papal Encyclical *Rerum Novarum*, on the Rights and Duties of Capital and Labour (1891). 'Perhaps there is nothing in recent history so striking or significant' as that encyclical, he remarked: 'In place of telling the masses that whatever they suffer is of God's will … [it] enters into an elaborate discussion of the social question and the means of dealing with it'.[54] Higgins was particularly impressed by its assumption 'that a State can, if it adopt the right means, and without the distribution of doles, alter the economic condition of the poor' – and by its insistence on a just and fair wage:

All masters of labour should be mindful of this – that to exercise pressure upon the indigent and the destitute for the sake of gain, and to gather one's profit out of the need of another, is condemned by all laws, human and divine. To defraud any one of wages that are his due is a great crime which cries to the avenging anger of Heaven. 'Behold, the

> hire of the labourers … which by fraud has been kept back by
> you, crieth; and the cry of them hath entered into the ears of
> the Lord of Sabaoth' (James 5:4).[55]

Higgins embedded the principle of the living wage into the system
of conciliation and arbitration: a secularised version of Catholic
teaching from the Scriptures. (Another key text, which became
something of a general maxim, was Luke 10:7 – 'The labourer is
worthy of his hire'.[56]) As such, the living wage is an example of a
three-step process of great significance to modern Australia: the
Bible was interpreted by a church which accepted it as God's word,
to produce theologies later appropriated by others in ways that did
not depend on orthodox faith – which then played a defining part
in Australian society.

Australian political parties

The resolution of the trade question helped settle the parliament
into two, rather than three sides. The two-party system remains a
feature of Australian political life, and itself points to the echo of
old debates about the Bible.

THE AUSTRALIAN LABOR PARTY (ALP) IS AUSTRALIA'S OLDEST
political party, having enjoyed continuous existence since the
1890s. Originating in the trade union movement and deeply linked
to Methodism, a branch of Christianity notable for its commitment
to the Bible as well as pragmatic social improvement, its early elec-
toral success was remarkable. Its first representatives were elected
to the South Australian and NSW parliaments in mid-1891. The

NSW election returned thirty-five Labor members, nine of whom were Methodists. Twelve more were convinced evangelicals of other Protestant varieties. The Methodist presence increased at the next election, prompting the Catholic *Freeman's Journal* to complain that 'the Labour Party is largely composed of pulpit-punchers and local preachers'![57]

Many of Labor's early politicians learned their craft in the churches – organising others, debating ideas and speaking publicly in such roles as Sunday school superintendents, youth leaders and lay preachers. Their ideals were nourished by the Bible too, especially the account of Jesus' teaching in the gospels. The first manifesto of the NSW party was reportedly drafted by the Methodist Frank Coffin, who is quoted as saying that 'his inspiration was derived from the Sea of Galilee, 1900 years ago, when the greatest of all social reformers had spoken'.[58]

In South Australia, the connections between Methodism, trade unionism and labour politics were especially marked. According to labour historian Denis Murphy, a significant proportion of the Party's early members there were 'ardent' Methodists.[59] The first Labor premier of the state, John Verran, was the son of a Cornish copper miner. Converted to Christianity as a teenager, Verran joined the Moonta Mines Primitive Methodist Church and developed a ministry as a Sunday school teacher and local preacher. A succession of clergy fed Verran's hunger for knowledge, and encouraged his support of trade unionism and interest in politics. Elected President of the Moonta branch of the Amalgamated Miners' Association in 1895, Verran entered the South Australian House of Assembly in 1901. In 1909, he was made leader of the state's parliamentary Labor Party, and in 1910, he won the election.[60]

It was an occasion of much rejoicing. Upon being sworn in, Verran and his ministerial colleagues made a special train trip to

Moonta, where more than 2000 residents of the old mining town joined them to celebrate. One of the speakers, another Methodist and future Labor premier Crawford Vaughan, got up and proclaimed: 'There have been many John's in history: John the Baptist, Prester John, King John, John Bunyan – and now John Verran!' The crowd knew their Bibles, as well as their Christian history, and roared with approval. When Verran rose to speak, full of emotion, he exclaimed: 'I am an MP because I am a PM (Primitive Methodist)!' Cries of 'Amen!' and 'Glory!' came from all parts of the hall. Verran went on to quote directly from the Bible: after years of struggle, grey-haired admirers of the labour movement in Moonta were saying 'Now, oh Lord, lettest thou thy servant depart in peace' – for they, like Simeon, had seen the salvation of the country.[61]

Federally, too, Methodists and other Protestants dominated the early Labor Party. Among the twenty-four members of the first caucus, there were six Presbyterians, including an ordained clergyman, five Anglicans, three Methodists, two Congregationalists, and a number of other Nonconformists. Only three were Catholics. These were not nominal affiliations, either: historian Stuart MacIntyre claims that half the Caucus attended church each week.[62]

By the early 1930s, however, Catholicism had eclipsed Methodism as the most influential Christian tradition in Australian Labor. The shift was related, in part, to issues of party discipline and leadership – issues which echoed, at least faintly, very old debates within Christian theology. For instance, the early Labor Party adopted a caucus model, under which its parliamentary representatives were required to vote according to the decisions of the party caucus. The pledge proved too difficult for some in the Protestant tradition to accept: it appeared to grate against the right of private judgment and individual freedom of conscience – and raised the spectre of Protestantism's chief historic enemy, Roman

Catholicism.[63] At the same time, collectivist aspects of the Labor Party resonated positively with Catholic social thinking and helped strengthen the connection between Catholicism and Labor.

This connection was not simple, however. Catholicism itself has encompassed a diversity of views and opinions, and Catholic elements within the Labor Party have always had to co-exist with, and indeed accommodate, more secular visions of the Labor program. Even as a source of tension, though, the influence of Catholicism has been important for Labor and Australian politics more generally. The most dramatic example is the split of the 1950s, during the height of the Cold War, when the Labor Party was torn apart by internal conflict over the perceived threat of Communism. Catholics played a notable role in a breakaway group, the Democratic Labor Party (DLP), which established rival branches in most states as well as a national committee. By directing preferences away from the ALP in favour of the anti-Communist Coalition, the DLP contributed to Labor's defeat at several elections and thus to the ALP's long absence from federal office.[64] This experience, in turn, has fed into popular (though problematic) assumptions about Labor as a party of opposition, and the Liberals as the 'natural' party of government. Even today, the Labor Party bears the marks – including a few scars – of the Bible's influence in Australian politics.

THE MODERN LIBERAL PARTY OF AUSTRALIA ROSE FROM THE ashes of its immediate forerunner, the United Australia Party, in 1945, but its lineage is usually traced back to the Deakinite liberals of the federation period. In its present form, it has proved the most enduring of the major non-Labor parties in Australian political history, and the most electorally successful. With its coalition partners, the Liberal party has governed Australia for roughly two-thirds of the post-war period.[65] The nation's two longest serving Prime Ministers, Robert Menzies and John Howard, were both Liberal leaders.

In significant ways, the Bible has influenced both the structure and culture of the Liberal Party. Protestant traditions of biblical interpretation have been particularly relevant. During the first years of the Commonwealth, Alfred Deakin and his supporters often worked constructively with Labor on a range of issues and policies. When it came to the mechanics of forming the party, though, their quintessentially Protestant notion of individual freedom of conscience grated with Labor's caucus pledge. To sign it, said Deakin, would require a man to give up what made him a man – 'his judgment and his conscience' – and that was something he and his supporters would not do. It was a definition of manliness with deep roots in 'the complex intertwined history of liberalism and Protestantism', as political scientist Judith Brett has said, and a striking example of the ongoing relevance of Reformation debates about the Bible to the evolving institutions of party politics.[66] In the event, Deakin ended up forging a non-Labor alliance, the Fusion Party, in 1909 – a forerunner of today's Liberals.

POLITICAL RHETORIC IN AUSTRALIA HAS USUALLY AVOIDED the more religious and idealistic flourishes characteristic of the United States. With a few exceptions, Australian politicians and political thinkers have been more reserved, more understated, more British in their expressions and habits of speech. As such, it can seem that the Bible has not been important to Australian political argument and conversation – especially compared with the United States. But the Bible *has* been a substantial source of political rhetoric and imagination. Leaders on all sides of parliament have explicitly appealed to Scripture to bolster a particular political claim, or to put forward a particular version of the Australian community, its values and its story. This is not just a past phenomenon, either: from the early to mid-2000s, there was an observable increase in religious language in federal parliament.[67] Perhaps more importantly, leaders on all sides have made more subtle appropriations of biblical concepts and images. Labor hero Ben Chifley did it when he spoke about 'the light on the hill' (see Matthew 5:14, the Sermon on the Mount). Liberal party icon Robert Menzies, Prime Minister from 1939 to 1941, and again from 1957 to 1966, owed a great debt to the Bible.

Born at Jeparit, Victoria, in 1894, Robert Menzies was raised in a devout, churchgoing household. His father James was a Presbyterian church elder turned Methodist local preacher and Sunday school teacher. His aunt was a missionary to Korea. His grandmother Elizabeth, with whom he boarded for a few years during school, was a serious Presbyterian who only allowed four books in her house: the Bible, the Presbyterian hymnal, *Ingoldsby Legends* and *Pilgrim's Progress*.[68] Menzies himself imbibed an apparently orthodox Presbyterian faith, which intensified during his time at Melbourne University. He attended Bible classes, joined the campus Christian union, and adopted what became a life-long habit of daily Bible reading. He later recalled that the catalyst for this last decision was a lecture he heard by the evangelical Anglican CH Nash, in which Nash held high his copy of the New Testament and proclaimed: 'In this book is all I know of Jesus Christ and all I need to know of what God has in store for me'.[69]

During his time in politics, Menzies' churchgoing was more sporadic, but his thought and language remained infused with the Bible. He read and understood it within certain cultural and intellectual traditions, too, which emerge in his famous 1941 radio address 'The Forgotten People'. Menzies argued that 'human nature is at its greatest when it combines dependence upon God with independence of man … the greatest element in a strong people is a fierce independence of spirit'. He identified the middle class as the people who embodied this spirit – 'the backbone of the nation', the people responsible for homes material, human and spiritual. Tellingly, he cited Robert Burns' poem 'The Cotter's Saturday Night', which his father had often read to him in childhood. It described a simple labouring family gathered together for a supper of milk and porridge, and worship around the family Bible. It evoked another world from urban, industrial, wartime Australia. But in the tradition of British puritanism, and in opposition to both the idle rich and the dependent poor, this was the kind of pious, frugal, self-reliant family that Menzies admired.

Menzies lauded the 'brave acceptance of unclouded individual responsibility' and identified a limited, enabling role for the state. But the Bible informed *and* tempered his view of individuality. When it came to the nation, he thought in the terms of civic Protestantism – imagining a Christian community, with a Christian calling that shaped its conduct in the world. His language was self-deprecating and understated, unlike the more messianic rhetoric typical of the American presidency. His decisions about going to war were also increasingly unpopular. But the trace of the Bible in his thought is unmistakable. Calling on Australians to enlist for service in the Korean War, in 1950, he spoke of a people 'with all our imperfections … believing in man's brotherhood, anxious to live at peace with our neighbour, willing to go the second mile to help him if he is less fortunate than we are'.[70] Much later and out of office in the 1970s, he gave a speech to the people of Kew, Melbourne:

You know I think it was the Apostle Paul who said that 'we are all members one of another'.[71] It is a lovely phrase, you know. It is a lovely expression. It means that no man lives to himself, that every man who lives in a community is a member of that community. He shares his membership with other people in it and, political friend or political foe, he owes them every good thing that he can contribute to the life of the country.[72]

Australia's political leaders have been diverse in both their personal responses to the Bible and their public uses of it. No one party has ever had a monopoly on biblical thought, values or rhetoric. Not even the parties that explicitly promote themselves as Christian can claim the adherence of most Bible-believing citizens. The remarkable thing is that politicians of varying beliefs, from across the political spectrum, have made such use of the Bible to express their political values and ideas. From the details of Australia's parliamentary procedures to the evolution of its major parties, the Bible has had a substantial influence on the nation's political life.

CHAPTER 9

WAR AND ITS AFTERMATH

Just a few days before Christmas 1917, after a six-week campaign, an expeditionary force including the Australian Light Horse captured the city of Jerusalem from the Ottomans. As the news filtered through to Australia, the press rejoiced. 'HOLY CITY AGAIN IN CHRISTIAN HANDS AFTER 700 YEARS', the Adelaide *Chronicle* proclaimed. Underneath a large picture, captioned 'General view of Jerusalem, taken from the Mount of Olives, where there was heavy fighting before the Turks were dispersed', it expressed great pleasure 'that the birthplace of Christianity should fall into the hands of a Christian Power almost on the anniversary of Christ's birth'.[1] Like many other papers, the *Sydney Morning Herald* stressed that General Allenby had taken care not to damage the 'holy city', and entered it 'reverently', on foot. 'Old women and girls threw flowers and palm leaves upon the road', it added, not needing to spell out for readers the parallel between Allenby and Jesus on Palm Sunday.[2] Most news agencies rightly pointed out that Jerusalem was holy to three major faiths, but there was no doubting that for many Australians this campaign, and the Great War more generally, was overlaid with Christian religious meanings.

Far away on the freezing Western Front, Australia's official war correspondent Charles Bean read the news about Jerusalem in the Paris edition of the *Daily Mail*. In the lead-up to capturing the city, there had been fighting at Bethlehem and on the Jericho road – familiar to any Sunday school student as the site for Jesus' famous parable of the Good Samaritan. Australian troops had also felt conscious of holding the very hills 'where Christ was supposed, according to the Bible, to have arose from the dead, and also to have fed the multitude from heaven from the five fish and three loaves of bread'.[3] After all, a significant proportion of the First Australian Imperial Force (1st AIF) came from an evangelical background, and of all the books available to servicemen at the front, 'the New Testament stood as the most widely owned and possibly the most widely read'.[4]

Reading a report of the capture of Jerusalem, Bean was troubled by the news of violence on and around the Mount of Olives:

> One couldn't help thinking … that if only the full meaning
> of that short sentence or two impressed itself upon the world,
> there would be no more fighting. The war would stop – it
> could not go on. The Mount – the Mount from which Christ
> spoke the wonderful sermon of brotherhood and charity
> and kindness – the mount held by a nest of active machine-
> guns and stormed by a magnificent charge at the point of the
> bayonet. One can hardly read it without feeling that heaven
> is going to crack and fall in like a broke ceiling. If ever there
> were a shocking sacrilege to a pure and wonderful idea! … I
> can't write or speak the things one feels – it chokes.[5]

Charles Bean was 'not much of a churchgoer' himself. His knowledge of the Bible was broad rather than detailed (he had not registered, for instance, that Jesus probably preached his famous sermon in Galilee, not on the Mount of Olives). He later admitted to thinking that the question of God's existence could not make much difference to a person's conduct.[6] But when it came to personal and national ethics, Bean believed in a fusion of classical and Christian ideals. The way to happiness, he once said, lay in 'the aims and virtues explained by Plato and Aristotle and raised in a different and much more powerful way by the founders of the great religions – and certainly most purely, most widely, and most effectively by the founder of Christianity'.[7] In late 1917, after three years of fighting, Bean worried that those 'pure' ideals were at the point of collapse. The contrast between the fight for Jerusalem and what Jesus had taught in the gospels gave an urgency to the question: what did the war mean for British civilisation? Could there be an ethical nationhood?

THE FIRST WORLD WAR HAD A DEEP IMPACT ON VIRTUALLY every Australian. Out of a total population of fewer than five million, more than 400 000 men and about 2500 women enlisted – including an estimated 1000 Aboriginal and Torres Strait Islander personnel.[8] The first naval and expeditionary force saw action in September 1914, successfully seizing German posts in Papua New Guinea. Much more famously, several 'ANZAC' units entered the fray as part of the Allied attack at Gallipoli, Turkey, in April 1915. Bean eulogised their feats in storming 'tier after tier of cliffs and mountains apparently as impregnable as Govett's Leap'.[9] The offensive ultimately failed, and Australian forces went on to long campaigns in western Europe and the Middle East. But Bean continued to write about the Gallipoli assault as an unrivalled moment of national revelation. 'The big thing in the war for Australia was the discovery of the character of Australian men. It was character which rushed the hills at Gallipoli and held on there.'[10] He suggested a cluster of ANZAC qualities which came to define popular ideas of an Australian spirit: 'reckless valour in a good cause, enterprise, resourcefulness, fidelity, comradeship, and endurance that will never own defeat'.[11] Bean's attempt to make meaning from the violence, to show that all the bloodshed had been worth something, produced ideas about national 'birth' and 'character', debated afresh by every generation of Australians since.

On the Australian home front, the First World War involved a mass civilian effort. Through the Red Cross, the Australian Comforts Fund, and many more localised charities, Australians devoted themselves to letter writing, sock knitting, book collecting, and fundraising. At the same time, the war exposed and exacerbated social divisions. Pacifist voices began to emerge publicly in 1915, and 1916 and 1917 saw increased industrial conflict, sectarianism, and bitter debates over conscription. By late 1918, when the fighting finally ended, every second family had been plunged into mourning. Almost 62 000 Australians had been killed, and another 156 000 returned having been gassed, imprisoned or wounded. The impact of such loss lasted longer than a single generation.

THE BIBLE WAS CRUCIAL TO THE WAYS AUSTRALIANS experienced the First World War. It was bound up with people's very understanding of why the war was being fought in the first place. It infused the whole spectrum of moral reflection from theories of just war to outright pacifism. The Bible was also part of the material, emotional and intellectual lives of many service men and women – one of their most common possessions at the front, and in many cases highly treasured. And as the war ground on and the terrible toll became clearer, the Bible provided a vocabulary for dealing with loss and salvaging meaning. It did not have a monopoly on the idiom of remembrance, but the Bible informed the ways the legacies of the war played out in Australian culture. After four transformational years, the question was sharper than ever: was there, could there be, such a thing as a Christian Australia?

Debating war

'It is hard to explain what is impelling me to go', wrote Owen Lewis to his father in 1915. 'But there is something allied to conscience which bids me go'. Nineteen-year-old Lewis was the top engineering student at Melbourne University that year, and the most devout member of a family attending Armadale Presbyterian Church. A consistent Christian who hated violence, he was nevertheless troubled by the news of war, and several of his friends and relatives had enlisted. According to his brother, Owen did not seek free beer, good pay, or the instant respectability of the uniform like more irreverent larrikin types did. He was a devout young man who did not smoke, drink, or pursue sex before marriage – 'puritanical in the best sense of the word', with a sense of 'deep moral compulsion' to volunteer.[12]

Seeking his parents' permission to enlist, Owen Lewis appealed both to the Protestant principle of conscience and the ideal of self-sacrifice he found in the Scriptures:

I believe in a hereafter and if following the will of
my conscience I enter it sooner than under ordinary
circumstances I do not think that anyone should regret it.
What comes to me a great deal is, that I am abiding here in
comfort while others … are fighting my battles and giving
their lives for me. Death must come to us all sooner or later
and there is no way so noble of leaving than that in which you
'Lay down your life for your friends'.[13]

In obedience to his parents, Lewis saw out the academic year and then enlisted in early 1916. He served on the Western Front, becoming a lieutenant in the newly formed Australian Flying Corps. Sitting beside my own relative, navigator George Best, he was shot down and killed in April 1918, meeting the early death he had contemplated so bravely.

In what circumstances, if any, should a nation go to war? What beliefs make it possible – or impossible – for an individual or community to become involved in conflict? For Lewis, the Bible underwrote a certain attitude towards life and death that helped him make sense of war and its risks, and propelled his decision to enlist. For Everard Digges La Touche, a young Ulster Protestant who taught theology at the Anglican college in Sydney, war service was a matter of discerning the will of God. He enlisted in the ranks, only to be killed leading a charge at Gallipoli. One of his contemporaries said, 'we did not all approve of a priest taking the sword – but nobody could discuss the question with Digges in his tent without realising that whether he was right or wrong … he had settled this question for himself with his Bible open before God'.[14]

Not every young soldier was so confident in the hereafter, nor as concerned with what the Bible taught. But at a time when 96 per cent of Australians identified as Christian at the census, and churches were among the most pervasive social institutions, virtually everyone in wartime Australia encountered and to some extent absorbed a Bible-infused understanding of the Great War.

WHEN BRITAIN DECLARED WAR ON GERMANY IN AUGUST 1914, the young Australian Commonwealth was automatically committed. But even aside from legal technicalities, people accepted that going to war alongside Britain was the proper way of things.

University professors came out in support; so did the major news-papers, politicians on all sides, and leaders of the churches. After all, the overwhelming majority of Australians felt a deep affinity with Britain. The new Commonwealth was bound to the Mother Country by culture, language, religion – and especially by what Henry Parkes had called 'the crimson thread of kinship'. As Labor leader Andrew Fisher had already declared, Australia would sup-port the empire to 'the last man and the last shilling'.

The Bible did not provide a straightforward endorsement of the Australian war effort, but it infused the general culture of the period. 'My parents were on the wharf waving ... Mum was crying', farmer Alan Broadribb recalled. 'Dad had been in Melbourne and got me a little Bible from the Bible Society. Dad always held his feelings in, but it was the last thing he gave me as we shook hands.'[15] Twenty-five-year-old Alf Stewart also took his Bible to war, having overcome a hesitation to volunteer because he could not bear the thought of killing. He joined in late 1915 hoping to become a stretcher-bearer, but got assigned to a rifle company that engaged in some of the fiercest fighting in France during 1916. Stewart's diary gives a picture of what Bible reading meant to him: 'for comfort's sake I read dear Ma's favourite chap-ter John 14. It took me out of myself for a while. During those terrible bombardments one can always find comfort in prayer, but the nerve strain is awful'. Another time, under intense fire, Stew-art admitted to feeling 'a bit afraid ... But suddenly it came to me, why should you be afraid, when you honestly believe that God is taking care of you; I felt ashamed and offered up a little prayer and instantly I lost all fear ... though I was shaking a bit'.[16] Stewart survived a wounding in August 1916, and made a point of going to as many church services as he could while recovering in Eng-land. Returned to the front, he was killed in September 1917: he ran into No Man's Land to rescue someone, and got shot in the attempt.

Taking the Bible to war was made easier by Christian organisations such as the Pocket Testament League, the Scripture Gift Mission, and the British and Foreign Bible Society. In just two years from 1914, the Bible Society alone distributed more than five million New Testaments in fifty languages – to troops on all sides and others caught up in the conflict. In this, it continued a long tradition of producing Bibles specifically for soldiers, which had begun in the 1640s when sections of the Geneva translation were printed in pocket size for members of Oliver Cromwell's Puritan army.[17] First World War Bibles were enabled by the new industrial print technologies, and buoyed by thousands of pounds in public donations – a remarkable example of how publishers and booksellers mobilised for war.[18] Such Bibles were sometimes given as departure gifts; along with other books and newspapers, they were also commonly included in care packages. Many Bibles were distributed by the YMCA and other charities. Chaplains also played a key role: William 'Fighting Mac' McKenzie gave out more than 1300 New Testaments in a two-day period on Gallipoli, reporting that 'the men rushed these testaments like wolves'.[19] William Dexter, on the Western Front, noted it was 'no uncommon thing to see a man in the trenches with his New Testament out reading it'.[20]

Some Christian diggers already read the Bible as a habit, and maintained it throughout their war service.[21] For others who were not especially religious, the circumstances, including boredom when not in the thick of fighting, as well as nostalgia for home and a desire for something familiar, may have driven them to take it up. One Australian soldier wrote home about how 'the reading of the Scriptures, the telling of our difficulties and our prayers for one another are a means of great help' in bringing peace of mind.[22]

John Gilbert Jacob found the Bible surprisingly reassuring in the midst of intense fighting. On the front lines one day during 1918, he picked up a New Testament belonging to a Scottish comrade. It was inscribed with the text of Joshua 1:9 – 'Be strong and of a good courage for the Lord thy God is with thee whitherso ever thou goest'. Jacob put it in his pocket while his trench was bombarded: it was 'the most magnificent barrage I have ever been under' he wrote, 'but it hardly made me quake, for those words kept sounding in my ears as loud as the approaching gazonkas'.[23]

Back at home, certain theologies drawn from the Bible informed the widespread acceptance of the war. One influential idea was commonly known as the 'just war theory', which provided a framework for going to war as right and necessary. It had classical roots, but was given shape by Christian thinkers such as Augustine and Aquinas.[24] Another important idea drew on Old Testament narratives of God's dealings with his chosen people. It involved an imperial theology that played into contemporary forms of British nationalism, prominent not only in Britain itself but also in its colonies. It nourished a belief that Britain held its empire by God's design, and for benevolent Christian purposes – a popular belief in godly nationhood that circulated widely.

This view had two important expressions in Australia. One was a sense of duty to aid the vulnerable, in parallel with an individual's calling to lay down their life for their friends. When Germany invaded Belgium, it seemed right for British peoples to defend that 'innocent and martyred nation', and resist the heresy of German militarism. The other was that war constituted a form of national discipline. It was a test, a trial, that would lead to spiritual renewal and moral purification. This was a line taken up by most Australian churches from 1914, reflecting an anxiety that the nation was not as Christian as the clergy would have liked. Methodist minister

Henry Howard went further than most in saying that war should be welcomed, because it could 'break down our trust in the material and strengthen our faith in the spiritual': it could be expected to purify a Christian society marred by 'intemperance, uncleanness, mutual distrust, commercial dishonesty, political chicanery'.[25]

A third theological discourse focused on threats to Christian civilisation: this was a confrontation between good and evil, Zion and Babylon.[26] It was not lost on many conservative Protestants that Germany had been the source of the new higher criticism, the fount of liberal scholarship, the apparent assault on traditional Biblicism. But in a much wider sense as well, Germany was considered an apostate nation. Didn't its leading theologians expound a doctrine of holy war? Didn't they claim to know the mind of God, insisting that he intended for Germany to dominate Europe and then the world? This view was preached from several Australian pulpits, giving the war a sense of religious conflict. But it went well beyond the churches, finding echoes in war propaganda and the secular press.[27] Even Norman Lindsay, the anti-clerical bohemian, drew posters of 'the frightful Huns'. In one, he depicted Germany not only as brutal and immoral, but as subverting the Christian gospel at every turn. Resisting such an enemy was a matter of rejecting the 'gospel of frightfulness' and the 'gospel of war', he said.[28]

Together, these ideas enabled and reinforced Australians' accepting response to the war on Germany. In fact, the almost universal initial support for the war is difficult to explain without understanding these theological elements. They involved interpretations of the Bible that blurred the lines between piety and patriotism, and filtered through popular culture in the more secular form of good versus evil. However, there were other interpretations, alternative visions of a Christian nation.

BERNARD LINDEN WEBB WAS THIRTY YEARS OLD WHEN HE AND his young family moved to Hay, in the Southern Riverina district of New South Wales, in 1914. As minister of the Methodist circuit there, it fell to him to pastor that congregation through the crisis. He went about the task in a remarkable way. In early 1915, Webb preached a series of three sermons arguing that the war could not be Christian. Regarding just war as a chimera, he expounded the Scriptures in favour of a positive pacifism. He argued that the kingdoms of this world maintained power by force, but the kingdom of Christ did so with self-sacrificing love. He cited Jesus' declaration, during his trial by Pontius Pilate: 'if my kingdom were of this world, then would my servants fight ... but now is my kingdom not from hence' (John 18:36). Webb stressed that Jesus refused the sword, 'even to save his life', and faced his followers with 'the tremendous responsibility of living for the same ideals'. 'This war', Webb argued, 'is not in keeping with our profession of Christianity; it is the outcome of materialism, worldliness, godlessness'.

Webb's pacifism turned on his understanding of the New Testament and an alternative vision of godly nationhood. He declared: 'No nation can be truly Christian till it will accept the ideals and act on the principles of the kingdom of Christ'. A Christian nation would forsake force for 'self-sacrificing love' and 'the way of the cross'. Such a nation would keep the peace 'not merely because the others have agreed to do the same, but because she dares be faithful to the ideals of her Lord no matter what it may cost her'. By this measure, Webb explained, there *was* 'no Christian nation in our time'. He realised strict pacifism was not 'immediately practical for a semi-Christian nation' like Britain or Australia, or for any of the nations in their present mood. 'But that doesn't make the war Christian, and the churches ought to be able to point out ... "a more excellent way"' (1 Corinthians 12:31).[29]

Webb's sermons comprised 'the most tightly argued case for biblical pacifism' produced during the First World War.[30] Published with the assistance of a Quaker friend, they established him as one of a small group of Australian ministers who openly and consistently opposed the war – including Methodists William Beale and Frank Walker, Queensland Presbyterian James Gibson, and the Sydney Congregationalist Albert Rivett, who founded the Australian Peace Alliance. The sermons received some sympathetic notice in the letters pages of the Methodist press, but in general such arguments were widely disparaged. Webb's Junior Circuit Steward resigned in disagreement, and fifteen men from his own congregation, out of a total adult membership of fifty, volunteered for military service. The wider Hay community was similarly untouched, recording one of the highest per capita rates of enlistment in the country.[31] Webb continued his ministry at Hay until October 1917, finally resigning during a virulent national debate about conscription, citing irreconcilable differences with his denomination's stance.

THE END OF THE GREAT WAR DID NOT SPELL THE END OF THE debate. Across the English-speaking world, Christians began to critique nationalism, imperialism, and even racism.[32] In Australia, several leaders re-evaluated nationalism with the resources of theology. The Anglican Archbishop of Brisbane found guidance in the act of God becoming human in Jesus: 'Faith in the incarnation engenders … an instinct of brotherhood which refuses to be confined within national boundaries'.[33] For the Bishop of Newcastle, the concept of idolatry seemed particularly useful: nationalism was 'the root evil of our time' because it made the state – rather than God – a 'source of all life's meaning'.[34] On university campuses, too, Christian students grappled with the tensions between the kingdom of Christ and the claims of the nation. At Sydney University, members of the Australian Student Christian Movement led a vibrant campus peace campaign. Many more supported the League of Nations, and especially the popular peace movement that gathered pace through the 1920s and 1930s.[35]

With the outbreak of the next world war in 1939, many of these dreams were shattered. Australian church leaders expressed patriotism far less strongly than they had in 1914, but most conceded that war against Germany embodied a just cause and that 'war was sometimes a necessary evil'.[36] Only a minority of people unconvinced by the moral necessity of the Second World War resisted the pressure to enlist. Between 1939 and 1945, almost 2800 Australian men claimed formal exemption on the grounds of conscientious belief. There were presumably many more of the same view among their wives, families and friends. A few of these were socialists or humanists, motivated by rationalist beliefs. But as historian Bobbie Oliver found, the overwhelming majority held 'strong Christian convictions'.[37]

The significance of religion to conscientious objection was not lost on the Australian Army: during the Second World War, it attempted to expose inconsistent objectors by debating their view of the Bible. A document issued in 1942 instructed Army interviewers to probe whether an objector accepted the Old and New Testaments as 'the infallible word of God and the only rule of life'. They were then to query whether the objector admitted 'contradictions', and whether he held that 'some parts are to be more believed than others'. In a disturbing instance of a state's attempt to adjudicate on the proper interpretation of the Scriptures, the Area Officer was then to 'prove' that God sanctioned violence by quoting mainly from the Old Testament, and to counter 'the contention that Christ did not use or sanction violence' with some tenuous speculations on certain verses from the gospels.[38] Christian pacifists were on much stronger biblical ground when they retorted that Jesus in fact rebuked his disciples when they drew swords in his defence, healed those whom they injured, and went calmly with his captors without resisting arrest (Luke 22). Or as one of the pacifist newspapers offered: 'One can't imagine [Jesus] turning a tommy gun on anybody or sticking a bayonet into a man's belly'.[39]

The courts, like the Army, found pacifist interpretations of the Bible unconvincing. Only 1.5 per cent of Australian Second World War objectors were granted an unconditional exemption from military duties. A full 60 per cent had their applications rejected or received orders to enlist as non-combatants. Those who still refused any kind of military service were sent to labour camps, or even to prison. There, an enquiry conducted by the ageing Linden Webb found that the Bible was the only permissible reading material for prisoners. But access to a copy was not always easy, and in a few cases the pages containing the Sermon on the Mount had been removed altogether – presumably because of Jesus' timelessly subversive statement:

Blessed are the peacemakers, for they will be called sons of God; Blessed are those who are persecuted because of righteousness, for theirs is the kingdom of heaven (Matthew 5:9–10).[40]

Memorials, public and private

The First World War robbed one generation of its sons, another of its uncles and fathers, and yet another of friends, brothers and husbands. Australian households and whole communities struggled to come to terms with such loss. The Bible was among the reference points for memorialising the dead, though in different ways in public and private settings.

A visitor to any Australian town is likely to see one – a memorial to local residents who served in war overseas. At so great a distance from the battlefields, and in the absence of bodies for funeral and burial, communities raised such memorials by the thousands after 1918. At Berridale, in south-east New South Wales, the people erected a fourteen-foot statue of a crucified Christ, inscribed: 'To the glory of God and in memory of the fallen of Berridale district who gave their lives for the Empire'.[41] Unveiled in November 1922, like every other local memorial it listed the names of the dead, but it was unique among community memorials in depicting a dying Christ.[42] A number of other towns opted for plain and unadorned crosses – but overall, as historian Ken Inglis showed, Christianity did not provide the primary symbolic repertoire for public sculpture. For each cross, Australians raised at least ten classical obelisks.[43]

As text, the Bible's place in memorials was more complex. In a few cases, it provided the inscription. Most common was the famous verse from John 15:13 – 'Greater love hath no man than this, that a man lay down his life for his friends'. At the Shrine of Remembrance in Melbourne, a memorial overwhelmingly Athenian in style and inspiration, the floor of the sanctuary was inscribed simply with the first phrase: 'Greater love hath no man'.[44] The fragment underscores that generation's familiarity with the New Testament: the assumption was that visitors could readily complete the sentence themselves. It also illustrates how biblical texts were used publicly in ways that relegated theology to the background. There was a palpable shyness, says John Moses, around the fact that the phrase came from Jesus, referring to his own sacrifice. Instead, it was made to highlight how people might ideally relate to one another. When the Bible *was* a source for such inscriptions, it was quoted in a manner open to non-denominational and even non-religious interpretations.

'Lest we forget': the most common phrase on Australian war memorials comes from the poem 'Recessional', written by Rudyard Kipling late in 1897, the year of Queen Victoria's diamond jubilee. Its ubiquity suggests the eclipse of biblical language as a vehicle for Australian public remembrance, and yet the persistence of biblically derived ideas about nationhood. The poem invoked the scriptural categories of a nation divinely called, blessed and chastened, referring to the text of Deuteronomy 6:12 – 'beware lest thou forget the Lord, who brought you forth out of the land of Egypt'. It also alluded to Psalm 95, which depicts the world in God's hands, and Psalm 51, in which a grave sinner offers up a humble and contrite heart. Crucially, it highlighted the dangers of imperial pride by contrasting the transience of human empires, per the biblical examples of Nineveh and Tyre, with the ancient yet enduring work of Christ.

The use of 'Lest we forget' illustrates how biblical ideas can move through a culture, becoming both less theological and widely influential in the process. Taken up in Australian war remembrance, the phrase remained open to a civic theology of nationhood – and this was arguably very important in the 1920s. But it could also be taken as a straightforwardly secular call to remember the nation's war dead.

Overall, these examples suggest the secularisation of the Bible's presence in culture. It was usually used in public to highlight ideals of human virtue, rather than to provide divine exhortation or instruction.[45] This reflected the need to unite rather than divide a religiously diverse population. It was also consistent with the non-sectarian, non-doctrinal use of the Bible to cultivate an ethical citizenship rather than a specific faith, by then a settled feature of Australian public discourse.

More personal memorials of the war dead offer a different view of its presence in Australian culture. Historian Colin Bale examined nearly 12 000 inscriptions chosen for Australians buried in First World War cemeteries in France and Belgium.[46] His remarkable study found notable differences between public and private remembrance. One was that bereaved relatives usually opted for personal messages, rather than ideas of patriotic duty or sacrifice. Owen Lewis' family, for instance, adopted the words of the English poet Edmund Spenser: 'Rest after toil, port after stormy seas'.[47] George Best, Lewis's colleague, was buried under the title of William Morris's poem 'Love is Enough'.[48]

Religious themes were also more common in personal memorials than in public ones. About one-third of Australian grave inscriptions included some kind of religious message. Two of the most popular texts – 'Thy will be done' (Matthew 6:10) and 'The Lord gave and the Lord hath taken away' (Job 1:21) – were familiar to many Australians from the Prayer Book burial service. Some cited a phrase from such hymns as 'Peace, perfect peace' – which itself drew on Isaiah 26:3.[49]

Biblical inscriptions also tended to function differently: in private remembrance, they 'tended to be more considerate of the theological purpose of the texts'.[50] This was partly because families were much freer than governments and community committees to express their beliefs. It may also point to a gendered element. While men were more prominent in making decisions about local war memorials, bereaved mothers and sisters were more likely to choose personal inscriptions. Perhaps the devotional Bible held more significance for ordinary women than for public men.

Australian families used the Bible to express the full range of responses to the death of their loved one.[51] Several turned to the Psalms to convey profound pain and disillusionment. For twenty-one-year-old Leonard Blackwood, who died of wounds in October 1917: 'Scatter thou the people that delight in war' (Psalm 68:30).[52] Other passages gave comfort to the bereaved. For Tom Cozens from Wangaratta, a young farmer killed in France: 'The eternal God is thy refuge and underneath are the everlasting arms' (Deuteronomy 33:27). Digges La Touche's wife chose 'Faithful unto death' (Revelation 2:10) and *'Quis Separabit'* – Latin for the opening words of Romans 8:35, 'Who shall separate us from the love of Christ? shall tribulation, or distress, or persecution, or famine, or nakedness, or peril, or sword?'[53] Yet others turned to the Scriptures to express hope for life beyond the grave.

My own relative, Sydney Moor Lake, served in Palestine with the Fourth Field Ambulance. He was killed in action in late 1917, on the day the Light Horse charged Beersheba. His devoutly evangelical mother chose the simple words 'With Christ', a fragment from the New Testament letter to the Romans: 'Now if we be dead with Christ, we believe that we shall also live with him'.[54]

How might such uses of the Bible be explained? For Pat Jalland, a historian of Australians' attitudes to death, they point to the residual trace of Christianity in the culture of the 1920s. In a time of crisis, she says, people reverted to customary and traditional forms, although they no longer attached real significance to them. For Bale, many biblical inscriptions seem to have an intensity that requires more explanation. In some cases, the choice of text surely reflected heartfelt Christian faith – including hope of resurrection, eternal life, and the ultimate defeat of death.[55] For a significant minority, at least, the theological Bible had an enduring ability to bring hope, meaning and comfort as they grappled with life and death.

Anzac Day and the sacred

Les Murray's verse novel, *The Boys Who Stole the Funeral* (1980), points to an enduring challenge in Australian society and culture: the challenge to make meaning from the devastation of war. It raises the question, too, about how much such meanings might rely on, or else repudiate, Christian ideas. The poem's protagonist, a journalist, quotes from the New Testament book of Hebrews 9:22 – 'without the shedding of blood there is no forgiveness of sins' as he discusses the First World War with a priest. In response, the priest refers to the very next chapter, 'Christ offered for all time a single sacrifice for sins' (Hebrews 10:12).

Nearly forty years after Murray's poem and a whole century after the First World War, the task of making meaning from war arguably remains a theological one. In Australia, its focus is Anzac Day, 25 April, presently observed as a de facto national day. The public ritual, mythology, and sense of sacredness that have become associated with Anzac Day open yet another window on to the complex and changing relationship of Bible and nation.

ANZAC DAY ITSELF EMERGED IN THE 1920S FROM A CONTEST of ideas about war and nation.[56] Some of its architects believed that the nation was a spiritual community, united under the sovereignty of Almighty God. They saw Anzac Day as an occasion to reflect on 'both the wickedness and cost of war; to do penance, commemorate the fallen and to render thanks for their sacrifice in the cause of freedom'. Preaching at St John's Anglican Cathedral in Brisbane on 25 April 1924, Canon David Garland laid out his ideas from the Bible, emphasising the parallels between the soldiers' sacrifice and Christ's, as well as 'the reality of that life beyond the veil where they live forevermore, and where some day, we too shall meet them', drawing on Hebrews 10:20. He concluded that:

> There is no room for anything but solemn observance of Anzac Day – the All Souls Day of Australia – and so we come before God … with tokens of Christian penitence and sorrow for the sins of the world which caused the sacrifice of these bright young lives, our dearest and our best.[57]

Garland was the life and soul of Brisbane's Anzac Day Commemoration Committee.[58] Aged fifty when war broke out, he had already devoted years of his life to making Australia a more seriously Christian nation – including by leading the Bible in State Schools campaign in several states as well as New Zealand. He had also served as chaplain to the Australian Light Horse in Palestine, becoming the first cleric to celebrate the Eucharist in the Church of the Holy Sepulchre after the Turks were expelled from Jerusalem. He saw Anzac Day as an opportunity 'to bring a community that had been largely alienated from God back into a proper relationship with him *as a nation*'.[59] As such, he designed a public liturgy for Anzac Day services, which included hymns, prayers, the Last Post and the world-leading innovation of a two-minute silence. These elements still feature in Anzac commemoration services nearly a century later.

Garland's vision of Anzac Day was rivalled by another, rooted in different ideas of war and nation. This second view was secular, military, and exclusively masculine. It saw 25 April as the day when Australia's soldiers won 'the credentials necessary to be recognised as an actor on the stage of history'. The NSW Returned Servicemen's League (RSL) outlined this view in the early 1920s:

> We are not quite in accord with the suggestion that Anzac
> Day should be a day of mourning … to the Australian Nation
> as a whole the day means more than a day on which many
> soldiers lost their lives. Its real significance lies in the fact that
> upon that day Australia proved itself a Nation and its soldiers
> proved that they were Men.[60]

In a similar vein, a 'mere digger' wrote to the *Daily Telegraph* 'to register a kick against petticoat control of war anniversaries': why privilege 'solemn grief-reviving' over the celebration of 'epic deeds' in 'dinkum' fashion?[61] Wasn't 25 April a day for celebrating such classical virtues as courage, comradeship, and bravery under fire? People of this view usually thought Anzac Day should be observed more as a holiday than a holy day, more like Australia Day than Good Friday.

In the end, each state legislated for Anzac Day in its own way. Typically, 25 April was marked by a closed holiday in the morning, to allow for services, and an open holiday in the afternoon, allowing for reunions at the pub and games of two-up. The competing concepts of war and nation continued to co-exist, unresolved. In 1965, the fiftieth anniversary of the Gallipoli landing, they came into outright conflict. With 25 April falling on a Sunday, the RSL asked churches to cancel their morning services in favour of a veterans' march at 9 a.m. The churches were shocked: Australians faced a 'sharp choice', said Methodist Alan Walker, between 'the worship of the state and its traditions and the worship of God'. (The RSL, he added, was 'one of the most pagan organisations in Australia'.[62]) In reply, the RSL's supporters took a dig at Walker's well-known pacifism, claiming that fighting for religious freedom and the 'spirit of sacrifice' expressed the true spirit of Christianity.[63]

The march went ahead at 9 a.m. Surprisingly, though, it

did not signal that Christian elements would be marginalised or excluded from Anzac commemoration. Hymns such as 'Abide with Me' are still sung at dawn services. The Lord's Prayer is still said, and the 'greater love hath no man' verse from John's gospel is still a defining text. As historian Michael Gladwin has argued, Christian chaplains also remain key participants, leading prayers and choosing Bible passages that resonate with themes of suffering, sacrifice and redemption.[64] Almost a century on, the Bible may well be more evident in Australian public life on Anzac Day than on any other occasion.

That said, an idea of the nation as a spiritual community has all but passed from popular understanding. Theological language like Garland's is much less common, at least beyond the contributions of participating clergy. The idea that nations exist under God's sovereign hand, and that national repentance might be appropriate, is relatively rare at official events. The biblical echoes of Kipling's 'Recessional' also go unrecognised by a more secular community. Anzac commemoration continues to borrow heavily from Christianity but in a less theological manner.

The early twenty-first century saw a remarkable surge in the popularity of Anzac events. Beginning in the 1980s and 1990s, the day – and the legend – came to enjoy unprecedented appeal, especially among younger generations. Tens of thousands of Australian backpackers began visiting Gallipoli each year. Dawn services and Anzac marches claimed swelling attendances. Various football leagues instituted 'Anzac derbies' featuring the Last Post, the national anthem and a minute's silence for remembrance. And for the centenary of the First World War (2014–18), Australian governments planned commemorative projects to the tune of nearly $325 million. Such spending was unparalleled around the world, outstripping the United Kingdom's by more than two to one.[65]

By 2015, the public appetite for 'Anzackery' may well have been sated, to judge from the modest ratings of Anzac television dramas and the apparent tiredness that met the torrent of commercial commemorative kitsch. But the idea that the war marked the birth of the nation continues to claim wide popular support, despite its vulnerability to a range of critiques. The Anzac legend has acquired an almost sacred status, such that certain public critics have been silenced with expressions of disapproval similar to the condemnation of blasphemy.[66]

What does this tell us about the shifting relationships between Bible, war and nation? Has the spirit of Anzac become a substitute religion for a post-Christian nation? Do Anzac services plug a gap once filled by the churches, as occasions for collective reflection on values, meaning and eternity? Perhaps Anzac observance points to both the secularisation of public culture, and the sacral qualities of Australian secularity.[67]

The Anzac legend itself relies in part on certain cultural appropriations of the Bible, particularly the gospel narratives of Jesus' suffering, death and eventual triumph through sacrifice. According to the New Testament, Jesus went to his death to open the way to eternal life (1 Corinthians 15); his ostensible defeat on the cross was in fact his crowning victory (Colossians 2:5). Similar reversals are required to interpret the soldiers' sacrificial death as the path to national life, and the comprehensive defeat at Gallipoli as a moment of true glory. Even if war is unchristian, as Linden Webb argued, the Bible helped create the cultural space to embrace tragic failure. Without its impact in culture, in a secularised way, the Gallipoli campaign could not have been so widely imagined as the birth of the nation. The enduring potency of this idea points to the Bible's residual influence in twenty-first-century Australia.

Reconsidering a Christian nation

In the years after 1918, Australians asked afresh what it might mean to live alongside one another: church and society; nation and empire; European and Asian and Indigenous Australian. And just as the Bible had been bound up with questions of nationhood before and during the war, it was part of the conversation in the decades that followed. For a number of post-war believers, the Bible's globalising qualities came to the fore. In a compelling few cases, the theological Bible offered a vision of a just and inclusive society, far richer and more Christ-like than the conventional Christian nation of newly federated Australia.

One expression of this new mood was a fresh Australian missionary effort. Turn-of-the-century visions of world evangelism survived the catastrophe of the Great War, and helped spur a fresh wave of international missionary activity in the Asia-Pacific. The movement involved a considerable number of Australian Christians: even as the Commonwealth implemented exclusionary immigration policies, scores of young people volunteered for service in India, China, Japan, Korea, and elsewhere. Missionary women had outnumbered men by as many as two to one in the period 1880 to 1913, and this trend continued after the war.[68]

Some Australian missionaries trained at one of the new Bible and missions colleges: the Chapman-Alexander Bible Institute in Adelaide (opened 1914); the Sydney Missionary and Bible College (1916) or the Bible Institutes of Melbourne, Adelaide and Perth, all formed in the 1920s. These Protestant colleges typically stood 'four-square for the whole-hearted acceptance of the entire sacred volume of the Old and New Testaments as from God'.[69] Together, they equipped hundreds of people for Christian missions. (By 1980, about 8000 students had enrolled in Australian Bible Colleges.[70])

Especially for women, though, perhaps the crucial influence was the Student Volunteer Movement, the missionary arm of the Australian Student Christian Movement (ASCM). These university-educated missionaries often went to work in the areas of public health, education and social welfare, and made substantial, long-term contributions to the well-being of their host communities. As feminist historian Renate Howe has found, such women saw themselves as 'a new type of missionary who aimed to build up Indigenous resources in church and society … [they] did not fully identify with either the cultural imperialism of the Americans or the colonial imperialism of the British-based missions'.[71] They represented a more tolerant, internationalist Christian citizenship. In the longer term, their relative openness to Asian cultures, their rejection of white racism, and their insistence on 'the principles and practice of Christian brotherhood'[72] gradually filtered back to the Australian churches, contributing to new understandings of the nation's place in the world.[73]

CLOSER TO HOME, INDIGENOUS CHRISTIANS OFFERED AN urgent critique of white Australia's track record of living out its professed faith. For them, the crucial context was that war had not ended in 1918: frontier violence and other attacks on their communities persisted much longer into the twentieth century. In the north of the continent, massacres continued – most famously at Forrest River, Western Australia, in 1926, and in connection with Coniston Station, Northern Territory, in 1928. In the south-east, Indigenous communities faced a second wave of dispossession from their land. A Naboth's Vineyard scenario played out again and again, as reserves held by Indigenous communities were turned over to white farmers. In South Australia, by 1913, 64 of the

97 reserves gazetted for Aboriginal people since the 1830s had been leased or sold to Europeans.[74] In New South Wales, in 1911, there were 27000 acres of Aboriginal reserve land. A mere sixteen years later, half of that had been revoked and another quarter leased out to settlers.[75] At Coranderrk, in Victoria, the whole station was shut down in the 1920s. Parliament refused to hand the remaining land over to Aboriginal returned servicemen, selling it off instead.[76]

Yorta Yorta man William Cooper grew up in a world shaped by these realities, and spent decades of his adult life challenging its injustice. Cooper had learned to read and write, and converted to Christianity, at Daniel and Janet Matthews' Maloga mission on the Murray River. He was one of a number of Aboriginal people who, around that time, began to forge lasting Christian communities. Within the constraints of their various contexts, Aboriginal Christians began to exercise more and more leadership. This development was paralleled by the formation of no fewer than forty-five new missions among Indigenous Australians between 1914 and 1939, including several affiliated with the Aborigines Inland Mission (AIM). In 1938, the AIM opened the first Aboriginal Christian training college.[77] Its publications for Aboriginal people celebrated conversions as well as instances of Indigenous initiative and independence in sharing the Bible with others. In time AIM networks, and emerging Indigenous churches more generally, provided a conduit for all kinds of Indigenous social and political activism – including those concerned with civil rights and land ownership.

As early as 1887, William Cooper was appealing to his local member of parliament with biblical arguments for land tenure: 'As there have been no grants of land made to our tribe … I do trust that you will be successful in securing this small portion of a vast territory which is ours by Divine Right'.[78] In 1893 he married Agnes Hamilton, one of the exiles from Coranderrk, and joined in the campaign against closing the reserves. When war broke out in 1914 their son Daniel enlisted. A member of the 24th Australian Infantry battalion, Private Cooper was killed in action in Belgium on 20 September 1917. He was buried in Perth Cemetery, Ypres, under a cross inscribed 'Father's Son'. The bereaved William came to think that Australia did not deserve the loyalty of its Indigenous people: 'the Aboriginal now has no status, no rights, no land … he has no country and nothing to fight for but the privilege of defending the land which was taken from him by the white race without compensation or even kindness'.[79]

Cooper devoted his own life to what he called the 'uplift' of 'the whole dark race'. He helped forge the Australian Aborigines League, which sought to work with white Christians to achieve 'emancipation'. Paying tribute to the 'generally unselfish … work of all denominations among the Aboriginal population', he looked for missionary co-operation. At the same time, he insisted that his own people held the potential to achieve transformation: 'The Aboriginal must be a partner in his own uplift … he must "work out his own salvation"' (Philippians 2:12).[80]

Much of Cooper's activism fell on deaf ears. Only small groups within the settler community seemed able to hear such ideas and critiques – in some cases enabled by a connection to Indigenous Christian missions, and a Christian theology that made space to admit wrongdoing. 'The time is past when we can close our eyes to facts and our hearts to the sorrows of these people', wrote Annie Thompson in the magazine *Ministering Women*. 'So shall Australians begin to make reparation for the deeds for which the world condemns us and the people of this fair land realise their responsibilities to those whom we have dispossessed.'[81] Or as the journal of the usually conservative Anglican Mothers Union put it in an article in the 1930s: 'The shame of it all lies like a black stain over the fair face of our nation's history. Do we not owe them reparation? What can we do to atone for the past?'[82]

In 1938, when white Australia marked its 150th anniversary, most non-Indigenous people saw cause to celebrate rather than to repent and atone. To Cooper and several of his colleagues, it was abundantly clear that this was not, in practice, a mature Christian nation. At Cooper's suggestion, Indigenous leaders gathered in Sydney to observe 26 January as a Day of Mourning. As white Australians celebrated, Cooper and his colleagues directed attention to all their people had lost, and to their aspiration for full citizenship.[83] This powerful political gesture made headlines, and instigated a public critique of Australia Day that remains potent decades later. In the 1940s, Cooper's associated efforts to establish the nearest Sunday as a National Aborigines Day was taken up by several churches, and eventually led to the designation of NAIDOC (National Aborigines and Islanders Day Observance Committee) week.

Crucially, for Cooper, the theological Bible helped expose the failures of settler Australia. It was a text that crossed cultural boundaries, that in his hands undermined imperial and nationalist conceits. At the same time, he found in the Bible an affirmation of the inherent equality and dignity of Aboriginal people, of their right to fair treatment, and of their ownership of the land as a God-given heritage. In Cooper's hands, the Bible not only sharpened his critique of colonialism, it nourished his vision for a more truly Christian community. He called on white politicians, as Christians, to live out the principles of their shared Scriptures.

In March 1938, Cooper wrote to Prime Minister Lyons 'from the standpoint of an educated black who can read the Bible upon which British constitution and custom is founded':

White men … claimed they had 'found' a 'new' country – Australia. This country was not new, it was already in possession of and inhabited by millions of blacks, who, while unarmed, excepting spears and boomerangs, nevertheless owned the country as their God-given heritage.

I marvel at the fact that while the textbook of present civilisation, the Bible, states that God gave the earth to man, the 'Christian' interferes with God's arrangement and stop not even at murder to take that which does not belong to them but belongs to others by right of prior possession and by right of gift from God.

Every shape and form of murder, yes, mass murder, was used against us and laws were passed and still exist, which no human creature can endure. Our food stuffs have been destroyed, poison and guns have done their work, and now white men's homes have been built on our hunting and camping grounds. Our lives have been wrecked and our happiness ended. Oh! Ye whites!

How much compensation have we had? How much of our land has been paid for? Not one iota. Again we state that we are the original owners of the country. In spite of force, prestige, or anything else you like, morally the land is ours. We have been ejected and despoiled of our God-given right and our inheritance has been forcibly taken from us.

When we learn … the history of the manner in which we have been treated these last 150 years, our confidence in the professed Christian nation – standing for good government justice and freedom – is sadly shaken.

It is unfair to treat us as a people of low mentality with treacherous tendencies who cannot be taught anything … In the sight of God we are as valuable as other men, and we feel sure that we could be taught, and we merely ask for an opportunity to prove that we can.

Are you prepared to admit that, since the Creator said in his Word that all men are of 'one blood' we are humans with feelings like yourselves in the eyes of Almighty God, that we can have joys and our sorrows, our likes and our dislikes, that we can feel pain, degradation, and humiliation just as you do? If you admit that, will you like true men do your bit to see a great injustice at least mollified by agitating for us to get a fair deal before it is too late?[84]

Cooper's questions – his challenge to white nationhood – remain significant today. They go to the heart of what it might mean for the Bible to continue to shape the Australian nation.

PART 4

A SECULAR AUSTRALIA?

Robert Menzies was the guest of honour at the opening of Bible House, Canberra, in February 1960. Comfortably ensconced as prime minister of Cold War Australia, he gave a speech outlining his views on the Bible's place in the nation and the world. The Bible Society itself, for which the building provided new headquarters, had 'a more truly international character' than any other organisation he could think of, he said: 'Its business is to make the Bible, or portions of the Bible, available to as many millions or hundreds of millions as can be reached'. The occasion certainly pointed to the expanding work of hard-copy distribution around the world. In Menzies' era and beyond, the globalising Bible was alive and well.

The opening of Bible House also suggested the privileged position of Christian institutions and ideas in Australian society. The federal government had donated £15 000 towards its construction. Its location, in central Canberra, embodied the idea that the Bible was to be held and valued at the heart of the nation. The prime minister himself imagined a Christian Australia – a nation in which 'we ought to read' and 'many of us ... constantly *do* read' the Bible. Menzies believed that 'this great and immortal book' was the proper focus of households and the root of true citizenship. It could bind a nation together, providing a point of unity even for those who disagreed on the finer points of theology. He told the crowd: 'The story is there, the history is there, the great gospel is there, the whole spirit of Christianity is there'. In Menzies' view, the Bible was 'the repository of our faith and of our inspiration'.

Menzies acknowledged that not everyone in Australia was willing to identify as Christian. According to the census of 1961, 0.7 per cent of people adhered to another religion, 0.4 per cent claimed to have none at all, and about 10 per cent gave no answer. But Menzies expected the Bible to engage virtually everyone – including agnostics and atheists – as 'the greatest piece of literature in the history of man'. He thought the Bible far superior to what passed for political discourse, for instance, and recommended the Authorised Version to anyone who wanted to understand English at its finest. Altogether, for Menzies, the Bible was a religious and cultural treasure – the text that defined the Australian people.[1]

The Bible was a visible presence in Menzies's Australia. By certain external measures, the nation was more Christian in the 1950s than it had been at federation. But there were changes afoot that soon became pronounced, affecting the churches, the shape of belief, and the ways Australians interacted with the Bible. These changes do not conform to a simple narrative of secularisation or religious decline. But they have transformed the Australian story of the Bible.

CHAPTER 10

THE TURNING POINT

By the sheer test of numbers, Robert Menzies governed an over-whelmingly Christian population. At census time the majority identified with one of the major denominations, and actual church participation increased during the 1950s – as it did in the United States, the United Kingdom, Canada and New Zealand.[1] Especially in the new suburbs of Australia's major cities and among the young families of the baby boom, both Sunday school enrolments and membership of Christian youth associations rose. Adults, too, became more seriously involved in churches. In Brisbane, for instance, Presbyterian church membership increased by more than a third in the five years to 1960. Methodist membership grew by a quarter, and Anglican confirmations swelled by 50 per cent in ten years.[2] The upswing meant that, by 1960, one in three Australian adults claimed to attend church almost weekly or more.[3] It was as if a generation sought in the churches the nurture and stability they craved after the devastation of war.

The significance of religion went well beyond people's denominational identities and churchgoing habits. In the political sphere, Menzies' own long incumbency was enabled partly by the divisions in the Labor Party, which themselves had much to do with certain expressions of political Catholicism. In education, Catholic schools received a boost from Menzies' 1963 decision to reverse nearly a century of settled policy and reintroduce direct government funding for church-affiliated schools. In the public system, too, religious education was growing. Legislative change made religious instruction permissible in South Australia in 1940, while Victoria allowed it in normal school hours – not just outside them – from the 1950s on. School-based student groups, such as Crusaders and the Inter School Christian Fellowship, were well attended through the 1940s, 1950s and 1960s. On university campuses, affiliates of the Student Christian Movement and the evangelical Intervarsity Fellowship engaged the attention of many hundreds of students. Many of them went on to their professional lives carrying something of their campus Christian experience. Future Labor Prime Minister Bob Hawke and Sir Ronald Wilson – High Court judge, Human Rights Commissioner and co-author of the *Bringing Them Home* Report – were among them.[4]

In popular culture, too, religion was a notable presence. American film after film offered creative reinterpretations of Bible stories for mass audiences: this was the heyday of the Hollywood Bible epic, eagerly watched by moviegoers when they were shown in Australian cinemas. Blockbusters included *Samson and Delilah* (1949), *Quo Vadis* (1951), *The Robe* (1953), *Ben Hur* (1959), and *The King of Kings* (1961) – all making use of the narrative and setting of the Christian Scriptures. The most extravagant film of this genre was Cecil B DeMille's *The Ten Commandments* (1956), starring Charlton Heston as Moses and Yul Brynner as Rameses II. The Technicolor version of 1956 was even more lavish than his 1920s original, as DeMille, by then in his seventies, pursued his vision with little humility and few limits: 'My ministry has been to make religious movies and get more people to read the Bible than anyone else ever has'.[5] When adjusted for inflation, global takings place *The Ten Commandments* among the most successful films in box office history.

On radio, religious broadcasting was also reaching its peak. Kenneth Thorne Henderson was an Oxford graduate, former war chaplain and ordained Anglican minister. He headed the first department of religious programming for the Australian Broadcasting Commission (ABC) from 1949 through to the mid-1950s. Aiming 'at supplementing the work of the churches', he built up a list of twenty-eight programs, covering doctrinal, mythological, ethical, ritual, experimental and social dimensions of religion, including by presenting the Christian church at worship. Monday to Saturday there was a *Daily Devotion* and a reading from the Bible.[6] By the late 1940s, virtually all commercial stations also featured regular religious programs. Dr Leslie Rumble, a Catholic priest, had a weekly *Question Box* program that ran for an extraordinary forty years, initially on 2UE and then on 2SM. He spoke in a voice 'like worn sandpaper, giving an effect of common sense and rationality', and when anyone asked what the Church taught on a subject, he quoted the Bible.[7] (His replies were republished as short books that went on to sell millions of copies around the world.) Other well-known presenters included the Seventh Day Adventist Laurie Naden, whose half-hour program was syndicated to more than fifty commercial stations by 1950, and Methodist Alan Walker, whose polished Christian drama series rated solidly across the country.[8]

The visibility of the Bible reached its twentieth-century peak in 1959, when the American evangelist Billy Graham toured Australia and New Zealand. For fifteen weeks, Graham preached a message of sin, judgment, forgiveness and salvation – emphasising his key points with that favourite phrase 'The Bible says ...'. Welcomed by politicians, judges and the mainstream press, he spoke on radio and television, and gave interviews to *Women's Weekly* and the local press. He preached at 114 separate meetings to a total audience numbering in the millions. Graham's final rally, at the Melbourne Cricket Ground, attracted 143 750 people – the largest crowd he had ever addressed and still a ground attendance record. It was a triumph of organisation and interdenominational co-operation, the pinnacle of public religion in post-war Australia.

Graham's crusade assumed that Australia was a Christian nation in need of renewal: it assumed people had a working knowledge of the Bible but needed to hear the call to personal conversion. For novelist Patrick White, hearing Graham confirmed that evangelical presentations of Christianity were inadequate to meet the needs of the times or the longings of the human heart. White went on to write several books and plays preoccupied with the possibilities of belief, yet unsatisfied with Christian theology. For others, though, hearing Graham involved a fresh and enlarging understanding of the Scriptures. Deane Meatheringham recalled going along reluctantly and feeling uncertain during the service. The evangelist preached on Noah, and then appealed for people to come forward:

> I just stood there, resolved that I could never do that. But as the crowds moved to the front, Billy kept repeating Ephesians 2.8–9 – 'For by grace are ye saved through faith; and that not of yourselves: it is the gift of God: Not of works, lest any man should boast'. Almost imperceptibly … it dawned on me … Salvation was something God gave me. It was as though I was let out of a box. I was free. I wanted to run, and I did.[9]

Overall, nearly 131 000 Australians – roughly 1.24 per cent of the whole population – 'went forward' in response to Graham's message. In the immediate aftermath, church congregations swelled, theological college enrolments rose, and there was a spike in requests for Bible reading guides published by Scripture Union (SU).[10] In fact, national SU membership almost doubled to 104 400 people between March 1958 and November 1959.[11] A number of those who became Christians at that time went on to became leaders and missionaries of the Australian churches – including Meatheringham, who became a Methodist minister, and Peter Jensen, Anglican Archbishop of Sydney.

THE VISIBLE RELIGION OF THE 1950s HIGHLIGHTS THE NEED for a more complex view of the twentieth century than simple secularisation. To at least some in the churches, the modest religious boom of the 1950s suggested that Australia was finally embracing the kind of 'righteousness that exalteth a nation'. But after the early 1960s, there was a pronounced contraction in the social reach and position of the churches in Australian life – and with it, a decline in most people's Christian socialisation and exposure to the theological Bible. A changing media landscape affected the Bible's visibility in mainstream culture, while shifting habits of reading reduced the Bible's prominence in many people's personal lives. Overall levels of Bible engagement fell, and the social base of biblical literacy shifted and shrank.

From the 1960s, those who remained felt the effects of Vatican II, which reshaped the place of the Bible in Catholic life and worship, and the formation of the uniquely Australian Uniting Church.[12] At the same time, for these churchgoers, as for Australians more generally, political movements for women's liberation, anti-racism, and demanding social, economic or environmental justice all posed tough questions about the Bible's meaning and relevance. Rather than a simple case of the secular clashing with the religious, or 'the world' opposing 'the church', these movements were partly related to new theologies and new ways of understanding Scripture. In the longer term, they added heat and complexity to the question of what the Bible might have to offer Australian society.

Going to church

John Button, a church minister's son, spent much of his childhood at church – playing sport in a Presbyterian cricket team, going to Presbyterian socials, and attending Sunday services. This was not unusual in the 1930s and 1940s, as many suburban congregations hosted their own sports clubs, youth groups, musical ensembles, and Scout and Guide troops. By the 1980s, though, when Button served as a minister in the Hawke Labor government, such a childhood was no longer possible in Australia. The churches did not have the same social reach, and far fewer people went along on Sundays or for special services. Between 1972 and 2014, the proportion of Australians attending worship at least once a month fell by more than half from 36 to 15 per cent.[13] More occasional forms of church participation – to mark major life events, for instance – also dropped sharply. After 1973, when the Whitlam government allowed civil celebrants to marry people in various settings, not just at the registry office, the number of marriages conducted with a religious rite declined from 84 per cent to just 27 per cent by 2013.[14] Baptisms and funerals are harder to track, but a similar trend is apparent.[15] This suggests that, while Prayer Book phrases like 'for richer, for poorer' still reverberate in popular culture, biblical commentary on baptism, marriage and death has become unfamiliar, even strange, to significant sections of the population. More generally, far fewer Australians encounter certain theological ideas, ethics and interpretations of the Bible through the churches. Since the 1960s, this has mattered enormously to its place in society and culture.

LARGE-SCALE DISAFFILIATION FROM THE CHURCHES HAS been evident in most other parts of the late twentieth-century West. It is one element of what historians have sometimes called the crisis of Christianity in its former strongholds of Europe, north America, and white-majority settler societies such as Australia and New Zealand. But it does not make up the whole story of the twentieth-century church in global perspective – nor is it the only significant feature of church life in Australia.[16] Here, too, the reach and influence of the church changed in uneven ways – with consequences for who, exactly, commonly encountered the theological Bible through the institutions of faith.

In Australia, the narrative of church decline correlates most closely with the experience of the older, British-origin Protestant denominations – Anglican, Presbyterian and Methodist. For well over a century, these three plus the Catholic church claimed the affiliation of at least 80 per cent of Australians. Between 1961 and 2016, however, their proportion of adherents dropped by half, accounting for much of the overall decline in levels of Christian affiliation at the census.[17] It is hard to know how much of this drop was *caused* by rising disbelief in the theological Bible, but one *effect* was that a shrinking proportion of Australians came within the orbit of the mainstream churches and regularly interacted with the Bible through them.

Still, some remarkable examples of vibrancy, transformation and renewal emerged. Some related to the gradual unravelling of the White Australia Policy in the post-war decades and the emergence of a positively multicultural nation in the 1980s. The increasingly diverse population bolstered the presence of non-Christian religions in the general community; it also added new texture and richness to Australian Christianity. Australian Catholicism, for instance, had been distinctly Irish before 1947, but was gradually reshaped by Italian, Maltese, Yugoslav, Polish, German, Dutch, Hungarian, Baltic, Lebanese, Indian, Sri Lankan, Vietnamese and Philippine Catholic immigrants.[18] (This is in fact a major reason why the proportion of Australians identifying as Catholic remained fairly stable over the second half of the twentieth century.) Hovering between 23 and 27 per cent of the population, Catholics have, since 1981, comprised the largest single Christian denomination in Australia.

At the same time, post-war migration spurred a rise in churches associated with non-British cultural groups, and introduced significant new communities who practised other forms of Christianity. To name just a few: Russians, Greeks, Lebanese and many others brought various forms of Orthodoxy; the Dutch brought the Reformed tradition; Indians brought Mar Thoma and other Christianities. By the early 1990s, there were fifty-two Korean churches just in Sydney, and over 75 per cent of Koreans living in Australia claimed to be Christian, compared with about 20 per cent in Korea itself.[19] Chinese immigrants formed distinct congregations within many Christian denominations. All together, new migrant churches added both vibrancy and strength to Christianity in Australia, bucking the trend of declining church affiliation that characterised the older British denominations.

Each Christian tradition expresses the Bible differently in their cultures and liturgies, has specific versions and translations of the text itself, and uses and interprets it in particular ways. As such, new migrant churches have been conduits for non-British forms of the Bible in Australia. They have also provided new centres for the theological and devotional Bible in the wider community. By the 1990s, people born in non-English-speaking countries were much more likely to attend church frequently than those born here (31 compared to 19 per cent).[20] In the early 2010s, twice as many recent immigrants attended religious services at least once a month as did Australians born of Australian parents.[21] Just as the global church is no longer predominately Western, the church in Australia is heading in a similar direction – adding urgency to the task of sifting the Bible from its British cultural trappings.

The spectacular growth of Pentecostalism adds another complication to the story of church decline in the post-war era. The movement had congregations in Australia from the early twentieth century, but entered a phase of rapid growth in the 1970s and 1980s – the very time when many people were leaving or avoiding the mainstream denominations. Pentecostals tended to value the Bible as the accurate and authoritative word of God, applicable to everyday life, while emphasising the Holy Spirit more than many traditional Protestant churches. Offering a more contemporary form of worship and stressing the possibility of a direct experience of God, Pentecostal churches attracted significant numbers of young people. Overall, in the fifty years from 1961 to 2011, Australian Pentecostals grew in number from roughly 16 000 to around a quarter of a million. In the process they formed more than 1000 congregations and created the largest churches ever seen in Australia – such as Hillsong in Sydney, Paradise Community Church (now Influencers Church) in Adelaide, Planetshakers in Melbourne and Hope Centre in Brisbane.[22]

A third area of post-war transformation occurred in the sphere of school education. In the public system, large numbers of schools, particularly at primary level, offered some form of religious education. The private system, comprising mainly Catholic and other church-affiliated schools, saw enrolments rise from 22 per cent of all Australian students in 1970 to just under 35 per cent in 2016.[23] In contrast to the level of church participation, this rise in enrolments suggests another shift, since the 1960s, in where Australians actually engage with the Bible. Of course, there has been (and still is) considerable variation in the overt religiosity of church-affiliated schools: how many such schools, like charities, have relegated Christianity to the heritage category? Even schools that see the presentation and cultivation of Christian faith as central to their mission may in practice provide a patchy biblical education. That said, most schools in the non-government sector have afforded their students some interaction with Christianity and its Scriptures – perhaps though religious education classes, chaplaincy groups, special assemblies, school masses or chapel services.

Half a century after Menzies, about 8 per cent of Australians can be found in church on any given Sunday.[24] This means participating in church remains a relatively significant occupation. For instance, twice as many Australians go to a service at least monthly as attend all AFL, NRL, A League and Super Rugby games combined per month during the football season.[25] There are more people in the pews from week to week than in all of South Australia.[26] The social reach of the churches extends even further in terms of the schools, preschools, care and welfare services that are part of the lives of many Australians. In all their variety, too, churches are thickly interwoven into the fabric of a multicultural nation.

Overall, however, levels of church involvement are much lower in the 2010s than in the 1950s, and possibly lower than at any other time since the British arrived. The overarching fact is that, over the past half-century, fewer and fewer Australians have been exposed to the public reading and preaching of the theological Bible, to its inculcation though church liturgy, to the repetition of its phrases through song and hymnody. A shrinking proportion of people have belonged to a community in which the Bible was openly valued as God's word. This, in turn, has made the theological Bible less prominent in the ways people construct their personal identities and life narratives, as well as the ways they understand their society, the world, and God.

Fragments in the air

Alan Walker had high hopes for the Australian media. As leader of the Methodist 'Mission to the Nation' in the early 1950s, Superintendent of Sydney's Wesley Mission and founder of the Lifeline phone counselling service, he anticipated that the public broadcaster, in particular, would play 'a very real part' in a 'quickening of Christian faith' around the nation.[27] After all, the mainstream press had played a substantial role in placing the Bible before the people, reporting sermons, lectures and the activities of various Christian organisations, as well as the latest popular scholarship and controversies. Both public and commercial radio broadcasters designated significant space to religious programs, including daily readings from the Bible, often aired in the morning prime time, right before the news.[28] By 1956, when Ken Henderson retired from religious programming at the ABC, it had a suite of shows including some that depicted the churches at worship, and others that presented the Christian faith in creative ways to unchurched audiences.

Like the churches, however, Australian radio and print media experienced major changes from the 1960s on, not least in the way the Bible was placed before the general population. At the ABC, weekday Bible readings became the focus of secular antagonism during the 1970s. In 1984 they became sacred readings that included texts from other religions and secular writers, finally ceasing entirely in early 1991. On the commercial stations, daily Bible readings and similar segments were increasingly re-scheduled outside of peak periods, and the free airtime allowed for religious programs came under increasing pressure. (As the number of free hours dropped, religious groups increased the number of hours they sponsored – a shift that fringe groups seemed to make more readily than the mainstream churches.) One consequence was that consumers of mainstream media in the 1970s and 1980s were less likely to have an incidental encounter with the Bible than people a generation earlier.[29]

A more significant trend concerned the way in which religion was actually presented – a trend away from its devotional aspects towards more detached, secular reportage. An early sign of this shift was the introduction of the *Frontier* program on the ABC. It was the initiative of Henderson's successor as head of religious programing, the Reverend Dr John Munro, an Anglican minister from Victoria with degrees in philosophy, comparative religion and social anthropology. Munro believed that the way Christian faith responded to the ultimate questions raised by human experience had a particular status in a society historically shaped by Christianity. But he also recognised that they could not properly claim a monopoly of the airwaves in what he judged to be a modern, plural society. Surely other world religions and secular ideologies also had a legitimate place – and the key was to convey 'the struggle of all involved ... to face the truth honestly'? In 1958, Munro introduced *Frontier* as an international religious news program. It broke new ground in offering a journalistic treatment of religious issues, reporting *about* religion from the outside rather than presenting it from the inside, according to its adherents.[30]

The less devotional, more secular presentation of religion on the ABC continued after the mid-1970s. The reference panel of church leaders was disbanded and not replaced by any other external consultative group, leaving program-makers to be guided by their own knowledge, interests and judgment. In this context, historian Alison Healey has noted a growing 'predominance of programs in the form of documentaries, interviews, news and comment'. Such programs covered different religious and spiritual paths more comprehensively, but offered a narrower range of listening experiences.[31] This probably meant that the Bible had a less theological presence on the ABC than it had in the 1950s – that it was presented less often in authoritative terms, or as part of devotional life and practice.

THE CHANGES OF THE LATE 1960s AND AFTERWARDS DID NOT spell the end of the Bible in public conversation, or in Australian culture more broadly. The churches were still relatively prominent, often allied closely to civil authorities. Religion was still a significant theme of print and radio journalism, and biblical phrases continued to surface in both casual language and political discourse. From the novels of Patrick White and the paintings of Arthur Boyd to the hit 1970s musicals *Godspell* and *Jesus Christ Superstar*, the Bible remained a vivid dialogue partner in the arts. But compared with the 1950s, and especially with the great age of the Bible, the Bible was less visible in late twentieth-century culture and society. The extent to which institutions like the media and the church actually placed the Bible before the people was decreasing. Crucially, it was the theological Bible, rather than the Bible in a more secular guise, whose presence in common culture receded most. People continued to encounter it outside Christian communities and institutions – but less often, and less deeply, as the Word of God. By the 1980s, familiarity with the theological Bible was no longer a typical by-product of an Australian upbringing or socialisation.

Reading the Bible

Once, in the winter of 1982, Ian Sexton found himself on an Aboriginal mission station in the very north of western Australia – sleeping within ten metres of live estuarine crocodiles, separated by mere chicken wire![32] Sexton was a 'flying Bibleman', employed by the Bible Society to carry the good book to people in rural and remote communities. He survived the crocodiles at Kalumburu to visit mining towns, cattle stations and other Indigenous missions scattered over one million square kilometres, from the Kimberley region through the whole Northern Territory to western Queensland and the Torres Strait.[33] His job as an aerial colporteur was to make Bibles available where they were otherwise difficult to obtain, to preach and teach the Word, and to provide local Christians with pastoral care, help and encouragement. It was a ministry the Bible Society maintained for decades from 1968 until 2015, a sign of its undiminished commitment to making the Bible available to literally every Australian.

HARD COPY BIBLES REMAINED UBIQUITOUS IN TWENTIETH-century Australia. In terms of new distribution, the overall trajectory was one of growth until at least the 1970s. To give a snapshot, the Bible Society circulated nearly 116 890 Scriptures throughout Australia in 1914; between 169 000 and 203 000 a year during the Depression decade of the 1930s; and over 400 000 a year right through the second half of the 1960s. In 1971, for the first time, the figure for Australia cracked half a million. These totals include full Bibles, New Testaments and 'portions' comprising at least one book (often one of the gospels). The Society also circulated shorter 'selections' at a rate of tens or even hundreds of thousands annually.[34] It is not surprising, then, that in 1960 nine out of ten Australians had a Bible in their homes – rivalled only by a cookery book and a dictionary (owned by 91 and 89 per cent of people, respectively). It far outdid atlases, encyclopedias and works by Shakespeare (owned by 42 per cent of people), and every other kind of book.[35]

From the 1960s on, levels of new Bible distribution were buoyed by the appearance of new English translations. The publication of the *New English Version* in 1961 caused a spike in Bible Society sales. It also gave a welcome shock to some Australian readers like John Harris: 'It was so exciting. You've got no idea. This new Bible was in our contemporary language!'[36] Then in 1966, the *Good News* translation of the New Testament appeared, followed by a complete *Good News Bible* in late 1976. Highly readable, it was a runaway hit – far outselling every other book previously published in Australia's history. In just fifteen months, sales topped a quarter of a million.[37] By October 1982, a million Good News Bibles had been sold across the country, meaning that one in every fifteen Australians had a copy.[38] Over the same period, the *New International Version* also sold over 100 000 copies.[39] Such demand for fresh translations underscores that there were still plenty of shekels in the Bible business, into and beyond the 1980s. It raises the question: what did Australians *do* with all these Bibles? How and how much did people read them? Was Bible reading an increasingly individual, private activity, as the institutions promoting it in society declined?

In 1960, a Gallup poll found that nine out of ten people had a Bible in their homes, but, in 39 per cent of cases, it was just gathering dust. The other 61 per cent of Bible owners picked it up at least once a year, including 38 per cent who had read it within the previous two weeks. That's a high level, compared to the 2010s: more than a third of adults read the Bible at least once a fortnight. But even so, a lot of the reading seems to have been shallow, rather than deep. The same poll found that only 15 per cent of respondents could agree, correctly, that the New Testament book of Acts did *not* give an account of Jesus' life on earth (it traces the expansion of the church after Jesus' ascension to heaven). A similar poll, conducted a few years earlier in the 1950s, found that only 23 per cent of Australian adults had read their Bibles for *at least ten minutes* in the previous fortnight – suggesting that many only read it in a brief, cursory manner, if at all.[40]

Even as reading habits continued to shift, printed texts themselves lost some of their weight and significance. Especially in the post-war era, reading of any kind became just one of many possible leisure activities. The relaxation of Sabbath laws, rising car ownership, and above all the advent of television meant that people had a lot more choice about how to spend their free time – especially their Sunday afternoons and evenings. Television became available in Australia in 1956, just in time for the Melbourne Olympics. Most households had a set by the mid-1960s.[41] For the Bible, the rise of television exposed huge new audiences to the great Hollywood biblical epics – in this sense, television carried Bible stories to thousands who would not have read them.[42] But more substantially, watching television soon eclipsed reading as a leisure activity. By the late 1990s, Australians spent at least four times as long watching television as reading anything.[43] In 2006, Australian adults spent an average of just twenty-three minutes a day reading, and only 48 per cent of people read any kind of book at least once a week.

How did Bible-reading fare? There is some evidence to suggest it stood up better than most other books. In 2002, a random sample of Australian adults was asked what they had read in relation to religion during the previous year. By far the most common response was the Bible, nominated by 29 per cent of people.[44] Notably, 8 per cent of respondents also claimed to read the Bible *frequently*. Overall, though, the comparison between 2002 and 1960 is very revealing: the proportion of annual Bible readers had dropped by half, and regular readers by three-quarters. In little more than a generation, the proportion of Australians who never picked up a Bible for themselves had leapt to seven out of ten.[45]

A challenge to authority

Germaine Greer grew up in war-time Melbourne, in a home she later described as one of relative cultural deprivation. There were only twenty books in the maple bookcase of her parents' sitting room, including a collection of Shakespeare, but not a Bible among them. She attended local Catholic schools, in step with her mother's professed faith. In 1952, she won a scholarship to a convent school, Star of the Sea College, Gardenvale, run by the Irish order of the Sisters of the Presentation of the Blessed Virgin Mary. There she learned about art and languages and the mysterious power of sex – taking it upon herself, at times, to read more on that subject.

One of Greer's younger schoolmates, Moira Curtin, recalls Greer taking her to the library. It was housed in a classroom with locked glass-fronted cupboards:

> I don't know whether she forced the lock, or whether some
> books like the Bible were left open. But she'd say: 'If you want
> to come up to the library, I'll show you the dirty bits in the
> Bible'. I used to go staggering up, absolutely intrigued. I'd
> never heard of Onan and his seed.[46]

(Greer showed Curtin the story, in Genesis chapter 38, about a young man who ejaculated on to the ground rather than fulfil his legal duty to his brother's widow – thus preventing a pregnancy, preserving his own inheritance, and displeasing the Lord.)

One of the nuns, Sister Eymard, tried to teach the girls the philosophical proofs of the existence of God. Greer recalls that she 'thereby destroyed my faith completely because she didn't know them. Rather, she did know them but they weren't valid'. (Greer later mused that perhaps she should have been taught by Jesuits, who would have taken such matters more seriously.) At any rate Greer abandoned her earnest teenage faith in the year after she left school:

> One of the sources of conflict that was distressing me during
> my first year of university was the collapse of my Catholic faith
> and my unwilling arrival at the conclusion that there was no
> God. Once that had been decided, there were no rules about
> anything else, either. I found myself thinking very hard about
> virginity and the morality of all that petting in parked cars.[47]

Greer's vibrant university career was capped by a scholarship to Cambridge, where she wrote a doctoral thesis on 'The Ethic of Love and Marriage in Shakespeare's Early Comedies'. Combining an academic career with radical journalism and devotion to women's liberation, she became an international celebrity when

The Female Eunuch was published in 1970. It was a wide-ranging manifesto, but among other things, it railed against the 'Christian' virtues claimed by her mother's generation, and the church's traditional teaching on the family from the Bible. 'We could see that our mothers black-mailed us with self-sacrifice, even if we did not know whether or not they might have been great opera stars or the toasts of the town if they had not borne us.' Similarly at school, Greer and other girls were 'encouraged to deny ourselves in order to give to others' – only to find that, again, the rhetoric rang hollow. 'We ate no sweets and put our pennies in a red and yellow box with a piccaninny on the front for the missions, if we were holy that is … The essential egotism of the practice was apparent to many of us in the demeanour of the most pious girls, for the aim of the exercise was ultimately to earn grace in the eyes of the Lord. Every such act had to be offered up, or else the heavenly deposit was not made to our account.' It was hardly divine grace, if it had to be earned – but to the adult Greer, the hypocrisy of the scenario was all too obvious.

When it came to Christian teaching on women, sexuality and the family, Greer argued that much of what passed for a timeless norm was a culturally embedded myth. The whole idea of falling in love and getting married, for example, was a middle-class Protestant invention, foreign to the medieval period. The Bible itself also had much to answer for, Greer said. Genesis, in particular, provided a precedent for blaming and shaming women for men's failures: 'The woman tempted me, and I did eat'. At the same time, Greer suggested, the Bible was a more complex text than the churches usually allowed: 'the grandsons of Adam consorted with the daughters of the flesh'; the Old Testament patriarchal family was 'ambiguous'; and somewhere in the Apocrypha lurked Lilith, 'the destructive woman, who offered love and licentiousness and threatened the family structure'.[48]

Greer articulated a furious challenge to traditional authority and demanded a new way of being that came to characterise the cultural upheavals of the 1960s and 1970s. Her critique of the church and its Bible was bound up with a larger criticism of structures that she judged limiting for women and obstructive to their full self-expression. It also resonated, at least faintly, with radical new movements in Christian theology, which produced new ways of approaching and interpreting the Bible.

THE FERMENT OF THE 1960s AND 1970s INCLUDED VIGOROUS disputes about the Bible's authority in social life. Some of that was part of a wider, intergenerational argument about traditional versus post-traditional society. Some of it, though, was concerned specifically with the Bible. How did Scripture, and particularly mainstream church interpretations of Scripture, contribute to cultures and structures that oppressed certain groups – women, the poor, people of colour? Was the Bible part of the problem, or part of the solution? Germaine Greer had her views, but her contemporaries in Australia expressed a broad spectrum of responses.

At one end were people outside the churches who had already abandoned the Bible as an authoritative theological text – and who came to see it as irrelevant and unnecessary in social and moral terms as well. Greer, for instance, had decided that Christianity was untrue and that church teaching on morality therefore had no ultimate basis. The Bible and its various interpretations were not divine revelations but the cultural products of a certain time and place, to be criticised and discarded because they obstructed the goal of women's liberation.

More common, perhaps, were those who found the churches' teaching on social and moral issues unhelpful, even oppressive, for life in the sixties – and as a result left their former community of faith and, with it, its Scriptures. Historians have noted that many young Australian Catholics felt pushed to this point by the papal encyclical *Humanae Vitae* of 1968. Among other things, it reaffirmed a negative view of birth control, shaped in part by the story of Onan in Genesis. The contraceptive pill had been available for seven years by then, and a fair proportion of Catholic women in Australia apparently did not, in practice, accept the church's pronouncements against it. Some also came into painful conflict with their priests and other members of their congregations over the issue. Historian Anne O'Brien suggests that so many younger women were lost to the church this way that no Catholic feminist group formed in these years.[49] Despite this exodus, women still made up the majority of regular church attenders in Australia.[50]

AUSTRALIANS HAD ALWAYS DEBATED EXACTLY WHAT Christian ethics entailed, and held a diversity of views about how ethics and law properly related. But for the long period from the colonial Church Acts of the 1830s to the 1950s, the idea that religion, and specifically a common, non-dogmatic kind of Christianity, nourished an ethical citizenship, had been a mainstay of public policy, and probably also of popular opinion. Even in the late nineteenth century, when popular debates about the new science and higher criticism were at their loudest, few had denied that Christianity was a sound cradle for morality and a proper basis for civil life. By the 1970s, however, this seemed to be changing as people reappraised the family, marriage, divorce, abortion and sexual ethics more generally.

In this context, some readers interacted more closely and attentively with the Bible – either to review and reaffirm traditional theologies, or to explore new questions and perspectives. What did the Bible actually say about women? About the family? About liberation? What was the relationship between the text, the teachings of the church, and wider cultures that privileged the experiences and aspirations of men? A precedent for feminist readings had been set back in the 1890s, when the ageing American radical, Elizabeth Cady Stanton, had initiated *The Woman's Bible* (1895).[51] For many Christians in post-1960s Australia, the crucial issue was not the Bible's authority, but how to interpret it.

Marie Tulip was born in 1935, four years before Germaine Greer, into a middle-class Presbyterian home in Mackay, north Queensland. After boarding school in Brisbane and an Arts degree with Honours in French, she went to Illinois, in the United States, where she completed a higher degree and became a tertiary teacher. Returning to Australia in the 1960s, she worked at Sydney and Macquarie universities, where she introduced a postgraduate diploma in the Teaching of English as a Second Language and became the driving force behind the publication of texts which gave special help to migrant women.[52]

During this period, Tulip read feminist work emerging from America by Betty Friedan, various theologians, and poets like Denise Levertov. (A few years later, she also read Germaine Greer.) Seeing the relevance to her own life, she became engrossed in feminist theology and politics. In 1968, Tulip founded Christian Women Concerned, the first explicitly religious feminist organisation in Australia. Its newsletter, *Magdalene*, was full of the language of women's liberation as well as the language of Scripture. Paul's words in Galatians 3:28 were often cited: 'there can be no male or female, for we are all one in Jesus Christ'.[53]

Tulip became one of Australia's 'warrior women of liberation theology'.[54] She developed university courses on feminism and religion that introduced students to new ideas, authors and perspectives, and eventually published several works in the field. From 1973, she also co-ordinated the NSW Council of Churches' Commission on the Status of Women. According to social historian Shurlee Swain, the Commission's conferences attracted women from across the country, while its involvement with International Women's Year in 1975 'injected a spiritual element into what had until then been a very secular women's movement'.[55]

In 1980, Tulip explained her vision with phrases borrowed from Jesus' declaration that 'I came that they may have life, and have it abundantly' (John 10:10), as well as his famous challenge to Nicodemus: 'No one can see the kingdom of God unless they are born again' (John 3:3). She wrote, full of hope, of the threefold 'mission of women':

> To bring to women the good news that they may indeed have life if they have the courage to claim it; to bring to men the good news that they may have life if they have the power to give up their power and privilege; and to bring to the church the good news that the kingdom can be reborn as the new community, where with trust and tenderness and real sharing we enable ourselves and one another to discover our full humanity.[56]

When it came to the Bible, feminist scholars focused attention on the women present in the text itself – Eve, the first woman, Mary, the mother of Jesus, and numerous other individuals mentioned in the Old and New Testaments, including as leaders and prophets of faith communities. By the 1980s, feminists studying the representation of women in biblical texts, and the roles and experiences of women in the worlds producing those texts, had raised cutting-edge questions about how to understand the Bible, and about the interpretive process itself.[57] Taking up these questions, feminist theology became associated with a deeper interest in the social and cultural context of the text's original composition, a greater awareness of the impact of the reader in interpretation, and a critical approach to male dominance in the work of theology through history. Elaine Wainwright and Dorothy Lee were two Australian biblical scholars who helped develop and apply such approaches to the study of Scripture. From the 1990s, their books and articles offered fresh readings of New Testament texts, particularly the gospels of Matthew and John. Like other scholarship influenced by feminist theology and hermeneutics, their work problematised 'the traditional reliance on male epistemologies'.[58]

Feminist scholars were also interested in the language used about God, both in the biblical text and in Christian theology more generally. They examined the persistence of male pronouns for God, the metaphor of 'Father', and the male gender of Jesus of Nazareth. Some post-Christian American writers concluded that Christianity was irredeemably patriarchal and sexist, and advised women to leave it. Others retrieved feminine images of God from the biblical text, emphasised Jesus' radically inclusive interactions with women, and suggested ways of interpreting male God-talk that made room to recognise the full humanity of women. Among the many outcomes of all this was a debate about how best to translate the Bible into English.

Jean Skuse, an Australian Methodist, was the first female General Secretary of the Australian Council of Churches. She served in that role from 1976 for more than a decade, speaking out on the status of women, among many other issues of social justice, from a Christian perspective.[59] In 1981, she argued publicly that the Bible had been used by churches 'to reinforce the second-class status of women'. She also criticised modern English translators for reproducing the sexist assumptions of their own times and contexts. Surely it was better to refer to 'children of God', rather than 'sons of God', for example, and help women feel included?[60]

Many Christians in Australia and elsewhere were sensitive to the issues Skuse identified. The debate about gendered language highlights how social movements could reshape biblical texts, and the inherent politics of translating the Bible for new and different contexts.

In wider perspective, feminism helped draw attention to the Bible's complexity. It highlighted the challenge – as well as the urgency – of interpreting Scripture for the present. As Elaine Wainwright recalled just before she retired as Professor of Theology at Auckland University, the feminist readings of the 1980s had 'reflected what was happening socially and were cutting-edge at the time. Feminist work was a natural extension of earlier involvement in social justice'. By the early 2000s, there was 'a whole variety of contemporary frameworks for interpreting the Bible, that bring it into the ethical life of Christians'. These included liberation, feminist and postcolonial hermeneutics, and more recently an ecological hermeneutic that considered the Bible from the perspective of the earth, in dialogue with an emerging ecological consciousness.[61]

The question of how to interpret the Bible is not going to go away. Competing views of what the Bible says, how it should be interpreted, and what authority it has anyway, remain a dynamic element of public conversation. The issues facing Australians in the 2010s range enormously – from gender and sexuality to the treatment of people seeking asylum to climate justice and sustainability. It is difficult to know what the longer-term outcomes of debate in all these areas will be, what beliefs and policy positions will gain the cultural assent of a majority of Australian people. But among the many public voices on such issues, there are some that draw on the Christian Scriptures. Part of the complication, though, is that they rest on diverse approaches to interpretation that are in turn changing with remarkable rapidity. This poses the challenge to the way Australians negotiate religion in the public sphere.

IN LATER LIFE, GERMAINE GREER SETTLED ON A VIEW OF THE Bible as a 'silly' book, a 'grand delusion' that could not possibly reveal God to people. Taking the Bible as God's word could in fact get a person 'into a real mess', she told a crowd at the 2012 Brisbane writers festival. Such views were a far cry from those of Robert Menzies, half a century previously. But not so differently to Menzies, Greer also commended the Bible as worth reading for its enormous cultural influence. Its translation into English had subverted the society that existed and created the modern one, she suggested. And as literature, it was a soaring testament to human yearning. If a person never read the Bible, they would 'not know how strong human yearning is for God, social justice, peace and transcendence'.[62]

It had not been Greer's experience, but a religious yearning for social justice had played its part in movements to recognise and affirm the full humanity of women. It was evident in the activism of Australian Christian feminists during and after the 1970s. It remained significant in some early twenty-first-century efforts to combat the endemic problem of family and domestic violence.[63] And in deeply personal ways, too, it brought healing to individual women who, like actor Anna McGahan, had a transformative encounter with the theological Bible.

Well known for her roles in *Underbelly*, *House Husbands*, *Anzac Girls* and *The Doctor Blake Mysteries*, McGahan initially picked up a Bible to prove to herself 'how bigoted the faith actually was': 'I had a liberal arts education, I had come from the LGBT community … a group of people that had felt so rejected by the church'. After a series of spiritual encounters that unsettled her assumptions, though, she resolved to 'detangle' herself from religion by reading the Bible for critical purposes herself. Finding a copy in the drawer of a hotel where she was staying, she turned to the New Testament and began reading. Within just a few pages, McGahan was undone:

> I remember clutching the book to my chest, laughing, and saying out loud: 'The Christians don't get Jesus. They actually don't get him!'… The Bible made Christianity markedly clear to me … [Jesus] was not exclusive. He did not favour the scholars, the puritans and the priests. He favoured *me* … The Jesus of the Bible was interested in taking the concept of God out of its stuffy, legalistic box, and replacing religion with relationship.

McGahan was humbled by the experience, 'broken by it and remarkably healed'. She thought: 'If this is true, it will change the whole world, and I don't know why no one has ever told me'.[64] Her story points to the disruptive impact of the Bible in the hands of an individual who interpreted it independently of church teaching and tradition. In McGahan's case, it led to personal transformation, a radical change of perspective, and a new vision of Christian community.

RE-IMAGINING AUSTRALIA

One million people, maybe more, turned out to see the young Queen Elizabeth arrive at Farm Cove, Sydney, in late summer 1954. As many as nine million – a full three-quarters of the population – sought a glimpse of her at some point during her eight-week Australian tour. In every major city, and dozens of smaller towns, she was greeted with virtually universal expressions of affection and loyalty. As the Irish Catholic premier of New South Wales, Joseph Cahill, had gushed on her arrival in his state: 'Our origin is British, our soul is British, we think British, we act British'.[1] This familiar sentiment was very common in Menzies' Australia. 'God save the Queen' was not replaced as the national anthem for another two decades.

In Australia, the Bible had long been associated with Britishness. It had arrived with British colonists and informed the process of settlement. It had provided a model of the English language and shaped ideas of the British nation. Many also took the Bible to be the source of England's greatness – and assumed a similar role for it in Australia, as part of greater Britain. But within a decade of the Queen's visit, the Britishness of the Bible, and of Australia itself, was beginning to crumble.

Even before the Second World War, Menzies had described Asia as Australia's near north – a proximity brought into alarming focus by Japanese air raids across the Top End, and submarine attacks on Sydney and Newcastle. War service also gave hundreds of thousands of people first-hand experience of the world beyond Australia, including in Europe, North Africa, Syria, Singapore, Borneo and Papua New Guinea. Their children, the baby boomers, explored even more widely as air travel became more accessible. In 1968, for the first time, more Aussie travellers opted for Asia than the United Kingdom. In 1973, Melbourne residents Tony and Maureen Wheeler published the first Lonely Planet guidebook, *Across Asia on the Cheap*, followed by *Southeast Asia on a Shoestring*. The hippy trail, so appealing to the Beatles, attracted tens of thousands of Australian backpackers in the 1970s. Part of the enticement was an encounter with the region's religions and spiritualities.[2]

In other ways, too, Australians reassessed their place in the global order. A number of Christians opted for missionary service in post-war Asia. For people like Frank Coaldrake, a pacifist Anglican from Brisbane who ministered to Japan for a decade from 1947, the Bible transcended Western culture, and enabled even once-warring nations to heal discord. Other Christians went to Indonesia and other parts of decolonising Asia, to support and partner with local churches among Australia's newly independent neighbours.[3]

At home, a few radical thinkers launched public criticisms of the White Australia policy. One of the earliest and most prominent was Methodist leader Alan Walker, who argued in 1946 that 'Christianity and racialism in any form are absolutely incompatible':

Jesus planted the idea of the fatherhood of God and the brotherhood of man too deeply within the Christian conscience … Paul held up the ideal of there being 'neither Jew nor Greek, bond nor free' (Galatians 3:28) too vividly for

> the Christian to accept colour-consciousness …
> The Christian knows he must rethink this business of a
> White Australia in the light of the principles of the gospel.[4]

From 1947, some 180 000 displaced Europeans were resettled in Australia, marking a decisive break with previous immigration policies that favoured British settlers. In the 1950s, hundreds of students began arriving from Asia to study at Australian universities under the Colombo Plan, a government initiative to strengthen regional relationships by sharing resources and expertise – another key crack in the edifice of White Australia. The task of formally unravelling that policy was finally completed in the early 1970s. The new trajectory of demographic change – and public policy – was from overwhelmingly 'British' to 'multicultural' Australia. By 2016, almost 30 per cent of people in Australia had been born overseas, with especially large and growing cohorts from China and India. As many as 300 languages were spoken throughout the community, the most common after English being Mandarin, Arabic, Cantonese and Vietnamese.

These new realities meant old certainties were ending. Britain was not necessarily 'home' to the baby boomer generation. Nor was their Australia self-evidently British, white, or Christian. By the 1970s, such longstanding ideas about Australia, its culture and identity, were publicly contested. To social commentator Donald Horne, there seemed to be a 'commendable emptiness in Australians about their place in the world, the need for a new rhetoric, a new approach, as if Australia were beginning again'.[5] Some Christians found this changing situation deeply threatening: one of the buttresses of the Bible's cultural authority – Britishness – was collapsing from under it. But for others, it presented a remarkable opportunity. The loosening of old allegiances between God, king and empire promised a new beginning not only for Australia, but for Australian spirituality and its scriptures.

Repackaging the theological Bible

One response to the changes of the 1960s and 1970s was to repackage the Bible and offer it to people afresh – as a text relevant to them not as Britons but as Australians. This impulse was especially marked among groups of white churchgoers who wondered if Christianity was 'failing' in their time, because it was too old-worldly, too worn out, too foreign for this place. Had Australian churches failed to give people a language in which they could speak authentically about and to God? Believing that the Bible was God's word, with a unique and enduring message of salvation, they attempted to express the gospel in a more compelling way.

Efforts ranged from the quietly creative renovation of denominational liturgy – exemplified by the first Anglican *Prayer Book of Australia* (1978) – to the radical recasting of Scripture in an Australian idiom.[6] In the 1970s, for instance, members of the evangelical Jesus Movement tried retelling some of Jesus' parables in Australian slang, and canvassed the possibilities of a 'gum-leaf theology'.[7] Uniting Church minister Bruce Pewer produced a volume of *Australian Psalms* (1979) that went through seventeen printings in twelve years. His *Australian Prayers* (1983) were also widely read.[8] Keith Murray attempted an ocker rendition of popular New Testament stories in *The Day the Grog Ran Out and Other Stories from the Big Book* in the mid-1980s – the top-selling item in ABC shops that Christmas. In the early 2000s, radio personality Kel Richards took this enterprise to a whole new level with the *Aussie Bible*:

> There was this sheila who came across a snake-in-the-
> grass with all the cunning of a con man. The snake asked
> her why she didn't just grab lunch off the tree in her
> garden. God, she said, had told her she'd be dead meat if
> her fruit salad came from that tree, but the snake told her
> she wouldn't die. So she took a good squiz and then a bite
> and passed the fruit on to her bloke. Right then and there,
> they'd realised what they'd done and felt starkers.[9]

Ocker Bibles were great fun, and hugely successful in terms of sales. (The first instalment of Richards' *Aussie Bible* was a runaway bestseller, moving 100 000 copies in three years and prompting a second volume.) Their colloquial style made the Bible fresher and clearer to some people; the Bible Society said they helped hospital and prison chaplains, in particular, introduce the text to new readers. In a sense, they were just the latest expression of the longstanding impulse to translate God's word into the vernacular.

At the same time, their production reflected a certain moment in Australian history, when defining a post-British identity was a national preoccupation. Ocker Bibles reflected the wider challenges of that project. They often embraced the mythology of the bush when society was in fact highly urbanised. They frequently invoked tropes of mateship – and referred to 'booze', 'mates', and 'sheilas' – in ways easily criticised as crude, blokey, even chauvinistic.[10] And though ocker Bibles shed the trappings of formal, traditional English, they embraced a kind of slang that did not suit the realities of a multicultural community. John Harris, a retired Bible translation consultant, remembers seeing Aussie Bibles given out in the square between St Andrew's Cathedral and Town Hall in Sydney: 'I doubt if many of the people taking them understood "Out of the blue

God knocked up the whole bang lot" or "Mary was a very special sheila"'.[11]

The Bible Society's attempts to connect the Bible to everyday life were similarly motivated by Christian mission. In the mid-1970s, the 'good news for everywhere' campaign centred on distributing Bible booklets to specific locations.[12] 'Good news for Dapto', for example, was directed to the residents of a suburb of Wollongong. It contained short passages from Scripture, along with photographs of the local area. Booklets for the Gold Coast and other locations similarly reflected the idea that suburbs and towns were the locus of people's experience and identity, and implied that the Bible 'spoke' to these. It is hard to measure the booklets' uptake and effect, but in 1975 the Bible Society recorded remarkable distribution figures: in twelve months, the society had circulated a total of over 2.47 *million* Bibles, testaments, gospels and Bible portions within Australia.[13]

Another initiative, from the early 1980s, involved Bibles for particular workforces. Building on the tradition of soldiers' Bibles, the first of these were produced for the armed forces. Unlike the Bibles produced during the two world wars, these new publications did not contain the whole New Testament, but portions chosen in discussion with chaplains to help ensure that they would have a meaningful message for readers. Interleaved with photographs of real service situations, they were also given titles and covers specific to each branch of the defence force ('On wings as eagles' in Air Force blue; 'Fighting together for the Faith' in Army green).[14] *The Miner's Bible* (1995), containing the New Testament and Psalms, was published in pocket size and bound in bright orange. It included the personal testimonies of several Australian Christians who worked in the mining industry, as well a Bible Society foreword that suggested connections between the Christian God and mining. (For example: 'As you search for precious stones and minerals, remember that our chief pursuit in life is for Jesus Christ. He is the stone who is precious to God but rejected by many. When we find him we are truly rich' – alluding to Matthew 13:44.[15]) Written to encourage a worker in faith, especially in difficult moments, such a foreword clearly departed from the historic principle of printing Bibles 'without note or comment'. It pointed to the reality that sectarianism had long faded as a significant barrier to engaging with the Bible. The Bible's relevance to everyday life was becoming a more urgent factor.

The *Surfer's Bible* rode the wave of niche Bible production all the way to the beach. It began with *The Grommet's Guide to God* (1994), a booklet edition of the gospel of Mark, including the famous story of Jesus walking on the water, and study tips especially for surfers. A collaboration between the Bible Society in Australia, Scripture Union and the board-riding fellowship Christian Surfers, it went through three reprints in three years. By late 1997, there were more than 18 000 copies in circulation and a sequel was due for release – *The Grommet's Guide to Growth*, an edition of the book of Romans. These Australian innovations grew into a full-text *Surfer's Bible* (2002), incorporating personal stories from well-known riders who were also Christians, explaining how they made sense of life beyond surfing.[16] The first edition sold 75 000 copies globally, and the Bible Society and Christian Surfers knew they had a winner. The second, published in 2008, featured a water-proof zip cover and came with a DVD about a surfing trip to Nias in Indonesia.[17] Editions were also produced in Spanish, French, Japanese and Portuguese – all featuring study tips and personal testimonies of local and professional Christian surfers.

For all the success of the *Surfer's Bible*, the trend towards producing and marketing Bibles for particular groups never became as pronounced in Australia as in the United States. There, it was a much larger and more consciously commercial venture. Companies such as Zondervan and Thomas Nelson, both now owned by News Corporation, developed large catalogues of Bibles tailored to various audiences, among them a *Spirit-filled Life Bible* (1991), a *Woman's Study Bible* (1995) and an *American Patriot's Bible* (2009) – ironically available in the King James translation. Many of these titles were also available in Australia, but Bible production has not engaged the substantial interest of Australian publishers. It has largely remained the work of Christian organisations such as the Bible Society. These groups, while existing and competing in a commercial market, retained a distinctly evangelistic concern for spreading the Bible as God's word.

The bicentenary of white settlement prompted one more attempt to Australianise the Scriptures. In 1988, the Bible Society published the first complete, all-Australian edition of the Old and New Testaments. It involved an adaptation of the American Good News version to suit Australian grammar and expression – replacing wildfire with bushfire, for instance, and field or meadow with paddock. Journalists could not resist suggesting that a properly Australian Bible would surely render the story of Jesus feeding the five thousand as a backyard barbeque. But this time, as the Bible Society explained, the claim to being Australian rested not on ocker language but primarily on the Bible's material production: it was typeset, printed and bound domestically, rather than imported from one of the large British or American Bible printers.[18] More than a million copies of the *Australian New Testament* were sold or given out, as part of 'Operation Good News 88'.

Australianising the cultural Bible

'I must have been eleven or twelve', Arthur Boyd recalled. '[My grandmother] still read to me – stories from an illustrated Bible. The book was full of marvellous tinted engravings, which had a memorable effect on me. Some were quite bizarre and grotesque, others were very gruesome.'[19] Born in 1920, Boyd came from a devout and deeply artistic family. His father Merrick, a ceramic artist, was a prophet-like figure – intensely religious with a reverence for the Scriptures. Throughout Boyd's childhood and early adulthood, prayer and communal Bible reading were part of the family's routine. For all that, though, Arthur did not develop a personal devotion to God: 'I can't remember ever having a belief in God. I didn't think it was necessary; it just didn't crop up'.[20] His biographer comments: 'despite his father's Bible readings, Arthur found no comfort there'.[21]

At first glance, Boyd's story suggests a pattern often thought of as typical in twentieth-century Australia: older generations were prone to devotional Bible reading, including in the family circle, but the faith of zealous parents and pious grandparents was not taken on by the next generation. Younger people might retain some familiarity with the Bible's ideas and narratives as a legacy of their childhood, but for them the Bible was more a hangover text, an old-time story, than a relevant word from God.

The departure from traditional beliefs and identities is a common element of the story of generational change among white Australians. But it is not universal or inevitable, nor as simple as a blanket term like 'secularisation' might make it seem. The decline of a British, white and Christian national identity marked a major cultural shift, but it did not spell the end of the cultural Bible. In fact, several mid-twentieth-century artists such as Boyd actively reconsidered the Bible – not as a repository of faith so much as a storehouse of myth and symbol. In most cases, their work involved a mature borrowing from the longer traditions of European art and creativity, alongside a fresh attentiveness to the Australian experience and setting. The result was an unprecedented flowering of religious art by European Australians, more biblical in its concerns and allusions than any of the settler art produced in the century and a half up to the 1940s. This fresh, creative use of the Bible did not gesture towards a post-British Australian Christianity, as ocker Bibles and gum leaf theology did. But it foregrounded the Australian experience, in conversation with the Scriptures, as part of an open-ended exploration of a post-Christian Australian spirituality.

From very early in his career, Arthur Boyd's work was marked by a creative interaction with the Bible. After his discharge from the Army in 1945, amid further revelations of the horrors of the Nazi war, he turned to the Bible as he grappled with the moral chaos he observed. He painted *The Mockers* (1945) and *The Mourners* (1945), which located the crucifixion of Christ amid a disorderly crowd in a distinctly Australian environment – by the shore of Port Phillip Bay with the Melbourne skyline on the horizon. Within a few years, his work included numerous ceramics and several major paintings canvassing biblical themes.

In the late 1960s and early 1970s, Boyd returned to biblical subjects with several works on Jonah and an extraordinary series on King Nebuchadnezzar.[22] There was no precedent, in any period of Western art, for such a sustained interest in the narrative of Daniel chapter 4. But Boyd successfully fused the story of a proud king reduced to madness with representations of local landscapes, to plumb the depths of human feeling – from the futility of suffering to the possibility of redemption. This unique expression of an

Australian imagination steeped in the Scriptures was a triumph of modern art, worthy of a symphony.[23]

Especially in the late 1940s, 1950s and 1960s, it was common for Australian creatives to grapple with the Bible. Several artists and writers entered into fresh dialogue with it as they responded to the horror of war and the collapse of old assumptions about European faith and civilisation. Russell Drysdale, Roy de Maistre, Robert Curtis, Eric Smith, Weaver Hawkins, Albert Tucker, and Brett Whiteley all took the crucifixion as their subject at some point.[24]

Among female modernists, Grace Cossington Smith pursued her own sense of the divine in the ordinary. She was a devout Anglican whose approach to art was deeply rooted in her spirituality. As she once explained, alluding to the New Testament texts of Philippians 4:8 and 2 Corinthians 4:18, 'art is the expression of whatsoever things are lovely, at the same time expressing things unseen – the golden thread running through time'.[25] During the 1950s, she completed two overtly biblical paintings now held by the National Gallery of Australia. *Then One of Them, Which Was a Lawyer, Asked Him a Question* (1952) depicts the conversation in Matthew 22 that prompts Jesus' famous parable of the Good Samaritan. *I Looked, and Behold, a Door Was Opened in Heaven* (1953) is a radiant interpretation of John's vision in Revelation 4:1. It positions the central figure, and the viewer, outside a door gazing up into heaven. Soon after completing this work, Cossington Smith turned to domestic interiors, producing a series – 'her most moving works' – for which she is justly famous.[26] These interiors celebrate the golden light entering doors and windows from the verandahs and the garden. As the writer Drusilla Modjeska remarked, 'It is as if she pushed open that door, stepped through, and found that the vision of heaven was where she was all the time – in her own bedroom'.[27]

Around the same time, Margaret Preston also took up explicitly biblical subjects. By then in her seventies, her quest for a distinctly Australian visual vocabulary was already well developed. Her biblical prints included *Noah's Ark* (c. 1950), *Golgotha* (1950) and *Christ Turning the Water into Wine* (1951), which located Jesus' miracle at the wedding in Cana in a paddock, with guests looking on from a veranda roofed with corrugated iron. Most striking was her version of *Adam and Eve in the Garden of Eden* (1950). She explained: the Garden was 'obviously here in Australia, the oldest land of all' – and properly populated with Sturt desert peas, flannel flowers, a koala, kangaroo, emu, echidna, kookaburra and platypus. Equally obviously, she added, 'Adam and Eve would be black'. Preston's subsequent print *The Expulsion* (1952) depicted a white angel holding a whip and sword, casting a black Adam and Eve out of the Australian Eden. The gate is locked behind them.[28]

From the 1960s, the move towards abstraction in the visual arts altered the Bible's overt presence in European Australian painting, but other creatives, especially writers and musicians, continued to grapple with the horizons of an Australian spirituality into the early twenty-first century. In the meantime, the theme of Indigenous culture and spirituality, and its interaction with Christianity, surged to the forefront of public consciousness. In Aboriginal art, theology and politics, the end of the British imperial Bible involved radically reassessing gospel and culture.

Indigenising the Bible

Most evenings, missionary Len Harris went down to the riverbank to read aloud from a little handwritten bundle of war-issue paper. It was 1942, and he had overstayed the evacuation of the CMS mission on Groote Eylandt, in the Gulf of Carpentaria, to act as a coast watcher for the Navy. With time on his hands, he had sought out the best local student, Grace Yimambu, and Bidigainj, a woman who spoke local languages but no English, to translate Bible passages into the Arnhem land language of Wubuy. They began with the Lord's Prayer, then the prayer for peace from the Anglican liturgy, and then started on Mark's gospel. For the opening words, they chose *Anawuluwulur anambalaman analawu* – 'The beginning of the Good Story'. Harris would take their work in progress to the riverbank and read it to the people by the campfire.

One night, the Nunggubuyu leader Madi Murungun suddenly got up and walked away. He did not return for several weeks, when he again surprised Harris by the fire. Harris recalled:

Glimpsing Madi, I held up my handwritten sheets of paper. '*Anambalaman analawu*', I said. The Good Story.

'*Yuwai. Idjubulu*', Madi replied. Yes. It is true.

Sixty people emerged from the shadows to crowd around the fire. Madi had brought them to hear the Good News of Jesus Christ in their own language. Urged by the people I read it over and over again, long into the night. Eventually, Madi came forward and asked to hold in his hands the 'leaves' I had written on. I knew he could not read.

'*Idjubulu*', he said again. It is true. He used to think Jesus was only a white man's God, he said, but now he understood that Jesus was also the God of black people. I asked him what had convinced him that the life of Jesus was true. He looked down at the sheets of paper and looked up at me again.

'Now I know that Jesus speaks Wubuy.'[29]

Translation into Indigenous languages marked the most important step away from the British Bible in Australia. In one sense, it could not be otherwise: vernacular translation always acted to dissolve the strict association of God's word with any one language or culture. At the same time, though, translation work did not end the politics of cross-cultural contact and negotiation.[30] Even as it opened the door to alternative interpretations and applications of the text, and even produced movements of indigenisation and cultural liberation, the actual dynamics of Bible translation only belatedly shed the old habits of European colonialism.[31]

After decades of isolated projects, the catalogue of Indigenous Scriptures began to grow slowly in the 1930s and 1940s. The most substantial and collaborative new project involved the community of Ernabella (Pukatja) Presbyterian mission, in the Musgrave range of South Australia. Superintendent Bob Love had previously worked at Kunmunya in the Kimberley, where he had made preliminary translations of the gospels of Mark and Luke into Worora, and translated some Worora stories into English. At Ernabella, he began compiling a vocabulary and making grammatical notes on the Pitjantjatjara tongue. Mission school teacher Ronald Trudinger published a grammar, and together with residents including Jacky Tjupuru and Nganyintja, the missionaries completed a gospel of Mark, later published as *Tjukurpa Palja Markaku* – 'the good story' or 'the good dreaming'. Over the next decade, the community translated all four gospels, the Book of Acts, and the epistles Ephesians, James and 1 John, as well as a catechism, the Apostle's Creed and a songbook of one hundred hymns.[32]

Elsewhere, individual missionaries took up translating the Bible alongside local people, but it was not yet missionary policy.

In the north of Australia, Nell Harris belied her formal status as a 'missionary's wife' to translate Mark and the first letter of John into Gunwinggu, a west Arnhem Land tongue. In the early 1950s, Beulah Lowe, a teacher at the Milingimbi Methodist mission in north-east Arnhem Land, received patient instruction in the Yolngu Martha language from local expert Badaltja Dhurrkay, among many others. The eventual results included literacy materials; a collection of hymns, choruses, and prayers; a published translation of Mark's Gospel (1967) and other Bible selections; as well as a widely used Yolngu Martha dictionary.[33] Around the same time, on Groote Eylandt, missionary linguist Judith Stokes worked with locals to develop a range of written materials in the Anindilyakwa language, including literacy aids, reading primers, descriptions of traditional songs, and parts of the Bible.[34] In central Australia, linguist Ted Strehlow spent years meticulously revising his father Carl's translation of the whole New Testament into western Aranda, finally published in 1956.

A sustained and substantial movement to translate the Bible into Indigenous languages emerged in the 1960s and 1970s. This was a momentous development, enabled by the growth of the Indigenous church, an increased emphasis on translation in missionary policy, the development of university studies in Aboriginal linguistics, and changes in government policy that at last *encouraged* the use of Indigenous tongues. Arguably the most significant venture was the Kriol Bible translation project, which began in the 1970s. This reflected some of the long-term effects of British colonisation as well as the transformative impact of Bible translation on Indigenous communities. Its result, thirty years later, was the *Holi Baibul* (2007) – the first full Bible published in an Indigenous Australian language.

The story of the Kriol Bible begins back at the turn of the

twentieth century, when the encroachments of the pastoral industry as well as outright settler violence made southern Arnhem Land a dangerous place for its Indigenous inhabitants. In 1908, the Church Missionary Society established a station at Ngukurr (Roper River), with the idea of creating a refuge for survivors of frontier conflict where they could be introduced to 'civilisation' and Christianity. Initially staffed by three white missionaries from Victoria and three Indigenous missionaries from Yarrabah in Queensland, the CMS station grew quickly, incorporating people from various trauma-tised language groups. Within a few years, dozens of children were living on the mission separately from their parents – perhaps not entirely voluntarily. (As one contemporary mission report put it, Indigenous parents had been 'influenced' by a resident Protector to leave their children there.[35])

It was routine for students at the early mission school to learn reading and writing in English, while being prohibited – on pain of punishment – from speaking local languages. Outside school, however, young people at the mission continued to speak to one another in their own ways, using a kind of pidgin that eventually creolised into a new language with its own distinctive vocabulary, sound system and grammar. During the middle decades of the century, Kriol spread through much of the remote north, becoming the mother tongue of thousands and the most widely spoken Aboriginal language in Australia. In the 1960s and 1970s, the work of academic linguists and missionary translators was crucial to Kriol becoming recognised as an actual language, not merely a corrupted form of English. Bible translation, in particular, helped define a standard Kriol, privileging one among several co-existing variations to express God's word.

'Finding the right meaning', as community translator William Hall put it, was a substantial challenge. Over a period of three decades, a team of up to thirty people including Hall, his wife Marjorie, and Ishmael and Irene Andrews worked through all sixty-six books of the Bible, as well as a range of related Bible story books and literacy materials. The process required deep reflection on the meaning of the text in divergent cultural contexts. 'We have a lot of different language translations of Bibles, some of which do tell us the truth and some of which do not', as Hall once put it. 'You have to find the right meaning for it – I believe this because I am a translator and I do translate in my own language for my own people. That is how I got involved with my understanding of God's word, so that I could share it with my own people.'[36]

The publication of the *Holi Baibul* was followed by several other Indigenous Scriptures. The Ngaanyatjarra Shorter Bible was the culmination of translation work begun by United Aborigines Mission (UAM) missionaries back in the 1950s and eventually involving a team of at least forty Ngaanyatjarra and Ngaatjatjarra speakers. Published in May 2008, it included the whole New Testament as well as Psalms, Proverbs, Daniel and Ezekiel.[37] The Yolngu Matha (Djambarrpuyngu) New Testament appeared a month later, bringing to fruition work begun by Beulah Lowe. One of its translators, Mr Maratja Dhamarrandji, explained the significance: 'It is an awesome thing for the Word of God to be in the heart language of the people because it is Jesus coming to become like an Aboriginal person, knowing the people, their feelings, the hurts, the pain, their whole identity'.[38] In 2010, nearly seventy years after Len Harris, Grace and Bidigainj began translating Mark's gospel, the Wubuy Shorter Bible appeared, containing the whole New Testament with Genesis chapters 1 to 11 and the books of Ruth and Jonah.[39] Work on the Pitjantjatjara Old Testament, begun in 2011, involved second-generation translators including Makinti Minutjukur. She volunteered to help in light of her parents' experience of completing the Pitjantjatjara New Testament, published in 2002: 'We saw the strength it gave them and the people that read it'.[40] By the end of 2014, the catalogue of published Indigenous Australian Bibles included the full Kriol Bible, thirteen New Testaments or Shorter Bibles and smaller portions of Scripture in at least thirty further languages.

UNRAVELLING THE BIBLE FROM THE BAGGAGE OF EUROPEAN culture and imperialism is a far larger enterprise than even translating the text or conveying the gospel across cultures. As the poet Oodgeroo Noonuccal hinted in the 1970s, it also matters *how* the Bible is applied in contexts where the colonial past lives into the present:

> Though baptised and blessed and Bibled,
> We are still tabooed and libelled.
> You devout salvation sellers
> Make us equals, not fringe dwellers.[41]

By the mid-twentieth century, there was a significant tradition of Indigenous Australian Christians drawing on the Bible in response to colonialism. It stretched back at least as far as the 1830s, when Thomas Brune, Wouraddy and others on Flinders Island interpreted the experiences of Indigenous Tasmanians in light of Scripture. It developed further from the 1860s, with the emergence of more permanent Indigenous Christian communities, and swelled again from the 1930s. Enabled in part by mission networks and the increasing recognition of Indigenous leadership, such appropriations of the Bible reached unprecedented visibility from the 1960s. Indigenous Christians led nation-shaping movements for the recognition of their civil and land rights – from the 1967 referendum removing discriminatory references from the federal constitution, to the landmark *Mabo* case. They responded creatively and critically to the Bible in art, music and literature. And they forged distinctive Aboriginal and Torres Strait Islander theologies that, in fundamental ways, reframed the relationship between Bible and culture.

Kuku Yalanji man Don Brady, whom pastor Charles Harris called 'the Martin Luther King of the Aboriginal race', was born at Palm Island Aboriginal settlement, north Queensland, in 1927. He embraced Christianity at an early age, and after a period as a farm labourer and professional tent boxer, trained as a missionary at the Aborigines Inland Mission (AIM) college near Newcastle, New South Wales. Among the first Aboriginal students to receive AIM training, Brady and his wife Aileen served in several rural communities in New South Wales and southern Queensland, raising their young family in very poor conditions.[42] Eventually moving to Brisbane, Brady did two years of further study at the Methodist Training College and Bible School. In 1964, he began work as a lay pastor with the West End Methodist Mission, ministering to urban-dwelling Aboriginal people. His work soon expanded to include the Christian Community Centre in Spring Hill, which provided both spiritual care and welfare assistance to some three thousand people. He opened a sports club, too, where he taught boxing as well as traditional songs, dances and crafts in an attempt to support young Indigenous men and foster their pride in culture.

Brady's political activism for racial justice was galvanised by an overseas trip in 1969. As the first Indigenous Australian recipient of a prestigious Churchill scholarship, he studied the social and political situation of Indigenous peoples in Fiji, New Zealand and the United States.[43] The civil rights movement in America had achieved recent victories with the passage of the *Civil Rights*

Act (1964) and the *Voting Rights Act* (1965), but the persistent realities of de facto segregation and profound economic inequality remained major grievances. Brady was present at race riots in Chicago on the first anniversary of Martin Luther King's assassination. While there, Brady later recalled, he also heard a call from God: 'Don arise, you are going to do a new thing'.[44] He was one of several Australian activists of his generation to be informed by wider international experiences, networks and ideas challenging racial discrimination.

Upon his return to Australia, Brady threw himself into campaigns for Aboriginal rights – leading street marches, publicly burning a copy of the oppressive *Queensland Aborigines Act*, and forming Indigenous-only organisations, including what became the National Tribal Council. He conducted a memorial service for those 'thousands of our people who have died' since white invasion, and provided interstate support for the new Aboriginal Tent Embassy outside Canberra's Parliament House.[45] He recognised that 'God is present in the sufferings of [hu]man[ity]', and proclaimed: 'Go forth in the struggle of God, in the power of God. Fight for freedom, for the cause of humanity, for God loves all'.[46]

In late 1971, Brady was arrested at what the press called 'the first Aboriginal race riot' – and a few months later the Brisbane Methodist Mission asked him to resign as a pastor. Effectively defrocked, he took a position in the reorganised Community Centre, subsidised by government and focused on physical and social welfare. He also established an independent Black Christian Community Church where he continued his pastoral ministry.[47] Increasingly isolated from the groups that had fostered his early career – the AIM and the Methodist church – Brady soon reminded a younger Indigenous minister, Graham Paulson, of John the Baptist, 'trying to maintain that energy, trying to maintain the drive, without a basis and without support. He lost his economic, emotional, spiritual, personal support'.[48] The toll was very high.

Brady's understanding of the Bible continued to shape his vision. According to Indigenous theologian Anne Pattel-Gray, he felt 'that God was on the side of the oppressed and was leading his people out of bondage'. He revealed to Aboriginal Christians that the same God who freed the Israelites from Egyptian rule was 'with the Aboriginal people as they struggled for freedom from Western oppression, racist laws and imperialism'. He shared a hope that 'God would send the Holy Spirit, the Comforter, to be their strength, hope and courage', and raised the consciousness of his people that 'Christ came and died for them, and they too were free, and inheritors of the Kingdom'.[49]

It was a theological outlook that had much in common with black theologies emerging elsewhere around the world, which took Aboriginal experiences seriously as a context for interpreting the Scriptures. It did away with default equations between Christianity and whiteness, and instead looked for links between the gospel and Aboriginality. Its key biblical touchstones included the Exodus narrative of liberation from slavery, the gospel accounts of Christ's personal humility and suffering, and Jesus' own mission 'to set at liberty those who are oppressed' (Luke 4:18–19).[50]

Don Brady was tragically isolated in his particular place and time, but he was not unique in relating the Bible to the lived experiences of his people and demanding social justice. Elsewhere in Australia, other key figures included Gladys Nicholls and her husband Pastor Doug Nicholls (1906–1988), a Yorta Yorta man whose remarkable public career included periods as an Aussie Rules footballer, political organiser, church pastor, and Governor of South Australia. During the 1950s, Nicholls co-founded the Federal Council for the Advancement of Aboriginal and Torres

Strait Islanders (FCAATSI), which played a leading role in the 1967 referendum campaign, and the Victorian Aborigines Advancement League, perhaps the first Indigenous body to petition the United Nations on land rights.[51] Another Yorta Yorta leader, Margaret Tucker, was a member of the Stolen Generations who devoted her life to promoting the rights of Aboriginal people as well as openly sharing her Christian faith. With her sister, she co-founded the first national body for Indigenous Australian women, the United Council of Aboriginal and Islander Women.[52]

Among the Bandjalung, Pastor Frank Roberts (1899–1968) worked to develop Cubawee settlement, near Lismore, New South Wales as a self-managing Aboriginal Christian community. He actively resisted the interventions of the Aborigines Protection Board and denounced its failures, publicly urging the Board to 'obey the biblical injunction and let truth prevail'.[53] One outcome of Roberts' ministry was the creation of a Christian network across Bundjalung communities – in turn crucial to their reassertion of land rights in the 1960s.[54]

Charles Harris, from north Queensland, was a cane cutter and travelling evangelist mentored for a time by Pastor Roberts at Cubawee, and by the (white) Methodist minister Ed Smith. After periods of ministry in Ingham and Townsville, Harris moved to Brisbane to work at the church founded by Don Brady, then called the Urban Aboriginal Mission. He undertook theological study through Alcorn College in Brisbane and, externally, Nungalinya College in Darwin. In 1980, he became the first Indigenous minister ordained in the Uniting Church in Queensland. Similarly to Pastor David Kirk, who had been instrumental in forming the Aboriginal Evangelical Fellowship of Australia during the 1970s, Harris sought to develop a self-supporting, self-governing and self-propagating Aboriginal church, free from white structures and constraints. He was instrumental in forming the Uniting Aboriginal and Island Christian Congress, serving as its first president from 1985. Supporting Aboriginal and Islander congregations throughout the country, it became the largest non-government Indigenous agency in Australia, with 10–15 000 people involved.[55]

One thing all these activists had in common was the remarkable strength they drew from both their Christian faith and their Indigenous community. Many of them had been influenced by Christian missions, which, for all the limitations and obstructions of their white management, had fostered organisational experience, literacy, and leadership skills – and provided a widespread network of contacts. As Christians themselves, their activism was infused with a sense of moral cause as well as ambition for the common good. Most radically of all, they found in the Bible a vision of justice that seemed relevant to them precisely *as* Aboriginal people, not in spite of their culture and identity. They brought their culture to 'the good book' and reappraised it in ways shaped by their own histories and experiences, and also, in some cases, by international anti-racism movements and associated shifts in theology. In doing so, they helped disentangle the Bible from its British and imperial cultural trappings, and began indigenising the Scriptures.

IN THE 1970s AND 1980s, AN INCREASING NUMBER OF INDIGENOUS Christians took up the task of reading and reinterpreting the Bible in an Aboriginal way. In the words of the Reverend Djiniyini Gondarra, a Yolngu theologian from Elcho Island, Arnhem Land, in the mid-1980s: 'We no longer see Him as the white man's God or a God that the missionaries brought to us, but He is our God who has lived with us in history. But not only in history, He is living with us now in the person of the Holy Spirit. He has given us the vision for the Aboriginal Church to think and theologize the gospel in the language and culture of the people'.[56] The results of this often went well beyond what European missionaries and church leaders could have anticipated. They ranged across the arts as well as formal theology, to offer diverse and creative visions of the Bible in contemporary Australia.

Since the arts have always been integral to Indigenous life and spirituality, it is not surprising that they were a key site for reinterpreting Christianity and its Scriptures. Jarinyanu David Downs, a Wangkajunga-Walmajarri painter, printmaker and preacher, was born near Lake Gregory sometime around 1925 and initially lived a traditional life in the Great Sandy Desert of Western Australia. He moved to the Northern Territory in the late 1940s, working as a drover and miner. In the mid-1960s, as he entered his forties, he converted to Baptist-style Christianity and joined a church in the township of Fitzroy Crossing. His new faith was accompanied by new attitudes to traditional Law and culture, which in turn informed his painting. On the one hand, Jarinyanu vigorously denounced the contemporary practice of traditional Indigenous Law as inconsistent with the truth of Christianity. On the other, he pursued traditional arts, making shields, boomerangs and coolamons decorated with ochre, and painting the ancient Story-cycles celebrated in ceremonies. Many of his works produced from the 1980s feature the Snake Spirit Kurtal, who takes the form of a man, travels across the land and brings rain. Several of these works are now held by the National Gallery of Victoria.

Jarinyanu saw no tension between his new Christian attitudes and his Aboriginal artistic practices: since God was the power behind the creation of the world, it was perfectly acceptable to reverence his power in whatever local form they took – Kurtal was a vehicle for expressing God's creation.[57] At the same time,

Jarinyanu's cultural background led him to accept and understand Christianity in step with the assumptions of his Indigenous world view. And just as Walmajarri land forms, languages, kinship systems, behaviours and designs had been authorised through their particular mention in Dreaming Story cycles, so too, the stories of the Bible provided the basis for his understanding of contemporary Western society.

In the late 1980s, Jarinyanu painted a biblical story cycle including *Moses Leading the Jewish People Across the Red Sea*, now held by the National Gallery in Canberra, and two studies of *Moses Belting the Rock in the Desert*. The Red Sea painting drew on an ancestral narrative belonging to Western Desert peoples, in which Tingari creator beings are described as two figures leading a group of people across the desert. Jarinyanu later painted *Whale Fish with Jonah and His Family* (1993) and *God Been Send'im Elders All Over Place – Gotta Preach'im All the People* (1995). The central figure of the latter is at once God and the artist himself, who was known to preach from his Walmajarri Bible in public spaces in Fitzroy Crossing, and in Rundle Mall on visits to Adelaide.[58] Jarinyanu's preaching, like his painting, expressed his philosophy that we 'gotta make 'em whole lot one family'.[59]

One of the perplexing things about Christianity in Australia, it seemed to Jarinyanu, was that its story cycle was not related to local sites. One of his works, *Moses and God Making the Ten Commandments: Blue Lake Country, Mount Gambier* (1989), can be seen as an effort to identify a connection between such a story and a specific place. Now held by the Queensland Art Gallery, the painting gives the whole area a Christian reading. As he later explained:

The Blue Lake is Jesus country. He was born here, and you can see this from signs that are still here today. The mud of Bronwe's Lake is Jesus' blood, and the Centenary Tower is Calvary. The shape of the cement water tower is a sign that Moses and God were also here, making the Ten Commandments … When the volcano exploded it threw a huge rock into the sky that held the spirit of Jesus. This rock became the star that travelled overseas until it was above the place where Jesus was to be born … After this the star returned to Australia and crashed down at Wolfe Crater [an enormous meteor crater south of Hall's Creek, on the edge of Jarinyanu's traditional country].[60]

A concern to locate biblical narratives within Indigenous land-scapes has informed the work of many other artists in recent years, including several of the sixty-five contributors to *Our Mob, God's Story* (2017), a remarkable volume of Aboriginal and Torres Strait Islander artworks interpreting passages of Scripture.[61] It also defined the work of the first Indigenous recipient of the Blake Prize for Religious Art, *The Stations of the Cross* by Shirley Purdie (2008). Born in 1948, Purdie is a senior member of the Gija people of Warmun, north-eastern Western Australia. Described by one cura-tor as 'one of Australia's greatest living painters', her works are held by a number of major galleries including the National Gallery in Canberra.[62] Her prize-winning piece used the visual language of Gija artists to depict the story of Jesus' crucifixion. The figures of Jesus and the cross are inset into shapes representing the nearby hills of the Kimberley.[63]

Purdie's art illuminates her community's sustained contact with Christianity, which in time gave rise to new forms of worship combining the Gija people's own spiritual teaching with Chris-tian theology. Purdie's painting was – and still is – at the centre of the same cultural and religious negotiation. Her works helped create a new vocabulary of images and symbols, that express both a profound connection to the land and a two-way spirituality focused on the common ground between the Dreamings of the Gija and Catholic theology. It is an expression of Indigenous creativity and identity that reinterprets and relocates the narratives of the Bible in country.

WHILE SCORES OF ABORIGINAL ARTISTS ENTERED INTO creative conversation with the Bible, by the mid-1990s there were an estimated 200 thinkers ready to explore the relationships between their Indigenous traditions and the Christian gospel in some systematic way.[64] Part of the impetus for this, as Don Brady's story suggested, was the influence of non-Western forms of the globalising Bible – including theologies developed by black Christians in north America and decolonising Africa, liberation theologies emerging from poor communities in South America and, from the mid-1970s, the 'water buffalo theology' of a self-consciously Asian Christianity. In all their diversity, each of these movements drew attention to the relationship between gospel and culture, and suggested new perspectives on Christian experience and theology.

A key question facing Indigenous theologians in the aftermath of European colonisation was: 'How did the Word become flesh in our culture?'[65] Some of the people prominent in debating the answer during the 1980s and 1990s had experienced the overt denunciation of their cultures and identities by white Christians. Dr Anne Pattel-Gray, a religious scholar from central Queensland, experienced an 'oppressive Jesus' in the post-war Australian church: 'the gospel came as so-called good news to our family in the midst of the oppression brought by church and government … We found Jesus in our midst, not in the church, where we experienced racism'. Others, such as Wiradjuri pastor Cecil Grant, experienced abuse from the police rather than from missionaries: 'Not all of the missionaries were oppressive; there were many gracious, godly women among them … they taught us the gospel … For me it brought liberation from alcoholism. I was transformed by a conversion experience which took me back to my cultural roots'. In turn, Graeme Mundine recalled how the Catholic mission at Bathurst had 'changed the lifestyle of our people … creating dependency on the one hand and gratitude for rescuing people from a conflict situation on the other'.[66]

For all these Christians, the task was to identify the common ground, where Indigenous cultures and traditions intersected with Bible teaching. How was God's long presence with Indigenous Australians visible in their laws and ceremonies? Through what rituals, ceremonies and narratives was the Word visible to their communities? For George Rosendale, from the Lutheran community of Hope Vale in Queensland, the crucial point was that:

> Our stories are not fables or myths, as white people like to
> call them. Our stories are teachings – teachings about this
> book, the Bible. There is lots and lots of teachings about life
> and living; and that is what I believe the Bible is: a book that
> teaches me how to live the life that *Yirrmbal* gave to me. That
> is the teaching we had – all about life and how we are together.

He went on:

> The Bible is the written word, the universal word, the good
> news in Jesus Christ, but it can be used to oppress or to give
> life. The coming of the gospel is the coming of the word of
> life, but the white man's culture is not Christian culture.

> What we are trying to bring into our culture is God's culture, not white man's culture. We are trying to bring together our spirituality through the gospel.[67]

The ways particular communities did this mattered enormously for their contemporary life and identity. In Djinyini Gondarra's community of Galiwi'ku in north eastern Arnhem Land, for instance, a traditional cleansing ceremony was adapted for Christian baptism. Not only was the pouring of water central to both ceremonies, but the traditional one was accepted as conveying something of the essential meaning of baptism – freedom from bondage, an end to mourning, broadening horizons and new beginnings.[68] On Murray Island, in the eastern Torres Strait, priestly leaders came to see the ancient law of Malo as reaching its fulfilment in the gospel of Christ. As lawman Kebi Bala explained in the 1990s, 'Christ promised "I have come not to destroy but to fulfil" [Matthew 5:17]. So he came to fulfil and make much clearer his work at Murray. Malo came to prepare Murray Island for Christianity and it makes me very proud as a *Zogo le* [traditional priest] to see Malo playing that role … Jesus Christ is where Malo was pointing.'[69]

According to anthropologist Deborah Bird Rose, 'most Aboriginal religions are extraordinarily open to accommodating new events and ideas … any number of permutations, additions and accommodations are possible as long as the underlying principles are not challenged'.[70] Her own work documents several examples, including a remarkable account shared with her by Big Mick Kankinang, from the Victoria Downs District of the Northern Territory, about an Indigenous 'Ned Kelly' Dreaming figure who shared characteristics with both Noah and Jesus.[71] On Murray Island, the process of accommodation had nation-shaping consequences, for it informed the Islanders' relationship with their land, which they went on to defend, successfully, in the famous *Mabo* case.

For Kebi Bala, also known as Dave Passi, one of the original plaintiffs, the idea of *terra nullius* was:

> … like the statue in the vision of Nebuchadnezzar. We have a gigantic problem but we need to look at the clay feet … There is an obscene injustice about Captain Cook standing on an island off the coast and claiming the whole of Australia for the British crown. Ownership came from God. God gave the ownership to the Indigenous people.[72]

This was not just a casual appeal to the Bible, to explain things in a way that white Christians and other biblically literate people might understand. It was a prophetic pronouncement against the injustice of legal dispossession, as a violation of an eternal spiritual law – the law of Malo as affirmed by the law of the Bible. Passi liked to quote the verse in Proverbs that says: 'Do not move an everlasting boundary stone, set up by your ancestors' (Proverbs 22:28).[73]

It took ten years of legal wrangling, but the Islanders' claim was eventually upheld by the High Court. The 1992 decision finally abolished the long-standing legal fiction of *terra nullius*, that old Lockean by-product of the European Bible, and opened the way for the recognition of native title. Eddie Mabo himself did not live to see this result, but he was afterwards hailed by his people as a kind of Moses who had led them to freedom.[74] When his body was returned to Murray Island for reburial in 1996, it was welcomed in terms borrowed from the biblical Exodus story: '*Mama namarida Mose mara memegle e naosa gair mara omaskir Israil le*', 'You sent Moses your servant to lead the people of the Israelites from Egypt'. '*Ekuaida mama gurgab gur damrikie mari adgirlam ko abele.*' 'By your blessing the waters parted because you are the way.'[75]

Towards a reconciled nation

They carried a wooden cross, feeling its weight on their shoulders as they wound their way to Parliament House. It was 1988, the bicentenary year of settler Australia, and no fewer than 50 000 Christians had converged on Canberra to mark the opening of the new parliament building and to pray for the nation. There were songs, banners, shouts of celebration and euphoria – but as the huge procession regathered on the parliamentary lawns, the crowd fell silent as someone spoke Jesus' words from the Sermon on the Mount:

> If you are offering your gift at the altar and there remember
> that your brother or sister has something against you, leave
> your gift there in front of the altar. First go and be reconciled
> to them; then come and offer your gift (Matthew 5:23–4).

The church leaders who had carried the cross planted it into the ground. Its two simple beams came from the cattle yard at Myall Creek where Wirrayaraay people had been herded together and massacred by settler stockmen in 1838. One hundred and fifty years had passed, but the wounds of violence, racism and injustice were terribly raw. The challenge of repentance and reconciliation was one of the most urgent facing the church – and the wider Australian nation.

IN 200 YEARS, THE BIBLE HAD UNDERGONE A SERIES OF transformations in its place in Australia, especially in relation to Indigenous people. From the outset, it had been bound up with the culture and beliefs of the British colonisers, and had an impact on Aboriginal people in every form it took, from a word of life to a destructive tool of imperialism. In every generation since Boorong, some had responded by rejecting the Bible – or at least parts of it – as incompatible with their own flourishing. It could be very difficult to separate the Bible entirely from European imperialism and its profoundly disruptive impact on Indigenous families, communities and cultures. As one Aboriginal Christian remarked in conversation recently, reading the Old Testament was all but impossible for her, because it felt like a book of genocide.

At the same time, in every generation since Dickey Bennelong, there were also people who readily distinguished between European colonisation and the theological Bible. For many of the Indigenous Christians mentioned earlier, the issue was less with the Bible per se, than with how the Bible was interpreted and applied in relation to Indigenous Australians. In many cases, they recognised the Jesus of the gospels as someone who 'was not part of the religious system, but was with the outcasts, the polluted and the unclean … We could identify with the Jesus who was crucified and suffered'. For some people, the Old Testament also offered a word of justice, freedom and restoration. Pitjantjatjara translator Makinti Minutjukur even found 'wonderful stories' in the book of Joshua, which recounts the colonial conquest of Canaan: 'The way God took them into the land – as I was translating I felt I was there with those people going into the promised land. As God was taking them in, he was also taking me'.[76]

On the lawns of the new Parliament House, Indigenous Christians drew on all these experiences to give voice to a distinctive vision of the nation. Unlike British settler visions, it was not rooted in the idea of a chosen people, with a specific vocation in the world; it did not assume a covenantal community along the lines of Old Testament Israel, or involve a call to that righteousness that 'exalteth the nation'. Nor did it trade in images of Christ as the bushman's friend or the unionist's mate, a companion on the dusty road to building the worker's paradise in Australia. It was a vision more like the one William Cooper had expressed half a century earlier – a vision of a nation marked by love, practical justice and the profoundest reconciliation. In the words of pastor Charles Harris, as he lit a ceremonial fire on the capital Canberra grass:

> We now use this smoke, from the fire of God's creation, to come and burn the past away, leaving us free to build a new and equal community. Our small fire reminds us of the fire God sent in His own Son to consume greed, robbery, murder, rape, destruction of family, and every kind of wickedness. Let God's holy fire cleanse this nation, this very land on which this great new building stands, so that those who work in it may govern in righteousness and justice.

> We believe that only real forgiveness, and a true change of heart, and the coming of God's Spirit of love and justice in a new way, will enable us all to share in a changed and renewed future.

Such a vision has found some acceptance among non-Indigenous Australians. With a lingering familiarity with the ideas of the Bible, some have recognised, in their own worldviews, the call to listen, to admit wrongdoing, to seek justice and pursue reconciliation. Even at the time of the bicentenary, this receptive group went well beyond the crowd of 50 000 Christians present on the lawns of the new Parliament House. It included Prime Minister Bob Hawke, who made it the first substantive item of business, when the new parliament formally opened in August, to move a motion supporting church calls for the acknowledgment of 'the nation's Aboriginal history' and the need for real reconciliation.[77] It also included Paul Keating, soon to succeed Hawke, and many of those who recognised themselves in his famous 1991 Redfern speech:

> The starting point might be to recognise that the problem starts with us non-Aboriginal Australians. It begins, I think, with that act of recognition. Recognition that it was we who did the dispossessing … It was our ignorance and our prejudice. And our failure to imagine these things being done to us.

It inspired many of the hundreds of thousands of people who involved themselves in the popular reconciliation movement of the 1990s.[78] It was also a powerful factor in the flood of formal apologies that flowed from Australian churches, especially after the *Bringing Them Home* report (1996) made clear the damage they had done as agents of government child removal policies.

The vision of reconciliation with justice so clearly articulated by Indigenous Christians in 1988 has neither been exhausted nor realised in twenty-first-century Australia. Another generation on, there is in fact more reason than ever to keep listening, theologising and imagining a different kind of nation. There is the challenge of achieving the myriad reforms that would empower Aboriginal and Torres Strait Islander peoples to 'take a rightful place in our own country'. There is also the challenge of relating rightly, as a society, to the land around us. For Charles Harris, outside Parliament House, the land was a God-given gift to Aboriginal Australians. As the text of Acts 17:26 had it, 'God hath made of one blood all nations … and determined … the bounds of their habitation'. For Harris, this meant that Aboriginal peoples' spiritual connection to the land, including sovereignty, should be properly honoured by the non-Indigenous population. A comparable idea was reasserted by Indigenous leaders in the 2017 Uluru Statement: 'sovereignty is a spiritual notion … It has never been ceded or extinguished'.[79]

Honouring Indigenous connections to country involved land rights, in a legal sense, but went well beyond that too. It was bound up with the proper stewardship of creation, rather than environmental exploitation. In tears, Deaconess Dinah Garagji once asked the Anglican Synod of the Northern Territory: 'How can we obey God if they take away our land? How can we be good stewards of it if we only half own it and someone else can make the decisions about it?'[80] Or as George Rosendale explained, the land was to be cared for by its divinely appointed custodians, not reduced to mere property and treated badly by its 'owners':

> We are not the owners of the land. Look at Genesis 2:15 –
> 'The Lord took the man and put him in the Garden of Eden,
> to till it and keep it'. This is Aboriginal teaching too. God has
> given us the land to care for – not ownership, but stewardship.
> The Bible tradition is the same as ours. Our old people say
> 'Hey! This is the same as our teaching!' But the white man
> has said 'No, your teaching is bad, it is heathen'.[81]

One of the insights of Indigenous theology, then, may be a recovered understanding of the land and, even more deeply, of the stewardship of creation. Indigenous readings of the Bible not only challenge imperial assumptions about the inferiority of non-European societies, they may help overturn poor Western theologies of environmental domination. The link was certainly clear to the non-Indigenous South Australian scholar Norman Habel, whose 'Earth Bible' project represents a major Australian contribution to biblical studies internationally. And it will only become more important as societies everywhere grapple with climate change – a catastrophe from which science, on its own, has not brought salvation.[82]

CHAPTER 12

THE BIBLE IN THE NEW MILLENNIUM

Stalking on stage to the menacing pulse of drums, a prophet in a black suit tells the crowd to brace themselves. Hold your breath, close your eyes, pray if you think it helps. Whether or not you quite believe it, the age of the Anthropocene is upon us. Behold, the sea is bound for heaven. All that we love, we lose. For all our restless searching, there is nowhere safe on earth.[1]

When Nick Cave returned to Australia with his band the Bad Seeds in early 2017, he brought his old arguments with God carried on in songs with biblical lyrics – from the defiant 'Mercy Seat' to the love song 'Into My Arms'. In shows across the country, he hissed and spat like the Old Testament God that had preoccupied him in his twenties. He also channelled his creativity into tenderness like the Christ of the gospels, whom he had discovered in his thirties. Now on the cusp of his sixties, Cave's conversation with God had clearly taken yet another turn – expressed in newer songs of loss and grief as raw as the memory of his teenage son. In 'Jesus Alone' Cave sang of falling – and crash landing into a field, with no God there to catch him. Before a surging sea of fans, Cave's performance circled a devastating possibility – had he, and everyone else, been deserted by God right when they most needed Him?[2]

Cave's spiritual journey is hardly typical of early twenty-first-century Australians, but his music points to the Bible's enduring but unresolved place in contemporary culture. At a time when the majority of people are disengaged from the institutional church, and only a few, including Cave, persist with close and attentive Bible reading, the long conversation with the Bible goes on in other ways. The Bible retains a presence in the arts, for instance, from popular music to literature to painting. If there are prophets in Australia any more, they are more likely to be creative rather than clerical figures. The Bible also continues to inform political debate and public conversation. Here the diversity of interpretations has come to the fore on issues ranging from marriage and family relationships to the challenges of the Anthropocene, particularly climate change. The discussion is often fraught, and the answers are far from easy. But as Cave's recent work insists, the challenge is to learn to live with unresolved losses and competing possibilities.

THE KINDS OF INSTITUTIONS AND EXPERIENCES WHICH introduced Nick Cave to the Bible are no longer as effective as they were in fostering broad biblical literacy in Australian society. During the great age of the Bible, churches and schools placed the Bible before most ordinary Australians, helping to make it widely familiar and lending weight to certain interpretations. In the early twenty-first century, these institutions are still relatively prominent in making the Bible known, but their reach is much smaller, their activity more contested, with consequences for the place of the Bible in Australian culture. Most people do not go to church even to celebrate Christmas or attend a wedding. Although a slim majority still identify as Christians at the census, levels of such self-identification are dropping, and the churches' moral and cultural authority is subject to increasing scepticism. In 2017, as the Royal Commission into Institutional Responses to Child Sexual

Abuse brought its four-year investigation to a conclusion, a representative survey found that 90 per cent of Australians considered abuse by the clergy to have a negative influence on their perception of Christianity. More than half of respondents said it had a 'massively negative influence' – placing abuse by the church well ahead of 'religious violence', 'hypocrisy', and 'judging others' as a damaging factor in popular attitudes to Christianity.[3]

Alongside the extraordinary courage and persistence of the victims, one thing that has stood out from the exposure of abuse is the catastrophic, destructive gap between what is practised and what is preached. Offenders against children have not – and could not have – claimed that their abuse was somehow permitted or required by the text of Scripture. At the same time, a familiarity with the Scriptures did not, in itself, prevent them from inflicting deep and lasting harm on vulnerable people. Suggestions that victims should simply forgive their abusers, along with appeals to the biblical warning against taking fellow believers to court, sometimes obstructed proper and timely redress. As in the case of settler violence against Indigenous Australians, people who knew the Bible, and even claimed to believe it, have been guilty of great evil. The additional failure of certain churches to respond appropriately to the victims has given ordinary Australians good reason to think more negatively of the institution. Among the many consequences, it is probable that some Australians have perceived the churches' book, the Bible, less positively by association.

IN THE REALM OF EDUCATION, THE EARLY TWENTY-FIRST century has seen a growth in independent schools, many of them affiliated with churches. In the public system, there has been fresh debate about Special Religious Education or Instruction (SRE/

SRI) – often called 'scripture'. Provisions for SRE have always depended on each state's particular legislation, but in general terms, school scripture has contributed significantly to ordinary Australians' religious education. In 2015, an independent review conducted for the NSW Department of Education found that SRE classes were held in 92 per cent of the state's primary schools, and 81 per cent of its secondary schools. The majority were provided by Christian groups – Catholic, Protestant and Orthodox. Islamic, Hindu, Buddhist, Jewish, Baha'i, Vedic, and Sikh SRE was also available in some places. There is no centralised data on levels of student participation, but responses from principals suggested that some 71 per cent of New South Wales primary schoolers, and 30 per cent of high schoolers, received some kind of SRE.[4] For many of these students, the classes probably provided their most substantial interaction with the Bible and their primary opportunity to acquire some basic religious literacy.

In the 2010s, the provision and future of SRE is the subject of debate. In New South Wales, since 2011, an increasing number of primary schools have begun offering Special Education in Ethics (SEE) as an alternative to SRE. According to the provider group Primary Ethics, SEE was available in about a quarter of New South Wales schools in 2017, with the highest uptake among students in the inner suburbs of Sydney.[5] In Victoria, where secular education has always been defined and enacted differently to New South Wales, Special Religious Instruction was completely removed from ordinary classrooms in 2016. While principals retained the discretion to offer SRE outside of normal hours, classroom teachers were to implement new curriculum requirements on global cultures, ethics, traditions and faiths, and building strong and respectful relationships.[6] Whether or not the new curriculum will realise the ideal of producing the kind of religious literacy necessary for navigating a diverse world, one likely effect of the change is that students in Victorian public schools will rarely if ever read the Bible for themselves.

Given the broad social trends evident since at least the 1960s, it is likely that overall biblical literacy is lower in Australia now than at any other time since colonisation by the British. The public conversation with the Bible goes on, but fewer Australians are familiar with the text and its interpretation in a way that enables them to participate in that conversation critically and effectively.

ANDREW CHAN GREW UP IN SOUTH-WESTERN SYDNEY DURING the late 1980s and 1990s, the youngest child of first-generation migrants from China. After leaving school he got a job at a catering company. 'I don't think I was really going anywhere in life … though I had a stable job and all.' A drug user himself, he started dealing for a quick pay day.[7] Arrested for heroin smuggling in 2005, the ringleader of the Bali Nine found himself in an Indonesian prison. 'At first I thought it was no big deal, I'll get outta this. It wasn't until I ended up in solitary confinement that I realised I wasn't.' Feeling hopeless and alone, he decided that if they were going to kill him anyway, he would do it himself. He made a noose with his T-shirt, before remembering 'the heaven/hell issue'. Wanting to make sure he ended up in heaven, and thinking that perhaps he should pray, Chan looked up and said 'God if you're real …' and broke down crying.

Shortly afterwards, Chan got hold of a Bible and started reading it from Genesis. When a Christian came to visit him, he explained that he was reading it, 'but didn't get much out of it'. The visitor said to read the New Testament, but Chan did not know what that was: 'He had to explain it was part of the Bible'. Beginning with the Gospels, Chan read through the New Testament a couple of times, 'but I didn't really notice any change. I just didn't get it'.

Just before his court date, Chan came across a passage in Mark chapter 11, where it says that if you have enough faith you can say to this mountain, 'Be removed', and God will do it. Chan prayed, 'God if you're real and this is true, I want you to free me – and I'll serve you every day for the rest of my life'. The court convicted him of drug trafficking and handed down the death penalty.

When Chan got back to his cell, he complained 'God, I asked you to set me free, not kill me'. God replied, 'Andrew, I have set you free from the inside out, I have given you life!' It marked Chan's moment of conversion, the beginning of his new life as a Christian. Chan enrolled in a Bible ministry course through a Pentecostal college in Melbourne and began leading English-language church services in Kerobokan prison. He initiated projects to improve prisoner welfare and developed a mentoring relationship with many other inmates. Openly admitting that 'I have lost all my integrity and good will, and brought deep shame and outrageous suffering to my loved ones', he devoted himself to worshipping God and comforting and encouraging others. In March 2015, Chan was formally ordained a Christian pastor. Eight weeks later, he faced the firing squad – leading seven other condemned prisoners in singing 'Bless the Lord O My Soul' and 'Amazing Grace', right up to the moment of their deaths.

Andrew Chan's story points to some of the niche exceptions to the growing disconnect between Australians and the Bible. He encountered the Bible not through church or school but through reading it for himself. Initially finding it interesting but not very relevant, he eventually experienced it as the transformative Word of God. Drawn to a Pentecostal form of Christianity, he became a worship-leader and pastor, and was eventually farewelled in a funeral at Sydney's Hillsong church. In a sense, Chan became part of a vibrant minority in contemporary Australia – a minority of young, culturally diverse Christians with a highly devotional experience of the Word.

The rise of Pentecostalism in late-twentieth-century Australia led to the formation of the nation's largest ever churches. One of the most influential, Hillsong in north-west Sydney, was by 2017 a multinational megachurch, exporting its brand of Pentecostalism to other parts of Australia and to several countries around the world – including Brazil, Israel, Russia, England, the United States, South Africa, France and Sweden, among others.[8] Its 2016 annual conference in Sydney was a sellout, with 30 000 delegates. Thousands more attended parallel conferences in London and New York.

In all this, churches like Hillsong created a new centre or subculture in which hundreds of thousands of Australians commonly interacted with the Bible as God's Word – 'accurate, authoritative and applicable to our everyday lives'.[9] From day to day and week to week, the Bible is read, sung, studied and preached as part of the regular life of Pentecostal churches. Its phrases are also taken up, and its qualities proclaimed, in pop-rock worship songs even more widely repeated and marketed around the world:

The lamp unto my feet
The light unto my path

Your Word will not be shaken
Your Word will never fail me …
Your Word is revelation.[10]

People who attend Pentecostal churches are among the most likely, of all Australian Christians, to take the Bible literally, word for word. Even among Pentecostals, however, there is a diversity of attitudes. According to the National Church Life Survey (NCLS) – the largest recurring survey in Australia after the census – more than 90 per cent of all Australian churchgoers accept the Bible as itself the Word of God.[11] However, recent surveys have also disclosed that, beyond this consensus, churchgoers vary considerably on the question of *how* the theological Bible should be interpreted:

> As God's word, is the Bible:
> a.   to be taken literally, word for word;
> b.   to be interpreted in the light of its historical and cultural context; or
> c.   to be interpreted in the light of its historical context and the Church's teaching?

Results over the past twenty years have shown that Pentecostals have been more likely to opt for (a), and Catholics for (c) – but that no denomination is marked by unanimity about how the Bible should be understood. In many cases, no single position has claimed a majority among a denomination's ordinary worshippers. As such, it is simply not possible, in contemporary Australia, to speak categorically of a Catholic or Anglican or Pentecostal approach to Scripture, though virtually all accept it as God's word.

Recent NCLS data also suggests that a significant shift in interpretation is underway. To the surprise of lead researcher Dr Ruth Powell, the 2011 survey recorded a massive jump in the overall proportion of church attenders opting for (b), a contextual approach to Scripture – up from 29 per cent of all respondents in 2001 to 38 per cent a mere decade later. Over the same period, a preference for a literalist approach dropped from 26 to 24 per cent of Australian churchgoers. Alongside a decline in traditionalist responses, this means that, most commonly, Australian churchgoers prefer to keep the historical and cultural context of the Bible firmly in view.

Perhaps the growing strength of a contextual approach to the Bible is related to the relatively high – and rising – level of education of Australian churchgoers. Perhaps it reflects the longer-term impact of feminist and Indigenous biblical scholarship, which has helped draw attention to the perspectives and contexts which shaped the writing of Scripture. Popular Christian attitudes to interpretation may also be also consistent with the tendency towards more moderate and accommodating forms of Protestantism in Australia – where, even among evangelicals, fundamentalism has always been more marginal than mainstream. Whatever their causes, the NCLS results give good reason to pause before assuming that contemporary Christians typically take the Bible at face value: in fact, less than one-quarter do. They also point to an interesting difference between the attitudes of Christians in Australia and in the United States. In 2017, a Gallup poll found that 24 per cent of all US adults considered the Bible to be 'the actual word of God, to be taken literally word for word' – a proportion that rose to 35 per cent among Protestants, and to 41 per cent among those who said religion was 'very important' to them.[12] In this light, literalism in Australia is very weak – which may help explain some of the differences in the role of religion in our respective political cultures.

ALONG WITH THE COMPLEXITIES OF BIBLICAL INTERPRETATION, the early twenty-first century has been marked by a fresh revolution in the culture of reading. With the rise of the internet and the spread of digital texts, we may be in the midst of changes as significant in the history of the book as the innovation of the codex and the invention of the printing press. So far, the digital revolution has involved a reversion to some very old methods of reading, notably scrolling. At the same time, it has made a vast library of texts more readily available to more people, arguably contributing to a democratisation of information.

The question is: what kind of literacy will the digital revolution produce, and what will it mean for the way people engage with the Bible? Though it is still too early to tell, the advent of searchable digital Scriptures may allow, even encourage, a shallower, more casual and fragmented interaction with the text. Perhaps it displaces a more critical interaction with a particular book of the Bible in favour of a more selective, consumerist, me-centred model of reading? On the other hand, its very searchability may enable a person to more easily pursue a theme or keyword across the whole body of Scripture, as well as to compare translations. In this sense, it may help rather than hinder a more careful and critical interaction with the text.

At the very least, the digital revolution has enabled new insights into what contemporary Australian readers actually look for in their Bibles. Data from the leading website Biblegateway. com revealed that, in 2013, Australians most wanted to read about hope, peace, joy, faith and, above all, love. The most commonly searched chapter was Matthew 6, a portion of Jesus' Sermon on the Mount that discusses giving to those in need, prayer, fasting, treasures in heaven, and instructions not to worry.

By verse, the top five Australian searches were:

- John 3:16 – For God so loved the world that he gave his one and only Son, that whoever believes in him shall not perish but have eternal life.
- Jeremiah 29:11 – 'For I know the plans I have for you',

declares the Lord, 'plans to prosper you and not to harm you, plans to give you hope and a future'.

- Philippians 4:13 – I can do all this through him who gives me strength.
- 1 Corinthians 13:4–8 – Love is patient, love is kind. It does not envy, it does not boast, it is not proud. It does not dishonor others, it is not self-seeking, it is not easily angered, it keeps no record of wrongs. Love does not delight in evil but rejoices with the truth. It always protects, always trusts, always hopes, always perseveres. Love never fails.
- Romans 8:28 – And we know that in all things God works for the good of those who love him, who have been called according to his purpose.[13]

In 2015, a free Bible App developed by YouVersion recorded almost 334 000 new downloads in Australia – a sizeable number nevertheless dwarfed by the 280 million downloads the app recorded globally between 2010 and mid-2017. As well as enabling users to read and share Bible verses on social media, the Bible App offered a choice of hundreds of personal reading plans. In the five years from 2010, a quarter of a million such plans were completed in Australia – most commonly on topics like God's purpose for our lives, hope, busyness and God's renewal.[14] Bible reading persists as a significant activity for some Australians.

IN MELBOURNE, IN THE 1980S, WRITER HELEN GARNER SHARED a house with a friend who had recently been 'saved'. 'He was, at the time, one of the most maddening people I have ever known', she recalled.

> When confronted by life's setbacks, he used to say in a way I
> heard as smug, 'I've got a resource in these matters'. I feared
> he was determined to convert me. He carried a small black
> New Testament in his shirt pocket wherever he went, and kept
> the big fat Bible beside him on the dining room table while
> we ate. I hated this. The book seemed to radiate an ominous,
> reproachful righteousness.[15]

At one point, Garner's friend and fellow novelist Tim Winton came
to stay a night or two. Winton was a Christian who had grown
up in a gently fundamentalist church, with a growing reputation
for exploring faith and meaning in his writing about Australian
life. Garner's flatmate was keen to meet him, and had planned a
weighty theological discussion. The big Bible lay on the table as
the trio ate their cake. Unable to face the aggravation, Garner went
out for a walk around the park. When she returned an hour or so
later, Tim and the Bible were still at the table:

> 'Where's Steve?'
> 'Gone upstairs for a nap, I think.'
> 'What happened?'
> 'Oh … we talked. And in the end I said to him "Why don't
> you give the book a rest? Why don't you let your life be your
> witness?"'[16]

Garner does not remember why she started reading the Bible herself a few years later. She had a modest history with institutional
Christianity, having been exposed to Anglicanism through her
education, and receiving baptism, at age twenty, in 1962. She later
laughed her baptism off, but a persistent if at times uncertain spirituality remained important to her.[17] By the late 1980s she was living

in Sydney, finding it hard to believe Jesus was real, and struggling with a new novel:

> I remember buying for a dollar a battered old copy of a 1950s translation of the New Testament in the Cat Protection Society op shop on my way along Enmore Road. I remember taking it to my work room, reading a few pages, then deciding – *because my writing was going so badly* – to get hold of the KJV and the Jerusalem Bible as well, to go back to Genesis, to sit there and read the whole damn thing … I remember being astonished at the intensity of the reading pleasure I got as a writer from the Bible … there were passages of narrative in the Bible that made my hair stand on end – with horror, bliss, and *technical awe*.[18]

It was a turning point in both her spiritual and creative life, with visible effects on *Cosmo Cosmolino*, her subsequent novel.

IN A CULTURE WARY OF BIBLE BASHERS, THE ARTS ARE AN important arena where Australians continue to grapple with faith and doubt, morality and meaning. 'People are embarrassed', Garner has remarked. 'They're embarrassed about God, they're embarrassed by biblical imagery and angels and ideas of redemption and salvation.'[19] And yet, as Winton has put it, 'I think fiction can explain things to people and render experiences of people and of God in a way that is sometimes superior to theology and sermons … Everything has its place in communicating the grace of God'. Several of Winton's own works – including *That Eye, The Sky* (1986), *Cloudstreet* (1991), *The Turning* (2005), and *Eyrie* (2013) – employ biblical ideas and imagery as part of an ongoing exploration of 'what it is to be Australian, to be human and to make and question meaning'.[20] The poetry of Les Murray and Kevin Hart, among many others, is notable for its willingness to take the mystical seriously.[21] In the collections *Limited Cities* (2012) and *Lunar Inheritance* (2017), a young Chinese-Australian poet from western Sydney, Lachlan Brown, has captured moments of grace in the everyday. For Brown, who regularly reads the Bible in a devotional way, this sensitivity is rooted in a particular understanding of a Jesus who reveals God even to ordinary people, in ordinary situations. He explains, 'It's not Gerard Manley Hopkins, you know, "The world is charged with the grandeur of God". But what does Hopkins look like in this fallen place … [the suburbs] where humans have kind of proliferated?'[22]

For songwriter Paul Kelly, as for Nick Cave, the Bible has compelled a sustained creative conversation. 'I'm an atheist', Kelly has declared, but 'the stories … and the language of the Bible are part of the cultural air that we breathe'. 'I have written a lot of songs that come from the Bible'.[23] 'Love is the Law' (2001), for example, includes several lines lifted directly from 1 Corinthians chapter 13. The album *Stolen Apples* (2007) takes its title from the story of Adam and Eve, and includes a number of tracks with religious themes. The beautifully hymn-like 'Meet Me in the Middle of the Air' (2005) draws heavily on Psalm 23 and 1 Thessalonians 4. Kelly's collaboration with Yolngu artist Geoffrey Gurrumul Yunupingu on a bilingual version of 'Amazing Grace' is one of the highlights of Australian recorded music. Gurrumul himself grew up at Elcho Island, north-east Arnhem land, with the musical legacy of the Methodist mission there. Acclaimed as 'Australia's most important voice', his *Gospel Album* (2015) offers a profound re-imagining of biblically inspired songs he learned from his mother and aunts. Sung in Yolngu Martha, it is an extraordinarily beautiful expression of an Indigenised Christianity. Such music mediates the Bible to Australian audiences, with a power to move even those who do not claim to be believers.

AMONG VISUAL ARTISTS, MELBOURNE PAINTER ADAM LEE IS becoming internationally known for his works on Eden, exile, Babel, and other biblical themes.[24] Pop artist Reg Mombassa, whose work with the surfwear company Mambo made him one of Australia's most recognisable visual artists, has customised biblical scenarios in paintings such as *Temptation in the Industrial Garden*, *The Ten Comparisons*, *The Road to Clovelly*, and *The Miracle of the Pies and Beer*. Since the mid-1990s, Mombassa has also produced numerous works featuring his now-iconic figure 'Australian Jesus'.[25] According to *Nativity* (2004), Australian Jesus was born in Bethlehem caravan park, in the Hunter Valley, where there was an abundance of carpentry opportunities. A koala, a chicken and a kangaroo sought him out at birth, bearing gifts of a football, a pie and some chips. *The Young Australian Jesus* (2001) was well-groomed and smartly dressed. But after a trip to India, he donned a cape and sandals, grew a beard, and allowed his hair to grow long and scruffy.

Over several years, Mombassa's Jesus has displayed a well-developed sense of social justice – exemplifying the subversive use of the Bible in Australian art, and its potentially unsettling contribution on ethical matters. *Australian Jesus Welcomes the Boat People* (2002) was painted during a peak in the political victimisation of people seeking asylum in Australia. In the style of stained glass, it showed Australian Jesus in a red cape, on a white horse, with a case of Mambo Bitter under his arm – ready to offer the beer to refugees arriving at Sydney Harbour. *Australian Jesus Addresses the Bigots*

(2005) depicted a suited, haloed Jesus preaching in the suburbs, finger raised: 'Homophobic bullies are not good Christians. Find yourself a new collective noun'. And in *Australian Jesus Discusses Climate Change Policy with Superman*, the two men sit together enjoying tea and a sandwich, overlooking Sydney harbour. There's no hint, in the work, of exactly what they discussed – but *Australian Jesus with Eyes Popped Out* (2011) locates a distressed and possibly drowning Jesus amid flooded suburban houses. It appears Australia's climate change policies had been ineffective in stemming the tide of rising seas.

THE TREATMENT OF REFUGEES, HOMOPHOBIA, AND CLIMATE change are major ethical challenges facing contemporary Australians. Along with economic inequality, family violence, Indigenous recognition and euthanasia, they are prominent moral issues in the 2010s – especially as they relate to public policy and legislation. Bound up with even deeper questions to do with human flourishing, and how best to relate to others in and beyond Australia, they go to the heart of the kind of society which the present generation is shaping.

The Bible has an ongoing if inconclusive role in the public consideration of such matters. In the 2010s, it is cited by parliamentarians, lobbyists, activists, artists, church leaders, and media commentators – each of whom use it in different ways. In many cases, the Bible is treated religiously, as the authoritative text for Christian Australians. This is true of the Love Makes A Way activists who repeatedly risked arrest protesting the unjust treatment of people seeking asylum in Australia. Pointing to 'the enemy-loving Christ who was willing to suffer for the sake of others', their movement had become, by late 2017, the largest nonviolent mobilisation of ordinary Australian Christians since the Vietnam War generation.[26] At the same time, in the midst of the 2017 Marriage Law postal survey, the Anglican Archbishop of Sydney argued for the retention of exclusively male–female marriage on the basis of Genesis 1 and 2, Matthew 19, and Ephesians 5. He also argued that heterosexual marriage was appropriate not only for Christians, but a good thing for all Australians: 'If we love our neighbours … we should be prepared to speak up for God's good plan for marriage in the conversation our country is now having'.[27]

Both the refugee activists and the Archbishop represent attempts by Christian believers to put their particular biblical understandings into practice – and not only for themselves but in ways that serve what they consider to be the common good of all Australians. Such appeals to the Bible are anchored in an activist Christian citizenship, expressed both in personal life and in efforts to influence politics and wider society.[28] Yet Christian citizenship can draw on competing interpretations of the Bible. These issues reveal yet again that even Christians understand and apply the text in very diverse ways. On civil disobedience, for example, Love Makes A Way received criticism from other believers, particularly on the use of prayer in political actions occupying government offices. On marriage, some Christian groups urged a change in the law to allow same-sex marriage, precisely by putting forward an alternative understanding of the Bible's relevant principles. Clearly, the task of interpreting and applying Scripture remains complex and contested. And as always, Christians are to be found at virtually every point of the political spectrum.

ADDING TO THE CHALLENGE OF THE PUBLIC BIBLE IS THAT its uses – and users – can surprise and confound. When taken up for partisan political purposes, for example, it can be asked to bear meanings in deep conflict with mainstream Christian interpretations – as when former prime minister Tony Abbott cited the Genesis verse about humanity exercising dominion over the earth to reject what he called the 'religion' of climate change. (Abbott's argument was in direct opposition to the biblical theology of the Pope's 2015 encyclical *On Care for Our Common Home*, which denounced the treatment of the earth as a resource to be mastered and exploited and explicitly rejected attempts to justify such conduct in terms of Genesis 1:28. Rather, while 'each community can take from the bounty of the earth whatever it needs for subsistence … it also has the duty to protect the earth and to ensure its fruitfulness for coming generations'.[29])

The public use of the Bible does not correspond neatly with belief, either. This is apparent when secular critics deploy it *against* those who claim to believe it – as when *Sydney Morning Herald* cartoonist Cathy Wilcox re-wrote the Lord's Prayer to suggest the unchristian idolatry of politicians who advocate for the expansion of coal mining in the face of global warming: 'Our coal, which art beneath us … '. At the same time, Christian pressure groups sometimes advance their political arguments in overwhelmingly secular language as if their foundation in the Bible might invalidate their argument. Materials produced by the Australian Christian Lobby during the Marriage Law debate, for example, made very little use of the Bible – preferring instead the terminology of rights and values.

On one level, none of this is unique to the twenty-first century. The story of the Bible in Australia has never been confined to the story of the churches, or Christianity more broadly. Since the earliest days of British colonial settlement, it has been taken up by people with varied beliefs and agendas. Even the energy of

Christian activism has always run in multiple directions. The Bible's implications for social and political life have always been contested. But nearly two and a half centuries after the Bible's initial transmission to Australia, levels of Christian affiliation and participation are at a historic low, as are general levels of biblical literacy. In some quarters, there is a palpable uncertainty about the benefits – even the legitimacy – of religious arguments and perspectives in the public domain. In this novel contemporary context, what weight do biblical arguments carry? How and how much does the Bible matter?

AFTER ASCENDING THE FAMOUS FRONT STEPS OF VICTORIA'S Parliament House, visitors walk through the vestibule across a beautifully tiled floor. Those who care to look down see the imperial coat of arms and a verse from the book of Proverbs: 'Where no counsel is, the people fall: but in the multitude of counsellors there is safety'.[30] Laid down in the 1870s, it is an appropriate sentence for a place where formal political discussion and decision-making occurs. It stresses both that the people need counsel, and that there is value in multiple voices. And while Australia has changed a lot since the 1870s, it is still true that good government and a flourishing society require genuine wisdom, and that the public good is best served by a multitude of counsellors. The need is for a wise, robust, informed pluralism.

In this context, the Bible remains relevant in Australian life and public conversation. One reason is that the world in general remains highly religious, and Christian belief persists even in more secular societies like Australia. As such, the community and its many counsellors will continue to include adherents of the theological Bible, alongside adherents of other faiths and none.

To restrict or exclude religious voices, or to treat religious texts as illegitimate reference points in public conversation, runs counter to the ideal of a plural but inclusive polity and society. This does not mean that the Bible, or perspectives informed by it, is entitled to any particular privilege. Nor should it be immune from rigorous public critique. But a confident, robust pluralism requires tolerance of religious voices, including Christian ones in all their diversity. It requires a willingness to hear and even engage with arguments nourished by Scripture. As Gordon Ramsay, a former Uniting Church minister turned ACT Attorney General has put it: 'Good politics comes from good listening, good conversations'.[31]

The Bible also remains relevant because of its particular place in Australia since British colonisation. It has a history here that, while complicated, is difficult to outrun completely. It lingers, for instance, as part of the legacy of British colonialism – a diffuse and often problematic legacy that is being re-shaped in post-British and post-colonial ways. The Bible has influenced the ways both Indigenous and non-Indigenous people have related to the land, negotiated racial difference, and imagined the nation. In various cultural and theological guises, it has also informed efforts to educate the young, to extend the franchise, and to meet the challenges of poverty. It has been applied to the formation of trade unions, schools and charities, as well as all manner of religious organisations. In the hands of Indigenous Christians, the Bible has nourished movements for justice, for land rights, and for recognition and reconciliation.

In all this, the Bible has been intricately bound up with the way contemporary Australian society has taken shape. It has had social, cultural and institutional impacts that we continue to live with today. This does not make the Bible, or certain interpretations of it, somehow normative for contemporary Australia. Australia is not, and has never been, a straightforwardly Christian society. But an intelligent pluralism requires good historical memory – a substantial and nuanced understanding of the past as the background to the conversation which present generations are joining and continuing. As such, a degree of biblical literacy – along with critical skill in evaluating how the Bible has been taken up and interpreted in our history – can only help Australians grapple well with the choices that society faces.

PRIZEWINNING WRITER CHRISTOS TSIOLKAS, AUTHOR OF *The Slap,* grew up in the Greek Orthodox community of Melbourne, where his post-war migrant parents had met, married, and settled. In early high school, around the same time as realising he was homosexual, Tsiolkas got involved with a Pentecostal church. It was a very difficult experience involving a confronting idea of sin that led him, at fifteen, to make a sharp turn away from Christian things. 'I gave up God and I gave up the Christian faith', as he told Geraldine Doogue on *Compass*. He placed his hopes in Communism and politics, and was eventually disillusioned with those as well: 'These human-made systems not only often didn't work but they left horrific tragedy in their wake'.

By his late twenties, Tsiolkas was 'very unhappy … not in a good place at all'. One day, on a lunch break, he wandered into a Catholic church. Sitting down on a pew, his body fell into the posture of prayer. 'I had not allowed myself to pray for years. And I just found that release and that comfort that I think I was seeking at the time.' There was no sudden clarity, no experience of conversion. His subsequent novels, stories and plays could not be called 'Christian'. 'But I no longer run away from [faith] the way I did for those early years', he explained. He remained in critical dialogue with the Bible, especially, as part of his own post-Orthodox identity and creativity.

'Do I believe in God? I don't know, I am truly agnostic', he has said. But in searching for a code to live by, 'I am a product of my history' – and 'history, you can't outrun it':

> I think there is something of incredible value in Christianity … the notion of turning the other cheek is incredibly important and inspiring for me.

> What was the first story that I really responded to in the Bible? I remember thinking about it for days … 'He who was without sin cast the first stone' (John 8:7), the relationship between Mary Magdalene and Jesus.

> For someone who has grown up in a migrant patriarchal world, here is a prostitute defended by Jesus Christ. Obviously now my relationship to that story has gone through a whole history, but there is something powerful in that Christian message that has played a part in forming my ethics.

> I don't want to discard that essence of that, let me call it a philosophy … how important that moral tradition has been in forming what I think is best in our culture.[32]

Tsiolkas suggests a final reason why the Bible remains relevant in contemporary Australia: its enduring ability to inform moral and ethical values. At a time when society faces challenges that go to the heart of what we might believe about humanity, the world and how best to relate to one another, the Bible can help cultivate an expansive ethical imagination. This is certainly true for Christians like Viv Benjamin, from 2012 to 2014 the CEO of the Oaktree Foundation, a volunteer movement that brings young people together to end global poverty.

> My generation … know[s] that the paradigm of seeking more and more for yourself doesn't work … the system is not working. We need to imagine a different way. And we see that in issues like climate change; in movements like Occupy, protesting Wall Street greed.
>
> The politic of our world is to serve the powerful and to seek to be them. Whereas the politic of Jesus says, 'serve the vulnerable and the weak and the underdog – and identify with them'… It says in [the New Testament letter of] Philippians, that Jesus, though he was in very nature equal with God, chose to come down and make himself humble like a servant, to be the poorest of the poor even unto death. That downward journey is also part of what he calls [Christians] to – whereas the world calls us to upward mobility, to try and reach power for ourselves and assert power over others rather than to serve.[33]

Most twenty-first century Australians are not nearly as familiar with the New Testament as Benjamin. Nor have they internalised what she calls the radical 'politic of Jesus' as deliberately or as deeply. But even for those who, like Tsiolkas, no longer identify with Christianity, or perhaps never did, the Bible may still speak to the human condition, with something to offer the ethical imagination. After all, in the 3000 years since its first portions were authored, the Bible has given rise to one of the world's major reservoirs of ethical reflection. It underpins a long and diverse tradition of thought on social, moral and political questions. And while the church's own record has been very mixed, and at times patently destructive, the Bible, variously interpreted, continues to appear in startling ways – as a source of inspiration, power and practical wisdom.

SELECT BIBLIOGRAPHY

Alderton, Z, 'Nick Cave: a journey from an Anglican God to a creative Christ', *Literature & Aesthetics*, vol. 19, no. 2, 2009, pp. 169–186.

Atkinson, A, *The Europeans in Australia Volume 1: The Beginning*, OUP, Melbourne, 1997.

—— *The Europeans in Australia Volume 2: Democracy*, OUP, Melbourne, 2004.

—— *The Europeans in Australia Volume 3: Nation*, UNSW Press, Sydney, 2014.

—— 'How do we live with ourselves? The Australian national conscience', RAFT Fellowship essay, *Australian Book Review*, no. 384, 2016.

Austin, AG, *Australian Education 1788–1900: Church, State and Public Education in Colonial Australia*, 3rd ed., Pitman Pacific Books, Melbourne, 1972.

Bale, C, *A Crowd of Witnesses: Epitaphs on First World War Australian War Graves*, Longueville Media, Sydney, 2015a.

—— '"We will remember them": The use of the Bible in remembering the service and sacrifice of Australians in WWI' in J Harris (ed.), *Their Sacrifice. The Brave and their Bibles*, Bible Society Australia, Sydney, 2015b, pp. 117–125.

Bashford, A, & Macintyre, S (eds.), *Cambridge History of Australia. Volume 1: Indigenous and Colonial Australia*, CUP, Melbourne, 2015.

Blackburn, K, 'The living wage in Australia: a secularisation of Catholic ethics on wages, 1891–1907', *Journal of Religious History*, vol. 20, 1996, pp. 93–113.

Boer, R, *Last Stop Before Antarctica: The Bible and Postcolonialism in Australia*, 2nd ed., Society of Biblical Literature, Atlanta, 2008.

—— *Nick Cave: A Study of Love, Death, and Apocalypse*, Equinox Publishing, Bristol, 2012.

—— 'The absurdly ideal Jesus of Reg Mombassa' in C Blyth & N Vaka'uta (eds.), *The Bible and Art: Perspectives from Oceania*, Bloomsbury, London and New York, 2017, pp. 55–72.

Boer, R & Abraham, I, 'Australasia', in JFA Sawyer (ed.), *The Blackwell Companion to the Bible and Culture*, Blackwell, Oxford, 2006, pp. 232–249.

Bollen, JD, *Protestantism and Social Reform in New South Wales, 1890–1910*, MUP, Melbourne, 1972.

Brett, MG, 'A suitably English Abraham: emigration to Australia in the nineteenth century', in J Havea (ed.), *Postcolonial Voices from Downunder: Indigenous Matters, Confronting Readings*, Pickwick Publications, Eugene, 2017, pp. 110–121.

Brooke, JH & Numbers, RL (eds.), *Science and Religion Around the World*, OUP, Oxford and New York, 2011.

Broome, R, *Aboriginal Australians: A History since 1788*, 4th ed, Allen & Unwin, Sydney, 2010.

Butcher, BW, 'Darwin down under: science, religion and evolution in Australia', in R Numbers & J Stenhouse (eds.), *Disseminating Darwinism: The Role of Place, Race, Religion and Gender*, CUP, Cambridge, 1999, pp. 39–60.

Carey, H, *Believing in Australia, A Cultural History of Religions*, Allen & Unwin, Sydney, 1996.

—— 'Lancelot Threlkeld, Biraban, and the colonial Bible in Australia', *Comparative Studies in Society and History*, vol. 52, no. 2, 2010, pp. 447–478.

Chavura, S & Tregenza, I, 'A political history of the secular in Australia, 1788–1945', in T Stanley (ed.), *Religion after Secularization in Australia*, Palgrave Macmillan, New York, 2015, pp. 3–31.

Chilton, H, 'Evangelicals and the end of Christian Australia: nation and religion in the public square, 1959–1979', unpublished PhD thesis, University of Sydney, 2014.

Crumlin, R, *Images of Religion in Australian Art*, Bay Books, Sydney, 1988.

Daniell, D, *The Bible in English: Its History and Influence*, Yale University Press, New Haven, 2003.

Davison, G, *Narrating the Nation in Australia: Menzies Lecture 2009*, Menzies Centre for Australian Studies, London, 2009.

—— 'Religion', in A Bashford & S Macintyre (eds.), *The Cambridge History of Australia vol. 2: The Commonwealth*, CUP, Melbourne, 2013, pp. 215–236.

De Hamel, C, *The Book: A History of the Bible*, Phaidon Press, London and New York, 2001.

Elford, K, 'A prophet without honour: the political ideals of John Dunmore Lang', *Journal of the Royal Australian Historical Society*, vol. 54, no. 2, 1968, pp. 161–175.

Ely, R, *Unto God and Caesar: Religious Issues in the Emerging Commonwealth, 1891–1906*, MUP, Carlton, 1976.

—— 'The forgotten nationalism: Australian civic Protestantism in the Second World War', *Journal of Australian Studies*, vol. 11, no. 20, 1987, pp. 59–67.

—— 'Protestantism in Australian history: an interpretative sketch', *Lucas: An Evangelical History Review*, vol. 5, 1989, pp. 11–20.

Gascoigne, J, *The Enlightenment and the Origins of European Australia*, CUP, New York, 2002.

Gladwin, M, 'Australian Anglican clergymen, science and religion, 1820–1850', in P Clarke & T Claydon (eds.), *God's Bounty: The Churches and the Natural World*, Ecclesiastical History Society, Woodbridge, Suffolk, 2010, pp. 293–306.

—— 'Anzac Day's religious custodians', in T Frame (ed.), *Anzac Day Then & Now*, NewSouth Publishing, Sydney, 2016, pp. 90–111.

—— 'Preaching and Australian public life: 1788–1914', *St Mark's Review*, no. 227, 2014, pp. 1–14.

—— *Anglican Clergy in Australia, 1788–1850: Building a British World*, Royal Historical Society with Boydell & Brewer, Woodbridge, 2015.

Greenslade, SL (ed.) *The Cambridge History of the Bible vol. 3: The West from the Reformation to the Present Day*, CUP, Cambridge, 1963.

Gregory, JS, *Church and State: Changing Government Policies towards Religion in Australia; with Particular Reference to Victoria since Separation*, Cassell Australia, Melbourne, 1973.

Griffen-Foley, B, 'Radio ministries: religion on Australian commercial radio from the 1920s to the 1960s', *Journal of Religious History*, vol. 32, no. 1, 2008, pp. 31–54.

Harris, D, Hynd, D & Millikan, D (eds.), *The Shape of Belief: Christianity in Australia Today*, Lancer, Homebush West, 1982.

Harris, J, *One Blood: 200 Years of Aboriginal Encounter with Christianity: A Story of Hope*, Albatross Books, Sydney, 1990.

—— (ed.), *Their Sacrifice: The Brave and their Bibles*, Bible Society Australia, Sydney, 2015.

—— 'Words of justice in a secular society: the role of the King James Version of the Bible in Australia', in A Duran (ed.), *The King James Bible: Across Borders and Centuries*, Duquesne University Press, Pittsburgh, 2014, pp. 151–172.

Harrison, P, *The Bible, Protestantism, and the Rise of Natural Science*, CUP, Cambridge, 1998.

Healey, A, 'A critical alliance: ABC religious broadcasting and the Christian churches', *Journal of the Australian Catholic Historical Society*, vol. 26, 2005, pp. 15–28.

Hilliard, D, 'Australia: towards secularisation and one step back', in CG Brown & M Snape (eds.), *Secularisation in the Christian World: Essays in Honor of Hugh McLeod*, Ashgate, Farnham, 2010.

Howe, R, *A Century of Influence: The Australian Student Christian Movement 1896–1996*, UNSW Press, Sydney, 2009.

—— 'The Australian Student Christian Movement and women's activism in the Asia-Pacific Region 1890s–1920s', *Australian Feminist Studies*, vol. 16, no. 36, 2001, pp. 311–323.

Howsam, L, *Cheap Bibles: Nineteenth Century Publishing and the British and Foreign Bible Society*, CUP, Cambridge, 1991.

Hudson, W, *Australian Religious Thought*, Monash University Press, Melbourne, 2016.

Hutchinson, M & Campion, E (eds.), *Re-visioning Australian Colonial Christianity: New Essays in the Australian Christian Experience 1788–1900*, Centre for the Study of Australian Christianity, Sydney, 1994.

Hyslop, A, 'Temperance, Christianity and feminism: the Woman's Christian Temperance Union of Victoria, 1887–97', *Historical Studies*, vol. 17, no. 66, 1976, pp. 27–49.

Inglis, KS, *Sacred Places: War Memorials in the Australian Landscape*, Miegunyah Press, Melbourne, 1998.

Jupp, J (ed.), *The Encyclopaedia of Religion in Australia*, CUP, Cambridge, 2009.

Keary, A, 'Christianity, colonialism and cross-cultural translation: Lancelot Threlkeld, Biraban and the Awabakal', *Aboriginal History*, vol. 33, 2009, pp. 117–155.

Kenny, R, *The Lamb Enters the Dreaming: Nathanael Pepper & the Ruptured World*, Scribe Publications, Melbourne, 2010.

Kidd, C, *The Forging of Races: Race and Scripture in the Protestant Atlantic World 1600–2000*, CUP, Cambridge, 2006.

Killeen, K & Forshaw, P (eds.), *The Word and the World: Biblical Exegesis and Early Modern Science*, Palgrave Macmillan, Basingstoke, 2007.

Linder, RD, *The Long Tragedy: Australian Evangelical Christians and the Great War, 1914–1918*, Centre for the Study of Australian Christianity, Open Book Publishers, Adelaide, 2000.

—— 'The Methodist love affair with the Australian Labor Party 1891–1929', *Lucas: An Evangelical History Review*, no. 23 & 24, 1997–1998, pp. 35–61.

Lyons, M & Tasker, L, *Australian Readers Remember: An Oral History of Reading 1890–1930*, OUP, Melbourne, 1992.

McLeod, H (ed.), *The Cambridge History of Christianity Volume 9: World Christianities c. 1914–c. 2000*, CUP, Cambridge, 2006.

Melleuish, G, 'A secular Australia? Ideas, politics and the search for moral order in nineteenth and early twentieth century Australia', *Journal of Religious History*, vol. 38, no. 3, 2014, pp. 398–412.

O'Brien, A, 'Religion', in A Bashford & S Macintyre (eds.), *Cambridge History of Australia. Volume 1: Indigenous and Colonial Australia*, CUP, Melbourne, 2015, pp. 414–437.

—— *God's Willing Workers: Women and Religion in Australia*, UNSW Press, Sydney, 2005.

O'Brien, G & Carey, H (eds.), *Methodism in Australia: A History*, Ashgate, Farnham, 2015.

O'Farrell, P, 'Bible reading and related mental furniture', *Australian Cultural History*, vol. 11, 1992, pp. 16–27.

Oliver, B, *Peacemongers: Conscientious Objectors to Military Service in Australia 1911–1945*, Fremantle Arts Centre Press, Perth, 1997.

Pattel-Gray, A (ed.), *Aboriginal Spirituality: Past, Present, Future*, Harper Collins, Melbourne, 1996.

Pattel-Gray, A & Brown, J (eds.), *Indigenous Australia: A Dialogue about the Word Becoming Flesh in Aboriginal Churches*, World Council of Churches Publications, Geneva, 1997.

Paulson, G & Brett, M, 'Five smooth stones: reading the Bible through Aboriginal eyes', *Colloquium*, vol. 45, no. 2, 2013.

Phillips, W, *James Jefferis: Prophet of Federation*, Australian Scholarly Publishing, Melbourne, 1993.

—— 'Religious profession and practice in NSW 1850–1901: the statistical evidence', *Historical Studies*, vol. 15, no. 59, 1972, pp. 378–400.

—— 'The defence of Christian belief in Australia 1875–1914: the responses to evolution and higher criticism', *Journal of Religious History*, vol. 9, no. 4, 1977, pp. 402–423.

—— 'Religious response to Darwin in Australia in the nineteenth century', *Journal of Australian Studies*, vol. 26, 1990, pp. 37–51.

—— 'Seeking souls in the diggings: Christian missions to the Chinese on the Victorian goldfields', *Victorian Historical Journal*, vol. 72, nos. 1–2, 2001, pp. 86–104.

Piggin, S, 'Power and religion in a modern state: desecularisation in Australian history', *Journal of Religious History*, vol. 38, no. 3, 2014, pp. 320–340.

—— (ed.), *Shaping the Good Society in Australia*, Australia's Christian Heritage National Forum, Macquarie, 2006.

Piggin, S & Linder, RD, *The Fountain of Public Prosperity: Evangelical Christians in Australian History, 1740–1914*, Monash University Publishing, Melbourne, 2018 (forthcoming).

—— *Attending to the Australian Soul: Evangelical Christians in Australian History, 1914–2014* (forthcoming).

Prince, J & Prince, M, *Tuned in to Change: A History of the Australian Scripture Union, 1880–1980*, Scripture Union of Australia, Sydney, 1979.

Riches, J (ed.), *The New Cambridge History of the Bible: Vol. 4, From 1750 to the Present*, CUP, Cambridge, 2015.

Roberts, DA, 'Language to save the innocent: Reverend L Threlkeld's linguistic mission', *Journal of the Royal Australian Historical Society*, vol. 94, no. 2, 2008, pp. 107–125.

Sharp, N, *Malo's Law in Court: The Religious Background to the Mabo Case*, Charles Strong Memorial Trust, Adelaide, 1994.

—— *Stars of Tagai: The Torres Strait Islanders*, Aboriginal Studies Press, Canberra, 1993.

Sheehan, J, *The Enlightenment Bible: Translation, Scholarship, Culture*, Princeton University Press, Princeton, 2005.

Surgitharajah, RS, *The Bible and Asia: From the Pre-Christian Era to the Postcolonial Age*, Harvard University Press, Cambridge MA, 2013.

Swain, S, 'A long history of faith-based welfare in Australia: origins and impact', *Journal of Religious History*, vol. 41, no. 1, 2017, pp. 81–96.

Thompson, A, *Australia and the Bible: A Brief Outline of the Work of the British and Foreign Bible Society in Australia 1807–1934*, British and Foreign Bible Society, London, 1935.

Topham, J, 'Science, religion and the history of the book', in T Dixon, G Cantor & S Pumfrey (eds.), *Science and Religion: New Historical Perspectives*, CUP, Cambridge and New York, 2010, pp. 221–244.

Van Toorn, P, *Writing Never Arrives Naked: Early Aboriginal Cultures of Writing in Australia*, Aboriginal Studies Press, Canberra, 2006.

Williams, R, *In God They Trust?: The Religious Beliefs of Australia's Prime Ministers, 1901–2013*, Bible Society Australia, 2013.

Zaunbrecher, M, 'Henry Lawson's religion', *Journal of Religious History*, vol. 11, no. 2, 1980, pp. 308–19.

Web resources

Ganter, R (ed.), *German Missionaries in Australia – A web-directory of intercultural encounters*, Griffith University, 2016, <missionaries.griffith.edu.au>.

Australian Dictionary of Biography, National Centre of Biography, Australian National University, 2006–2017, <adb.anu.edu.au/>.

The Encyclopedia of Women & Leadership in Twentieth-Century Australia, Australian Women's Archives Project, 2014, <www.womenaustralia.info/leaders>.

e-Melbourne: the city past and present, School of Historical & Philosophical Studies, University of Melbourne, 2008, <www.emelbourne.net.au/index.html>.

NOTES

Introduction: Under the skin

1   R Clark, P Fidlon & RJ Ryan, *The Journal and Letters of Lt. Ralph Clark 1787–1792*, Australian Documents Library in Association with The Library of Australian History, Sydney, 1981, entry for Tuesday 1 May 1792.

2   H Maxwell-Stewart & I Duffield, 'Skin deep devotions: religious tattoos and convict transportation to Australia', in J Caplan (ed.), *Written on the Body: The Tattoo in European and American History*, Princeton University Press, Princeton, 2000, p. 134; S Barnard, *Convict Tattoos: Marked Men and Women of Australia*, Text Publishing, Melbourne, 2016, p. 26.

3   A Heuken, 'Christianity in pre-colonial Indonesia', in JS Aritonang & KA Steenbrink (eds.), *A History of Christianity in Indonesia*, Brill, Leiden, 2008, pp. 3–7. See more generally RS Surgitharajah, *The Bible and Asia: From the Pre-Christian Era to the Postcolonial Age*, Harvard University Press, Cambridge MA, 2013.

4   C Hamilton, 'Political correctness: the left won the war but should be wiser about its battles', *ABC Religion and Ethics*, 31 August 2015, <www.abc.net.au/religion/articles/2015/08/31/4303139.htm>.

5   Quoted in A Langmaid, 'All kids must read the Bible, federal opposition leader Tony Abbott says', *Herald Sun*, 18 December 2009, <www.heraldsun.com.au/archive/news/all-kids-must-read-the-Bible-federal-opposition-leader-tony-abbott-says/story-e6frf7l6-1225811885777>.

6   *Sydney Morning Herald*, 14–15 August 2010, News Review p. 4, cited in S Piggin, 'Power and religion in a modern state: desecularisation in Australian history', *Journal of Religious History*, vol. 38, no. 3, 2014, pp. 1–21.

7   J Sheehan, *The Enlightenment Bible: Translation, Scholarship, Culture*, Princeton University Press, Princeton, 2005.

8   See entry in WS Ransom & WS Ramson (eds.), *The Australian National Dictionary: A Dictionary of Australianisms on Historical Principles*, Oxford University Press, Melbourne, 1988.

9   P O'Farrell, 'Bible reading and related mental furniture', *Australian Cultural History*, vol. 11, 1992, p. 19.

10   J Hull, 'Bible in state schools question', *The Worker*, 19 February 1910, p. 13, cited in Y Perkins, 'Queensland's Bible in State Schools Referendum 1910: a case study of democracy', unpublished BA (Hons) thesis, University of Sydney, 2010, p. 41.

11 J Jefferis, 'How shall we read the Bible?', in his *Our Bible and Our Beliefs: Six Lectures Delivered in the Congregational Church, Pitt Street, Sydney, as a Help to Young Men of Free Thought*, Samuel Lees, Sydney, 1882, p. 1.

12 According to the 2006 census, 63 per cent of Australians identified as Christian; according to the Nielsen poll, 67 per cent of Australians did.

13 Nielsen poll, 'Faith in Australia, 2009', Survey report 16 December 2009, <www.smh.com.au/pdf/Nielsen%20Poll%20Faith%20Dec19.pdf>.

14 P Robertson, '"The one thing needful": three evangelical Anglican women in the Hunter Region of NSW, 1825–1850', *Lucas: An Evangelical History Review*, vol. 23 & 24, 1997–1998, pp. 5–34.

15 M Reeson, *Currency Lass,* Albatross Books, Sydney, 1985, p. 72.

16 J Jefferis, 'What has the Bible done?', in *Our Bible and Our Beliefs,* 1882.

Part 1: Colonial Foundations

1 G Worgan, *Journal of a First Fleet Surgeon*, Library Council of New South Wales in association with the Library of Australian History, Sydney, 1978, p. 1.

Chapter 1: In the beginning?

1 Augustine, *The City of God*, trans. M Dods, Digireads edition, 2009, Book 16, chapter 9, pp. 398–99 (first published in Latin in CE426).

2 'Magellan as preacher (1521)' extracted from Pigafetta's Journal in K Koschorke, F Ludwig & M Delgado (eds.), *A History of Christianity in Asia, Africa and Latin America, 1450–1990: A Documentary Source Book*, William Eerdmans, Grand Rapids, 2007, p. 21.

3 J Cook, *Endeavour* journal, entry for Friday 21 September 1770, National Library of Australia, Manuscript 1, page 318, online transcription at <nla.gov.au/nla.cs-ss-jrnl-cook-17700921>.

4 G Denning, 'Cook, James', in G Davison, J Hirst & S Macintyre (eds.), *The Oxford Companion to Australian History*, Oxford University Press (OUP), Melbourne, 2001.

5 D Daniell, *The Bible in English: Its History and Influence*, Yale University Press, New Haven, 2003, pp. 131–145, 429–430.

6 Johann Eck, *Enchiridion* (1525), cited in R Roldan-Figueroa, 'Bible in the Reformation', in R Benedetto (ed.), *New Westminster Dictionary of Church History vol. 1*, Westminster John Knox Press, Louisville and London, 2008, p. 88.

7 S Prickett, 'Eighteenth century and romantic: introduction', in R Lemon, E Mason, J Roberts & C Rowland (eds.), *The Blackwell Companion to the Bible in English Literature*, Wiley-Blackwell, Oxford, 2009, pp. 313–328.

8 J Newton, diary entry for Tuesday 8 July 1777, cited at <www.johnnewton.org/Groups/252728/The_John_Newton/new_menus/Whos_Who/Richard_Johnson/Richard_Johnson.aspx>.

9 See the list of books sent out with Johnson in N Macintosh, *Richard Johnson, Chaplain to the Colony of NSW: His Life and Times 1755–1827*, Library of Australian History, Sydney, 1978, pp. 105–106.

10 R Johnson, *An Address to the Inhabitants of the Colonies Established in New South Wales and Norfolk Island*, London, 1794, online at <acl.asn.au/pdf/Richard_Johnson's_Address.pdf> pp. 4–5.

11   G Browne, *The History of the British and Foreign Bible Society*, Bible Society,
     London, 1859, vol. 1, p. 3.
12   A Strachan, *Remarkable Incidents in the Life of the Rev. Samuel Leigh*, James
     Nichols, London, 1853, p. 26.
13   'Rev. William Henry to the London Missionary Society', Parramatta, 29 August
     1799, in FM Bladen (ed.), *Historical Records of NSW*, Government Printer, Sydney,
     1895, vol. 3, pp. 714–5. I thank Dr Stephen Chavura for this reference.
14   Reported in G Worgan, *Journal of a First Fleet Surgeon*, Library Council of New
     South Wales in association with the Library of Australian History, Sydney, 1978,
     p. 36, alluding to 2 Thessalonians 3:10.
15   A O'Brien, *God's Willing Workers: Women and Religion in Australia*, UNSW Press,
     Sydney, 2005, p. 22.
16   T Watling & G Mackaness, *Letters from an Exile at Botany-Bay to his Aunt
     in Dumfries*, Review Publications, Dubbo, 1979; 'George Barrington to a
     gentleman in the County of York', Cape of Good Hope, 1 July 1791 in FM
     Bladen (ed.), *Historical Records of NSW*, vol 2, Government Printer, Sydney,
     1893, p. 783; 'Letter from a female convict', 14 November 1788, Bladen 1893,
     pp. 746–747.
17   Cited in S Barnard, *Convict Tattoos: Marked Men and Women of Australia*, Text
     Publishing, Melbourne, 2016, p. 26.
18   J Bradley & H Maxwell-Stewart, 'Embodied explorations: investigating convict
     tattoos and the transportation system' in I Duffield & J Bradley (eds.), *Representing
     Convicts: New Perspectives on Convict Forced Labour Migration*, Leicester
     University Press, London, 1997, p. 196.
19   Barnard 2016, p. 27.
20   H Maxwell-Stewart & I Duffield, 'Skin deep devotions: religious tattoos and
     convict transportation to Australia', in J Caplan (ed.), *Written on the Body: The
     Tattoo in European and American History*, Princeton University Press, Princeton,
     2000, p. 130.
21   Maxwell-Stewart & Duffield 2000, p. 127.
22   Barnard 2016, p. 50.
23   It seems Isherwood already had these particular tattoos when he first arrived in
     Van Diemen's Land. See Barnard 2016, p. 24.
24   P O'Farrell, *The Catholic Church in Australia: A Short History 1788–1967*, Thomas
     Nelson, Melbourne, 1968, p. 13.
25   A Atkinson, *The Europeans in Australia Volume 1: The Beginning*, OUP,
     Melbourne, 1997, p. 178.
26   Maxwell-Stewart & Duffield 2000, pp. 129–31.
27   Maxwell-Stewart & Duffield 2000, p. 132.
28   A Thompson, *Australia and the Bible: A Brief Outline of the Work of the British and
     Foreign Bible Society in Australia 1807–1934*, British and Foreign Bible Society,
     London, 1935, p. 30.
29   P Cunningham, *Two Years in New South Wales*, Henry Colburn, London, 1827,
     vol. 1, pp. 253–254.
30   Cunningham 1827, vol. 1, p. 254.
31   Cunningham 1827, vol. 1, pp. 280–281.

32   Rev Richard Hill to Governor Macquarie 8 July 1819, cited in A Grocott, *Convicts, clergymen and churches: attitudes of convicts and ex-convicts towards the churches and clergy in New South Wales, 1788–1851*, Sydney University Press, Sydney, 1980, p. 49.

33   Extracts from Johnson's journal, cited in Macintosh 1978, p. 107.

34   JT Bigge 1822, cited in Grocott 1980, p. 45.

35   B Smith, *Australia's Birthstain: The Startling Legacy of the Convict Era*, Allen & Unwin, Sydney, 2008, p. 353.

36   D Baker, *Days of Wrath: A Life of John Dunmore Lang*, Melbourne University Press (MUP), Melbourne, 1985, p. 58.

37   Cited in Grocott 1980, p. 267.

38   J Hawes, 1830, cited in T O'Connor, 'Raising Lazurus', in L Frost & H Maxwell-Stewart (eds.), *Chain Letters: Narrating Convict Lives*, MUP, Melbourne, 2001, p. 148. My emphasis. The allusion is to Luke 23.

39   JD Merewether, *Diary of a Working Clergyman in Australia and Tasmania, Kept During the Years 1850–53*, Hatchard & Co, London, 1859, p. 59.

Chapter 2: Indigenous encounters

1   W Tench, *A Complete Account of the Settlement at Port Jackson in New South Wales*, Nichol & Sewell, London, 1793, p. 21.

2   A Atkinson, *The Europeans in Australia Volume 1: The Beginning*, Oxford University Press (OUP), Melbourne, 1997, p. 182.

3   D Collins, *An Account of the English Colony in New South Wales*, Cadell & Davies, London, 1798.

4   R Johnson to H Fricker, 9 April 1790, safe 1/121, Mitchell Library, State Library of NSW, digitised at <archival.sl.nsw.gov.au/Details/archive/110331129>.

5   See M Lake, 'Salvation and conciliation: First missionary encounters at Sydney Cove', in A Barry, J Cruickshank, A Brown-May & P Grimshaw (eds.), *Evangelists of Empire? Missionaries in Colonial History*, eScholarship Research Centre, Melbourne, 2008, pp. 87–102.

6   M Johnson, letter to Henry Fricker, 21 December 1795, MLMSS 6722, Mitchell Library, Sydney.

7   KV Smith, 'Bennelong among his people', *Aboriginal History*, vol. 33, 2009, pp. 7–30.

8   DA Roberts & M Reeson, 'Wesleyan Methodist missions to Australia and the Pacific', in G O'Brien & H Carey (eds.), *Methodism in Australia: A History*, Ashgate, Farnham, 2015, pp. 197–210.

9   W Walker to Secretary Wesleyan Missionary Society, 29 April 1823, cited in J Brook & JL Kohen, *The Parramatta Native Institution and the Black Town: A History*, UNSW Press, Sydney, 1991, p. 164.

10   W Walker, cited in J Colwell, *The Illustrated History of Methodism; Australia, 1812–1855, New South Wales and Polynesia, 1856–1902*, William Brooks & Co., Sydney, 1904, p. 176.

11   Walker to Watson, 20 February 1822, cited in Brook & Kohen 1991, p. 160.

12   Colwell 1904, p. 176.

13   *Sydney Gazette*, 27 September 1822, p. 2, <nla.gov.au/nla.news-article2181341>.

14   H Carey, *Believing in Australia, A Cultural History of Religions*, Allen & Unwin, Sydney, 1996, pp. 53–54.

15   W Carey, *An Enquiry into the Obligations of Christians to Use Means for the Conversion of the Heathens*, Leicester, 1792.

16   Richard Johnson to Joseph Hardcastle, 26 August 1799, *Evangelical Magazine*, 1800, p. 302.

17   R Kenny, *The Lamb Enters the Dreaming: Nathanael Pepper & the Ruptured World*, Scribe Publications, Melbourne, 2010, pp. 176–177, 199.

18   P Van Toorn, *Writing Never Arrives Naked: Early Aboriginal Cultures of Writing in Australia*, Aboriginal Studies Press, Canberra, 2006, p. 100 and chapter 5 more generally.

19   Walker, cited in Colwell 1904, p. 176

20   Roberts & Reeson, 2015, p. 199. Walker's mission was suspended on the basis of 'his unwillingness to cooperate with the rulings of his Methodist colleagues'.

21   P Brock, 'Christian missions to Aboriginal people', in J Jupp (ed.), *The Encyclopaedia of Religion in Australia*, Cambridge University Press (CUP), Cambridge, 2009, p. 96.

22   Brock 2009, p. 96.

23   See R Ganter, 'Introduction', in R Ganter (ed.), *German Missionaries in Australia – A web-directory of intercultural encounters*, Griffith University, 2016, <missionaries.griffith.edu.au/introduction>.

24   Brock 2009, p. 96.

25   Carey 1996, pp. 54–55.

26   E Fenn, 'The Bible and the missionary', *The Cambridge History of the Bible: The West from the Reformation to the Present Day*, vol. 3, CUP, Cambridge, 1963, pp. 383–407.

27   P Van Toorn 2006, p. 214.

28   T Brune, sermon, 20 April 1838, Robinson Papers, ML A7073 vol. 52 part 6, f.135 cited in Van Toorn 2006, p. 115.

29   For a detailed and probing discussion, see Van Toorn 2006, ch. 5.

30   T Brune, *Flinders Island Weekly Chronicle*, 17 Nov 1837, cited in A Heiss & P Minter (eds.), *Macquarie PEN Anthology of Aboriginal Literature*, Allen & Unwin, Sydney, 2008, pp. 10–11.

31   Wouraddy, address to the weekly meeting for prayer and mutual instruction, translated into English by Pieyenkomeyenner, April 1838. Journal annotations, 14 April 1838, quoted in Van Toorn 2006, p. 117.

32   G Taplin, 'Journal 1859–1879', entry for 31 January 1860, PRG 186-1/3, State Library of South Australia, transcription at <www.firstsources.info/ uploads/3/4/5/4/34544232/taplins_diary_1859-79.pdf>.

33   See J Harris, *One Blood: 200 Years of Aboriginal Encounter with Christianity: A Story of Hope*, Albatross Books, Sydney, 1990, pp. 357–370.

34   Djiniyini Gondarra, *Let My People Go*, 1986, cited in Van Toorn 2006, p. 118.

35   From the preface to Threlkeld's revised *Australian Grammar*, 1850, cited in H Carey, 'Lancelot Threlkeld, Biraban, and the colonial Bible in Australia', *Comparative Studies in Society and History*, vol. 52, no. 2, 2010, pp. 447–478.

36   When a young American philologist visited the mission in 1839, it was obvious

to him that 'McGill was accustomed to teach his native language, for when he was asked the name of anything he pronounced the word very distinctly, syllable by syllable, so that it was impossible to mistake it'. Horatio Hale, cited in C Wilkes, *Narrative of the United States Exploring Expedition*, vol. 2, Wiley & Putnam, London, 1845, p. 253.

37 Historic interactions with Muslims from Macassar did lead to the incorporation of Arabic-language elements into Yolngu, and a growing minority of Aboriginal people now identify as Muslim. But the Qur'an has not been the focus for translation projects here.

38 For example, 'Verily, we have made it an Arabic Qur'an, haply ye will comprehend it', Surah 43:3.

39 J Sheehan, *The Enlightenment Bible: Translation, Scholarship, Culture*, Princeton University Press, Princeton, 2005, chapter 1.

40 Cited in DA Roberts, '"Language to save the innocent": Reverend L Threlkeld's linguistic mission', *Journal of the Royal Australian Historical Society*, vol. 94, no. 2, 2008, p. 111.

41 Harper Biography, Wellington Valley Project, University of Newcastle, <downloads.newcastle.edu.au/library/cultural%20collections/the-wellington-valley-project/wellpro/h/harper.html>.

42 See DA Roberts & H Carey, '"Beong! Beong! (more! more!)": John Harper and the Wesleyan mission to the Australian Aborigines', *Journal of Colonialism and Colonial History*, vol. 10, no. 1, 2009.

43 See H Carey, 'Death, God and linguistics: conversations with missionaries on the Australian frontier 1824–1845', *Australian Historical Studies*, 2009, pp. 169–174, and J Harris, *One Blood: 200 years of Aboriginal Encounter with Christianity: A story of Hope*, Albatross Books, Sydney, 1990, pp. 60–61.

44 Cited in Harris 1990, p. 230.

45 After four years, Ridley was forced to abandon his efforts and return to parish ministry. He maintained a lifelong interest in Indigenous tongues, however, publishing *Kamilaroi, Dippil, and Turrubul: Languages Spoken by Australian Aborigines* in 1866, and a revised and enlarged version as *Kamilaroi and Other Australian Languages* in 1875. See N Gunson, 'Ridley, William (1819–1878)', *Australian Dictionary of Biography (ADB)*, Australian National University, first published 1976, <adb.anu.edu.au/biography/ridley-william-4477/text7309>.

46 BJ Blake (ed.), 'Wathawurrung and the Colac language of southern Victoria', ANU Research School of Pacific and Asian Studies, Canberra, 1998. <victoriancollections.net.au/media/collectors/52f0758a9821f40464f742c1/items/56c69086400d0c3518d14bdb/56d6732d2162f11c380e1440/original.pdf>; and further CA McCallum, 'Tuckfield, Francis (1808–1865)', *ADB*, National Centre of Biography, Australian National University, <adb.anu.edu.au/biography/tuckfield-francis-2747/text3887>.

47 DJ Mulvaney, 'Thomas, William (1793–1867)', *ADB,* National Centre of Biography, Australian National University, <adb.anu.edu.au/biography/thomas-william-2727/text3845>.

48 MH Fels, *'I Succeeded Once': The Aboriginal Protectorate on the Mornington Peninsula, 1839–1840,* ANU EPress, Canberra, 2011, p. 6.

49   Fels 2011, chapter 12.

50   Taplin journal, entry for 29 March 1860.

51   The results of his continued translation and ethnographic work, done partly in collaboration with James Uniapon (Ngunaitponi), included a *Native Book of Worship* (1874) and a number of ethnographic works, including *The Narrinyeri* (1874) and *The Folklore, Manners, Customs and Languages of the South Australian Aborigines* (1879).

52   Ganter 2016.

53   See WF Veit, 'Strehlow, Carl Friedrich Theodor (1871–1922)', *ADB*, National Centre of Biography, <adb.anu.edu.au/biography/strehlow-carl-friedrich-theodor-8698/text15221>; and A Kenny, *The Aranda's Pepa: An Introduction to Carl Strehlow's Masterpiece Die Aranda- und Loritja-Stamme in Zentral-Australien (1907–1920)*, ANU EPress, Canberra, 2013.

54   Quoted in NJB Plomley & GA Robinson, *Weep in Silence: A History of the Flinders Island Aboriginal Settlement with the Flinders Island Journal of George Augustus Robinson 1835–1839,* Blubber Head Press, Hobart, 1987, pp. 68–70.

55   See C Lockwood, 'Rev. Samuel Gottlieb Klose (1805–1889)', in R Ganter (ed.) *German Missionaries in Australia – A web-directory of intercultural encounters*, Griffith University, 2016, <missionaries.griffith.edu.au/biography/klose-rev-samuel-gottlieb-1805-1889>.

56   J Cruickshank & P Grimshaw, '"I had gone to teach but stayed to learn": Geraldine MacKenzie at Aurukun Mission, 1925–1965', *Journal of Australian Studies*, vol. 39, no. 1, 2015, pp. 54–65.

57   R Ganter, 'Cape Bedford Mission (Hope Vale) (1886–1942)', in R Ganter (ed.), *German Missionaries in Australia – A web-directory of intercultural encounters*, Griffith University, 2016, <missionaries.griffith.edu.au/introduction>.

58   Cited in Roberts 2008, p. 114

59   See Kenny 2010.

60   British and Foreign Bible Society, *After a Hundred Years: A Popular Illustrated Report of the BFBS for the Centenary Year 1903–4*, Bible House, London, 1904, p. 3.

61   The Lord's Prayer, translated from English into Nyul Nyul, and then from Nyul Nyul back into English by Herman Nekes, Pallottine missionary to the Kimberley, <missionaries.griffith.edu.au/biography/nekes-hermann-fr-prof-dr-1875-1948#Language_work_in_the_Kimberley>, citing 'Aborigines do tricks with tongues', *The Mail*, Adelaide, 8 April 1939, p. 5.

62   A scan of the manuscript can be viewed via the State Library of NSW, <acmssearch.sl.nsw.gov.au/search/itemDetailPaged.cgi?itemID=825646>.

63   Threlkeld and Biraban's Gospel of Mark Manuscript, p. 189, SLNSW, accessed at <acmssearch.sl.nsw.gov.au/search/itemDetailPaged.cgi?itemID=825646> digitised page.

64   Carey 2010, pp. 447–478.

65   See A Keary, 'Christianity, colonialism, and cross-cultural translation: Lancelot Threlkeld, Biraban, and the Awabakal', *Aboriginal History*, vol. 33, 2009, p. 138.

66   At Raukkan, Taplin came to a similar decision: 'I shall in future speak of our God by His name Jehova, and not use *Nurundere* for the name of God, lest the natives should think there was any resemblance between the God of the Bible and the corrupt offspring of their own imaginations', Taplin journal, 22 September 1859.

67   Keary 2009.

68   Threlkeld, '7th report 1837'; Threlkeld, 'Concluding remarks 1838'; Threlkeld, 8th annual report, all cited in Keary 2009, p. 140.

69   Carey 2010, p. 460, citing Threlkeld 1828–1846, p. 255. The reference is to Job 12: 23.

70   Van Toorn 2006, p. 46.

71   'Family Notices', *Sydney Morning Herald*, 1 May 1846, p. 3, <nla.gov.au/nla.news-page1517909>.

72   Cited at <www.newcastle.edu.au/school/hss/research/publications/awaba/language/missionaries.html>.

73   Collins 1798.

74   P McConvell & N Thieberger, *State of Indigenous Languages in Australia 2001*, Department of Environment and Heritage, Commonwealth of Australia, 2001, p. viii, p. 61, <minerva-access.unimelb.edu.au/handle/11343/34091>, and also Australian Human Rights Commission, *Social Justice Report*, 2009, <www.humanrights.gov.au/sites/default/files/content/social_justice/sj_report/sjreport09/pdf/sjr_ch3.pdf>, Chapter 3 'the perilous state of Indigenous languages in Australia'.

75   See J Troy, *The Sydney Language*, Panther Publishing & Printing, Canberra, 1994, <www.dharug.dalang.com.au/Dharug/reference/troy_sydney_language_publication.pdf>.

76   P Darcy, Aboriginal Languages Research and Resource Centre (The Languages Centre) website, NSW Department of Aboriginal Affairs, <www.alrrc.nsw.gov.au/>.

77   Carey 2009, p. 173.

78   Ganter 2016, citing R Amery, 'Beyond their expectations: Teichelmann und Schürmann's efforts to preserve the Kaurna language continue to bear fruit', in W Veit (ed.), *The Struggle for Souls and Science – Constructing the Fifth Continent: German Missionaries and Scientists in Australia*, Strehlow Research Centre Occasional Paper, 2004, pp. 9–28; MA Gale, *Dhangum Djorra'wuy Dhäwu – A History of Writing in Aboriginal Languages*; Aboriginal Research Institute, University of South Australia, 1997.

79   H Carey, 'Lancelot Threlkeld and missionary linguistics in Australia to 1850' in O Zwatjes & E Hovdhaugen (eds.), *Missionary Linguistics/Linguistica Misionera: Selected Papers from the First International Conference on Missionary Linguistics, Oslo, 13–16 March 2004*, John Benjamins Publishing Company, Amsterdam, 2004.

Chapter 3: God's immigrants?

1   JD Lang, 'Departure of the Ship *Fortitude*', *British Banner*, 13 September 1848.

2   G Davison, 'Population' in G Davison, J Hirst & S Macintyre (eds.), *The Oxford Companion to Australian History*, rev ed., Oxford University Press (OUP), Melbourne, 2001, pp. 520–22.

3   I Wyly, cited in D Fitzpatrick, *Oceans of Consolation: Personal Accounts of Irish Migration to Australia*, Melbourne University Press (MUP), Melbourne, 1995, chapter 3, 'These golden shores: Isabella Wyly 1856–77', pp. 96–138.

4   Stephen Doust to David Doust, 15 May 1857, cited in A Atkinson, *Camden*, 2nd ed., Australian Scholarly Publishing, Melbourne, 2008, pp. 256–257.

5   M Kiddle, *Men of Yesterday: A Social History of the Western District of Victoria 1837–1890*, MUP, Melbourne, 1961, p. 502.

6   A O'Brien, 'Religion', in A Bashford & S Macintyre (eds.), *Cambridge History of Australia. Volume 1: Indigenous and Colonial Australia*, Cambridge University Press (CUP), Port Melbourne, 2015, p. 426.

7   A Atkinson, 'Our first chance of kingdom come', *Push From the Bush*, no. 19, April 1985.

8   JD Lang, 'Journal of a voyage to Van Dieman's [sic] Land & New South Wales in the ship *Andromeda*', 15 October 1822, title page, Lang Papers vol. 1, Mitchell Library, Sydney.

9   JD Lang, 'Journal of a Voyage to Van Dieman's [sic] Land & New South Wales in the ship *Andromeda*', title page and entry for 15 October 1822, Lang Papers vol. 1, Mitchell Library, Sydney, cited in M Lake, '"Such spiritual acres": Protestantism, the land, and the colonisation of Australia 1788–1850,' PhD thesis, University of Sydney, 2008, p. 273.

10   D Baker, *Days of Wrath: A Life of John Dunmore Lang*, MUP, Melbourne, 1985, p. 73; M Prentis, *The Scots in Australia: A Study of New South Wales, Victoria and Queensland 1788–1900*, Sydney University Press, Sydney, 1983, pp. 58–64.

11   JD Lang, *Account of the Steps Taken in England, with a View to the Establishment of an Academical Institution or College in NSW; and to Demonstrate the Practicability of Effecting an Extensive Migration of the Industrious Classes from the Mother Country to that Colony*, Stephens & Stokes, Sydney, 1831, p. 17.

12   See Baker 1985, chapters 6, 15–18.

13   See Lake 2008, chapter 8.

14   JD Lang, *An Historical and Statistical Account of NSW: From the Founding of the Colony in 1788 to the Present Day*, Sampson Low, Marston, Low & Searle, London, 1875, title page to both volumes, citing Judges chapter 18; vol. 1, p. 127, citing Genesis 26:13; vol. 1, pp. 342, 343, 338, citing Deuteronomy 8:8–9.

15   Lang 1875, vol. 2, p. 411; see also JD Lang, 'Colonization in Australia', *British Banner*, 22 March 1848 and 21 June 1848, cited in Lake 2008, chapter 8.

16   See D Pike, *Paradise of Dissent: South Australia 1829–1857*, MUP, Melbourne, 1957.

17   J Stephens, *Land of Promise*, Smith, Elder & Company, 1839, p. 100, cited in H Carey, *God's Empire: Religion and Colonialism in the British World, c. 1801–1908*, CUP, Cambridge, 2011, p. 319.

18   P Gregory, 'Popular religion in New South Wales and Van Diemen's Land from 1788 to the 1850s', unpublished PhD thesis, University of New England, 1994, chapter 2: 'Deist foundations'.

19   Gregory 1994, chapter 2.

20   Cited in C Bradford, '"Providence designed it for a settlement": religious discourses and Australian colonial texts', *Children's Literature Association Quarterly*, vol. 24, no. 1, 1999, p. 4.

21   Stephens 1839, p. 6.

22   *SMH*, 27 March 1846, cited in M Gladwin, 'Australian Anglican clergymen, science and religion, 1820–1850', in P Clarke & T Claydon (eds.), *God's Bounty: The Churches and the Natural World*, Ecclesiastical History Society, Woodbridge, Suffolk, 2010, p. 301.

23   T Mitchell, *Three Expeditions into the Interior of Eastern Australia (1838)*, Libraries Board of South Australia, Adelaide, 1965.

24   Cited in R Waterhouse, *The Vision Splendid*, Curtin University Books, Fremantle, 2005, p. 166.

25   WA Broddribb, *Recollections of an Australian Squatter, or Leaves from My Journal since 1835*, John Ferguson and the Royal Australia Historical Association, Sydney, 1978, pp. 7–11.

26   Lang, 13 September 1848.

27   JM Stuart, *The Journals of John McDouall Stuart During The Years 1858, 1859, 1860, 1861, and 1862, When He Fixed the Centre of the Continent and Successfully Crossed It from Sea to Sea* (1864), entry for 9 October 1862, cited in R Boer, *Last Stop Before Antarctica: The Bible and Postcolonialism in Australia*, 2nd ed., Society of Biblical Literature, Atlanta, 2008, p. 61.

28   E Giles, *Australia Twice Traversed: The Romance of Exploration Being a Narrative Compiled from the Journals of Five Exploring Expeditions into and through Central South Australia, and Western Australia, from 1872 to 1876* (1889), cited in Boer 2008, pp. 103, 105.

29   E Giles, *Australia Twice Traversed* (1889), web edition by eBooks@Adelaide, University of Adelaide, 2014, <ebooks.adelaide.edu.au/g/giles/ernest/g47a/complete.html>, discussed in Boer 2008, chapter 3.

30   G Grey, *Journals of Two Expeditions of Discovery in NW and West Australia During the Years 1837, 38 and 39*, London, 1841, vol. 1, pp. 381, 393–4, cited in Boer 2008, pp. 58–59

31   G Bolton, H Vose & G Jones (eds.), *The Wollaston Journals, vol. 1, 1840–1842*, University of Western Australia Press (UWA Press), Nedlands, 1991, p. 128.

32   G Bolton, H Vose & G Jones (eds.), *The Wollaston Journals, vol. 2, 1842–1844*, UWA Press, Nedlands, 1992, pp. 122–123.

33   Bolton, Vose & Jones 1992, pp. 41, 58, 102.

34   See R Kenny, *The Lamb Enters the Dreaming: Nathanael Pepper & the Ruptured World*, Scribe Publications, Melbourne, 2010, pp. 24–25; also Lake 2008, chapter 4.

35   See J Gascoigne, *The Enlightenment and the Origins of European Australia*, CUP, New York, 2002.

36   WC Wentworth, *Statistical, Historical and Political Description of the Colony of New South Wales*, G & WB Whittaker, London, 1819, pp. 88–89.

37   J Atkinson, *An Account of the State of Agriculture and Grazing in New South Wales (1826)*, facsimile edition, Sydney University Press (SUP), Sydney, 1975, pp. 6–7.

38   E Macarthur, *Colonial Policy of 1840 and 1841 as Illustrated by the Governor's Despatches and the Proceedings of the Legislative Council of New South Wales*, John Murray, London, 1841, p. 35.

39   See J Gascoigne 2002, chapter 4.

40   J Locke, *Second Treatise of Government* (1690), web edition by eBooks@Adelaide, University of Adelaide, 2014, <ebooks.adelaide.edu.au/l/locke/john/l81s/complete.html>, chapter 5.

41   Quote is first given in J Walsh, 'Some particulars of Robert William von Steiglitz', *Victorian Historical Magazine*, vol. 12, 1928, pp. 150–152; cited in Kenny 2010, p. 140. Von Steiglitz went on: 'They were about the most uncivilized people in the world and the least intellectual, being, in fact, as was afterwards clearly proved,

incapable of civilisation; and Providence seems to decree that such should give way to the more intelligent race'.

42   *Sydney Herald*, 7 November 1838, cited in RHW Reece, *Aborigines and Colonists: Aborigines and Colonial Society in New South Wales in the 1830s and the 1840s*, SUP, Sydney, 1974, p. 171. Original italics.

43   L Ryan & N Smith, 'Trugernanner (Truganini) (1812–1876)', *Australian Dictionary of Biography (ADB)* online edition, <adb.anu.edu.au/biography/trugernanner-truganini-4752/text7895>, published first in hard copy 1976.

44   Quoted in L Ryan, *The Aboriginal Tasmanians*, 2nd ed., Allen & Unwin, Sydney, 1996, pp. 141f.

45   See N Clements, 'Tasmania's Black War: a tragic case of lest we remember?', *The Conversation*, 24 April 2014, available at <theconversation.com/tasmanias-black-war-a-tragic-case-of-lest-we-remember-25663>.

46   R Broome, *Aboriginal Australians: A History since 1788*, 4th ed., Allen & Unwin, Sydney, 2010, pp. 37–38.

47   See R Broome, 'The statistics of frontier conflict', undated, KooriWeb website, <www.kooriweb.org/foley/resources/story28.html>.

48   Niel Black diary, cited in P Russell, *Savage or Civilised? Manners in Colonial Australia*, UNSW Press, Sydney, 2010, p. 92.

49   Russell 2010, pp. 93–94.

50   Russell 2010, p. 97.

51   For an example of outright violence: John Bussell, the eldest son of an English clergyman, settled his extended family on land in the south-west of the Swan River settlement, WA. Every Sunday, he gathered his family in the sitting room and led them in worship. One day in 1841, 'the Bussell men were directly involved' in the massacre of Aborigines on the Vasse. See M Quartley, 'Authority and affection: John and Charlotte Bussell', in P Russell (ed.), *For Richer for Poorer*, MUP, 1994, p. 25.

52   F Jensz, *German Moravian Missionaries in the British Colony of Victoria, 1848–1908: Influential Strangers*, Brill, Leiden, 2010, p. 116; and Kenny 2010, pp. 134–145.

53   The point about evangelical exposure is made in S Piggin & RD Linder, *The Fountain of Public Prosperity: Evangelical Christians in Australian History, 1740–1914*, Monash University Publishing, Melbourne, 2018 (forthcoming); see also J Harris, 'Counting the bodies: Aboriginal deaths in colonial Australia', *Zadok Paper* S115, Spring 2001.

54   'Claims of the Aborigines', a sermon preached by the Rev. John Saunders, Bathurst Street Baptist Church, Sydney, 14 October 1838, reported in *The Colonist*, 17 October 1838, cited in Piggin & Linder, 2018.

55   Despatches relative to the massacre of various Aborigines of Australia in the year 1838', cited in Piggin & Linder 2018.

56   JD Lang, *National Sins, the Cause & Precursors of National Judgements: A Sermon preached in the Scots Church, Sydney on Friday November 2, 1838, being the day appointed by his Excellency, Sir George Gipps, as a day of fasting and humiliation on account of the late calamitous drought*, James Tegg, Sydney, 1838, pp. 13–15.

57   House of Commons Parliamentary Select Committee & Aborigines Protection Society, *Report of the Parliamentary Select Committee on Aboriginal Tribes*, Aborigines Protection Society, London, 1837.

58   *Report of the Parliamentary Select Committee on Aboriginal Tribes*, 1837, p. 60.

59   JD Lang, *Cooksland in North-Eastern Australia: The Future Cotton-field of Great Britain: Its Characteristics and Capabilities for European Colonization, with a Disquisition of the Origin, Manners and Customs of the Aborigines*, Longmans, Brown, Green & Longmans, London, 1847, p. 469.

60   Lang 1838, p. 22; Lang 1847, p. 469.

61   Cited in MG Brett, 'A suitably English Abraham: emigration to Australia in the nineteenth century', in J Havea (ed.), *Postcolonial Voices from Downunder: Indigenous Matters, Confronting Readings*, Pickwick Publications, Eugene, 2017, pp. 115–116.

62   Cited in A O'Brien, '"Kitchen fragments and garden stuff": Poor Law discourse and Indigenous people in early colonial New South Wales', *Australian Historical Studies*, vol. 39, 2008, p. 151; also H Reynolds, *The Law of the Land,* Penguin, Melbourne, 2003.

63   Saunders 1838, cited in Piggin & Linder 2018.

64   See *The Encylopaedia of New Zealand* website, <teara.govt.nz/en/treaty-of-waitangi>.

65   O'Brien 2008.

66   See J Boyce, *1835: The Founding of Melbourne & the Conquest of Australia*, Black Inc, Melbourne, 2011, chapter 7.

67   The Letters Patent of February 1836 said: 'Nothing in those our Letters Patent … shall affect or be construed to affect the rights of any Aboriginal Natives of the said Province to the actual occupation or enjoyment in their own Person or in the Persons of their Descendants of any Land therein now actually or enjoyed occupied by such Natives'. The Resident Commissioner was instructed: 'You will see that no lands which the natives may possess in occupation or enjoyment be offered for sale until previously ceded by the natives to yourself. You will furnish the protector of the Aborigines with evidence of the faithful fulfilment of the bargain or treaties, which you may effect with the Aborigines for the cessation of lands'. Both cited in Brett 2017, p. 111.

68   W Hull, *Remarks on the Probable Origin and Antiquity of the Aboriginal Natives of New South Wales*, 1846, cited in Kenny 2010, p. 35.

69   See C Kidd, *The Forging of Races: Race and Scripture in the Protestant Atlantic World 1600–2000*, CUP, Cambridge, 2006.

70   Brett 2017, p. 118.

71   Kidd 2006, p. 25.

72   Kenny 2010, p. 30.

73   SL Chase, 'Faith the Antidote to Despair; or Hope for the Aborigines: a sermon', Goodhugh & Hough, Melbourne, 1857.

74   See J Lyndon, 'Christian heroes?: John Gribble, Exeter Hall and antislavery on Western Australia's frontier', *Studies in Western Australian History*, no. 30, 2016, pp. 59–72.

75   JB Gribble, *Dark Deeds in a Sunny Land, or Blacks and Whites in NW Australia (1886)*, UWA Press, Nedlands, 1987.

76   'Gribble, John Brown (1847–1893)', *ADB*, National Centre of Biography, Australian National University, <adb.anu.edu.au/biography/gribble-john-brown-3668/text5727>, 1972; also Broome 2010, pp. 117–118.

77 Lillie Matthews to Alick Crawford, 22 July 1883, cited in P O'Farrell, *Letters from Irish Australia 1825–1929*, UNSW Press, Melbourne, 1984, pp. 76–77 and chapter 5 more generally.

78 Edward Stone Parker (1854), quoted in Kenny 2010, p. 63.

Part 2: The Great Age of the Bible

1 On Livermore, see *54th British and Foreign Bible Society Report*, London, 1858, p. clxi; 'Bible Society', *Tasmanian Times*, 1 June 1867, p. 4; 'River Don', *Launceston Examiner*, 3 March 1868 p. 3; *55th BFBS Report*, 1859, p. 238; 'The late venerable Isaac Livermore', *Weekly Examiner* (Launceston), 8 March 1873, p. 7.

2 Reflections from the NSW Auxiliary, in the *52nd BFBS Report,* London, 1856, p. cliii.

3 The American Bible Society printed 6 million copies in thirty years from 1816, and within a generation commanded the market. It had printed more than 32 million Bibles by 1880 – all in the King James translation, free of legal restriction as it was based outside of England.

4 C De Hamel, *The Book: A History of the Bible*, Phaidon Press, London and New York, 2001, pp. 261–263.

Chapter 4: Spreading the Word

1 J Backhouse, *A Narrative of a Visit to the Australian Colonies*, Hamilton, Adams & Co, London, 1843, p. 389 and online at <downloads.newcastle.cdu.au/library/cultural%20collections/pdf/backhouse.pdf>.

2 JD Lang, *An Historical and Statistical Account of New South Wales, Both as a Penal Settlement and as a British Colony*, Cochrane & M'Crone, London, 1834, vol. 2, pp. 85–126.

3 A Keary, 'Christianity, colonialism and cross-cultural translation: Lancelot Threlkeld, Biraban and the Awabakal', *Aboriginal History*, vol. 33, 2009, pp. 117–155. For reports of the military operation in the Hunter River Valley see R Darling, 'Dispatches, September 1826', Mitchell Library, A 1197, Reel CY 522.

4 J Backhouse, 'Journal', 28 April 1836, cited in Keary 2009, p. 127.

5 Backhouse 1843, p. 390. Note that the population of Maitland in 1836 was about 1160.

6 B Kingston, *The Oxford History of Australia, Volume 3, 1860–1900: Glad, Confident Morning*, Oxford University Press (OUP), Melbourne, 1993.

7 Note that ballot box/secret voting was first used in South Australia and Victoria in the elections of 1856. See <www.aph.gov.au/binaries/senate/pubs/pops/pop37/sawer.pdf>.

8 'The Great Northern Railway: opening of the railway', *Maitland Mercury and Hunter River General Advertiser*, 31 March 1857, p. 2.

9 L Howsam, *Cheap Bibles: Nineteenth Century Publishing and the British and Foreign Bible Society*, Cambridge University Press (CUP), Cambridge, 1991, pp. 3, 35–36.

10 All from his farewell sermon to his congregation at Maitland: GK Rusden, *Sermon, Selected to Preach in St Peters Church East Maitland on Sunday March 20 1859*, Henry Thomas, West Maitland, 1859.

11   Anne Rusden to Rose Selwyn, 28 November 1854, cited in P Curthoys, 'State support for churches 1836–1860', in B Kaye (ed.), *Anglicanism in Australia: A History*, Melbourne University Press (MUP), Melbourne, 2002, p. 41.

12   J Allan, *Rose Scott: Vision and Revision in Feminism*, OUP, Melbourne, 1994, p. 34. Rose Scott was the Reverend GK Rusden's granddaughter.

13   R Bourke, cited in J Gascoigne, *The Enlightenment and the Origins of European Australia*, CUP, Melbourne, 2002, p. 29.

14   See WG Broughton's address on the laying of the foundation stone of St Peter's East Maitland, 20 March 1838, citing Ephesians 2:20, reported in the *Sydney Herald*, 29 March 1838.

15   A O'Brien, 'Religion', in A Bashford & S Macintyre (eds.), *Cambridge History of Australia. Volume 1: Indigenous and Colonial Australia*, CUP, Melbourne, 2015, pp. 414–437. For more on the *Church Acts*, see D Stoneman, 'The Church Act: the expansion of Christianity or the imposition of moral enlightenment', PhD thesis, University of New England, 2011.

16   E Hodder, *George Fife Angas,* Hodder & Stoughton, London, 1891, p. 98.

17   S Piggin, *Spirit of a Nation: The Story of Australia's Christian Heritage,* Strand Publishing, Sydney, 2004, p. 49.

18   JD Bollen, *Protestantism and Social Reform in New South Wales, 1890–1910*, MUP, Melbourne, 1972, p. 4.

19   Cited in Piggin 2004, p. 49.

20   A Trollope, *Australia and New Zealand*, Chapman & Hall, London, 1873, cited in D Hilliard, 'Australia: towards secularisation and one step back', in CG Brown & M Snape (eds.), *Secularisation in the Christian World: Essays in Honor of Hugh McLeod*, Ashgate, Farnham, 2010, pp. 75–92.

21   W Phillips, 'Religious profession and practice in NSW 1850–1901: the statistical evidence', *Historical Studies*, vol. 15, no. 59, 1972, pp. 378–400.

22   For wider context, see W Gibson, 'The British sermon 1689–1901: quantities, performances and culture' in W Gibson & KA Francis (eds.), *Oxford Handbook of the British Sermon*, OUP, Oxford, 2012, pp. 3–30.

23   M Gladwin, 'Preaching and Australian public life: 1788–1914', *St Mark's Review*, no. 227, 2014, p. 2.

24   Calculation is based on 10 000 a year in the 1830s and 1840s; 30 000 a year in the 1850s; 40 000 a year in the 1860s; 50 000 a year in the 1870s; 60 000 a year in the 1880s. This is conservative at several points – Gladwin's initial calculation was based on only two sermons a week for Anglican clergy; my extrapolation from 30 000 in the 1850s to 60 000 in the 1880s relies on the fact that clergy numbers in all the major denominations doubled or nearly doubled between 1870 and 1890.

25   J Damousi, *Colonial Voices: A Cultural History of English in Australia 1840–1940*, CUP, Cambridge, 2010, p. 70, discussed in Gladwin 2014, pp. 7–8.

26   See, for example, all the 'reception by denomination' essays in J Riches (ed.), *The New Cambridge History of the Bible: Vol. 4, From 1750 to the Present*, CUP, Cambridge, 2015.

27   Concordance entry on 'Holy Scriptures', citing 2 Peter 3:16 and 2 Peter 1:20, in *The Holy Bible translated from the Latin Vulgate, diligently compared with the Hebrew, Greek and other editions in divers languages; the Old Testament first*

published by the English college at Douay AD 1609; and the New Testament, first published by the English college at Rheims AD1582, with annotations, references and an historical and chronological index. Stereotype edition, Richard Coyne, Dublin, 1833, in the David Scott Mitchell collection, State Library of NSW. Note that catechisms which addressed the topic of 'scripture' tended to repeat similar warnings. See P O'Farrell, 'Bible reading and related mental furniture', *Australian Cultural History*, vol. 11, 1992, pp. 16–27.

28   On music and Australian methodism, see J Mansfield, 'Music – a window on Australian Christian life', in M Hutchinson & E Campion (eds.), *Re-visioning Australian Colonial Christianity: New Essays in the Australian Christian Experience 1788–1900*, Centre for the Study of Australian Christianity, Sydney, 1994, pp. 131–152; J Mansfield, 'The music of Australian revivalism', in M Hutchinson, E Campion & S Piggin (eds.), *Reviving Australia: Essays on the History and Experience of Revival and Revivalism in Australian Christianity*, Centre for the Study of Australian Christianity, Sydney, 1994, pp. 123–142.

29   Article VI: 'Holy Scripture containeth all things necessary to salvation: so that whatsoever is not read therein, nor may be proved thereby is not to be required of any man that it should be believed as an article of the Faith, or be thought requisite or necessary to salvation', Anglicans Online website, <anglicansonline. org/basics/thirty-nine_articles.html>.

30   Probably the most cited book in English, after the Bible itself, the *Book of Common Prayer* was not only responsible for phrases like 'for richer, for poorer; in sickness and in health'; it made particular biblical terms and ideas deeply familiar to generations of churchgoing people. See M Gladwin, 'The Book of Common Prayer in Australia and the British Empire 1788–1918', *St Mark's Review*, no. 222, 2012, pp. 75–89.

31   GK Rusden, *A Sermon Preached at St Peters Church Maitland, on 11th February 1849*, R Jones, Maitland, 1849.

32   CJ Blomfield to L Edwards, 15 March 1831, cited in P Robertson, '"The one thing needful": three evangelical Anglican women in the Hunter Region of NSW, 1825–1850', *Lucas: An Evangelical History Review*, vol. 23 & 24, 1997–1998, pp. 5–34.

33   See M Lyons & L Tasker, *Australian Readers Remember: An Oral History of Reading 1890–1930*, OUP, Melbourne, 1992, chapter 3.

34   Gladwin 2014.

35   'A wife's allowance', *The Dawn*, 1 November 1896, p. 32.

36   Australian Religious Tract Society, *Fourth Annual Report of the Australian Religious Tract Society*, George Howe, Sydney, 1827, p. 12.

37   Australian Religious Tract Society, *Tenth Annual Report of the Religious Tract Society in Australia*, Stephen & Stokes, Sydney, 1833, p. 8; *Report of the Religious Tract Society in Australia for the 30th year*, 1853, p. 13 and *Report for 50th (Jubilee) Year*, Cook & Co, Sydney, 1874, p. 12.

38   See Jonathan Topham, 'Science, religion, and the history of the book', in T Dixon, S Pumfrey & G Cantor (eds.), *Science and Religion: New Historical Perspectives*, CUP, Cambridge, 2010, pp. 221–244.

39   Estimate of Rev Michael Henry Becher, visiting agent of the BFBS. 'Report of a Mission to the Colonies of Australia and Tasmania', Appendix Four to the *53rd*

BFBS Report, London, 1857, p. 79. Note that the oldest of the colonial auxiliaries, at Sydney, had issued just over 5200 copies by 1827 and about 11700 by 1841. Circulation increased markedly through the 1840s and early 1850s, reaching nearly 39300 by 1853 and a total of 57000 Scriptures by 1856. (Figures from the NSW section of BFBS Annual Reports for the relevant year.)

40 BFBS, *71st Report*, London, 1875, p. 181; *75th Report*, London, 1879, p. 168. Note one BFBS agent said 'Melbourne and suburbs contributed far less to Bible Society work than other parts of the colony' (BFBS 1875, p. 185).

41 Particularly Lady Richardson-Bunbury and her daughters at Picton; Miss Elinor Clifton at Leschenault and Mr Edward Parker of Dangin, near York.
    See 'Obituary: Miss EK Clifton', *Western Mail* (Perth), 2 April 1904, p. 16; 'Obituary: Mr ER Parker', *Western Mail,* 5 August 1905, p. 46; and more generally A Thompson, *Australia and the Bible: A Brief Outline of the Work of the British and Foreign Bible Society in Australia 1807–1934*, British and Foreign Bible Society, London, 1935, chapter 10, 'Winnowings from the west'.

42 Thompson 1935, pp. 113–114.

43 Total circulation since the foundation of the NSW society is given as 73203 in 1859 and as 401425 in 1895, an increase of 328222 during the intervening years. See BFBS annual reports for the relevant years.

44 'A report of 130 years of Bible Society women's work in Queensland, previously called Moreton Bay Settlement', typescript by Lily Butters, 1985.

45 The quote is from 'Bible Missions', *Evening Journal* (Adelaide), 4 November 1873, p. 2. On the formation and early work of the Surry Hills group, see 'Branch Bible Association – Darlinghurst and Surry Hills', *The Empire* (Sydney), 9 May 1857, p. 4.

46 To use a phrase from BFBS 1856, p. cliv.

47 Hilliard 2010, p. 78.

48 BFBS, *51st Report*, London, 1855 citing 37th report from NSW, p. cviii.

49 BFBS 1855, citing 37th report from NSW, p. cviii.

50 Cited in BFBS 1859, p. 238.

51 See J Harris, 'Words of justice in a secular society: the role of the King James Version of the Bible in Australia', in A Duran (ed.), *The King James Bible: Across Borders and Centuries*, Duquesne University Press, Pittsburgh, 2014, pp. 151–172; the 1823 figure is reported in BFBS, *19th Report*, London, 1823, p. lxiv.

52 Key sources on missions among the Chinese include: K Cronin, *Colonial Casualties: Chinese in Early Victoria*, MUP, Melbourne, 1982, chapter 6; D Austin, 'Citizens of heaven: overseas Chinese Christians during Australian federation', in S Couchman, S Fitzgerald & P Macgregor (eds.), *After the Rush: Regulation, Participation and Chinese Communities in Australia, 1860–1940*, Otherland Literary Journal, Melbourne, 2004, pp. 75–88; K Cole, *The Anglican Mission to the Chinese in Bendigo and Central Victoria 1854–1918*, Keith Cole Publications, Bendigo, 1994.

53 BFBS Report, 1857, p. cci.

54 See W Phillips, 'Seeking souls in the diggings: Christian missions to the Chinese on the Victorian goldfields', *Victorian Historical Journal*, vol. 72, nos. 1–2, 2001, p. 91.

55   The British and Foreign Bible Society published the New Testament in 1813, and the whole Bible in 1822. This was the first known entire printed version of the Scriptures in Chinese. A Wylie, 'The Bible in China: a record of various translations of the Holy Scriptures', in A Foster, *Christian Progress in China: Gleanings from the Writings and Speeches of Many Workers*, Religious Tract Society, London, 1889, pp. 29–46.

56   According to the BFBS report for 1856, for example, the Melbourne Auxiliary applied for a grant of 3500 Bibles in Chinese; and Geelong ordered 875 copies in Chinese as well as other Scriptures. Two years later in 1858, the BFBS reported that Moreton Bay had received 1080 Scriptures in the year, as well as a grant of 700 German and Chinese Scriptures.

57   M Tjalkabota, 'Recollections', first told to FW Albrecht in Aranda, and later translated into English by Paul Albrecht. Published as an Appendix to P Albrecht, *From Mission to Church 1877–2002: Finke River Mission*, Finke River Mission, Hermannsburg, NT, 2002.

58   P Albrecht, 'Tjalkabota, Moses (1869–1954)', *Australian Dictionary of Biography (ADB)*, Australian National University, <adb.anu.edu.au/biography/tjalkabota-moses-13219/text23937>, published first in hard copy 2005.

59   FW Albrecht, 1950, cited in R Radford, 'Moses Tjalkabota (1869–1954)', *Australian Dictionary of Evangelical Biography*, Evangelical History Association of Australia, 2004, <webjournals.ac.edu.au/ojs/index.php/ADEB/article/view/757/754>.

60   P Brock, 'New Christians as evangelists', in N Etherington (ed.), *Missions and Empire*, OUP, Oxford and New York, 2005, pp. 132–152.

61   Tjalkabota 2002.

62   See A Kenny, *The Aranda's Pepa: An Introduction to Carl Strehlow's Masterpiece Die Aranda- und Loritja-Stamme in Zentral-Australien (1907–1920)*, ANU EPress, Canberra, 2013.

63   Albrecht 2005, accessed online 27 May 2017.

64   Brock 2005, pp. 148–149.

65   L Latai, 'Covenant keepers: a history of Samoan (LMS) missionary wives in the Western Pacific from 1839–1979', unpublished PhD thesis, ANU, 2016, Appendix 7, pp. 323–324, <openresearch-repository.anu.edu.au/bitstream/1885/110679/1/Latai%20Thesis%202016.pdf>.

66   D Wetherell, 'From Samuel McFarlane to Stephen Davies: continuity and change in the Torres Strait Island churches, 1871–1949', *Pacific Studies*, vol. 16, no. 1, 1993, pp. 1–32.

67   See J Cruickshank, 'Aboriginal Missions', *The Encyclopedia of Women & Leadership in Twentieth-Century Australia*, Australian Women's Archives Project, 2014, <www.womenaustralia.info/leaders/biogs/WLE0336b.htm>.

68   For a brilliant study of Pepper, see R Kenny, *The Lamb Enters the Dreaming: Nathanael Pepper & the Ruptured World*, Scribe Publications, Melbourne, 2010.

69   P Brock, 'Christian Missions to Aboriginal People', in J Jupp (ed.), *The Encyclopaedia of Religion in Australia*, CUP, Cambridge, 2009, pp. 99–100.

70   *Fourth Annual Report of the Apsley Aboriginal Mission*, 11 January 1845, p. 271. Thanks to Stephen Chavura for this reference.

71   G Taplin, Journal 1859–1879, entries for the week of September 3–7, 1864, PRG 186-1/3, State Library of South Australia, transcription at <www.firstsources.info/uploads/3/4/5/4/34544232/taplins_diary_1859-79.pdf>.

72   P Jones, 'Unaipon, James (1835–1907)', *ADB*, Australian National University, <adb.anu.edu.au/biography/unaipon-james-13227/text7247>, published first in hard copy 2005.

73   J Harris, 'The first Aboriginal evangelists', Bible Society website, 9 July 2015, <www-archive.biblesociety.org.au/news/the-first-aboriginal-evangelists>.

74   See P Jones, 'Unaipon, David (1872–1967)', *ADB*, Australian National University, <adb.anu.edu.au/biography/unaipon-david-8898/text15631>, published first in hard copy 1990.

75   'Queen Emma dead', *Sunday Times* (Sydney), 3 December 1916, p. 26.

76   M Nugent, 'Timbery, Emma (1842–1916)', *ADB*, Australian National University, <adb.anu.edu.au/biography/timbery-emma-13218/text23935>, published first in hard copy 2005.

77   See J Kociumbas, 'Noble, James (1876–1941)', *ADB*, Australian National University, <adb.anu.edu.au/biography/noble-james-7853/text13641>, published first in hard copy 1988; S Swain, 'Noble, Angelina (c. 1879–1964)' in *The Encyclopedia of Women & Leadership in Twentieth-Century Australia*, Australian Women's Archives Project, 2014, <www.womenaustralia.info/leaders/biogs/WLE0502b.htm>.

78   R Ganter, 'Pingilina, Johannes', in R Ganter (ed.), *German Missionaries in Australia – A web-directory of intercultural encounters*, Griffith University, 2016, <missionaries.griffith.edu.au/biography/pingilina-johannes>.

Chapter 5: Seeking the good society

1   BH Lee, *One of Australia's Daughters: An Autobiography of Mrs Harrison Lee*, Ideal Publishing Union, London, 1900, pp. 21, 24–28.

2   On her activism, see P Grimshaw, 'Lee, Betsy (Bessie) Harrison (1860–1950)' in *The Encyclopedia of Women and Leadership in Twentieth-Century Australia*, Australian Women's Archives Project, 2014, <www.womenaustralia.info/leaders/biogs/WLE0622b.htm>; also AM Mitchell, 'Lee, Betsy (Bessie) (1860–1950)', *Australian Dictionary of Biography (ADB)*, National Centre of Biography, Australian National University, <adb.anu.edu.au/biography/lee-betsy-bessie-7144/text12331>, published first in hard copy 1986.

3   A Atkinson, 'How do we live with ourselves? The Australian national conscience', RAFT Fellowship essay, *Australian Book Review*, no. 384, 2016, online at <www.australianbookreview.com.au/abr-online/current-issue/185-september-2016-no-384/3531-how-do-we-live-with-ourselves-the-australian-national-conscience-by-alan-atkinson>.

4   J Jefferis, *Our Bible and Our Beliefs: Six Lectures Delivered in the Congregational Church, Pitt Street, Sydney, as a Help to Young Men of Free Thought*, Samuel Lees, Sydney, 1882, lecture 6, 'How shall we read the Bible?'.

5   A O'Brien, *God's Willing Workers: Women and Religion in Australia*, UNSW Press, Sydney, 2005, p. 64.

6   BM Bubacz, 'The female and male orphan schools in New South Wales, 1801–

1850', unpublished PhD thesis, University of Sydney, 2008, p. 62.

7   Hassall to George Burder, postscript of 19 August to a letter dated 5 August 1801, extracted in FM Bladen, *Historical Records of NSW, vol. 4*, Government Printer, Sydney, 1896, pp. 446–447; AT Yarwood, *Samuel Marsden*, Oxford University Press (OUP), Melbourne, 1968, pp. 87, 111.

8   S Marsden to M Stokes, 24 August 1801, 'Letters from the Marsden family to Mary and John Stokes, 1794–1824', MLMSS719, Mitchell Library, State Library of NSW, transcript at <acms.sl.nsw.gov.au/_transcript/2015/D00007/a1755.html>.

9   Quoted in Yarwood 1968, p. 87.

10   For analytical overviews see S Swain, 'A long history of faith-based welfare in Australia: origins and impact', *Journal of Religious History*, vol 41, no. 1, 2017, pp. 81–96; S Swain, 'Welfare work and charitable organisations', in J Jupp (ed.), *The Encyclopedia of Religion in Australia*, Cambridge University Press (CUP), Cambridge, 2009, pp. 685–694.

11   Society for Promoting Christian Knowledge and Benevolence, Minute Book, A7269, ML cited in S Piggin & RD Linder, *The Fountain of Public Prosperity: Evangelical Christians in Australian History, 1740–1914*, Monash University Publishing, Melbourne, 2018 (forthcoming).

12   Piggin & Linder 2018.

13   *Regulations of the New South Wales Saving Bank: A Depositary for the Savings of the Poor*, G. Howe Government Printer, Sydney, 1819, pp. 4–5, available via the State Library of NSW at <acms.sl.nsw.gov.au/album/albumView.aspx?itemID=888098&acmsid=0>.

14   Piggin & Linder 2018.

15   G Blainey, *A History of the AMP 1848–1998*, Allen & Unwin, Sydney, 1999, p. 33.

16   B Zimmerman, *The Making of a Diocese: Maitland, its Bishop, Priests and People 1866–1909*, Melbourne University Press (MUP), Melbourne, 2000, pp. 138–141.

17   Swain 2017, p. 83.

18   C Walch, 'Hopkins, Henry (1787–1870)', *ADB*, National Centre of Biography, Australian National University, <adb.anu.edu.au/biography/hopkins-henry-2197/text2837>, published first in hard copy 1966.

19   See R Teale, 'Goodlet, John Hay (1835–1914)', *ADB*, National Centre of Biography, Australian National University, <adb.anu.edu.au/biography/goodlet-john-hay-3631/text5645>, published first in hard copy 1972; J Mansfield, 'Goodlet, Ann Alison (1824–1903)', *ADB*, National Centre of Biography, Australian National University, <adb.anu.edu.au/biography/goodlet-ann-alison-12941/text23387>, published first in hard copy 2005; and for a more detailed account see PF Cooper, *More Valuable Than Gold: The Philanthropy of John and Ann Goodlet*, Eider Books, The Ponds, 2015.

20   Piggin & Linder 2018.

21   Luke chapter 14 says: 'When thou makest a feast, call the poor, the maimed, the lame, the blind: And thou shalt be blessed; for they cannot recompense thee: for thou shalt be recompensed at the resurrection of the just'.

22   This sermon is no. 66 in the Moore College collection of Marsden's sermons. The paper on which it is written is watermarked 1833. David Pettett's transcriptions are at <myrrh.library.moore.edu.au:443/handle/10248/5508>. See Piggin and Linder 2018.

23   For discussion, see M Lake, 'Samuel Marsden, work, and the limits of evangelical
     humanitarianism', *History Australia*, vol. 7, no. 3, 2010; M Lake, '"Promoting the
     welfare of these poor heathens": contextualising Marsden's attitudes to Indigenous
     peoples', in P Bolt & D Pettett (eds.), *Launching Marsden's Mission: The Beginnings
     of the Church Missionary Society in New Zealand, viewed from New South Wales*,
     The Latimer Trust, London, 2014.

24   S Judd & A Robinson, 'Christianity and the social services in Australia: a
     conversation', in S Piggin (ed.), *Shaping the Good Society in Australia: Australia's
     Christian Heritage*, Australian Christian Heritage National Forum, Macquarie
     University, Sydney, 2006, pp. 109–126.

25   Transcript, *Q&A*, ABC television, Monday 7 September 2015, <www.abc.net.au/
     tv/qanda/txt/s4286225.htm>.

26   'Telegraphing the Bible from Queenscliff' in 'History of The Argus, 1846–1926:
     Eighty Years in Outline', Supplement to *The Argus*, 9 September 1926, p. 6.

27   E Ihde, *A Manifesto for New South Wales: Edward Smith Hall and the Sydney
     Monitor, 1826–1840*, Australian Scholarly Publishing, Melbourne, 2004, p. 38–39.

28   Hall, *Sydney Monitor*, 11 June 1836, p. 4, cited in Ihde 2004, p. 39.

29   MJB Kenny, 'Hall, Edward Smith (1786–1860)', *ADB*, National Centre of
     Biography, Australian National University, <adb.anu.edu.au/biography/hall-
     edward-smith-2143/text2729>, published first in hard copy 1966.

30   Hall, *Sydney Monitor*, 18 February 1828, cited in Ihde 2004, p. 38.

31   Hall, *Sydney Monitor*, 23 April 1836, p. 2, cited in Ihde 2004, pp. 41–42.

32   Kenny 1966.

33   Useful interpretive histories of the colonial press include RB Walker, *The
     Newspaper Press in New South Wales 1803–1920*, Sydney University Press, Sydney,
     1976; D Cryle, *The Press in Colonial Queensland: A Social and Political History
     1845–1875*, University of Queensland Press (UQP), Brisbane, 1989.

34   See I Breward, *Australia: The Most Godless Nation Under Heaven?*, Beacon Hill
     Books, Melbourne, 1988, pp. 30–31; M Gladwin, 'The journalist in the rectory:
     Anglican clergymen and Australian intellectual life, 1788–1850', *History Australia*,
     vol. 7, no. 3, 2010, pp. 1–28.

35   On Lang radicals and the press see Cryle 1989, chapter 2. On Kerr and Swan, see
     L Gardiner, 'Kerr, William (1812–1859)', *ADB*, National Centre of Biography,
     Australian National University, <adb.anu.edu.au/biography/kerr-william-2304/
     text2981>, published first in hard copy 1967; C Lack & AA Morrison, 'Swan,
     James (1811–1891)', *ADB*, National Centre of Biography, Australian National
     University, <adb.anu.edu.au/biography/swan-james-4677/text7737>, published
     first in hard copy 1976.

36   Note, however, that the Congregationalist Barzillai Quaife wrote for the *SMH*'s
     rival *Empire*.

37   See 'Stephens, John (1806–1850)', *ADB*, National Centre of Biography, Australian
     National University, <adb.anu.edu.au/biography/stephens-john-2697/text3781>,
     published in hard copy 1967.

38   See S Macintyre, *A Colonial Liberalism: The Lost World of Three Victorian
     Visionaries*, OUP, Melbourne, 1991; CE Sayers, 'Syme, David (1827–1908)', *ADB*,
     National Centre of Biography, Australian National University, <adb.anu.edu.au/

biography/syme-david-4679/text7741>, published first in hard copy 1976.

39 Piggin & Linder 2018.

40 M Gladwin, *Anglican Clergy in Australia, 1788–1850: Building a British World*, Royal Historical Society with Boydell & Brewer, Woodbridge, 2015, p. 159.

41 J Horne & G Sherrington, 'Education', in A Bashford & S Macintyre (eds.), *Cambridge History of Australia. Volume 1: Indigenous and Colonial Australia*, CUP, Melbourne, 2015, pp. 367–390.

42 J Kociumbas, *Australian Childhood: A History*, Allen & Unwin, Sydney, 1997.

43 GK Rusden, *A Sermon Preached at St Peter's Church East Maitland on 9th November 1856*, Joseph Cook, Sydney, 1856, p. 14.

44 AG Austin, *Australian Education 1788–1900: Church, State and Public Education in Colonial Australia*, 3rd ed., Pitman Pacific Books, Melbourne, 1972, p. 51.

45 Regulations of the National Board of Education, as to the government of schools with respect to attendance and religious instruction, *Votes and Proceedings, NSW Legislative Council 1849*, extracted in AG Austin, *Select Documents in Australian Education 1788–1900*, Pitman Pacific Books, Melbourne, 1963, p. 104–105.

46 See JS Gregory, *Church and State: Changing Government Policies Towards Religion in Australia; with Particular Reference to Victoria since Separation*, Cassell Australia, Melbourne, 1973, p. 62.

47 Speech made at a meeting at Yan Yan Gurt, 17 November 1849, reproduced in AG Austin, *George William Rusden and National Education in Australia 1849–1862*, MUP, Melbourne, 1958, pp. 129–137.

48 Petition from the parishioners of East Maitland, opposing the introduction of the British and Foreign School Society system of education, *Votes and Proceedings, NSW Legislative Council 1839*, extracted in Austin 1963, pp. 75–76.

49 A Atkinson *The Europeans in Australia Volume 2: Democracy*, OUP, Melbourne, 2004, pp. 188–189.

50 Report of the Intercolonial Conference Sydney, 1883, cited in W Phillips, *James Jefferis: Prophet of Federation, Australian Scholarly Publishing*, Melbourne, 1993, p. 142.

51 Regulations of the National Board, cited in Austin 1958, pp. 28–29.

52 See C Campbell, 'Free, compulsory and secular Education Acts', *Dictionary of Educational History in Australia and New Zealand* (DEHANZ) website, 2014, <dehanz.net.au>.

53 Gregory 1973, pp. 117–118.

54 See JD Bollen, *Protestantism and Social Reform in New South Wales, 1890–1910*, MUP, Melbourne, 1972; Piggin & Linder 2018; also RN Warren, 'Instructing them in "the things of God": the response of the Bishop and the Synod of the Church of England in the Diocese of Sydney to the *Public Instruction Act 1880* (NSW) regarding religious education for its children and young people, 1880–1889', MEd thesis, University of Sydney, 2014.

55 R Lawson, *Brisbane in the 1890s*, UQP, Brisbane, 1973, pp. 225f.

56 *A Century of Journalism: The Sydney Morning Herald and Its Record of Australian Life 1831–1931*, John Fairfax & Sons Limited, Sydney, 1931, p. 656.

57 Examples taken from an 1880 report prepared for the Victorian Legislative Council, as described in Gregory 1973, appendix G, pp. 275–277.

58   AE Selwyn, *Address to Synod July 22, 1890*, T Dimmock, West Maitland, 1890, p. 14.

59   Cited in SV Mosma & JC Soper, *The Challenge of Pluralism: Church and State in Five Democracies*, Rowman & Littlefield, Lanham, 1997, p. 93.

60   AW Black, 'Religious studies in Australian Public Schools: an overview and analysis', *Australian Education Review*, vol. 7, no. 3, 1975.

61   R Ely, *Unto God and Caesar: Religious Issues in the Emerging Commonwealth, 1891–1906*, MUP, Melbourne, 1976, p. 56; E Sweetman, C Long & J Smyth, *A History of State Education in Victoria*, Education Department of Victoria, Melbourne, 1922, pp. 145–149.

62   See R Fogarty, *Catholic Education in Australia, 1806–1950*, MUP, Melbourne, 1959.

63   See P Byrt, 'Simon Wonga, Aboriginal leader (c. 1824–1874)', *Victorian Historical Journal*, vol. 76, no. 1, 2005, pp. 3–24.

64   DJ Mulvaney, 'Thomas, William (1793–1867)', *ADB*, National Centre of Biography, Australian National University, <adb.anu.edu.au/biography/thomas-william-2727/text3845>, published first in hard copy 1967.

65   Thomas to Redmond Barry, quoting Wonga, cited in Byrt 2005.

66   Later, in 1860s, the Taungurong restaged this significant journey for the colonial photographer Charles Walters. The resulting images, 'Setting off for the Acheron' and 'Giving Thanks', continued to play on the biblical narrative. See J Lydon, '"Watched over by the indefatigable Moravian missionaries": colonialism and photography at Ebenezer and Ramahyuck', *La Trobe Journal*, no. 76, Spring 2005.

67   See R Broome, *Aboriginal Australians: A History since 1788*, 4th ed., Allen & Unwin, Sydney, 2010, pp. 81ff.

68   D Barwick, *Rebellion at Coranderrk*, Aboriginal History Inc, Canberra, 1998, p. 63.

69   'Simon', *The Australian News for Home Readers*, 25 August 1865, p. 13.

70   Cited in 'Simon' 1865, p. 13.

71   Barwick 1998, p. 75.

72   B Attwood, *Rights for Aborigines*, Allen & Unwin, Sydney, 2003, p. 12.

73   See R Broome, '"There were vegetables every year Mr Green was here": right behaviour and the struggle for autonomy at Coranderrk Aboriginal reserve', *History Australia*, vol. 3, no. 2, 2006; Attwood 2003, pp. 7–12; Barwick 1998, p. 55.

74   State Library of Victoria, 'Coranderrk Mission', <ergo.slv.vic.gov.au/explore-history/fight-rights/Indigenous-rights/coranderrk-mission>; Attwood 2003, p.10.

75   P Van Toorn, *Writing Never Arrives Naked: Early Aboriginal Cultures of Writing in Australia*, Aboriginal Studies Press, Canberra, 2006, p. 133.

76   Attwood 2003, p. 28.

77   J Evans & G Nanni, 'Re-imagining settler sovereignty: the call to law and the Coranderrk Aboriginal reserve, Victoria 1881 and beyond', in Z Laidlaw & A Lester (eds.), *Indigenous Communities and Settler Colonialism: Land Holding, Loss and Survival in an Interconnected World*, Palgrave Macmillan, Basingstoke, 2015, pp. 24–44.

78   See J Gillison, 'Bon, Ann Fraser (1838–1936)', *ADB*, National Centre of Biography, Australian National University, <adb.anu.edu.au/biography/bon-ann-fraser-5284/text8911>, published first in hard copy 1979.

79   B Attwood, 'Coranderrk', e-Melbourne: The City Past and Present website,

<www.emelbourne.net.au/biogs/EM00405b.htm>, first published in hard copy 2005.

80   Cited by Aunty Joy Murphy Wandin, in the foreword to G Nanni & A James, *Coranderrk: We Will Show the Country*, Aboriginal Studies Press, Canberra, 2013, <aiatsis.gov.au/sites/default/files/products/book/coranderrk-foreward.pdf>.

81   William Barak to the *Argus*, 1889, cited in J Cruickshank, 'Sorry (Not Sorry): Australia's history of ambivalence to Aboriginal activism', ABC Religion and Ethics website, 26 May 2016, <www.abc.net.au/religion/articles/2016/05/26/4469930.htm>.

82   Attwood 2005.

Chapter 6: Re-evaluating the text

1   HH Richardson, *The Fortunes of Richard Mahoney*, introduction by M Ackland, Penguin, Melbourne, 2008 (first published in three volumes, 1917–29). The reference to Paul comes from 2 Corinthians 13:8.

2   G Serle, *The Rush to Be Rich: A History of the Colony of Victoria*, Melbourne University Press (MUP), Melbourne, 1971, p. 127.

3   In a vast literature, see P Harrison, *The Bible, Protestantism, and the Rise of Natural Science*, Cambridge University Press (CUP), Cambridge, 1998; K Killeen & P Forshaw (eds.), *The Word and the World: Biblical Exegesis and Early Modern Science*, Palgrave Macmillan, Basingstoke, 2007; JH Brooke & RL Numbers (eds.), *Science and Religion Around the World*, Oxford University Press (OUP), Oxford and New York, 2011; P Harrison, 'Original sin and the problem of knowledge in early modern Europe', *Journal of the History of Ideas*, vol. 63, no. 2, 2002, pp. 239–259.

4   M Gladwin, 'Australian Anglican clergymen, science and religion, 1820–1850', in T Claydon & P Clarke (eds.), *God's Bounty? The Churches and the Natural World*, Boydell & Brewer, Suffolk, 2010, pp. 293–306.

5   LA Gilbert, 'Plants and parsons in nineteenth century NSW', *Historical Records of Australian Science*, vol. 5, no. 3 (1982) pp. 17–32.

6   See 'James Hutton, founder of modern geology', American Natural History Museum website, <www.amnh.org/explore/resource-collections/earth-inside-and-out/james-hutton-the-founder-of-modern-geology/>.

7   W Neil, 'The criticism and theological use of the Bible, 1700–1950', in SL Greenslade (ed.), *The Cambridge History of the Bible vol. 3: The West from the Reformation to the Present Day*, CUP, Cambridge, 1963, pp. 238–293.

8   A Mozley, 'Evolution and the climate of opinion in Australia, 1840–76', *Victorian Studies*, vol. 10, no. 4, 1967, pp. 411–430.

9   WS Macleay to WB Clarke, 4 July 1842 cited in Mozley 1967, pp. 416–417.

10   Cited in Mozley 1967.

11   BW Butcher, 'Darwin down under: science, religion and evolution in Australia', in R Numbers & J Stenhouse (eds.), *Disseminating Darwinism: The Role of Place, Race, Religion and Gender*, CUP, Cambridge, 1999, pp. 39–60.

12   WB Clarke, inaugural vice-presidential address to NSW Royal Society, cited in Mozley 1967, p. 423.

13   Cited at <www.victorianweb.org/victorian/religion/colenso.html>.

14   See EC Turnley, 'Cole, Edward William (1832–1918)', *Australian Dictionary of Biography (ADB)*, Australian National University, <adb.anu.edu.au/biography/cole-edward-william-3243/text4897>, published first in hard copy 1969; W Kirsop, 'Cole's Book Arcade: 'marvellous Melbourne's palace of intellect' in J Hinks & C Armstrong (eds.), *Worlds of Print: Diversity in the Book Trade*, British Library, London, 2006, pp. 31–40.

15   H Jackson, *Australians and the Christian God*, Mosaic Press, Preston, 2013, p. 111; quote is from 'Hanson, Sir Richard Davies (1805–1876)', *ADB*, Australian National University, <adb.anu.edu.au/biography/hanson-sir-richard-davies-3710/text5821>, published first in hard copy 1972; see also G Taylor, *Sir Richard Hanson*, The Federation Press, Annandale, 2013.

16   R Twopenny, *Town Life in Australia*, Elliot Stock, London, 1883, available via Project Gutenberg at <www.gutenberg.org/files/16664/16664-h/16664-h.htm>.

17   S Macintyre & S Scalmer, 'Colonial states and civil society', in A Bashford & S Macintyre (eds.), *The Cambridge History of Australia Vol. 1: Indigenous and Colonial Australia*, CUP, Melbourne, 2013, p. 213.

18   A Atkinson, 'The rise of the newspaper and the fall of the sermon: the case of World War One', paper delivered at the Preaching Australia Conference, Canberra 2013, cited in M Gladwin, 'Preaching in Australian public life 1788–1914', *St Mark's Review*, no. 227, 2014, pp. 1–14. Note it was the early nineteenth-century German philosopher Georg Hegel who said the newspapers were coming to serve modern people as a substitute for morning prayers. Cited in B Anderson, *Imagined Communities: Reflections on the Origin and Spread of Nationalism*, revised edition, Verso, London, 1991, p. 35.

19   A Atkinson, *The Europeans in Australia Vol. 3: Nation*, UNSW Press, Sydney, 2014; Macintyre & Scalmer 2013, p. 212.

20   G Higinbotham, *Science and Religion: The Relations of Modern Science with the Christian Churches: A Lecture*, Samuel Mullen, Melbourne, 1883, p. 8.

21   Cited in Atkinson, *The Europeans in Australia Volume 3: Nation*, pp. 101–102.

22   GK Rusden, *A Sermon Preached at St Peters Church Maitland, on 11th February 1849*, R Jones, Maitland, 1849.

23   Cited in FB Smith, 'Rusden, Henry Keylock (1826–1910)', *ADB*, Australian National University, <adb.anu.edu.au/biography/rusden-henry-keylock-4524/text7407>, published first in hard copy 1976. Rusden also called himself 'a determinist in philosophy, a Malthusian and radical in sociology and an ultra free-trader'.

24   'Christ in the Sepulchre, 5 May 1867', in 'Iconoclastes' (signed HK Rusden), *Tough Morsels of Theology*, Melbourne, 1868.

25   HK Rusden, *The Power of the Pulpit: A Lay Sermon Dedicated to the People and Clergy of Victoria*, E Purton & Co, Melbourne, 1877.

26   'Religious Tract and Book Society', *Sydney Mail and New South Wales Advertiser*, 18 January 1873, p. 86.

27   See A Fyfe, *Science and Salvation: Evangelical Popular Science Publishing in Victorian Britain*, University of Chicago Press, 2004.

28   See J Topham, 'Science, religion and the history of the book', in T Dixon, G Cantor & S Pumfrey (eds.), *Science and Religion: New Historical Perspectives*,

CUP, Cambridge and New York, 2010, pp. 221–244.

29   Jackson 2013, p. 111.

30   'Adelaide Literary and Scientific Association and Mechanics' Institute', *Southern Australian*, Wednesday 28 August 1839, p. 3.

31   C Perry, *Science and the Bible: A Lecture Delivered by Request, on Monday, September 20, 1869*, Mason, Firth and Co, Melbourne, 1869.

32   D Hilliard, 'Intellectual life in the Diocese of Melbourne,' in B Porter (ed.), *Melbourne Anglicans: The Diocese of Melbourne, 1847–1997*, Mitre Books, Melbourne, 1997, pp. 27–48.

33   *Address of James Moorhouse, DD Bishop of Melbourne, to the Church of England Assembly, Melbourne, Tuesday, September 16, 1879*, Church of England Book Depot, Melbourne, 1879; and generally M Sturrock, *Bishop of Magnetic Power: James Moorhouse in Melbourne, 1876–1886*, Australian Scholarly Publishing, Melbourne, 2005.

34   Hilliard 1997, p. 32

35   Higinbotham 1883, pp. 17f.

36   C Strong, Preface to *Christianity Re-interpreted and Other Sermons*, George Robertson & Co, Melbourne, 1894.

37   Hilliard 1997, p. 29; D Hilliard, 'Australia: towards secularisation and one step back', in C Brown & M Snape (eds.), *Secularisation in the Christian World*, Ashgate, Farnham, 2010, p. 79.

38   J Roe, *Beyond Belief: Theosophy in Australia 1879–1939*, UNSW Press, Sydney, 1986, p. 29.

39   AG Stephens, 'For Australians' (1899), cited in G Davison, 'Religion', in A Bashford & S Macintyre (eds.), *The Cambridge History of Australia Vol. 2: The Commonwealth*, CUP, Melbourne, 2013, p. 221.

40   A O'Brien, 'Religion', in Bashford & Macintyre, vol. 1, 2013, p. 434.

41   Hilliard 2010, p. 79.

42   H Jackson, *Churches and People in Australia and New Zealand 1860–1930*, Allen & Unwin, Sydney and Wellington, 1987, chapter 5.

43   D Harris, 'Counting Christians', in D Harris, D Hynd & D Millikan (eds.), *The Shape of Belief: Christianity in Australia Today*, Lancer, Homebush West, 1982, p. 236.

44   See E Hartrick, 'Consuming illusions: the magic lantern in Australia and Aotearoa/New Zealand 1850–1910', unpublished PhD thesis, University of Melbourne, 2003, <minerva-access.unimelb.edu.au/handle/11343/39479>, especially chapters 6 and 7.

45   O Chadwick, *The Secularization of the European Mind in the Nineteenth Century*, CUP, Cambridge, 1975, p. 175.

46   JH Brooke & RL Numbers (eds.), *Science and Religion Around the World*, OUP, Oxford and New York, 2011, p. 2.

47   W Phillips, 'Religious response to Darwin in Australia in the nineteenth century', *Journal of Australian Studies*, vol. 26, 1990, pp. 37–51.

48   S Piggin & RD Linder, *The Fountain of Public Prosperity: Evangelical Christians in Australian History, 1740–1914*, Monash University Publishing, Melbourne, 2018 (forthcoming).

49   I am indebted to Dr Geoffrey Treloar for discussions and advice on this topic, and for the details of this paragraph. See further Piggin & Linder 2018; S Piggin & RD Linder, *Attending to the Australian Soul: Evangelical Christians in Australian History, 1914–2014* (forthcoming); and for the wider international context, GR Treloar, *The Disruption of Evangelicalism: The Age of Torrey, Mott, McPherson and Hammond*, InterVarsity Press, Downers Grove, 2017, especially chapter 4.

50   D Chambers, 'Harper, Andrew (1844–1936)', *ADB*, Australian National University, <adb.anu.edu.au/biography/harper-andrew-6567/text11295>, published first in hard copy 1983.

51   Australian National Church Life Survey results indicate that 26 per cent of churchgoers in 2001, and 24 per cent in 2011, said that the statement 'The word of God, to be taken literally word for word' most closely matched their view of the Bible. R Powell, 'Trends in Australian Church Vitality: Denominational Briefing: CLS Research Report', NCLS Research, Sydney, 2015. Kindly shared with the author by Dr Ruth Powell.

52   Cited in Gladwin 2010, pp. 295–296.

53   W Phillips, 'The defence of Christian belief in Australia 1875–1914: the responses to evolution and higher criticism', *Journal of Religious History*, vol. 9, no. 4, 1977, pp. 402–423.

54   M Ackland, *Henry Handel Richardson: A Life*, CUP, Cambridge, 2004, p. 28.

55   J Prince & M Prince, *Tuned in to Change*, Scripture Union, Sydney, 1979, pp. 15–19, 29.

56   Figure cited is from 1886. J Prince & M Prince, *Tuned into Change: A history of the Australian Scripture Union, 1880–1980*, Scripture Union of Australia, Sydney, 1979, p. 23.

57   The main study in Australia is J Roe 1986.

58   EF Hughes, 'Various aspects of conscience in relation to religion', a lecture given under the auspices of the Victorian Association of Progressive Spiritualists, reported in *Harbinger of Light*, August 1875, cited in FB Smith, 'Religion and freethought in Melbourne, 1870–1890', Masters research thesis, School of History, University of Melbourne, 1960, available via <hdl.handle.net/11343/39410>, pp. 25–26.

59   W Hudson, *Australian Religious Thought*, Monash University Press, Melbourne, 2016, p. 12.

60   C Strong, 'The differences and unity of the Gospels and Epistles', in *Christianity Re-interpreted and Other Sermons*, George Robertson, Melbourne, 1894, pp. 19–56.

61   Comments originally published in *The Contemporary Review*, December 1870, reprinted in TH Huxley, *Critiques and Addresses*, MacMillan, 1873.

Part Three: Bible and Nation

1   H Lawson, 'Song of the heathen', in C Roderick (ed.), *Collected Verse of Henry Lawson*, Angus & Robertson, Sydney, 1967–69, vol. 3, p. 64.

Chapter 7: Advancing Australia Fair

1   T Dingle, 'Depressions', in *e-Melbourne: The City Past and Present*, School of Historical & Philosophical Studies, University of Melbourne, 2008, <www.

emelbourne.net.au/biogs/EM00460b.htm>, and further M Bellanta, 'Rethinking the 1890s', in A Bashford & S Macintyre (eds.), *The Cambridge History of Australia vol. 1: Indigenous and Colonial Australia*, Cambridge University Press (CUP), Melbourne, 2013, pp. 218–241.

2   B Judd, *He That Doeth: The Life Story of RBS Hammond*, Marshall, Morgan & Scott, London, 1951.

3   A O'Brien, 'Religion', in Bashford & Macintyre 2013, p. 434.

4   M Lake, *Faith in Action: HammondCare*, UNSW Press, Sydney, 2013, pp. 11–69.

5   F Lees & D Burns, *The Temperance Bible Commentary*, National Temperance Publication Depot, London, 1894 (sixth edition) – with Hammond's signature inside the front cover, above the Dymocks shop sticker. Now in possession of the HammondCare historical archives, Sydney.

6   Lees & Burns 1894, 'Preliminary dissertation', p. xxviii.

7   Most local option laws did not go far enough for temperance advocates, who wanted all residents, including women and tenants – not just ratepayers – to have the power not only to reduce the concentration of licences or limit the granting of new ones, but to revoke all licences and establish 'dry' areas. A Blainey, 'Australia', in J Blocker, D Fahey & I Tyrrell (eds.), *Alcohol and Temperance in Modern History: An International Encyclopedia vol. 1 A-L*, ABC-Clio, Santa Barbara, 2003, pp. 75–79.

8   The Reverend JW Gillett of the Evangelical Council of New South Wales, cited in H Chilton, 'Evangelicals and the end of Christian Australia: nation and religion in the public square, 1959–1979', unpublished PhD thesis, University of Sydney, 2014, p. 57. Along the same lines, R Broome notes that 'many clergy seriously alleged that the Christian Sunday was the basis of the British Empire'; *Treasure in Earthen Vessels: Protestant Christianity in New South Wales Society, 1900–1914*, University of Queensland Press (UQP), St Lucia, 1980, p. 132.

9   Chilton 2014, p. 57.

10   On Australia see R Ely, 'Protestantism in Australian history: an interpretative sketch', *Lucas: An Evangelical History Review,* vol. 5, 1989, pp. 11–20; R Ely, 'The forgotten nationalism: Australian civic Protestantism in the Second World War', *Journal of Australian Studies*, vol. 11, no. 20, 1987, pp. 59–67; K Massam & J Smith, 'Images of God: civil religion and Australia at war 1939–1945', *Australian Religion Studies Review,* vol. 11, no. 2, 1998; Chilton 2014.

11   R Ely 1989, p. 15.

12   S Piggin & RD Linder, *The Fountain of Public Prosperity: Evangelical Christians in Australian History, 1740–1914*, Monash University Publishing, Melbourne, 2018 (forthcoming).

13   W Lawton, *The Better Times to Be: Utopian Attitudes to Society among Sydney Anglicans, 1885 to 1914*, UNSW Press, Sydney, 1990, p. 162.

14   Cited in Piggin & Linder 2018.

15   *Echo*, 17 September 1883, p. 4, cited in E Wilson, '"Wandering stars": the impact of British evangelists in Australia, 1870s–1900', PhD thesis, University of Tasmania, 2011, p. 137, available at <eprints.utas.edu.au/12522/2/Revised_thesis.pdf> (Hampson is the focus of pp. 134–144). See also S Swain, 'In these days of female evangelists and hallelujah lasses: women preachers and the redefinition of

gender roles in the churches in late nineteenth-century Australia', *Journal of Religious History*, vol. 26, no. 1, 2002, pp. 65–77.

16 BH Lee, *One of Australia's Daughters: An Autobiography of Mrs Harrison Lee*, Ideal Publishing Union, London, 1900, p. 75, referring to Matthew 7: 1–3. Interestingly, Lee quotes the first verse in a form slightly different to the King James text, which reads: 'Judge not, that ye be not judged'.

17 See Lee 1900, pp. 79–81.

18 H Jones, *In Her Own Name: A History of Women in South Australia from 1836*, Wakefield Press, Adelaide, 1986, p. 86.

19 P Grimshaw, 'Gender, citizenship and race in the Woman's Christian Temperance Union of Australia, 1890 to the 1930s', *Australian Feminist Studies*, vol. 13, no. 28, 1998, pp. 199–214.

20 Cited in A Hyslop, 'Temperance, Christianity and feminism: the Woman's Christian Temperance Union of Victoria, 1887–97', *Historical Studies*, vol. 17, no. 66, 1976, pp. 27–49.

21 'WCTU Page' of the *Alliance Record*, 11 January 1890, cited in Hyslop 1976, p. 39. Note the biblical phrases, ideas and allusions here – for example to 1 Corinthians 8:9.

22 Blainey 2003, pp. 75–79.

23 I Tyrrell, 'International aspects of the Woman's Temperance Movement in Australia: the influence of the American WCTU, 1882–1914', *Journal of Religious History*, vol. 12, no. 3, 1983, pp. 284–304.

24 M Lake, *Getting Equal: The History of Australian Feminism*, Allen & Unwin, Sydney, 1999, p. 27.

25 P Grimshaw, 'Suffragists', *The Encyclopaedia of Woman and Leadership in Twentieth Century Australia*, online at <www.womenaustralia.info/leaders/biogs/WLE0453b. htm>.

26 S Magarey, *Passions of the First Wave Feminists*, UNSW Press, Sydney, 2001, p. 25.

27 B Matthews, *Louisa*, McPhee Gribble, Melbourne, 1987, p. 396.

28 H Radi, 'Lawson, Louisa (1848–1920)', *Australian Dictionary of Biography (ADB)*, Australian National University, <adb.anu.edu.au/biography/lawson-louisa-7121/ text12285>, published first in hard copy 1986.

29 Cited in Radi 1986.

30 L Lawson, 'Inaugural address to the Dawn Club', 23 May 1889, cited in Matthews 1987, pp. 251–252, quoting Isaiah 65:17, 2 Peter 3:13 and Revelation 21:1.

31 'The biblical side of the question', *The Dawn* (Sydney), 4 December 1892, pp. 9–10.

32 'Demonstration in the evening', *The Daily Telegraph* (Sydney), 20 November 1893, p. 6.

33 See M Zaunbrecher, 'Henry Lawson's religion', *Journal of Religious History* vol. 11, no. 2, 1980, pp. 308–319.

34 See S Piggin, 'Australia's Jesus and Australian values', in S Piggin (ed.), *Shaping the Good Society in Australia: Australia's Christian Heritage*, Australia's Christian Heritage National Forum, Sydney, 2006.

35 *The Bulletin*, 27 January 1894, cited in J Barnes, '"The secret of England's greatness": a note on the anti-imperialism of *Such Is Life*', *Journal of the Association for the Study of Australian Literature*, vol. 13, no. 1, 2013.

36 CMH Clark, 'Furphy, Joseph (1843–1912)', *ADB*, Australian National University, <adb.anu.edu.au/biography/furphy-joseph-6261/text10785>, published first in hard copy 1981.

37 Cited in Clark 1981.

38 'Britain and the Bible', *Southern Cross* (Catholic newspaper), Adelaide, 5 November 1909, p. 8.

39 'Jingo', 'Righteousness exalteth a nation', *Daily Herald* (Adelaide), 1 July 1911, p. 4.

40 'Jingo', 'Righteousness exalteth a nation', *Daily Herald* (Adelaide), 1 July 1911, p. 4.

41 RD Linder, 'Spence, William Guthrie (1846–1926)', *Australian Dictionary of Evangelical Biography*, <webjournals.ac.edu.au/ojs/index.php/ADEB/article/view/830/827>.

42 WG Spence, *The Ethics of New Unionism: Delivered in Leigh House, Sydney, N.S.W., on Sunday Night, June 12th, 1892, Under the Auspices of the Australian Socialist League*, Martin & Grose, Creswick, 1892.

43 RD Linder, 'McGowen, James Sinclair Taylor (1855–1922)', *Australian Dictionary of Evangelical Biography*, Evangelical History Association of Australia, 2004, <webjournals.ac.edu.au/ojs/index.php/ADEB/article/view/993/990>; Piggin & Linder 2018; B Nairn, 'McGowen, James Sinclair (1855–1922)', *ADB*, Australian National University, <adb.anu.edu.au/biography/mcgowen-james-sinclair-7360/text12785>, published first in hard copy 1986.

44 A O'Brien, *God's Willing Workers*, UNSW Press, Sydney, 2005, p. 64; W Birman & E Wood, 'Beadle, Jane (Jean) (1868–1942)', *ADB*, Australian National University, <adb.anu.edu.au/biography/beadle-jane-jean-5163/text8671>, published first in hard copy 1979.

45 J Harris, 'Words of justice in a secular society: the role of the King James Version of the Bible in Australia', in A Duran (ed.), *The King James Bible Across Borders and Centuries*, Duquesne University Press, Pittsburgh, 2014, pp. 151–172.

46 Recent examples include the many church pronouncements that opposed the abolition of Sunday penalty rates for low-paid workers in 2017, as well as the ongoing advocacy of Christian charities seeking to address homelessness, unemployment and other issues.

47 RM Williams with O Ruhen, *Beneath Whose Hand: The Autobiography of RM Williams*, Macmillan, Melbourne, 1984, p. 91.

48 Williams 1984, p. 17.

49 Williams 1984, p. 155, referring to the story of Jesus' visit to the home of Martha and Mary in Luke 10:38–42.

50 Williams 1984, pp. 125, 193, 194. Bible references added.

Chapter 8: Politics and the Bible

1 Standing orders, as cited in GV Puig, 'Parliamentary Prayers and Section 116 of the Australian Constitution', *Papers on Parliament,* no. 51, June 2009, available at <www.aph.gov.au/About_Parliament/Senate/Research_and_Education/pops/pop51/puig>. The Lord's Prayer is recorded, in slightly different ways, in Matthew 6:9–13 and Luke 11:1–4.

2 From reports in the *Age* (Melbourne), 10 May 1901, pp. 7–8 and the *Argus*, 10 May 1901, p. 5.

3   K Elford, 'A prophet without honour: the political ideals of John Dunmore Lang',
     Journal of the Royal Australian Historical Society, vol. 54, no. 2, 1968, pp. 161–175;
     J Reynolds, 'West, John (1809–1873)', *Australian Dictionary of Biography (ADB)*,
     Australian National University, <adb.anu.edu.au/biography/west-john-2784/
     text3965>, published first in hard copy 1967.

4   *Sydney Morning Herald*, 30 January 1888, cited in W Phillips, *James Jefferis:
     Prophet of Federation*, Australian Scholarly Publishing, Melbourne, 1993 p. 170.

5   *Sydney Morning Herald*, 23 January 1888, cited in Phillips 1993, p. 169.

6   *Sydney Morning Herald*, 9 April 1898, cited in A Atkinson, *The Europeans in
     Australia Volume 3: Nation*, UNSW Press, Sydney, 2014, p. 290. Emphasis added.

7   Atkinson 2014, p. 297; D Hilliard, 'Australia: toward secularisation and one step
     back', in CG Brown & M Snape (eds.), *Secularisation in the Christian World: Essays
     in Honor of Hugh McLeod*, Ashgate, Farnham, 2010, p. 81.

8   J Hirst, *The Sentimental Nation: The Making of the Australian Commonwealth*,
     Oxford University Press (OUP), Melbourne, 2000, p. 18.

9   Hirst 2000, p. 4.

10   The allusion is to John 19:23–24.

11   J Hirst, 'Federation: destiny and identity', Papers on Parliament No. 37,
     November 2001, available at <www.aph.gov.au/senate/~/~/link.aspx?_id=
     8D6A81550F0F4F22A6CBE7691B59BB98&_z=z> and more generally Hirst 2000.

12   These words conclude his work *Fifty Years in the Making of Australian History*,
     Longmans, Green & Co, London, 1892; digital version available via <setis.library.
     usyd.edu.au/ozlit/pdf/fed0024.pdf>.

13   Deakin, not long after his election to the 1898 convention. Cited in R Williams,
     In God They Trust?: The Religious Beliefs of Australia's Prime Ministers, 1901–2013,
     Bible Society Australia, 2013, p. 36.

14   Barton, speaking in Sydney to recommend the Constitution Bill, 19 April
     1898, cited in R Ely, *Unto God and Caesar: Religious Issues in the Emerging
     Commonwealth, 1891–1906*, Melbourne University Press (MUP), Carlton, 1976,
     pp. 105–106. See more generally Williams 2013, pp. 28–32.

15   Atkinson 2014, p. 264.

16   WR Schoobridge (Convenor of the Good Citizenship committee of Glenora
     Christian Endeavour society), 'The Christian aspect of Federation', *The Mercury*
     (Hobart), 28 May 1898, p. 4.

17   *Evening News* (Sydney), 8 February 1897, cited in Atkinson 2014, p. 214.

18   J Murnane, 8 February 1898, 'Federation', *Eastern Districts Chronicle* (York, WA),
     12 February 1898, p. 3.

19   See Williams 2013, pp. 33–44.

20   See Williams 2013; Al Gabay, *The Mystic Life of Alfred Deakin*, Cambridge
     University Press (CUP), Cambridge and New York, 1992.

21   *Register*, 2 January 1901, cited in Phillips 1993, p. 248.

22   Glynn at the Adelaide convention, 1897, cited in Ely 1976, p. 33, see also Atkinson
     2014, p. 269.

23   Atkinson 2014.

24   Ely 1976.

25   R Garran, *Commentaries on the Constitution of the Commonwealth of Australia*,
     Angus & Robertson, Sydney, 1901.

26   See A Atkinson, 'Federation, democracy and the struggle against a single Australia', *Australian Historical Studies*, vol. 44, no. 2, 2013, pp. 262–279, as well as Atkinson 2014. He notes that between one-fifth and one-quarter of qualified citizens voted against federation.

27   J Roe, *Social Policy in Australia: Some Perspectives 1901–1975*, Cassell, Sydney, 1976, p. 3.

28   *The Australian Sentinel and Herald of Liberty*, first issue, May 1894, cited in Ely 1976, pp. 28–29.

29   See Ely 1976, pp. 29–30.

30   J Rickard, 'Higgins, Henry Bournes (1851–1929)', *ADB*, Australian National University, <adb.anu.edu.au/biography/higgins-henry-bournes-6662/text11483>, published first in hard copy 1983. See further J Rickard, *HB Higgins: The Rebel as Judge*, Allen & Unwin, Sydney, 1984.

31   For an introductory summary of that debate, see M Maddox, 'Religion, state and politics in Australia', in J Jupp (ed.), *The Encyclopaedia of Religion in Australia*, CUP, Cambridge, 2009, pp. 608–620, and as a counterpoint S Chavura, 'The separation of religion and state: context and meaning', *Nebula*, vol. 7, no. 4, 2010, pp. 37–46.

32   S Chavura & I Tregenza, 'A political history of the secular in Australia, 1788–1945', in T Stanley (ed.), *Religion after Secularization in Australia*, Palgrave Macmillan, New York, 2015.

33   Ely 1976, p. 124.

34   Chavura & Tregenza 2015.

35   I am indebted to Dr Stephen Chavura for clarifying conversations on this point.

36   1898 Australasian Federation Conference, Third Session Debates, 2 March 1898, online at <parlinfo.aph.gov.au/parlInfo/search/display/display. w3p;query=Id%3A%22constitution%2Fconventions%2F1898-1120%22>; see also Ely 1976, pp. 122–123. In 1901, the NSW, Tasmanian and SA legislatures, and the Victorian Legislative Assembly, did not have prayers at all.

37   Maddox 2009, p. 614.

38   Cited in Ely 1976, p. 123.

39   Cited in Maddox 2009, p. 614.

40   Editorial, *Sydney Morning Herald*, 8 June 1901, cited in Ely 1976, p. 124 – my emphasis.

41   Cited in Maddox 2009, p. 614.

42   For more on this point, see J Dickson, 'Letting go of the Lord's Prayer in Parliament', *The Drum*, 17 January 2014, at <www.abc.net.au/news/2014-01-17/ dickson-parliament-prayer/5203930>.

43   J Ireland, 'Heaven help those trying to scrap Lord's Prayer in Parliament', *Sydney Morning Herald*, 18 January 2014, <www.smh.com.au/federal-politics/political-opinion/heaven-help-those-trying-to-scrap-lords-prayer-in-parliament-20140117-310mr.html>. The Fairfax poll had 5447 respondents, of whom 67 per cent opposed a change.

44   See 'Oaths and affirmations made by the executive and members of Federal Parliament since 1901', Parliamentary Library research paper 20,

<www.aph.gov.au/About_Parliament/Parliamentary_Departments/
Parliamentary_Library/pubs/rp/rp1314/OathsAffirmations>

45   M Tate, 'Personal explanations', Senate, *Debates*, 23 October 1984, p. 2208, cited in
     Parliamentary Library research paper, 'Oaths and affirmations'.

46   Cited in W Phillips, 'Jefferis, James (1833–1917)', *ADB*, Australian National
     University, <adb.anu.edu.au/biography/jefferis-james-3853/text6123>, published
     first in hard copy 1972.

47   G Long, 'White Australia, by the Bishop of Bathurst', *The East and the West:
     A Quarterly Review for the Study of Missionary Problems*, vol. 17, no. 68, October
     1919, p. 296.

48   EW Cole, *The White Australia Question*, EW Cole Book Arcade, Melbourne, 1903.

49   G Melleuish, 'A secular Australia? Ideas, politics and the search for moral order in
     nineteenth and early twentieth century Australia', *Journal of Religious History*,
     vol. 38, no. 3, 2014, pp. 398–412.

50   See generally S Macintyre, 'A fair wage', in his *Winners and Losers: The Pursuit of
     Social Justice in Australian History*, Allen & Unwin, Sydney, 1985.

51   Harvester Judgement (Ex parte McKay), *Commonwealth Arbitration Reports*, 1907,
     pp. 4, 21, <www.aph.gov.au/binaries/library/intguide/law/harvester.pdf>.

52   Francis Castles, *The Working Class and Welfare: Reflections on the Political
     Development of the Welfare State in Australia and New Zealand, 1890–1980*, Allen &
     Unwin, Wellington and Sydney, 1985.

53   K Blackburn, 'The living wage in Australia: a secularisation of Catholic ethics on
     wages, 1891–1907', *Journal of Religious History,* vol. 20, 1996, pp. 93–113; Chavura
     & Tregenza 2015, p. 21.

54   HB Higgins, *Another Isthmus in History: A Lecture Before the University Historical
     Society on July 13th, 1896*, Martin & Gorse, Creswick, 1896, pp. 17–18.

55   Pope Leo XII, *Rerum Novarum* (1891), section 21, available at <w2.vatican.
     va/content/leo-xiii/en/encyclicals/documents/hf_l-xiii_enc_15051891_rerum-
     novarum.pdf>.

56   See Macintyre 1985, pp. 44–45.

57   Cited in RD Linder, 'The Methodist love affair with the Australian Labor Party
     1891–1929', *Lucas: An Evangelical History Review,* no. 23 & 24, 1997–1998,
     pp. 35–61.

58   Cited in K Rudd, 'Politics', in S Piggin (ed.), *Shaping the Good Society in Australia*,
     Australia's Christian Heritage National Forum, Sydney, 2006, p. 165.

59   D Murphy, *Labor in Politics: The State Labor Parties in Australia, 1880–1920*,
     University of Queensland Press (UQP), St Lucia, 1975, p. 250.

60   Linder 1997–1998, pp. 35–61.

61   'Mr Verran lionised', *Mount Barker Courier*, 24 June 1910, p. 3. The allusion is to
     Luke 2:25–32.

62   S Macintyre, 'The first caucus', in J Faulkner & S Macintyre (eds.), *The True
     Believers: The Story of the Federal Parliamentary Labor Party,* Allen & Unwin,
     Sydney, 2001, p. 24.

63   J Brett, *Australian Liberals and the Moral Middle Class: From Alfred Deakin to John
     Howard*, CUP, Melbourne, 2003, p. 42.

64   See C Madden, 'The Democratic Labor Party: an overview', Parliamentary

Library Research Publications, 18 July 2011, <www.aph.gov.au/About_
Parliament/Parliamentary_Departments/Parliamentary_Library/pubs/BN/2011-
2012/DPLOverview>.
65 See <www.liberal.org.au/our-history>. For general introductions, see I Hancock,
'Liberal Party of Australia' and B Galligan, 'Liberal Party predecessors', both in
B Galligan & W Roberts (eds.), *Oxford Companion to Australian Politics*, OUP,
Melbourne, 2007.
66 Brett 2003, p. 40.
67 A Crabb, 'Invoking religion in Australian politics', *Australian Journal of Political
Science,* vol. 44, 2009, pp. 259–279.
68 AW Martin, 'Menzies, Sir Robert Gordon (Bob) (1894–1978)', *ADB*, Australian
National University, <adb.anu.edu.au/biography/menzies-sir-robert-gordon-
bob-11111/text19783>, published first in hard copy 2000, and AW Martin, *Robert
Menzies: A Life, vol. 1, 1894–1943*, MUP, Carlton South, 1993.
69 D Paproth, *Failure Is Not Final: A Life of CH Nash*, Centre for the Study of
Australian Christianity, 1997, pp. 127–128 and 236.
70 Robert Menzies, 6 July 1950, cited in H Chilton, 'Evangelicals and the end
of Christian Australia: nation and religion in the public square, 1959–1979',
unpublished PhD thesis, University of Sydney, 2014, p. 77.
71 Ephesians 4:25.
72 H Henderson, *Letters to My Daughter: Robert Menzies, Letters, 1955–1975*, Pier 9,
Millers Point, 2011, p. 272.

Chapter 9: War and its aftermath
1 'The taking of Jerusalem', *Chronicle* (Adelaide), 22 December 1917, p. 24.
2 'Entry to Holy City', *Sydney Morning Herald*, 18 December 1917, p. 9.
3 Trooper Ernest Pauls, cited in P Daley & M Bowers, *Armageddon: Two Men on an
Anzac Trail*, Miegunyah Press, Melbourne, 2011, p. 92.
4 See RD Linder, *The Long Tragedy: Australian Evangelical Christians and the Great
War, 1914–1918*, Centre for the Study of Australian Christianity & Open Book
Publishers, Adelaide, 2000; S Piggin & RD Linder, *Attending to the National Soul:
Evangelical Christians in Australian History, 1914–2014* (forthcoming). On the
availability and prevalence of Bibles among Australian service personnel, see
M Gladwin, *Captains of the Soul: A History of Australian Army Chaplains*, Big Sky
Publishing, Sydney, 2014; C Bale, '"We will remember them": The use of the
Bible in remembering the service and sacrifice of Australians in WW1', in J Harris
(ed.), *Their Sacrifice: The Brave and Their Bibles,* Bible Society Australia, Sydney,
2015b, pp. 117–125. On its role in the intellectual lives of Australian soldiers, see
A Laugesen, *'Boredom Is the Enemy': The Intellectual and Imaginative Lives of
Australian Soldiers in the Great War and Beyond*, Ashgate, Farnham, 2013, p. 40.
5 Bean Diary, December 1917, cited in D McCarthy, *Gallipoli to the Somme: The
Story of CEW Bean*, John Ferguson, Sydney, 1983, p. 308.
6 See KS Inglis, 'Bean, Charles Edwin (1879–1968)', *Australian Dictionary of
Biography (ADB)*, Australian National University, <adb.anu.edu.au/biography/
bean-charles-edwin-5166/text8677>, published first in hard copy 1979. Bean's
comment was made in 1948.

7   See G Lindsay, 'Be substantially great in thyself: getting to know CEW Bean; barrister, judge's associate, moral philosopher', 2013, <www.forbessociety.org.au/wordpress/wp-content/uploads/2013/03/bean.pdf>, pp. 41–42.

8   C Wilcox, 'World War One', in G Davison, J Hirst & S Macintyre (eds.), *The Oxford Companion to Australian History*, Oxford University Press (OUP), Melbourne, 2001; M Oppenheimer, *Australian Women and War*, Dept. Veterans Affairs, Canberra, 2008; N Riseman, 'Diversifying the black diggers' histories', *Aboriginal History*, vol. 39, 2015, p. 137.

9   *Commonwealth of Australia Gazette*, no. 39, Monday 17 May 1915, <www.gallipoli.gov.au/battle-of-the-landing/charles-bean.php>.

10   Inglis 1979.

11   CEW Bean, *Anzac to Amiens*, Australian War Memorial, Canberra, 1946, p. 181, <www.awm.gov.au/histories/chapter.asp?volume=1>.

12   B Lewis, *Our War: Australia During World War I*, Melbourne University Press (MUP), Melbourne, 1980, p. 134.

13   Owen Gower Lewis to his father James Lewis, 27 April 1915, cited in Linder 2000, p. 47.

14   LB Radford, cited in M Hutchinson & J Wolffe, *A Short History of Global Evangelicalism*, Cambridge University Press (CUP), New York, 2012, p. 152.

15   J Harris (ed.), *Their Sacrifice: The Brave and Their Bibles*, Bible Society Australia, Sydney, 2015, p. 101.

16   A Stewart, *Diaries of an Unsung Hero*, compiled by Margaret Willmington, Mark Webb of B-in-Print, Blaxland, 1995, discussed in Piggin & Linder (forthcoming).

17   S Mill & R Huber, *The Bible: A History: The Making and Impact of the Bible*, Lion Hudson, Oxford, 2015 [2003], p. 308.

18   R Steer, *Good News for the World: The Story of the Bible Society: 200 Years of Making the Bible Heard*, Monarch Books, Oxford, 2004, p. 316; Laugesen 2013, pp. 27, 36.

19   Linder 2000, p. 46.

20   Linder 2000, p. 46.

21   For examples, see Linder 2000, pp. 20, 113–114.

22   Cited in Laugesen 2013, p. 27. Note there are lots more stories in Harris 2015.

23   Letter 14 April 1918, cited in Laugesen 2013, pp. 40–41. Jacob was killed three months later in July 1918.

24   I am not suggesting that these ideas and ideals sprang straight or simply from the text, or that their sole roots lie in the Christian Scriptures. Indeed, their particular forms, in the western European tradition, owe much to the particular settlements between classical and early Christian thought achieved by Augustine, and later in relation to humanism (with Aquinas). For overviews, see R Cox, 'The ethics of war up to Thomas Aquinas', in S Lazar & H Frowe (eds.), *The Oxford Handbook of the Ethics of War*, published online October 2015 (hard copy forthcoming), and S Lazar, 'War', in EN Zalta (ed.), *The Stanford Encyclopedia of Philosophy*, <plato.stanford.edu/archives/spr2017/entries/war/>, first published 3 May 2016.

25   Cited in M McKernan, *The Australian People and the Great War*, Thomas Nelson, Melbourne, 1980, p. 18.

26   For an account of an intriguing millenarian variation on this theme, see

F Bongiorno, 'The Devil and Kaiser Bill: Victor Kroemer and the world crisis of 1914–15', *Australian Journal of Politics and History,* vol. 53, no. 3, 2007, pp. 420–435.

27 For instance, a regional Victorian paper commented on Germany's 'brutal and material' ideals, 'blown up with high conceits, engendering pride which, according to Milton, are the motives of the apostate angel': 'War against war', *Casterton Free Press and Glenelg Shire Advertiser* (Victoria), 11 March 1915, p. 2.

28 N Lindsay cartoon from *The Bulletin*, 1916, reproduced in Linder 2000; N Lindsay drawings of *Voice of Germany*, in *The collection of war posters, featuring cartoons by Norman Lindsay, for the purpose of promoting enlistment in the armed forces*, State Library of NSW, online at <acms.sl.nsw.gov.au/album/albumView. aspx?itemID=1014662&acmsid=0>.

29 BL Webb, *The Religious Significance of the War*, Christian World, Sydney, 1915, p. 20.

30 Linder 2000.

31 'Hay during World War I: Rev B Linden Webb and the Hay Methodist Congregation', *Hay Historical Society Web-Site Newsletter* October 2007, no. vii, <users.tpg.com.au/hayhist/NewsletterSeven.html>.

32 In the United Kingdom, Archbishop William Temple advocated a robust Christian ecumenicalism that would surmount all dividing barriers. See E Loane, *William Temple and Church Unity: The Politics and Practice of Ecumenical Theology*, Springer International, Switzerland, 2016. In the United States, Reinhold Niebuhr and other Christian internationalists 'rejected exceptionalist frameworks and eschewed the dominant '"Christian nation" imaginary as a lens through which to view US foreign relations': MG Thompson, *For God and Globe: Christian Internationalism in the United States Between the Great War and the Cold War*, Cornell University Press, Ithaca, 2015.

33 S Donaldson, 'Christianity and international relations', Address to the Lambeth Conference, July 1920, cited in B Fletcher, 'Anglicanism and nationalism in Australia', *Journal of Religious History*, vol. 23, no. 2, 1999, p. 227.

34 Batty to Burgmann, 30 November 1937, cited in Fletcher 1999, p. 227.

35 See R Howe, 'The Australian Student Christian Movement and women's activism in the Asia-Pacific region 1890s–1920s', *Australian Feminist Studies*, vol. 16, no. 36, 2001, pp. 311–323; M Lake, 'Faith in crisis: Christian university students in peace and war', *Australian Journal of Politics and History,* vol. 56, no. 3, 2010, pp. 441–454.

36 Gladwin 2014, p. 101.

37 B Oliver, *Peacemongers: Conscientious Objectors to Military Service in Australia 1911–1945*, Fremantle Arts Centre Press, Perth, 1997, pp. 10, 87.

38 Oliver 1997. According to the Army, Luke 22:38 was 'proof' that Jesus had his disciples armed with swords to protect him: 'They said Lord, behold, here are two swords. And he said unto them, "It is enough"'. Another of the Army's favourite verses was John 2:15, which describes Jesus clearing the temple by driving out the money changers with a lash.

39 Oliver 1997, p. 118.

40 Oliver 1997, p. 134.

41   See the description at Monuments Australia, <monumentaustralia.org.au/
      themes/conflict/multiple/display/20323-berridale-war-memorial>; KS Inglis,
      Sacred Places: War Memorials in the Australian Landscape, Miegunyah Press,
      Melbourne, 1998, pp. 152–153.

42   Crucified Christs were erected, though, in the grounds of a few churches and
      church schools – particularly those of a Catholic or Anglo-Catholic variety. For
      examples see Inglis 1998, pp. 151–152.

43   Inglis 1998.

44   Description of Shrine of Remembrance in 'The Shrine Story' brochure available
      at <www.shrine.org.au/files/ShrineStory_English_Web.pdf>.

45   Bale 2015b.

46   His PhD was published as *A Crowd of Witnesses: Epitaphs on First World War
      Australian War Graves*, Longueville Media, Sydney, 2015a.

47   See the Commonwealth War Graves Commission record of his headstone, <www.
      cwgc.org/find-war-dead/casualty/64432/LEWIS,%20OWEN%20GOWER>.

48   Commonwealth War Graves Commission record of his headstone, <www.cwgc.
      org/find-war-dead/casualty/64135/BEST,%20GEORGE%20WILLIAM>.

49   Written by the evangelical leader Edward Bickersteth, this hymn was itself
      inspired by Isaiah 26:3: 'You will keep in perfect peace him whose mind is
      steadfast, because he trusts in you'.

50   Bale 2015b, pp. 117–125.

51   C Bale, 'Grief, religion and national identity', *St Mark's Review*, no. 231, 2015c,
      pp. 86–97.

52   Private LS Blackwood, killed age 21 in October 1917, J Laffin, *We Will Remember
      Them: Australian Epitaphs of World War I*, Kangaroo Press, Sydney, 1995, p. 99.

53   Cited in Bale 2015b, p. 124.

54   Commonwealth War Graves Commission record of his headstone, <www.cwgc.
      org/find-war-dead/casualty/644815/LAKE,%20SYDNEY%20MOOR>.

55   Bale 2015b, pp. 117–25 and further Bale 2015a.

56   J Moses, 'The struggle for Anzac Day 1916–30 and the role of the Brisbane Anzac
      Day Commemoration committee', *Journal of the Royal Australian Historical
      Society*, vol. 88, no. 1, 2002, pp. 54–74.

57   Cited in Moses 2002, p. 59.

58   WM Mansfield, 'Garland, David John (1864–1939)', *ADB*, National Centre of
      Biography, Australian National University, <adb.anu.edu.au/biography/garland-
      david-john-6278/text10821>, published first in hard copy 1981.

59   J Moses, 'The Faith of Canon David John Garland (1864–1939) – an Australian
      Gladstonian imperialist', *St Mark's Review*, no. 225, 2013, pp. 71–84.

60   RSSILA NSW branch, 21 March 1921, cited in Moses 2002, p. 63.

61   Cited in M Gladwin, 'Anzac Day's religious custodians', in T Frame (ed.), *Anzac
      Day Then & Now,* NewSouth Publishing, Sydney, 2016, p. 99.

62   Wright, *Alan Walker: Conscience of the Nation*, Openbook Publishers, Adelaide,
      1997, p. 182; H Chilton, 'Battling for the nation's soul: the RSL vs. the churches,
      Anzac Day 1965', *Teaching History*, vol. 49, no. 1, 2015, p. 34–37.

63   Cited in Gladwin 2016, p. 98.

64   M Gladwin, 'The one request of all ranks', in J Harris (ed.), *Their Sacrifice: The*

Brave and their Bibles, Bible Society Australia, Sydney, 2015, pp. 55–69.

65   See J Brown, *Anzac's Long Shadow: The Cost of Our National Obsession*,
      Black Inc, Melbourne, 2014, extracted at <www.themonthly.com.au/blog/
      james-brown/2014/02/17/1392601420/anzacs-long-shadow-cost-our-national-
      obsession>.

66   See for example: M Whitbourn, 'SBS presenter Scott McIntyre sacked over
      "inappropriate" Anzac Day tweets', *Sydney Morning Herald*, 26 April 2015,
      <www.smh.com.au/national/ww1/sbs-presenter-scott-mcintyre-sacked-over-
      inappropriate-anzac-day-tweets-20150426-1mtbx8.html>; C Ford, 'The hypocrisy
      that lies behind the reaction to seven words from Yassmin Abdel-Magied', *Sydney
      Morning Herald*, 28 April 2017, <www.smh.com.au/lifestyle/news-and-views/
      opinion/over-the-top-reaction-to-seven-words-from-yassmin-abdelmagied-brings-
      this-country-into-disrepute-20170428-gvueno.html>.

67   W Hudson, *Australian Religious Thought*, Monash University Press, Melbourne,
      2016, chapter 2.

68   M Allen, 'Missionaries abroad', in *The Encyclopedia of Women & Leadership in
      Twentieth-Century Australia*, Australian Women's Archives Project, 2014,
      <www.womenaustralia.info/leaders/biogs/WLE0442b.htm>.

69   WS Clack, *We Will Go: The History of 70 Years Training Men and Women for World
      Missionary Ministry*, Melbourne Bible College of Victoria, Melbourne, 1990, p. 14.

70   Piggin & Linder (forthcoming).

71   Howe 2001, pp. 311–323.

72   Examples from A O'Brien, *God's Willing Workers: Women and Religion in Australia*,
      UNSW Press, Sydney, 2005, pp. 76–77.

73   See for instance F Engel, *Christians in Australia: Volume Two, Times of Change,
      1918–1978*, Joint Board of Christian Education, Melbourne, 1993, chapter 7;
      M Lake, 'Western heritage, Asian destiny: the Australian Council of Churches'
      activity in Asia, 1950–1965', *ERAS Journal*, no. 7, 2005; Hudson 2016, p. xxii.

74   C Rowley, *Outcasts in White Australia*, Penguin, Melbourne, 1972, p. 90.

75   H Goodall, *Invasion to Embassy*, Allen & Unwin, Sydney, 1996, p. 137.

76   R Broome, *Aboriginal Australians: A History since 1788*, 4th ed., Allen & Unwin,
      Sydney, 2010, p. 95; 'Coranderrk', Australian Heritage Database, Department
      of Environment and Energy, Australian Government, <www.environment.gov.
      au/cgi-bin/ahdb/search.pl?mode=place_detail;place_id=106033>. In 1998, in
      the aftermath of the Wik decision, the Indigenous Land Corporation purchased
      eighty-one hectares of the original Coranderrk reserve, recognising its ongoing
      importance to the Kulin people and the descendants of its residents. The reserve
      remains owned and managed by an Aboriginal organisation.

77   Piggin & Linder (forthcoming).

78   W Cooper, *Blood from a Stone: William Cooper and the Australian Aborigines
      League*, edited with an introduction by A Markus, Monash Publications in
      History no. 2, Melbourne, 1986, p. 7.

79   Cooper 1986, p. 18.

80   Cooper to Mr Paterson, Hon Minister for the Interior, 31 October 1936, in
      B Attwood, *Rights for Aborigines*, Allen & Unwin, Sydney, 2003, pp. 41–45.

81   Cited in O'Brien 2005, p. 78. O'Brien notes that, in the 1920s, Australian

missionary thought began to move towards a more positive view of Indigenous culture, and to acknowledging the role of white Australians in colonisation.

82   Cited in O'Brien 2005, p. 83.

83   Attwood 2003, p. 17.

84   Cooper to the Prime Minister, 31 March 1938, in Cooper 1986, pp. 77–83.

Part 4: A Secular Australia?

1   R Menzies, 'Speech at the opening and dedication of the Canberra Bible House on February 13, 1960' [sound recording], Menzies collection MS 4936, National Library of Australia, online at <nla.gov.au/nla.obj-222158841>.

Chapter 10: The turning point

1   Australian Bureau of Statistics data cited in D Harris, 'Counting Christians', in D Harris, D Hynd & D Millikan (eds.), *The Shape of Belief: Christianity in Australia Today*, Lancer Press, Sydney, 1982, pp. 229–288.

2   D Hilliard, 'Popular religion in Australia in the 1950s: a study of Adelaide and Brisbane', *Journal of Religious History* vol. 16, no. 2, 1988, pp. 228–229.

3   D Hilliard, 'Australia: toward secularisation and one step back' in CG Brown & M Snape (eds.), *Secularisation in the Christian World: Essays in Honor of Hugh McLeod*, Ashgate, Farnham, 2010, p. 81.

4   See R Howe, *A Century of Influence: The Australian Student Christian Movement 1896–1996*, UNSW Press, Sydney, 2009, pp. 398–399.

5   Cecil B DeMille cited in K Orrison, *Written in Stone: Making Cecil B DeMille's Epic* The Ten Commandments, Vestal Press, Lanham, Maryland, 1999.

6   See A Healey, 'A critical alliance: ABC religious broadcasting and the Christian churches', *Journal of the Australian Catholic Historical Society*, vol. 26, 2005, pp. 15–28, and also KS Inglis, *This Is the ABC: The Australian Broadcasting Commission 1932–1983*, Black Inc, Melbourne, 2006, p. 176.

7   E Campion, 'Rumble, Leslie Audoen (1892–1975)', *Australian Dictionary of Biography (ADB)*, Australian National University, <adb.anu.edu.au/biography/rumble-leslie-audoen-11584/text20679>.

8   See B Griffen-Foley, 'Radio ministries: religion on Australian commercial radio from the 1920s to the 1960s', *Journal of Religious History,* vol. 32, no. 1, 2008, pp. 31–54.

9   Deane E Meatheringham, cited in S Piggin, 'Billy Graham in Australia, 1959 – was it revival?', *Lucas: An Evangelical History Review,* no. 6, 1989 available at <webjournals.ac.edu.au/ojs/index.php/LUCAS/article/view/8790/8787>.

10   Piggin 1989.

11   J Prince & M Prince, *Tuned in to Change: A History of the Australian Scripture Union, 1880–1980*, Scripture Union of Australia, Sydney, 1979, p. 166.

12   See generally P Neuner, 'The reception of the Bible in Roman Catholic tradition', trans. L Archibald, in J Riches (ed.), *The New Cambridge History of the Bible vol.4: From 1750 to the Present*, Cambridge University Press (CUP), Cambridge, 2015, pp. 537–562.

13   McCrindle Research, 'A demographic snapshot of Christianity and church attendance in Australia', 2014, <mccrindle.com.au/the-mccrindle-blog/a-demographic-snapshot-of-christianity-and-church-attenders-in-australia>.

14   For the 2013 figure, see <www.abs.gov.au/ausstats/abs@.nsf/mf/3310.0>.

15   Hilliard 2010, p. 84.

16   For an overview, see H McLeod, 'Introduction', in H McLeod (ed.), *The Cambridge History of Christianity Volume 9: World Christianities c. 1914–c. 2000*, CUP, Cambridge, 2006, pp. 1–14.

17   In 1961, 34.9 per cent responded Anglican, 24.9 Catholic, 10.2 Methodist and 9.3 Presbyterian and Reformed – a total of 79.3 per cent. In 2016, 22.6 of Australians responded Catholic and 13.3 Anglican. A further 3.7 affiliated with the Uniting Church, formed in 1977 and incorporating virtually all Methodists, Congregationalists and most Presbyterians. 2.3 per cent of people in 2016 said they were Presbyterian/Reformed.

18   G Bouma, *Australian Soul: Religion and Spirituality in the 21st Century*, CUP, Cambridge, 2006, p. 64.

19   Christian Research Association, 'Korean churches in Australia', *Pointers* (CRA Bulletin), vol. 5, no. 2, 1995, reporting data from Gil Soo Han, *Social Sources of Church Growth: Korean Churches in the Homeland and Overseas*, University Press of America, Maryland, 1994, data from 1991.

20   Australian Community Survey (1998) reported by P Kaldor, R Dixon, & R Powell et al, *Taking Stock: A Profile of Australian Church Attenders*, Openbook Publishers, Adelaide, 1999, p. 22. Note however that lower levels of involvement among second-generation immigrants have been documented in P Bentley, T Blombery & P Hughes, *Faith Without the Church?: Nominalism in Australian Christianity*, Christian Research Association, Melbourne, 1992.

21   P Hughes (ed.), *Charting the Faith of Australians: Thirty Years in the Christian Research Association*, Christian Research Association, Melbourne, 2016, p. 30.

22   Hughes 2016, p. 35.

23   McCrindle Research, 'National education report: a snapshot of schools in Australia in 2015', 20 April 2015, <www.mccrindle.com.au/the-mccrindle-blog/national-education-report-a-snapshot-of-schools-in-australia-in-2015>; Australian Bureau of Statistics, 'Schools, Australia, 2016', 2 February 2017, cat. no. 4221.0, <www.abs.gov.au/ausstats/abs@.nsf/mf/4221.0>; and for wider discussion, P Hughes & C Pickering, 'Bible engagement among young Australians', Christian Research Association, April 2010, <www.cra.org.au/Bible_Engagement_Report.pdf>.

24   Harris 1982, p. 236 and Hilliard 2010, p. 82.

25   McCrindle Research 2014 notes 3.495 million monthly churchgoers, compared to 1.684 million sport attendees.

26   McCrindle Research 2014 suggests there are 1.8 million in church compared to 1.6 million in SA.

27   Inglis 2006, p. 177.

28   Griffen-Foley 2008, pp. 31–54.

29   Griffen-Foley 2008.

30   Healey 2005, pp. 15–28.

31   Healey 2005, p. 26.

32   *The Sower*, Magazine of the Bible Society Australia, no. 103, January 1983, p. 6.

33   'Farewell to pilot', *The Sower*, no. 105, July 1983, p. 1.

34   These figures are drawn from Bible Society reports of annual circulation, included
      in Bible Society publicity such as *The Sower* magazine. Notably, such reportage
      usually included figures for New Guinea along with figures for each of the
      Australian states. The New Guinea figures have been omitted from the Australian
      totals given here, though Bible Society work in New Guinea and the assumption
      that New Guinea was an 'extension' of Australia deserves much further discussion
      and exploration.

35   Data cited in H Mol, *Religion in Australia: A Sociological Investigation*, Nelson,
      Melbourne, 1971, p. 21.

36   M Lake & J Harris, 'John Harris's Bibles', *St Mark's Review*, no. 240, 2017,
      pp. 76–92.

37   The 250 000th copy was presented to the Governor General by the president of the
      United Bible Societies in March 1978. 'Bible for Sir Zelman', *Canberra Times*,
      15 March 1978, p. 22.

38   M Dunlevy, 'Plenty of shekels in the Bible business', *Canberra Times*, 28 August
      1982, p. 14.

39   Dunlevy 1982, p. 14. NIV sales figures are for the period between its publication
      in 1979 and August 1982.

40   Data from both polls cited in Mol 1971, p. 21.

41   D Carter & B Griffen-Foley, 'Culture and media', in A Bashford & S Macintyre
      (eds.), *The Cambridge History of Australia. Volume 2: The Commonwealth of
      Australia*, CUP, Melbourne, 2015, p. 252.

42   P O'Farrell, 'Bible reading and related mental furniture,' *Australian Cultural
      History*, vol. 11, 1992, p. 25.

43   Christian Research Association, 'What people do with their free time', *Pointers*
      (CRA Bulletin), vol. 10, no. 2, 2000, drawing on ABS Time Use survey 1997.

44   Wellbeing and Security Survey (2002) results, reported in P Hughes & L Fraser,
      Life, Ethics and Faith in Australian Society: Facts and Figures, Christian Research
      Association, Melbourne, 2014, p. 60.

45   Wellbeing and Security Survey (2002) results reported in Hughes & Fraser 2014,
      p. 60.

46   Cited in C Wallace, *Germaine Greer: Untamed Shrew*, Pan Macmillan, Sydney,
      1997.

47   C Wallace 1997.

48   G Greer, *Female Eunuch*, Farrar, Straus and Giroux, London, 1970.

49   A O'Brien, *God's Willing Workers: Women and Religion in Australia*, UNSW Press,
      Sydney, 2005, p. 237.

50   Women have long outnumbered men among church attenders in Australia. In
      2001, the ratio was 3:2. See National Church Life Survey, 'Gender profile of
      church attenders', <www.ncls.org.au/default.aspx?sitemapid=137>.

51   See D Rogers, 'Elizabeth Cady Stanton (1815–1902)', *The Internet Encyclopedia of
      Philosophy*, <www.iep.utm.edu/stanton/#SH4a>, and further the local review:
      'The Woman's Bible', *South Australian Register*, 20 May 1897, p. 6.

52   L Nicklin & E White, 'Marie Tulip highly involved in the women's movement
      in times of great social change', *Sydney Morning Herald*, 11 February 2016,
      <www.smh.com.au/comment/obituaries/marie-tulip-highly-involved-in-the-

womens-movement-in-times-of-great-social-change-20160210-gmr2pz.html>.

53   O'Brien 2005, p. 237.

54   Nicklin & White 2016.

55   S Swain, 'Tulip, Marie', *The Encyclopedia of Women and Leadership in Twentieth-Century Australia*, Australian Women's Archives Project, 2014a, <www.womenaustralia.info/leaders/biogs/WLE0457b.htm>.

56   Marie Tulip, 'Women and the kingdom', *International Review of Mission*, vol. 69, no. 274, 1980, pp. 135–142, cited in Swain 2014a.

57   E Wainwright, 'In fear and great joy: forty years of feminist biblical scholarship', *Compass: A Review of Topical Theology*, vol. 39, no. 1, 2005, <compassreview.org/autumn05/7.html>.

58   Phrase from W Hudson, *Australian Religious Thought*, Monash University Press, Melbourne, 2016, p. 183.

59   See S Swain, 'Skuse, Jean', *The Encyclopedia of Women and Leadership in Twentieth-Century Australia*, Australian Women's Archives Project, 2014b, <www.womenaustralia.info/leaders/biogs/WLE0329b.htm>.

60   *Sydney Morning Herald*, 2 April 1981, cited in Swain 2014b.

61   E Wainwright, 'Our stories', University of Auckland website, n.d., <www.auckland.ac.nz/en/for/the-media/ourstories/elaine-wainwright.html>.

62   G Hohnberg, 'Reading the Bible is good for you? Rachel Sommerville & Germaine Greer', City Bible Forum submission, 2012, <cityBibleforum.org/city/brisbane/blog/reading-Bible-good-you-rachel-sommerville-germaine-greer>.

63   For some recent media discussions, see S Dorney, 'Good Book helps Solomon Islands' domestic violence', *Correspondents Report*, ABC Radio, 27 October 2012, <www.abc.net.au/radio/programs/correspondentsreport/good-book-helps-solomon-islands-domestic-violence/4337532>; and for Australian perspectives, J Baird & H Gleeson, 'Submit to your husbands': women told to endure domestic violence in the name of God,' ABC News website, 10 August 2017, <www.abc.net.au/news/2017-07-18/domestic-violence-church-submit-to-husbands/8652028>; H Gleeson & J Baird, 'Anglican Diocese of Sydney makes apology to victims of domestic violence', ABC News website, 11 October 2017, <www.abc.net.au/news/2017-10-11/anglican-diocese-of-sydney-apologises-to-abuse-victims/9038410>.

64   A McGahan, 'The ache of co-existence', blog post, 18 September 2017, <www.aforbiddenroom.com/spirit/the-ache-of-co-existence/> and A McGahan, 'I don't judge anyone, except Christians', *Life and Faith* podcast, Centre for Public Christianity, 3 August 2017, <www.publicchristianity.org/i-dont-judge-anyone-except-christians/>.

Chapter 11: Re-imagining Australia

1   Cited in N Meaney, '"In history's page": identity and myth', in D Schreuder & S Ward (eds.), *Australia's Empire*, Oxford University Press (OUP), Oxford, 2008, pp. 363–386.

2   A Sobocinska, *Visiting the Neighbours: Australians in Asia*, NewSouth Publishing, Sydney, 2014, pp. 121, 123.

3   See M Lake, 'Western heritage, Asian destiny: the Australian Council of Churches'

activity in Asia, 1950–1965', *Eras Journal*, vol. 7, 2005, <artsonline.monash.
edu.au/eras/eras-journal-lake-m-western-heritage-asian-destinythe-australian-
council-of-churches-activity-in-asia-1950-1965/>.

4   A Walker, *White Australia*, Christian Distributors' Association, Sydney, 1946;
     H McQueen, *Gallipoli to Petrov: Arguing with Australian History*, Allen & Unwin,
     Sydney, 1984, p. 146.

5   Cited in Meaney 2008, pp. 363–389.

6   RJW Shiner, 'Speaking to God in Australia: Donald Robinson and the writing
     of an Australian Prayer Book (1978)', *Studies in Church History,* vol. 53, 2017,
     pp. 435–447.

7   See H Chilton 'Evangelicals and the end of Christian Australia: nation and
     religion in the public square, 1959–1979', unpublished PhD thesis, University of
     Sydney, 2014, chapter 7, 'Radical renewal'.

8   B Pewer, *Australian Psalms*, Lutheran Publishing House, Adelaide, 1979; Shiner
     2017, pp. 437–438.

9   L Morris, 'And God said: Let's have some light, mate', *Sydney Morning Herald*,
     13 July 2006, <www.smh.com.au/news/national/and-god-said-lets-have-some-
     light-mate/2006/07/12/1152637740437.html>; see K Richards, *The Aussie Bible
     (Well, bits of it anyway!)*, Bible Society, Sydney, 2003.

10   Chilton 2014, p. 290.

11   M Lake & J Harris, 'John Harris's Bibles', *St Mark's Review*, no. 240, 2017,
     pp. 76–92.

12   *The Sower*, British and Foreign Bible Society in Australia, Sydney, April 1976.

13   Portions made up the vast majority of the figure, which was itself a rise of 17 per
     cent on the previous year. See *The Sower*, 1976, p. 10.

14   'Specialised selections for different audiences', *The Sower*, no. 96, April 1981, p. 5.

15   Introduction, *The Miner's Bible: New Testament and Psalms*, Bible Society, 1995.

16   Surfer's Bible website, <www.christiansurfers.net/surfers-Bible/>.

17   'New Surfer's Bible takes off', *Inside: CSA Newsletter*, Summer 08–09, p. 1.

18   J Harris, 'An Aussie Bible: do we need another translation?' *Zadok Perspectives*,
     no. 21, March 1988, pp. 3–6, 9.

19   D Hart, *Australian Painters of the Twentieth Century*, The Beagle Press, Sydney,
     2000.

20   Boyd to Fuller, *Modern Painters*, vol. 3, no. 2, Summer 1990, cited in D Bungey,
     Arthur Boyd: A Life, Allen & Unwin, Sydney, 2007, p. 577.

21   Bungey 2007, p. 83.

22   The Jonah collection was a collaboration between Boyd and poet Peter Porter.
     See A Boyd & P Porter, *Jonah*, Secker & Warburg, London, 1973; A Boyd,
     Nebuchadnezzar: 34 Paintings and 18 Drawings, with text by TSR Boase, Thames
     and Hudson, London, 1972. In the same period, Boyd also produced several
     works on the medieval saint Francis of Assisi. See M Pont, *Arthur Boyd and Saint
     Francis of Assisi: Pastels, Lithographs & Tapestries, 1964–1974*, Macmillan Art
     Publishing, Melbourne, 2004.

23   Bungey 2007.

24   See R Crumlin, *Images of Religion in Australian Art*, Bay Books, Sydney, 1988.

25   Cited in Crumlin 1988, p. 26

26 D Thomas, 'Smith, Grace Cossington (1892–1984)', *Australian Dictionary of Biography (ADB)*, Australian National University, <adb.anu.edu.au/biography/smith-grace-cossington-8469/text14893>, published first in hard copy 1988.

27 D Modjeska, *Stravinsky's Lunch*, Picador, Sydney, 1999, p. 322.

28 Crumlin 1988, pp. 40–45.

29 J Harris, 'The coastwatcher and the Aborigines', in J Harris (ed.), *Their Sacrifice: The Brave and their Bibles*, Bible Society Australia, Sydney, 2015, pp. 137–145.

30 For a detailed discussion, see L Rademaker, 'Language and the mission: talking and translating on Groote Eylandt 1943–1973', unpublished PhD thesis, ANU, 2014.

31 For example L Sanneh, 'Bible translation, culture and religion', in L Sanneh & MJ McClymond (eds.), *The Wiley Blackwell Companion to World Christianity*, Wiley/Blackwell, Hoboken, NJ, 2016, pp. 265–281.

32 JH Love, 'Love, James Robert Beattie (1889–1947)', *ADB*, Australian National University, <adb.anu.edu.au/biography/love-james-robert-beattie-7241/text12541>, published first in hard copy 1986; P Eckert & J Nicholls, 'A brief history of the Pitjantjatjara Bible Translation Project', August 2014, <www.papertracker.com.au/wp-content/uploads/2014/12/Bible-Translation-History-of-Pitjantjatjara-Aug-2014.pdf>.

33 See B Lowe, 'Yolngu–English Dictionary', ARDS Inc, 2004, <www.aurhim.net/test/journal/B.Lowe_Web_Dict.pdf>. Thanks to Laura Rademaker for this reference.

34 For an overview of Stokes' linguistic work, see G Koch & J Waddy, 'Obituary: Judith Stokes OAM', *The Free Library*, 22 September 2003, at <www.thefreelibrary.com/Judith+Stokes+OAM.-a0123582188>. For a detailed exploration, see Rademaker 2014.

35 1911 Mission Report, cited at 'Roper River Mission (1908–1988)', Find & Connect Web Resource Project for the Commonwealth of Australia, 2011, <www.findandconnect.gov.au/guide/nt/YE00010>.

36 W Hall, 'Dreams, visions and Aboriginal spirituality', in A Pattel-Gray (ed.), *Aboriginal Spirituality: Past, Present, Future*, Harper Collins, Melbourne, 1996, pp. 37–40.

37 Ngaanyatjarra Bible, online edition, <aboriginalBibles.org.au/Ngaanyatjarra/root.htm>, first published in 2007.

38 Cited in 'Bible Translation support', Bible Society Australia website, <www-archive.Biblesociety.org.au/projects/Indigenous/Bible-translation-support>.

39 At that time, many older adults in and around Numbulwar spoke or at least understood Wubuy. Since young people at Numbulwar spoke Kriol as their first language, however, Wubuy was considered an endangered language. See 'e-Baibul, Bible text in Australian Aboriginal languages' website, <aboriginalBibles.org.au/Wubuy/root.htm>.

40 T Holgate & B McLellan, 'Bible translation runs in the family for these Indigenous women', *Eternity*, 10 July 2017, <www.eternitynews.com.au/good-news/Bible-translation-runs-in-the-family-for-these-Indigenous-women/>.

41 K Walker, 'Aboriginal Charter of Rights', lines 35 and 36. This poem was prepared for and presented to the Annual General Meeting of the Federal Council for Advancement of Aborigines and Torres Strait Islanders, Adelaide, 1962, and later

published in K Walker, *Stradbroke Dreamtime*, Angus & Robertson, London, 1972, available at <www.poetrylibrary.edu.au/poets/noonuccal-oodgeroo/aboriginal-charter-of-rights-0719030>.

42   'A Cherbourg saint', *Journey*, Uniting Church in Australia: Queensland Synod, 2008, <journeyonline.com.au/local-church-news/a-cherbourg-saint/>.

43   R de Costa, *A Higher Authority: Indigenous Transnationalism and Australia*, UNSW Press, Sydney, 2006, p. 100.

44   de Costa 2006, p. 100; A Pattel-Gray, 'Australian Indigenous religions: Aboriginal Christianity', *Encyclopedia of Religion*, Thomson Gale, 2005, <www.encyclopedia.com/environment/encyclopedias-almanacs-transcripts-and-maps/australian-Indigenous-religions-aboriginal-christianity>.

45   S Taffe, *'Don Brady', Collaborating for Indigenous Rights 1957–1973*, National Museum of Australia, 2014, <Indigenousrights.net.au/people/pagination/don_brady>; Y Best, 'Brady, Donald (Don) (1927–1984)', *ADB*, Australian National University, <adb.anu.edu.au/biography/brady-donald-don-12246>, published first in hard copy 2007.

46   Cited in A Pattel-Gray, 'Methodology in an Aboriginal theology', in DN Hopkins & EP Antonio (eds.), *The Cambridge Companion to Black Theology*, CUP, Cambridge, 2012, p. 283.

47   Taffe 2014.

48   Paulson cited in Pattel-Gray 2012, p. 284.

49   Pattel-Gray 2012, p. 282; and further Taffe 2014; Best 2007.

50   See generally Pattel-Gray 2012, pp. 278–297.

51   R Broome, 'Nicholls, Sir Douglas Ralph (Doug) (1906–1988)', *ADB*, Australian National University, <adb.anu.edu.au/biography/nicholls-sir-douglas-ralph-doug-14920/text26109>, published first in hard copy 2012.

52   See J Farquharson, 'Tucker, Margaret Elizabeth (Auntie Marge) (1904–1996)', *Obituaries Australia*, National Centre of Biography, Australian National University, <adb.anu.edu.au/biography/tucker-margaret-elizabeth-auntie-marge-1556/text1618>.

53   Cited in J Cruickshank, 'Christians and the Referendum', Common Grace blog, 28 May 2017, <www.commongrace.org.au/christians_and_the_1967_referendum>.

54   H Radi, 'Roberts, Frank (1899–1968)', *ADB*, Australian National University, <adb.anu.edu.au/biography/roberts-frank-11535/text20579>, published first in hard copy 2002.

55   T Blake, 'Harris, Charles Enoch (1931–1993)', *ADB*, National Centre of Biography, Australian National University, <adb.anu.edu.au/biography/harris-charles-enoch-18183/text29753>, published online 2017; Pattel-Gray 2005; D Bell, 'Aboriginal theologies', in J Jupp (ed.), *Encyclopedia of Religion in Australia*, CUP, Melbourne, 2009, p. 92.

56   D Gondarra, *Let My People Go*, Bethyl Presbytery, Darwin, 1986, pp. 13–14, cited in P Van Toorn, *Writing Never Arrives Naked: Early Aboriginal Cultures of Writing in Australia*, Aboriginal Studies Press, Canberra, 2006, p. 118.

57   D Kentish, *You Listen Me! An Angry Love: Writings in Honor of Jarinyanu David Downs*, Duncan Kentish Fine Art, Adelaide, 1995, p. 3.

58   Kentish 1995, p. 14. Note the Walmajarri Bible is made up of translations of nine Old Testament and eight New Testament books.

59   Quoted at <www.portrait.gov.au/portraits/2005.61.4/jarinyanu-david-downs>. Downs was represented in many group exhibitions in the 1980s and 1990s. The National Gallery of Victoria holds fifteen of his works.

60   Cited in Kentish 1995, p. 5.

61   L Sherman & C Mattingley (eds.), *Our Mob, God's Story*, Bible Society Australia, Sydney, 2017.

62   Lachlan Warner, McGlade Gallery Director, cited in 'Artists interpret Stations of the Cross for ACU's innovative Easter Exhibition', *Catholic Communications*, Sydney Archdiocese, 24 March 2015, at <www.sydneycatholic.org/news/latest_news/2015/2015324_1804.shtml>.

63   E Bähr, 'The impact of Christianity on Australian Indigenous art,' 2013, article at <www.aboriginal-art.de/EN/themen_christentum.htm>.

64   G Trompf, 'Foreword', in Pattel-Gray 1996.

65   See A Pattel-Gray & J Brown (eds.), *Indigenous Australia: A Dialogue about the Word Becoming Flesh in Aboriginal Churches*, World Council of Churches Publications, Geneva, 1997.

66   A Pattel-Gray, C Grant & G Mundine, 'The gospel as good news', in Pattel-Gray & Brown 1997.

67   G Rosendale, cited in Pattel-Gray & Brown 1997, pp. 16, 19.

68   See R Bos, *Didgeridoo Theology: The Development of an Authentic Christian Symbolic Life Among Australian Aboriginal People*, Nungalinga College, Darwin, 1980.

69   Cited in N Sharp, *Malo's Law in Court: The Religious Background to the Mabo Case*, Charles Strong Memorial Trust, Adelaide, 1994, p. 13; N Sharp, *Stars of Tagai: The Torres Strait Islanders*, Aboriginal Studies Press, Canberra, 1993, pp. 99, 106–110.

70   Cited in Sharpe 1994, p. 8.

71   See DB Rose, *Ned Kelly Died for Our Sins*, Charles Strong Memorial Trust, Adelaide, 1988, and R Boer & I Abraham, 'Australasia', in JFA Sawyer (ed.), *The Blackwell Companion to the Bible and Culture*, Blackwell, Oxford, 2006, pp. 232–249.

72   Father Dave Passi, quoted in Pattel-Gray & Brown 1997, p. 45.

73   David Passi commonly referred to this text in explaining his participation in the Mabo case that discovered native title on his island of Mer. Reported in G Paulson & M Brett, 'Five smooth stones: reading the Bible through Aboriginal eyes', *Colloquium*, vol. 45, no. 2, 2013, p. 203.

74   G Davison, *Narrating the Nation in Australia: Menzies Lecture 2009*, Menzies Centre for Australian Studies, London, 2009, pp. 22–23.

75   Davison 2009, p. 23. Quotes from the service were originally reported in M Finlay, 'Eddie Mabo comes home', *Good Weekend*, 1 June 1996.

76   Holgate & McLellan 2017.

77   A Pratt, 'Practising reconciliation? The politics of reconciliation in the Australian Parliament, 1991–2000', Parliamentary Library Research Publications, 2005, <www.aph.gov.au/binaries/library/pubs/monographs/pratt/practisingreconciliation.pdf>, p. 13.

78   For discussion, see M Phillips, 'Aboriginal reconciliation as religious politics: secularisation in Australia', *Australian Journal of Political Science*, vol. 40, no. 1, 2005, pp. 111–124.

79   Uluru Statement, 2017, via <www.referendumcouncil.org.au/sites/default/files/2017-05/Uluru_Statement_From_The_Heart_0.PDF>.

80   J Harris, 'Justice, Aboriginal land rights, and the use and abuse of Scripture', *Zadok Perspectives*, no. 18, 1987, pp. 3–10.

81   G Rosendale, cited in Pattel-Gray & Brown 1997, pp. 13, 14.

82   Norman Habel (ed.), *The Earth Bible*, five vols., Sheffield Academic Press, Sheffield, 2000–2002. See outline at 'The Earth Bible', Centre for Theology, Science & Culture, Flinders University, <www.flinders.edu.au/ehl/theology/ctsc/projects/earthbible/>. See also Pope Francis, 'Encyclical Letter *Laudato Si*' on care for our common home', 2015, <w2.vatican.va/content/francesco/en/encyclicals/documents/papa-francesco_20150524_enciclica-laudato-si.html>.

Chapter 12: The Bible in the new millennium

1   Paraphrased lyrics of 'Anthrocene', from *Skeleton Tree*, first song on the setlist at the ICC show, Sydney 21 January 2017.

2   M Molyneux, 'Album review: Nick Cave and the Bad Seeds *Skeleton Tree*', 13 September 2016, Howl and Echo website, <howlandechoes.com/2016/09/album-review-nick-cave-and-the-bad-seeds-skeleton-tree/>. On Cave's interaction with the Bible, see accounts in N Cave, 'Introduction', *The Gospel According to Mark*, Canongate, Edinburgh, 1998; N Cave, *The Secret Life of the Love Song/The Flesh Made Word*, 2000. For discussion, see Z Alderton, 'Nick Cave: a journey from an Anglican God to a creative Christ', *Literature & Aesthetics*, vol.19, no. 2, 2009; R Boer, *Nick Cave: A Study of Love, Death, and Apocalypse*, Equinox Publishing, Bristol, 2012, and Boer's several further essays.

3   McCrindle Research, Faith and Belief in Australia survey, May 2017, McCrindle Research, Sydney, 2017, available at <mccrindle.worldsecuresystems.com/blog/2017/05/Faith%20and%20Belief%20in%20Australia%20Report_McCrindle_2017.pdf>.

4   *2015 Review of Special Religious Education and Special Education in Ethics in NSW Government Schools*, NSW Department of Education, 23 March 2016, p. xv <education.nsw.gov.au/media/schools-operation/2015_review_sre_see.pdf>.

5   K Munro, 'Ethics classes in NSW primary schools growing despite barriers to enrolment', *SMH*, 29 January 2017, <www.smh.com.au/national/education/ethics-classes-in-nsw-primary-schools-growing-despite-barriers-to-enrolment-20170124-gtxppa.html>.

6   'Special Religious Instruction', School Policy and Advisory Guide, Victoria State Government Department of Education and Training website, <www.education.vic.gov.au/school/principals/spag/curriculum/Pages/sri.aspx>.

7   Cited in M Davis, 'The condemned' (transcript), *Dateline*, SBS Australia, 14 November 2010, <www.sbs.com.au/news/dateline/story/condemned>.

8   'Locations' list, Hillsong church website, <hillsong.com/>.

9   'Our beliefs', Australian Christian Churches website, <www.acc.org.au/about-

us/>. ACC is the main Pentecostal umbrella group in Australia, with which Hillsong is affiliated.

10   'Your word', by Chris Davenport/Hillsong Worship (*Let There Be Light* album, 2016) drawing on Psalm 119:105.

11   Data in the following section comes from R Powell, *Trends in Australian Church Vitality: Denominational Briefing* (NCLS Research Report), NCLS Research, Sydney, 2015. With thanks to Dr Powell for sharing this with me. Summary publicly available as 'Religious beliefs of Church attenders' via <youtu.be/ bpV8meXj0cI>. See also the fact sheet 'View of the Bible', based on the 1996 NCLS results, at <www.ncls.org.au/default.aspx?sitemapid=146>.

12   Gallup Research, 'Poll: values and beliefs, 3–7 May 2017', summarised at <www.gallup.com/poll/210704/record-few-americans-believe-Bible-literal-word-God.aspx>.

13   McCrindle Research, 'Bible reading not dead in Australia', 2014, <www.mccrindle. com.au/resources/Bible-Reading-in-Australia_McCrindle-Research_Blog.pdf>.

14   See K Payne, 'Australia's most popular Bible verse for 2015 is …', *Eternity News*, 27 December 2015, <www.Biblesociety.org.au/news/australias-most-popular-Bible-verse-for-2015-is>.

15   H Garner, 'On being bad at reading the Bible', *Portland Magazine*, Winter 2004.

16   H Garner, 'Eight scenes from a friendship', in H McPhee (ed.), *Tim Winton: A Celebration*, National Library of Australia, Canberra, 1999, p. 5.

17   B Brennan, *A Writing Life*, Text Publishing, Melbourne, 2017, p. 107.

18   H Garner, 'Dreams, the Bible and *Cosmo Cosmolino*', in *True Stories: Selected Non-fiction*, Text, Melbourne, 1996, pp. 137–141.

19   H Garner, 'On turning fifty', in *True Stories*, p. 160; Brennan 2017, p. 118.

20   L McCredden & N O'Reilly, 'Introduction', in *Tim Winton: Critical Essays*, UWA Publishing, 2014, p. 3.

21   See T Davison, *Christian Mysticism and Australian Poetry*, Cambria Press, Amherst, 2013.

22   F Wright & L Brown, 'Six degrees from the city: Episode 1 Lachlan Brown', *Sydney Review of Books* podcast, 29 August 2017, transcript at <sydneyreviewofbooks.com/six-degrees-city-episode-1-lachlan-brown/>.

23   Cited in S Bennett, 'The Gospel according to Paul', *Herald Sun*, 27 June 2011, <www.heraldsun.com.au/entertainment/the-gospel-according-to-paul/story-e6frf96f-1226082193294>.

24   Adam Lee artist website, <adamlee.com.au/>.

25   For discussion see R Boer, 'The absurdly ideal Jesus of Reg Mombassa', in C Blyth & N Vaka'uta (eds.), *The Bible and Art: Perspectives from Oceania*, Bloomsbury, London and New York, 2017, pp. 55–72; G Clarke, 'The Australian Jesus of Reg Mombassa', 29 January 2010, Centre for Public Christianity website, <publicchristianity.org/library/the-australian-jesus-of-reg-mombassa>; A Blanch, 'Reg Mombassa's Australian Jesus', *Transpositions: Theology, Imagination and the Arts*, c. 2010, <www.transpositions.co.uk/reg-mombassas-australian-jesus/>.

26   G Broughton, 'Crossing over: can love make a way for those languishing on Manus Island?' *ABC Religion and Ethics*, 8 November 2017, <www.abc.net.au/

religion/articles/2017/11/08/4761842.htm>.

27   'What has God joined together?', Sydney Anglicans website, <sydneyanglicans.
      net/marriage/the-same-sex-marriage-debate>.

28   They did not always convince other people. In the case of the Marriage Law
      Survey, for instance, 61.6 per cent of all respondents ultimately favoured a change
      in the law to allow same-sex couples to marry.

29   Pope Francis, 'Encyclical letter *Laudato Si*' on care for our common home',
      2015, paragraphs 65–67, <w2.vatican.va/content/dam/francesco/pdf/encyclicals/
      documents/papa-francesco_20150524_enciclica-laudato-si_en.pdf>.

30   Parliament of Victoria, *Inside the Parliament of Victoria*, Melbourne, 2012,
      <www.parliament.vic.gov.au/images/stories/documents/education/Inside_
      Parliament_2014_small.pdf>.

31   Cited in T Hassan, 'Left behind? Progressive Australians' reluctance to talk
      religion', *SMH*, 17 June 2017, <www.smh.com.au/comment/left-behind-
      progressive-australians-reluctance-to-talk-religion-20170616-gwsmv6.html>.

32   C Tsiolkas, interviewed by Geraldine Doogue, 'Christos Tsiolkas: man behind
      The Slap', *Compass* (ABC), 9 October 2011, <www.abc.net.au/compass/s3315704.
      htm>.

33   V Benjamin interviewed by A West, *Religion and Ethics Report* (ABC
      Radio National), 29 August 2012, <www.abc.net.au/radionational/
      programs/religionandethicsreport/new-ceo-for-the-oaktree-
      foundation/4231018#transcript>.

ACKNOWLEDGMENTS

Telling true stories always involves a community – from the moment the first curious questions get asked, to the point a narrative finally emerges. This book has been no exception. Greg Clarke helped seed the idea back in 2014 and remained an encouraging reader throughout. I have also been helped and taught by many other generous thinkers who shared their insights and expertise, including by reading and commenting on parts of the draft. Thank you so much Stephen Chavura, Hugh Chilton, Joanna Cruickshank, Emily Deller, Andrew Errington, Michael Gladwin, John Harris, Sian Lim, Natasha Moore, Stuart Piggin, Ruth Powell, Malcolm Prentis, Laura Rademaker, Geoff Treloar, and Richard White. Each of you made this a much better book, and me a better historian and writer.

In facing the basic challenge of creating the conditions to write, I relied for more than two years on the financial support of my partner Joel and the availability of a spare desk in various public libraries. I am especially grateful to Julie Olsten and Erin Mollenhauer at Moore Theological College; Susan Phillips at St Mark's National Theological Centre; and staff at Campsie local library, the University of Sydney and the NSW State Library. Critical, too, was the personal support of friends and family, including John and Kristine Morrison, Denise Lake, Peter and Jenny Lake, and Steph Olsen, who hosted me or helped care for my children from time to time. The encouragement of the diverse congregations of Campsie Baptist Church and All Saints Petersham, and my friends Lauren Errington, Erin Gavin, Megan James, Cath Finney Lamb, Byron Smith, Jessica Smith and Mandy Tsang, was also vital.

In the project's final twelve months, I benefited enormously from a Senior Research Fellowship at Anglican Deaconess Ministries, Sydney. This provided such essential tools as a work space and steady income, and I could not have asked for better colleagues than Alix Beeston, Jo Chew, Annette Pierdziwol, Kate Harrison Brennan, and the staff at ADM.

In transforming the manuscript into a book, it has been a delight to work with Elspeth Menzies at NewSouth Publishing, and especially with editor Jocelyn Hungerford, who made this a much sharper, shorter piece than I could have. I am also grateful for the help of Bec Lawson with referencing, and Rhiannon Davis with both referencing and preparing the index. Without knowing names, I also want to thank every reader who gave this book – and its writer – the gift of their time and attention.

Through it all, Joel, Jemima and Hamish have patiently shouldered this project's heaviest burdens, all while bringing profound joy to my life. Their love and grace on the journey has been a wonderful thing – and yes kids, it really is finished now.

Most of this book was written on the traditional lands of the Eora nation, with an acute awareness of my structural privilege as a white Australian. In its own small way I hope it points to the urgency and importance of pursuing reconciliation with justice. I offer it to my children and God-children, in the hope that they may one day grapple with the Bible for themselves.

INDEX